Xiang Wang

Ximing Monastery

History and Imagination in Medieval Chinese Buddhism

LAP LAMBERT Academic Publishing

Impressum / Imprint

Bibliografische Information der Deutschen Nationalbibliothek: Die Deutsche Nationalbibliothek verzeichnet diese Publikation in der Deutschen Nationalbibliografie; detaillierte bibliografische Daten sind im Internet über http://dnb.d-nb.de abrufbar.
Alle in diesem Buch genannten Marken und Produktnamen unterliegen warenzeichen-, marken- oder patentrechtlichem Schutz bzw. sind Warenzeichen oder eingetragene Warenzeichen der jeweiligen Inhaber. Die Wiedergabe von Marken, Produktnamen, Gebrauchsnamen, Handelsnamen, Warenbezeichnungen u.s.w. in diesem Werk berechtigt auch ohne besondere Kennzeichnung nicht zu der Annahme, dass solche Namen im Sinne der Warenzeichen- und Markenschutzgesetzgebung als frei zu betrachten wären und daher von jedermann benutzt werden dürften.

Bibliographic information published by the Deutsche Nationalbibliothek: The Deutsche Nationalbibliothek lists this publication in the Deutsche Nationalbibliografie; detailed bibliographic data are available in the Internet at http://dnb.d-nb.de.
Any brand names and product names mentioned in this book are subject to trademark, brand or patent protection and are trademarks or registered trademarks of their respective holders. The use of brand names, product names, common names, trade names, product descriptions etc. even without a particular marking in this work is in no way to be construed to mean that such names may be regarded as unrestricted in respect of trademark and brand protection legislation and could thus be used by anyone.

Coverbild / Cover image: www.ingimage.com

Verlag / Publisher:
LAP LAMBERT Academic Publishing
ist ein Imprint der / is a trademark of
OmniScriptum GmbH & Co. KG
Heinrich-Böcking-Str. 6-8, 66121 Saarbrücken, Deutschland / Germany
Email: info@lap-publishing.com

Herstellung: siehe letzte Seite /
Printed at: see last page
ISBN: 978-3-659-67671-0

Zugl. / Approved by: Palo Alto,Stanford University,Diss.,2012

Ximing Monastery

History and Imagination In Medieval Chinese Buddhism

by

Wang Xiang

Lambert Academic Publishing

Saarbrücken   Germany

2015

To My Father Wang Shi'en

TABLE OF CONTENTS

LIST OF FIGURES AND TABLE

iv

ACKNOWLEDGEMENTS

Many people assisted in the writing of this book, providing documents, offering editorial help, and reviewing portions of the manuscript. First of all, I would like to thank the members of my Stanford dissertation committee, Professor Carl Bielefeldt, Professor Paul Harrison, as well as Dr. Dongfang Shao 邵東方, without whose dedication and support, this book would not have been possible. My principal advisor, Professor Carl Bielefeldt, has had to endure my academic immaturity and ignorance in the long course of my writing; he has shown only patience in return. I got to know Professor Paul Harrison late in my graduate career but he nonetheless meticulously read my dissertation and offered valuable advice. In particular, I also want to thank Dr. Shao, Chief of the Asian Division in the Library of Congress, for his unremitting assistance and moral support at many difficult times. Professor Hester Gelber and the late Professor John McRae kindly stepped in to round out the proposal committee and dissertation defense committee when I had no one to call on.

This book is the product of a decade-long fascination with Buddhist Chang'an that was begun at Yale University in 2002, continued in the Department of Religious Studies at Stanford University, and completed with the help of research grant provided by Beijing Normal University-Hong Kong Baptist University United International College (UIC) 聯合國際學院. It was shaped by conversations with many Chinese scholars during my visit to Beijing University. First and foremost, I am grateful to Dr. Zhanru 湛如, who generously shared his preliminary research on Ximingsi with me. I greatly appreciate the support of Professor Rong Xinjiang 榮新江 and Dr. Chen Huaiyu 陳懷宇, who gave me the opportunity to publish a part of an early version of chapter 6 in the prestigious journal *Tang yanjiu* 唐研究 (Tang Studies). Some of the other chapters also emerged out of my presentations made at different international conferences, in which the warm atmosphere and scholarly interaction among scholars have been a great source of personal and intellectual pleasure. The project was also made possible through many grants from a variety of organizations, including the Center of East Asian Studies, Department of Religious Studies and Center of South Asia at Stanford University, the China Times Cultural Foundation, Overseas Young Chinese Foundation, Chinese Government Award, and UIC Research Grant.

During the final stages of the writing in 2012, I was great aided by the Stanford East Asian Library, which provided me a private table where I could spread out hundreds of books and concentrate on my research. I would also like to thank my fellow classmates, Yang Zhaohua and Ho Chiew Hui in particular, for their encouragement during my year at Stanford. Many thanks also go to my family, especially my wife and my mother, for their support for and assistance with my work on this project. Finally, this book is affectionately dedicated to the memory of my father, Wang Shi'en 王世恩 (1946-2009), whose passing a few years ago was a great loss to me. Over a period of ten years, he remained an ardent supporter of the long and arduous journey of my academic career.

Dr. Shawn Wang
(Wang Xiang 王翔)
Friday, February 06, 2015
Shanghai

ABBREVIATIONS

BZJ   *Daizong chao zeng sikong dabianzheng guangzhi sanzang heshang biaozhiji* 代宗朝贈司空大辨正廣智三藏和上表制集

CFYG   *Cefu yuangui* 冊府元龜

DNBZ   *Dai Nihon bukkyō zensho* 大日本佛教全書

EBTEA   *Esoteric Buddhism and the Tantras in East Asia* (Brill, 2011)

FDLH   *Ji gujin fodao lunheng* 集古今佛道論衡

IBK   *Indogaku bukkyōgaku kenkyū* 印度學佛教學研究, Tokyo.

JTS   *Jiu Tang shu* 舊唐書

Mochizuki   *Mochizuki bukkyō daijiten* 望月仏教大辭典

NDL   *Da Tang neidian lu* 大唐內典錄

Ono   *Chūgoku Zui Tō Chōan jiin shiryō shūsei* 中國隋唐長安寺院史料集成 (*Kaisetsuhen* 解說篇 and *Shiryōhen* 史料篇)

P   Chinese manuscripts from Dunhuang in the Pelliot Collection

QTS   *Quan Tang shi* 全唐詩

QTW   *Quan Tang wen* 全唐文

S   Chinese manuscripts from Dunhuang in the Stein Collection

SGSZ   *Song gaoseng zhuan* 宋高僧傳

SKQS   *Yingyin Wenyuange siku quanshu* 景印文淵閣四庫全書

SZFSZ   *Da Ci'ensi sanzang fashi zhuan* 大慈恩寺三藏法師傳

T   *Taishō shinshū daizōkyō* 大正新修大藏經

TB   *Ximingsi tabei* 西明寺塔碑

THY   *Tang huiyao* 唐會要

XTS   *Xin Tang shu* 新唐書

XZJ   *Xuzang jing* 續藏經

ZYL   *Zhenyuan xinding shijiao mulu* 貞元新定釋教目錄

ZZTJ   *Zizhi tongjian* 資治通鑒

The River of Jiao (Jiaoqu 交渠)

Figure. 1   Bird's Eye View of Ximingsi 西明寺. Source: Heng Chye Kiang, *Tang Chang'an de shuma chongjian* 唐長安的數碼重建, 22.

1

Chapter One

Introduction

Chang'an and Ximingsi

When the firm edifice of Tang China (618-907) rose over East Asia, the capital of the empire, historically known as Sui-Tang Chang'an 長安, emerged as perhaps the greatest city in the world from the seventh to the tenth century (Figure. 2).[1] Actuated by the enterprising spirit of the empire, Chang'an was continuously filled with strangers from every part of the world, who brought with them the exotic cultures of their native countries. At the height of its power and opulence, the city became the very embodiment of culture and spirituality, with its citizens practicing a remarkable range of religions, including Confucianism, Buddhism, Islam, Nestorianism, Zoroastrianism, Manichaeism and Daoism. In spite of the priority given to Daoism by the Tang founders, Buddhism, which possessed greater institutional strengths, became the most popular of all the faiths. The support given to Buddhism by most of

---

[1] The city of Tang Chang'an inherited its name from its monumental predecessor flourishing in the earlier Han Empire. In 202 B.C., to the south of the old Qin capital Xianyang 咸陽, Liu Bang 劉邦 (256-195 B.C., r. 202-195 B.C.), the first emperor of the Han Dynasty, established the city of Han Chang'an 漢長安. Rhapsodic descriptions of the capital are available in some Chinese classics such as *Wenxuan* 文選 (Literary Selections) and *Sanfu huangtu* 三輔黃圖 (Description of the Three Capital Districts). For the establishment of Han Chang'an, see Wu Hung, *Monumentality in Early Chinese Art and Architecture* (Stanford, Calif: Stanford University Press, 1995), 143-88; Victor Cunrui Xiong, *Sui-Tang Chang'an* (Ann Arbor: Center for Chinese Studies, University of Michigan, 2000), 7-14; Mark Lewis, *The Early Chinese Empires Qin and Han* (Belknap Press of Harvard University Press, 2007), 19. For detailed studies of Sui-Tang Chang'an, see Song Suyi 宋肅懿, *Tangdai Chang'an zhi yanjiu* 唐代長安之研究 (Taipei: Dali chubanshe, 1983); Thomas Thilo, *Chang'an: Metropole Ostasiens und Weltstadt des Mittelalters 583-904* (Wiesbaden: Harrassowitz, 1997); Xiong, *Sui-Tang Chang'an*; Thomas Thilo, *Chang'an 2, Gesellschaft und Kultur* (Wiesbaden: Harrassowitz, 2006).

2

the Tang emperors was reflected in the unprecedented political powers of the clergy during this time.

The city of Chang'an was built after the pattern prescribed in the classical texts *Kaogong ji* 考工記 (Records for the Scrutiny of Crafts) and *Yijing* 易經 (Book of Changes). The city plan of Sui-Tang Chang'an was conceived on a grand scale unmatched anywhere in the ancient world.[2] In this great metropolis, huge residential wards (*fang* 坊) were everywhere erected along invisible vertical and horizontal lines. Each of the "urban villages" was equally defined by mud walls with central gates. The total number of villages reached one hundred over the course of the three centuries of Tang rule. The grand city was divided into east-west components called the two streets (*liangjie* 兩街) by a 150-meter wide demarcation zone, known as the Avenue of the Vermillion Bird (*zhuque* 朱雀). As art historian Nancy Steinhardt says, "The strict adherence to a grid pattern for the streets and the almost perfect symmetry of the city were emphasized by the streets' lengths: Twenty-five of them, fourteen longitudinal and eleven latitudinal, ran the entire distance of the outer wall."[3] Travelers and pilgrims who entered Chang'an for the first time would find numerous thoroughfares leading to the Western Market (*xishi* 西市), a huge bazaar of international trade and foreign modes of worship. The Islamic geographer Abu Zayd Hasan (9th c.), recorded the impressions of an Arab visitor to Tang Chang'an, Ebn Wahab, as follows:

> He told us the City was very large, and extremely populous; that it was divided into two great Parts, by a very long and very broad Street; that the emperor, his chief Ministers, the Soldiery, the supreme Judge, the Eunuchs, and all belonging to the imperial Household, lived in that Part of the City which is on the right hand Eastward...The Part on the left hand Westward, is inhabited by the People and the Merchants, where are also great Squares, and Markets for all the Necessaries of Life.[4]

---

[2] *Kaogong ji* 考工記 (Records for the Scrutiny of Crafts) is the sixth part of *Zhouli* 周禮 (Rites of Zhou), known as *Dongguan kaogongji* 冬官考工記 (Winter offices, Records of the Scrutiny of Crafts), for an introduction of the text, see Michael Loewe, *Early Chinese Texts: A Bibliographical Guide* (Berkeley, Calif.: Institute of East Asian Studies, 1993), 24-32. On the construction of Sui-Tang Chang'an, see Xiong, *Sui-Tang Chang'an*, 37-54.

[3] Nancy Shatzman Steinhardt, *Chinese Imperial City Planning* (Honolulu: University of Hawai'i Press, 1990), 94.

[4] Abu Zayd Hasan bin Yazid, *Ancient Accounts of India and China*, trans. Eusebius Renaudot (London: S.

Introduction

Standing in awe on the wide street adjacent to the facade of the southeastern corner of the huge market, any foreign traveler would easily identify the rooftops of a gorgeous monastery located in the diagonal residential ward by the name of "Prolonging Health" (Yankang fang 延康坊). This magnificent religious institution is the central topic of the present study: Ximing (Western Brightness) Monastery (hereafter referred to as Ximingsi 西明寺), a premier center of Buddhism and pivot point of international cultural exchange across Asia during the Tang dynasty.

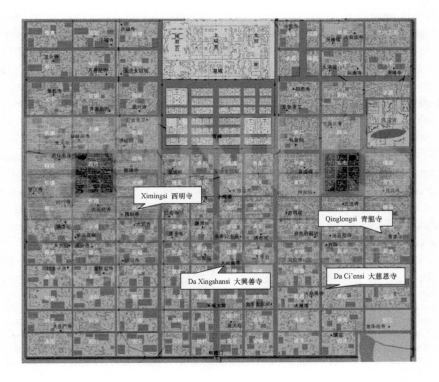

Figure. 2   Plan of Sui-Tang Chang'an.
Source: Heng Chye Kiang, *Tang Chang'an de shuma chongjian*, CD-ROM.

Harding, 1733), 58-59. In the present book, all the translations are mine, unless otherwise indicated.

Introduction

Among the more than one hundred Buddhist monasteries in Chang'an during its heyday, Ximingsi was exceptional in many ways.[5] Its great prestige not only attracted gifted young men to forsake worldly pomp for the life of a monk, but also collected a galaxy of preeminent scholars contributing to Ximingsi's reputation as a nexus of Buddhist learning. The following thematic chapters will discuss at length some of the most illustrious of these masters, including Xuanzang 玄奘 (600-664); Daoxuan 道宣 (596-667); Yuanzhao 圓照 (8th c.) and Xuanchang 玄暢 (796-875). The scholastic training at Ximingsi engaged its clergy in the tasks of scriptural translation, editing and composition. Those diligent monks had produced a series of holy texts or commentarial works essential to East Asian Buddhism, among which we may find: *Foding zunsheng tuoluoni* 佛頂尊勝陀羅尼 (Skt. *Sarvadurgati pariśodhana uṣṇīṣavijayadhāraṇī*, Dhāraṇī of the Jubilant Buddha-Corona, T967); *Jin guangming zuishengwang jing* 金光明最勝王經 (Skt. *Suvarṇaprabhāsottama sūtra*, Golden Light Scripture, T665) and *Renwang huguo bore boluomiduo jing* 仁王護國般若波羅蜜多経 (Perfection of Wisdom Sūtra for Humane Kings Protecting Their Countries, or *The Scripture for Humane Kings*, T246). Filled with such works, as well as secular texts of Chinese culture, the excellent collection at the Ximing Library made it a magnet for both talented scholars and young candidates of national exams. In the seventh century, the saintly abbot of Ximingsi, Daoxuan, reported that the national tripiṭaka found in the monastery library amounted to more than three thousand scrolls of manuscripts, all of which were contained in the celebrated bibliographical catalogue *Datang neidian lu* 大唐內典錄 (Buddhist Catalogue of the Great Tang, T2149).[6]

Accounts of highly esteemed foreign masters are also common in the literary notices of the monastery. For instance, the *Song gaoseng zhuan* 宋高僧傳 (The

---

[5] For studies on the number of Buddhist monasteries in Chang'an, see Xiong, *Sui-Tang Chang'an*, 303-20 (Appendix 3: "Buddhist Institutions"); Ono Katsutoshi 小野勝年, *Chūgoku Zui Tō Chōan jiin shiryō shūsei: shiryōhen* 中國隋唐長安寺院史料集成: 史料篇 (Kyoto: Hōzōkan, 1989), 453-70 (hereafter abbreviated as "Ono, *Shiryōhen*"). For an explanation of Ono Katsutoshi's table, see Xiong, *Sui-Tang Chang'an*, 253, note 96. The translation of "Ximing" as "Western Brightness" is based on Ono Katsutoshi's research, see Ono Katsutoshi, *Chūgoku Zui Tō Chōan jiin shiryō shūsei: kaisetsuhen* 中國隋唐長安寺院史料集成: 解說篇 (Kyoto: Hōzōkan, 1989), 147 (hereafter abbreviated as "Ono, *Kaisetsuhen*"). Ximingsi also reminds us of the Ximingge 西明閣 (Ximing Pavilion) of Chang'an in the Later Qin (384-417) period. It was the monastery where Kumārajīva 鳩摩羅什 (344-413) and his translation team of 800 monks rendered the *Mahāprajñāpāramitā-sūtra* into Chinese (*Mohe bore boluomi jing* 摩訶般若波羅蜜經, T223), see *Lidai sanbao ji* 歷代三寶紀 (Record of Three Treasures of Different Dynasties), T49, no. 2034, p. 79, a9-13.

[6] *Datang neidian lu* 大唐內典錄 (abbreviated as *NDL* in the footnotes), T55, no.2149, p. 302, c1-2.

5

Song-Dynasty Collection of Biographies of Eminent Monks, T2061), a collection of the biographies of eminent monks active in the Tang, has an account regarding Śubhakarasiṃha (Ch. Shanwuwei 善無畏, 637-735), the prince-monk of Orissa and tantric guru who resided at Ximingsi. When the 80-year old master arrived in Chang'an in 716 (Kaiyuan 開元 4), the Emperor Xuanzong 玄宗 (r. 712-756) received him in audience to show his respect. When asked to choose a monastery at which to settle down, the Indian master replied that what drew him to China was the reputation of Daoxuan, who rigorously upheld the Buddhist precepts (vinaya); therefore, he asked to be sheltered in his monastery and shared a cell with Daoxuan at Ximingsi.[7] Daoxuan was probably the greatest reformer of monastic codes in the Tang, and Śubhakarasimha is seen as one of the three Indian masters of the Kaiyuan period (*Kaiyuan sandashi* 開元三大士) who transmitted the seminal tantric text *Mahāvairocana-sūtra* (Ch. *Darijing* 大日經, Jap. *Dainichikyō*, T848) to the Chinese followers of esoteric Buddhism.[8] However, the story is anachronistic; since Daoxuan had passed away long before the Indian monk's arrival, there could have been no convergence of their life stories at Ximingsi.[9] Although the two masters represent two traditions, exoteric and esoteric Buddhism, it shows that, from the beginning, the Ximingsi had been a leading elite institution of traditional Buddhist scholasticism, and in the eighth century, it gradually became a far-famed cradle of the fresh teaching of esoteric Buddhism.

During its most flourishing years, from the seventh to the tenth century, aspiring

---

[7] *Song gaoseng zhuan* 宋高僧傳 (The Song-Dynasty Collection of Biographies of Eminent Monks, abbreviated as *SGSZ*), T50, no. 2061, p. 791, a29-b4. In many cases of citing the *SGSZ*, I also compare the original text with the digital edition of the *Song gaoseng zhuan*, an international project undertaken by Marcus Bingenheimer, Jen-Jou Hung, John Kieschnick and Boyong Zhang. Website accessed: http://buddhistinformatics.ddbc.edu.tw/songgaosengzhuan/, Monday, May 28, 2012. For Daoxuan's ordination movement, see Chen Huaiyu 陳懷宇, *The Revival of Buddhist Monasticism in Medieval China* (Peter Lang, 2007), 93-116.

[8] In Chinese, the text is styled in full as *Da piluzhena chenfo shenbian jiachi jing* 大毘盧遮那成佛神變加持經 (Skt. *Mahā-vairocanābhisaṃbodhi-vikurvitā-dhiṣṭhāna-vaipulya-sūtrendra-rāja-nāma-Dharmaparyāya*, T848). It is one of the three major scriptures of Chinese tantrism in the Tang. See, Mochizuki Shinkō 望月信亨, *Bukkyo daijiten* 佛教大辭典 (Kyoto: Sekai seiten kankō kyōkai, 1954-1971), 3376-377. The first six volumes of the *Bukkyo daijiten* are hereafter abbreviated as *Mochizuki*. The eighth volume (*zōho* 增補) and volumes nine to ten (*hoi* 補遺) are abbreviated as "*Mochizuki*, addendum 1" and "*Mochizuki*, addendum 2".

[9] Bernard Faure thinks their encounter represents two diametrically opposed types of Buddhist saints: the rigorist monk and the laxist monk, see Bernard Faure, *The Red Thread: Buddhist Approaches to Sexuality* (Princeton, N.J.: Princeton University Press, 1998), 5.

talents from the Asian periphery gathered at Ximingsi to share in the glories of the institution. The well-known debate between the Korean prince-monk Wŏn Chŭk 圓測 (Ch. Yuance, 613-696) and the Chinese master Kuiji 窺基 (632-682) catalyzed the Korean Yogācāra Sect, a school holding that all the phenomenal world is mind in its ultimate nature. The Gandhāran monk Buddhapāla (Ch. Fotuoboli 佛陀波利, 7th c.), who aimed to "sacrifice his life to benefit sentient beings," rendered the mantra *Uṣṇīṣavijayadhāraṇī* into Chinese with the assistance of the Ximing scholar Shunzhen 順貞.[10] The Japanese Shingon patriarch Kūkai 空海 (774-835), during his early days in the ninth-century Chang'an, was acquainted with a generation of vinaya masters and Indian translators at Ximingsi.[11] On the other hand, the Ximing prelates who chose to leave Chang'an occasionally also preached in small towns near Central Asia. From the seventh to the eighth century, the Tang empire included the lowlands of Guangzhong 關中, a dozen provincial territories, and the frontiers as far as the four garrison cities of the Western region (Anxi sizhen 安西四鎮).[12] During some chaotic moments in the Tang dynasty, some Ximing-schooled clerics devoted themselves to mendicant preaching and travelled widely throughout the northwestern territory. This was revealed through some Dunhuang Buddhist manuscripts analyzed by the Japanese scholar Ueyama Daishun 上山大峻, who brought to us the life and works of the Ximing scholar Tankuang 曇曠 (8th c.) in his brilliant *Tonkō bukkyō no kenkyū* 敦煌佛教の研究 (Studies on Buddhism in Dunhuang). Tankuang's *Dacheng ershier wen* 大乘二十二問 (Twenty-two Questions on Mahāyāna), composed in response to the inquiries of the great Tibetan dharma king Trisong Detsen (or Tibetan Wylie: Khri srong lde btsan, 742-797, Ch. Chisong dezan 赤松德贊), was one of the most valuable doctrinal elaborations on Mahāyāna composed in the eighth century.[13]

---

[10] Buddhapāla's *SGSZ* biography is located at T50, no. 2061, p. 717, c15-p. 718, b7. On the cultural history of the *dhāraṇī* that Buddhapāla translated at Ximing, see Liu Shufen 劉淑芬, *Miezui yu duwang: Foding zunsheng tuoluoni jingzhuang zhi yanjiu* 滅罪與度亡: 佛頂尊勝陀羅尼經幢之研究 (Shanghai: Shanghai guji chubanshe, 2008).

[11] *[Go]shōrai mukuroku* [禦]請來目錄 (Catalogue Submitted by Imperial Request), T55, no. 2161, p. 1060, b17-20, see *Mochizuki*, 2804.

[12] The four garrison towns were the four Tang protectorates in the western region, namely, Yutian 於闐 (Khotan), Shule 疏勒 (Kashgar), Suiye 碎葉 (Suyāb) and Yanqi 焉耆 (Karasahr).

[13] The manuscripts of *Dacheng ershier wen* 大乘二十二問 (Twenty-two Questions on Mahāyāna) are available in the collection of Dunhuang library, see Ueyama Daishun 上山大峻, *Tonkō bukkyō no kenkyū* 敦煌佛教の研究 (Kyoto: Hōzōkan, 1990), 42-43.

Introduction

Due to its close proximity to the Western Market of Chang'an and to its fame as a scenic spot of peony flowers, Ximingsi also became a site favored among lay visitors. The imposing monastic cloisters inspired many Tang poets, including the eminent Bai Juyi 白居易 (772-846), Yuan Zhen 元稹 (779-831), and Wen Tingyun 溫庭筠 (812-870), who help us to understand the monastic serenity and elegance with their first-hand accounts. Other less poetic sources tell us that Ximingsi was also remarkable for its architectural beauty, associated with the grandeur of the legendary Jetavana Monastery (Skt: Jetavana Anāthapiṇḍadasyārāma, Ch. Qiyuan jingshe 祇園精舍) near Śrāvastī (today's Gonda district of Uttar Pradesh), one of the six largest Indian cities during the Buddha's lifetime. Ximingsi later became the prototype for the royal Jing'ai (Reverence) Monastery (Jing'aisi 敬愛寺) in Luoyang 洛陽 and the official Daianji 大安寺 (Monastery of Great Peace, a.k.a. Nandaiji 南大寺) in Heijōkyō 平城京, the capital city of Japan during most of the Nara period (710-740 and 745-784). The story of Ximingsi that connected with the history of Daianji started in the ninth year of Tenpyō 天平 (727) when Emperor Shōmu 聖武天皇 (r. 724-749), the promoter of Nara Buddhism, ordered the construction of Daikandaiji 大官大寺 after the site plan of an ideal monastery.[14] According to *Honchō kōsō den* 本朝高僧伝 (Biographies of Eminent Monks of Japan), a hagiography written by the Japanese Rinzai monk Mangen Shiba 卍元師蠻 (1626-1710) in 1702, master Dōji 道慈 (d. 744), who studied the three fundamental treatises (Ch. *sanlun* 三論, Jap. *sanron*) of the Mādhyamika school in Chang'an, reported that he had experienced the splendor of Ximingsi, a scene so impressive that he resolved to build a monastery modeled on it upon his return to Japan.[15] True or not, the story reveals the great cultural prestige that Ximingsi enjoyed in medieval Japan. Its impact on Buddhism,

---

[14] The Tenpyō era (729-749) is known as one of the most brilliant in the history of Japanese culture, In 741 (Tenpyō 13), Emperor Shōmu ordered the establishment of the state-sponsored Kokubunji 国分寺 ([Nara Era] state-supported provincial temples) in each province. Archaeological excavations of the Kokubunji sites began in 1951 and have continued since. With the help of the priest Rōben 良弁 (689-773), Emperor Shōmu also authorized the establishment of the Tōdaiji 東大寺 (Great Eastern Monastery) and the casting of the Buddha image of Vairocana.

[15] For the biographical sketch of Dōji (*Washū Daianji shamon Dōji den* 和州大安寺沙門道慈傳), see *Honchō kōsōden* 本朝高僧伝 (Biographies of Eminent Monks of Japan), *Dai Nihon bukkyō zensho* 大日本仏教全書 (abbreviated as *DNBZ*), vol. 63, 39-40. *Sanlun* refers to the three treatises translated by Kumārajīva, on which the Three Treatise School (Skt. Mādhyamika, Ch. Sanlunzong 三論宗 or Zhongguanpai 中觀派) bases its doctrines. They are *Madhyamaka-śāstra* (Ch. *Zhonglun* 中論, T1564), *Dvādaśanikāya-śāstra* (Ch. *Shi'er men lun* 十二門論, T1568) and *Śata-śāstra* (Ch. *Bailun* 百論, T1569), see *Mochizuki*, 1702.

as we will see in subsequent chapters, was truly profound and far-reaching.

Methodological Concern and Chapter Outlines

Generally speaking, monasteries throughout the world, especially those centers of learning at the height of their greatness, have been the beneficiaries of sustained scholarly attention.[16] This vibrant tradition of critical enquiry, defined sometimes as "monastic studies," actually finds its origin in landscape studies and the archaeology of Anglo-Saxon religious communities as an approach to dating and phasing a monastery's structures in excavation.[17] In an investigation of religious houses in East Anglia, Tim Pestell tells us:

> Medieval monasteries long attracted the antiquary, and while scholarly study only intensified in the nineteenth century, many research agenda had, by then, already been set. In particular, the Romantic movement of the preceding century proved influential, stimulating interest in monastic ruins from an artistic perspective and in many cases leading to their manipulation.[18]

Likewise the antiquarian interest in the monasteries of Chang'an began in the Song dynasty and revived, long after the decline of Chang'an, in the nineteenth century. Some old scholastic classics, such as *Chōan shiseki no kenkyū* 長安史跡の研究 (Study of the Historical Sites of Chang'an), demonstrate similar interests in geography, crumbling monuments and the architectural remains of ancient Chinese

---

[16] The ancient monasteries are topics of intense research in the West, for some examples, see Jean Virey, *L'abbaye De Cluny* (Macon: Impr. Protat frères, 1921); Joan Evans, *Monastic Life at Cluny, 910-1157* (London: Oxford University Press, 1931); Lyn Rodley, *Cave Monasteries of Byzantine Cappadocia* (New York; Melbourne: Cambridge University Press, 1985); Lacarra Ducay and María del Carmen, *Monasterio De Leyre* (Pamplona: Gobierno de Navarra, 2001); Patrick Greene, *Medieval Monasteries* (London: Continuum, 2005); Elizabeth Fentress, *Walls and Memory: The Abbey of San Sebastiano at Alatri* (Turnhout: Brepols, 2005) and so forth. See William Johnston, ed., *Encyclopedia of Monasticism* (Chicago: Fitzroy Dearborn, 2000), 866-68.

[17] Tim Pestell, *Landscapes of Monastic Foundation: The Establishment of Religious Houses in East Anglia C. 650-1200* (Woodbridge, Suffolk: Boydell Press, 2004), 1-17; and see Sarah Foot, "What was an Early Anglo-Saxon Monastery?" in *Monastic Studies: the Continuity of Tradition*, ed. J. Loades (Bangor, Gwynedd: Headstart History, 1990), 48-57.

[18] Pestell, *Landscapes of Monastic Foundation*, 2.

monasteries.[19] However, for modern Buddhist studies scholars, philosophical inquiry and doctrinal study of a sect (Jap. *shūgaku* 宗學) are the dominant methods in the study of a Buddhist monastery.[20] These approaches treat saṃgha and scripture as the nuclei of Buddhist religion and the very prism through which much of the history of the Buddhist monastery is reflected. On the other hand, Birendra Prasad, in his survey of studies of Indian monasteries in the past century, suggests that current study of Indologists must move beyond the purely art historical domain and should be studies that reference wider societal processes and their interactions with other societal institutions.[21] Therefore, James Robson points out that a fault line runs through interpretations of both East Asian Buddhism and Southeast Asian Buddhism. He says:

> One of the main interpretive problems that scholars of Buddhism now face is the following: How we are to account for the real functioning of those institutions and at the same time capture perceptions of those sites as ideal settings that are somehow supposed to transcend the quotidian world that surrounds them?[22]

It is notable that recent monastery monographs and scholarly articles, not all of them written by Buddhist Studies scholars, start to suggest other profitable lines of enquiry, such as history of art, exorcism, ritual studies, religious anthropology and political history.[23] Instead of using "Monastic Studies" or "Buddhist Monasticism," I prefer

---

[19] Adachi Kiroku 足立喜六, *Choān shiseki no kenkyū* 長安史跡の研究 (Tokyo: Toyo bunko, 1933). From 1929 to 1933, Johannes Prip-Moller (1889-1943) visited hundreds of monasteries in Central China and drew the monastic plans to understand the function and location of the monastic buildings in modern China. See Prip-Moeller, *Chinese Buddhist Monasteries: Their Plan and Its Functions as a Setting for Buddhist Monastic Life* (Hong Kong: Hong Kong University Press, 1967).

[20] *Mochizuki*, addendum 2, 356-57.

[21] Birendra Nath Prasad, "Major Trends and Perspectives in Studies in the Functional Dimensions of Indian Monastic Buddhism in the Past One Hundred Years: A Historiographical Survey," *Buddhist Studies Review* 2, no. 1 (2008): 54.

[22] James Robson, "Introduction: 'Neither Too Far, nor Too Near': The Historical and Cultural Contexts of Buddhist Monasteries in Medieval China and Japan," in *Buddhist Monasticism in East Asia: Places of Practice*, eds. James Benn, Lori Rachelle Meeks, and James Robson (London: Routledge, 2010), 9.

[23] For a recent survey of Buddhist monasteries and monasticism in East Asia, see Pierre Pichard and François Lagirarde, eds., *The Buddhist Monastery: A Cross-Cultural Survey* (Paris: École française d'extrême-orient, 2003); Benn, Meeks, and Robson, *Buddhist Monasticism in East Asia*, 1-17. For recent scholarly investigations of Chinese Buddhist monasteries, see Antonino Forte, "The Origins and Role of the Great Fengxian Monastery at Longmen," *Annali* 56 (1996): 365-87; Kenneth J. Hammond, "Beijing's Zhihua

the term "Monastic Buddhism," which subsumes the profane as well as the sacred nature of Buddhist establishements, that is to say, the lived reality and history of a monastery and its function as an institution of spiritual transformation and Buddhist learning. Based on the relevant historical and religious accounts, what are presented here in a book of modest compass, are some selected perspectives, such as the political relationship between the state and the Buddhist church; art historical imaginaire versus archaeological discovery, as well as monastic scholarship such as bibliographical catalogues and Buddhist collections. As I will elaborate in the concluding chapter, in response to the interpretive problems posited by Robson, my future study of Ximingsi, which is to be written in Chinese, will include a number of new lines of enquiry as well as traditional studies of monasticism and scholasticism.

Having broadly outlined the relevant methodological concerns, I turn here to the significance of the study and how I plan to unfold the story. The limited scholarship on Ximingsi is colored by sketchy treatment of every conceivable perspective on the monastery, from monastic history and doctrinal debate to eminent masters. In the past twenty years, more confident steps have been taken to discuss the site plan the ruin and Buddhist collection of Ximingsi, but until today there is no book-length study in any language to shed light on this almost forgotten sanctuary. This is due to the fact that there is no central text or temple gazetteer of Ximingsi that we can rely on, and the body of historical and religious literature is extremely fragmentary as well as difficult to collect. The problem is especially acute with the excavated *objets d'art* which remain inaccessible to scholars outside the circle of professional archaeologists. A consequence of this imbalance in sources is that, where documentary material exists, it has often been seized upon without critical appreciation of other evidence. Based on sources and monastic records absent in the existing scholarship, the present study will examine thematic topics such as the

---

Monastery: History and Restoration in China's Capital," in *Cultural Intersections in Later Chinese Buddhism*, ed. Marsha Weidner (Honolulu: University of Hawai'i Press, 2001), 189-208; Duan Yuming 段玉明, *Xiangguosi: zai Tang Song diguo de shensheng yu fansu zhijian* 相國寺: 在唐宋帝國的神聖與凡俗之間 (Chengdu: Bashu shushe, 2004); Chen Jinhua 陳金華, "Images, Legends, Politics, and the Origin of the Great Xiangguo Monastery in Kaifeng: A Case-Study of the Formation and Transformation of Buddhist Sacred Sites in Medieval China," *Journal of the American Oriental Society* 125, no. 3 (2005): 353-378; idem., "The Statues and Monks of Shengshan Monastery: Money and Maitreyan Buddhism in Tang China," *Asia Major* (2006): 111-60; Meir Shahar, *The Shaolin Monastery: History, Religion, and the Chinese Martial Arts* (Honolulu: University of Hawai'i Press, 2008).

historic monastery; the temple's site plan and sacred space; and bibliographical catalogues and manuscript libraries.

I intend to group my topics into the two parts that Robson pointed out: the secular and quotidian world that surrounded the monastery, and the soterological function and idealistic aspect of the monastery. The book consists of two parts containing six chapters and a conclusion. The first part fills out the broad picture of the practical functioning of Ximingsi in the political life of the Tang sovereign as well as its role in the complicated social worlds within which it was situated. To elucidate the rich history and legend of Ximingsi, the first three chapters focus on the prehistory and history of the monastery. There is little doubt that for over a millennium, the boundaries between the real and the imagined monastery are shifting and slippery. This is particularly perplexing given that historical facts are often overshadowed by anecdotal literature and the literary imagination associated with the monastery. Robert Borgen, in his attempted reconstruction of the history of Dōmyōji 道明寺 in Osaka, poses a similar issue that we will encounter in our interpretation:

> The history of Dōmyōji, noteworthy though it may be, demonstrates a fundamental difficulty faced when trying to understand events from the ancient past. The data needed to answer all the questions one might like to pose are often missing. The clear focus and rigorous argumentation typical of modern scholarly writing may well veil the murky uncertainty that is the true picture left by the sources.[24]

We have the same problem here. Nevertheless, I shall try here for the first time to piece together scraps of ancient texts in an effort to reconstruct a comprehensive picture of the historical fact of Ximingsi. In chapter 2, I intend to investigate the prehistory of Ximingsi in the context of anecdotal stories and the social world of Sui-Tang Chang'an. Then, in chapters 3 and 4, I shall address the general position of Ximingsi in relation to the Tang monarchs. This is by no means to explore the full range of issues in the history of Ximingsi but to sketch out the major events that took place at Ximingsi and to show how the institution served the Tang Empire as a super monastery over two and a half centuries.

---

[24] Robert Borgen, "A History of Dōmyōji to 1572 (or Maybe 1575): An Attempted Reconstruction," *Monumenta Nipponica* 62, no. 1 (2007): 3-4.

Introduction

Next follows the second part of the book, which contains two thematic chapters dealing with less mundane aspects of Ximingsi. In the fifth chapter, I look into the space and artistic world of Ximingsi, a topic of interest to art historians and archeologists. Decorated with palatial opulence and furnished with didactic paintings and images in courtly styles, the monastery could also be aptly compared to a modern public museum. Revealed through textual sources and pictorial manuscripts, the original site plan of Ximingsi presents itself as something of a mystery. This chapter first documents the founding of the monastery and its architectural development under the abbotship of Xuanzang and Daoxuan. The question I explore is to what extent the monastery was related to the *Zhong tianzhu sheweiguo qihuansi tujing* 中天竺舍衛國祇洹寺圖經 (Illustrated Scripture of Jetavana Monastery of Śravāstī in Central Asia, T1899), an illustrated manuscript attributed to Daoxuan. It is also noted in ancient sources that Ximingsi had a remarkable influence upon the establishment of the Daianji Monastery in Japan. However, as the illustrated manuscript of Jetavana has posed questions for our understanding, scholars have long been puzzled by the relationship between Ximingsi and Daianji. This chapter will put forward a re-examination of key issues and evidence not carefully studied before. Since the final eclipse of the Tang Empire in the early tenth century, Ximingsi has lain in "two-meter deep" oblivion under the bustling city of modern Xi'an. As an integral part of the archaeological excavation of ancient Chang'an started after 1949, the excavation of Ximingsi took place in 1985 and 1992, revealing thousands of artifacts and architectural remains of a major monastic cloister.[25] Chapter 5 will attempt a partial reconstruction of the monastic plan on the basis of archaeological evidence and textual sources, in an effort to elucidate the intended religious use of the building complex and answer questions posed by art historians. It will then explore the disputed relationship of Ximingsi to its Indian and Japanese parallels.[26] My purpose here is not to provide comprehensive solutions to the art historical issues but merely to set out a departure point from which further investigations might proceed.

Chapter 6 then provides a glimpse of Ximingsi as a scholarly institution —— including the distinguished library and a cultural history of the renowned Buddhist

---

[25] For brief archaeological reports of Ximingsi, see An Jiayao 安家瑤, "Tang Chang'an Ximingsi yizhi fajue jianbao 唐長安西明寺遺址發掘簡報," *Kaogu* 考古 1 (1990): 45-55; idem, "Tang Chang'an Ximingsi yizhi de kaogu faxian 唐長安西明寺遺址的考古發現," *Tang yanjiu* 唐研究 6 (2000): 337-52.

[26] With regard to the dispute, see Hattori Masanobu 服部匡延, "Daianji wa saimyōji no mokentoiu setsu nitsuite 大安寺は西明寺の模建という説について," *Nanto bukkyō* 南都仏教 34 (1975): 24-39.

collection across medieval centuries. I will first focus on the seventh-century Buddhist bibliographical catalogue *Datang neidian lu* and a typical genre of Chinese Buddhist libraries entitled *jingzang* 經藏 (sūtra repository, Jap. *kyōzō*), which disappeared in post-Song China but prospered in Tang Chang'an. Next we will turn to a second Buddhist catalogue edited in 800, *Zhenyuan xinding shijiao mulu* 貞元新定釋教目錄 (Zhenyan Revised Catalogue of Canonical Buddhist Texts, T2157), and some special collections that testify to the transmission of manuscripts from China to Japan and sectarian traditions passed down at Ximingsi. This trajectory of investigation increases our understanding of Japanese monks who resided and studied in Ximingsi, including Kūkai, Dōji, Eichū 永忠 (743-816), and Enchin 円珍 (814-891), to name but a few.[27] Finally, at the end of the book, I will put emphasis on the legacy of Ximingsi and explore a variety of prospects for further study.

In general, this book is exploratory, not definitive. It may be used as a well-documented introduction to Ximingsi, but at this stage it does not offer a comprehensive survey of all the eminent scholar-monks in residence, nor does it deal with the great complexity of the monastery's scholastic tradition. In broad strokes, my point of departure is to explore this monastery in a range of methodological alternatives, especially those rarely touched by religious scholars. It is also important to note here that, by connecting with the rich cultural legacy of Chang'an, this project also contributes to the fledgling field of Chang'an Studies advocated by Chinese scholars.[28] Consequently, I hope the present study might well have set up a stage from which we can proceed to probe into the spiritual world and more complicated issues related to Ximingsi.

---

[27] For a pioneering study of Japanese student-monks in residence at Ximingsi, see Ono Katsutoshi, "Chōan no saimyōji to nittō guhōsō 長安的西明寺與入唐求法僧," in *Chūgoku mikkyō* 中國密教, ed. Matsunaga Yūkei 松長有慶 and Yoritomi Motohiro 賴富本宏 (Kyoto: Hōzōkan, 1994-1995), 65-86.

[28] This project also aims to remedy the deficiency in Chang'an studies noted by Chinese historian Rong Xinjiang 榮新江, see Rong Xinjiang, "Sui-Tang Chang'an yanjiu de jidian sikao 隋唐長安研究的幾點思考," *Tang Yanjiu* 9 (2003): 2-3. Chang'an studies is yet not comparable to the flourishing fields of Tokyo Studies (*Tōkyō gagu* 東京学), Edo Studies (*Edo gaku* 江戸学) and Kyoto Studies (*Kyōto gaku* 京都学); see, e.g., Ogi Shinzō 小木新造, *Edo Tōkyōgaku jiten* 江戸東京学事典 (Tokyo: Sanseidō, 1987); Ōgushi Natsumi 大串夏身, *Edo, Tōkyō gaku zasshi ronbun sōran* 江戸・東京学雑志論文総覧 (Tokyo: Seikyūsha, 1994); Murai Yasuhiko 村井康彦, *Kyōto gaku e no shōtai* 京都学への招待 (Tokyo: Asuka kikaku, 2002).

PART ONE

Imaginaire and Religio-Political History of Ximingsi

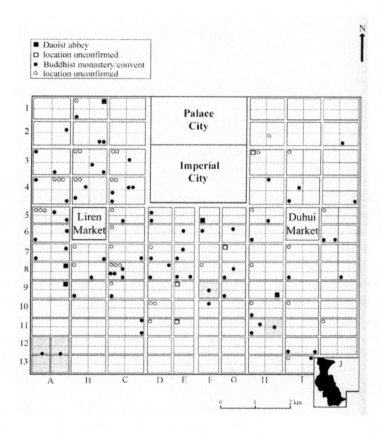

Figure. 3   Religious Institutions of the Sui City of Daxingcheng. Source: Victor Cunrui Xiong, *Emperor Yang of the Sui Dynasty: His Life, Times, and Legacy*, 158.

Chapter Two

The Prehistory of Ximingsi: Anecdotes and Imagining

The Birth of Tragedy: From General to Prince

For the first millennium of the Common Era, Chang'an was the gateway to the northwestern Silk Road and the very symbol of ancient China, the land known as *Cīna-sthāna* (Ch. *zhendan* 震旦 or *zhina* 支那) in Buddhist literature. Since the transmission of Buddhism to China, the Buddhist representatives from Serindia, seeking to spread their religion in China, had come to the city with the mission to impress the ruling class.[1] By the seventh century, through an arduous course against opposition, Buddhism had proved itself to be a persuasive religion compatible with Chinese tradition. Meanwhile, as seen in monks' travel diaries, Persian missionaries' steles, and diplomats' epitaphs, the city of Tang Chang'an, originally constructed as the Sui-dynasty city of Daxingcheng 大興城 (Figure. 3) in 613 (Daye 大業 9), rose to beome a prominent hub of religion and cultural splendor after the founding of the Tang in 618. It was a monumental metropolis, filled with theatres, temples, stūpas, gardens, and grand residences.

In the long history of China, Chang'an was the first city to gather hundreds of Buddhist monasteries in a single urban area. The subject of our study, Ximingsi,

---

[1] Chinese Buddhism was from the outset a distinctly urban phenomenon because Buddhism was brought to China with the merchants who traveled along the urban centers of the Silk Road in northwestern China. See Erik Zürcher, *The Buddhist Conquest of China: the Spread and Adaptation of Buddhism in Early Medieval China* (1959; repr., Leiden: Brill, 2007), 59. For other studies of this phenomenon, see, e.g., James Heitzman, "Early Buddhism, Trade and Empire," in *Studies in the Archaeology and Palaeoanthropology of South Asia*, ed. Kenneth Kennedy and Gregory Possehl (New Delhi: Oxford & IBH: American Inst. of Indian Studies, 1984), 121-37; Kathleen Morrison, "Trade, Urbanism, and Agricultural Expansion: Buddhist Monastic Institutions and the State in the Early Historic Western Deccan," *World Archaeology* 27, no. 2 (1995): 203-21.

while perhaps hardly typical of the Chang'an Buddhist institutions, provides one window into the little-known world of the medieval metropolitan monastery in China. It is inevitably a world combining fact and fiction. By the high point of the Tang period in the eighth century, urban authors and mendicant minstrels had created an anecdotal Chang'an that incorporated the street tales and popular stories of the citizens. Under such circumstances, the story of Ximingsi that comes down to us across the centuries is an ongoing dialogue between literature and history.[2]

The major part of Ximingsi, we know, was constructed on the site of an abandoned royal residence. Like many other imperial temples in Chang'an, it thus preserved the features of Chinese residential architecture, built around the traditional "cloister" (*yuan* 院).[3] Blinded, perhaps, by the later splendor of Ximingsi, scholars have hitherto ignored the monastery's prehistory that took place in the residence. Yet this prehistorical melodrama is not without its interest; for even a preliminary perusal of scattered Tang sources —— official annals, urban tales, anecdotes, hagiographies and literary accounts —— reveals a story that shaped the cultural image of Ximingsi in China and beyond. Hence, before exploring the critical history of Ximingsi in chapter 3, we will first contemplate here its prehistory, embellished by imaginaire and tragedies long forgotten. This drama unfolds with a Sui Dynasty general and concludes with a Tang Dynasty prince, although I do not always strictly follow the historical sequence.

In the Sui and first years of the Tang, Ximingsi was preceded by a magnificent residence huge in scale. Over three brief decades, the house became the property of dignitaries and members of the imperial family. The story begins with the ascendency of Yang Su 楊素 (d. 606), Director of the Department of State Affairs (*shangshu ling* 尚書令) in the short-lived Sui Dynasty. His lengthy biography in the *Suishu* 隋書 (Book of Sui) testifies to his significance in both domestic politics and military

---

[2] For some examples of imaginaire in cultural history, see Alain Godard and Marie-Françoise Piéjus, *Espaces, histoire et imaginaire dans la culture Italienne de la Renaissance* (Paris: Université Paris III Sorbonne nouvelle, Centre Censier, 2006); Jacques Le Goff and Michel Cazenave, *Histoire et imaginaire* (Paris, Poiesis: Diffusion Payot, 1986); Michel Morin and Claude Bertrand, *Le territoire imaginaire de la culture* (Montréal: Hurtubise HMH, 1979).

[3] In Buddhist literature, *yuan* 院 (Skt. *ārāma* or *paryāṇa*, Jap. *in*) refers to a cloister or a grove, *Mochizuki*, 172-73. For a brief introduction to the definition of Buddhist monastery (*si* 寺) in Chinese Buddhism, see Pichard and Lagirarde, *The Buddhist Monastery*, 309-10. For detailed discussion of this topic, see below, Chapter 5.

history in the sixth century.[4] Shortly after 584 (Kaihuang 開皇 4), the Sui sovereignty was afflicted by the calamites of war and revolt from the South. Yang Su was summoned by the first Sui emperor Yang Jian 楊堅 (r. 581-604) to crush the rebellion led by Wang Guoqing 王國慶, a viceroy stationed in the Southern port of Quanzhou. After he returned to Chang'an in victory, he was greatly rewarded by the emperor:

> Once he arrived in the capital, visitors called on him in succession. His son Yang Xuanjiang was promoted to the position of Yitong general. The emperor bestowed upon him 40 *jin* of gold; a silver jar filled with coins, 3000 bolts of thin silk; 200 horses; 2000 sheep; 100 hectares of public paddy and a district [to build his residence].

> 比到京師, 問者日至. 拜素子玄奬為儀同, 賜黃金四十斤, 加銀瓶, 實以金錢, 縑三千段, 馬二百匹, 羊二千口, 公田百頃, 宅一區.[5]

In this account, the last word deserves our attention; for, while the Chinese term "*yiqu* 一區" means "a district" or "a section," it may refer here to "a plot of ground" in the Sui city of Daxingcheng.[6] Built by the talented architect Yuwen Kai 宇文愷 (555-612) under the sponsorship of Wendi in 583, the city of Daxingcheng grew into power and opulence in Sui-Tang China, although much of the city remained unpopulated in early Tang.[7] It is hardly surprising that the land bestowed upon Yang

---

[4] For the Biography of Yang Su, see *Suishu* 隋書 (Book of Sui), 48.1281-92. For an explanation of the title *Shangshu ling* 尚書令, see Charles Hucker, *A Dictionary of Official Titles in Imperial China* (Stanford: Stanford University Press, 1985), 412. For a general introduction to Yang Su, see Xu Song 徐松 and Li Jianchao 李健超, *Zengding Tang liangjing chengfang kao* 增訂唐兩京城坊考 (Xi'an: Sanqin chubanshe, 2006), 207; Victor Cunrui Xiong, *Historical Dictionary of Medieval China* (Lanham, Md.: Scarecrow Press, 2009), 609; see also Gang Deng, *Maritime Sector, Institutions, and Sea Power of Premodern China* (Westport, Conn.: Greenwood Press, 1999), 10. The newly excavated epitaph of Yang Su also sheds light on his life; see Liang Jianbang 梁建邦, "Yang Su muzhi de faxian yu jiazhi 楊素墓誌的發現與價值," *Weinan shifan xueyuan xuebao* 渭南師範學院學報 1 (1990): 94-98.

[5] *Suishu* 48.1285; Liang Jianbang, "Yang Su muzhi de faxian yu jiazhi," 97.

[6] In some cases, *yiqu* 一區 also means "one residence"; see *Hanyu da cidian* 漢語大詞典 (Shanghai: Cishu chubanshe, 1986-1993), s.v. *yiqu*. In Japanese kanji, *ikku* 一区 refers to "a region", "a segment" or "an area"; see *Nihon kokugo daijiten* 日本国語大辞典 (Tokyo: Shōgakukan, 2006), s.v. *ikku*. The dictionary is hereafter abbreviated as *Nihon kokugo daijiten*.

[7] For a brief introduction of the two cities of Chang'an, see Xiong, *Historical Dictionary of Medieval China*,

Su was immediately used to build a magnificent residence, which can be dated approximately between 584 and 599. The extravagant building complex may have lasted into the seventh century when it was passed on to the hands of a Tang prince. It is believed that a part of the layout of this splendid residence was preserved when it was renovated as the Ximingsi several decades later.

Thanks to the military exploits of Yang Su, his son Yang Xuangan 楊玄感 (d. 618) was promoted to the senior position of Pillar of State (*zhuguo* 柱國).[8] Parvenu though it was, the Yang clan rose to become a power capable of monopolizing high government positions. They possessed thousands of lackeys and maidservants within the confines of their extravagant mansion, which was comparable to the Sui imperial palace.[9] However, shortly after Yang Su passed away, Yang Xuangan and his brothers broke their oath of loyalty to the throne and in 613 (Daye 大業 9) masterminded a rebellion against the Emperor Yang of the Sui (Suiyangdi 隋煬帝, r. 604-618). Unfortunately their mutiny failed as a result of the questionable strategy of besieging the eastern capital Luoyang. Xuangan, his brother Yang Jishan 杨积善, and the rebel force were practically destroyed in Shangluo 上洛 (Shang County, Shanxi). The end of the Yang family, the fate of the Yang brothers in particular, was tragic, as Victor Cunrui Xiong says:

At his own request, Xuangan was hacked to death by Jishan, who then stabbed himself. While the head of Xuangan was delivered to the emperor, his corpse was hauled to a marketplace in Luoyang, where it was quartered and, after being exposed in public for three days, ground up and burned. With Yangdi's permission, General Yuwen Shu had the wounded Jishan tied to a wooden shaft, enclosing his neck with a chariot wheel. Officials shot at him until his body was covered with arrows like a hedgehog. He was then dismembered. Xuangan's other brothers either died during the rebellion or were hunted down and killed by the Sui army. The lineage of the powerful Yang clan was exterminated.[10]

78-9; see also Okazaki Takashi 岡崎敬, "Zui・Daikō = Tō・Chōanjō to Zuitō・tōto Rakuyōjō —— kinnen no chōsa kekka o chūshin toshite 隋・大興 = 唐・長安城と隋唐・東都洛陽城 —— 近年の調査結果 を中心として," *Bukkyō geijutsu* 仏教芸術 51 (1963): 86-108.

[8] In 590, Yang Su crushed another revolt in the former Chen territory, a petty state founded on the fertile southern land of the empire. In the subsequent years of Renshou 仁壽 (601-604), Yang Su next subdued the Turkic army and forced them to retreat to the northern steppe.

[9] *Suishu*, 48.1285.

[10] Victor Cunrui Xiong, *Emperor Yang of the Sui Dynasty: His Life, Times, and Legacy* (Albany: State

As a result of this incident, the extravagant residence of the Yang clan was confiscated by the Sui government. We do not know the fate of the confiscated residence during the decade after the death of Yang Xuangan. From the point of view of Chinese popular religion, an abandoned residence is ridden with "contaminated elements." People of the time believed that in the wake of the tragedy of the Yang clan the house was filled with ominous airs (*yinqi* 陰氣) that should be expelled through apotropaic rituals. Shortly after the founding of the Tang Dynasty, in the middle of the reign of Wude 武德 (618-626), the forsaken residence was renovated and registered under the name of Princess Wanchun (Wanchun gongzhu 萬春公主), one of the nineteen daughters of Emperor Gaozu 高祖 (r. 618-626).[11] The life of princess Wanchun is unrecorded in history, but she probably lived in the house for ten years —— a period sufficient to overhaul and upgrade the residence to a level commensurate with the Tang imperial standard. After her brother, the empire's ironhanded ruler Taizong 太宗 (r. 626-649), seized the throne through fratricide, he bequeathed the house to his beloved fourth son Prince Li Tai 李泰 (618-652) around 636 (Zhenguan 貞觀 10), when the young Prince was granted the noble title "King of Wei" (*weiwang* 魏王). Well versed in literature, Li Tai was known for patronizing talented scholars and men of letters. Attracted to his literary enterprise, scholars gathered in the Wenxue guan 文學館 (Mansion of Literature) established within his residence.[12] I suspect that much of his private library and manuscripts preserved in this institution ended up, a few decades after, in the famed collection of Ximingsi. As we will see in chapter 6, the Ximingsi library also contained a substantial collection of secular texts and literary writings. Unfortunately Li Tai's ambition for power outweighed his literary taste. After an internecine struggle with his brother Li Chengqian 李承乾 (619-645), Li Tai was demoted and exiled to distant Junzhou 均

University of New York Press, 2006), 60.

[11] "Ono, *Shiryōhen*", 227; Xu Song and Li Jianchao, *Zengding Tang liangjing chengfang kao*, 208.

[12] Li Tai is also remembered as one of the noted geographers in the Tang period. Following the tradition of expounding one's ideas in writing, he and his guest writers spent five years editing the *Kuodizhi* 括地志 (Gazetteer of the Earth, 641), a geographical tome testifying to his talents in prose and vision. For Li Tai's biographies, see *JTS* 76. 2653-656; *XTS* 80. 3563. For the aristocratic residences of the Tang Dynasty princes, see Nunome Chōfū 布目潮渢, "Tōdai Choan ni okeru ōfu · ōtaku ni tsuite 唐代長安における王府·王宅について," In *Chūgoku shūrakushi no kenkyū* 中国聚落史の研究, ed. Tōdaishi kenkyūkai 唐代史研究会 (Tokyo: Tōsui shobō, 1980), 115-24. Sun Yinggang 孫英剛, "Sui-Tang Chang'an de wangfu yu wangzhai 隋唐長安的王府與王宅," *Tang Yanjiu* 9 (2003): 185-214.

州, south of the Yangtze River. After he passed away in 652 (Yonghui 永辉 3), the Tang government eventually bought back his residence.[13]

Anecdotal Accounts of Yang Su and Ximingsi

Anyone familiar with English literature knows the nineteenth century British epistolary novel, *The Moonstone* (1868), which tells a riveting story of a magic yellow diamond stolen from the forehead of the Indian Moon Goddess. From its loss to recovery, the gem claimed many lives among those who tried to take possession of it.[14] Like the moonstone, the residence of Yang Su was also a house that brought misfortune to its owners. Tales of the residence, most of which center on the powerful Yang Su, were known to the founders of Ximingsi, including Xuanzang and Daoxuan, who might very well have thought that it was not an ideal site on which to construct a monastery. However, the monastic community apparently appreciated such a merciless general, whose biography, edited by the Tang historians, is testament to his ironhandedness and power.[15] Surprisingly, discredited in Chinese history, he survived as a charismatic figure in both popular literature and Buddhist annals. In the apologetic writings of Buddho-Taoist debates, Yang Su was repeatedly cited as a pro-Buddhist official. The early Tang Buddhist scholar Falin 法琳 (572-640), in his treatise *Bianzheng lun* 辯正論 (Discerning the Correct, T2110), declares that Yang Su admired Buddhist dharma and constructed a Guangming Monastery (Guangmingsi 光明寺, Brightness Monastery) so that he could accumulate merit.[16] Another story, in Daoxuan's *Ji gujin fodao lunheng* 集古今佛道論論衡 (Collection of Critical Evaluations of Buddhism and Daoism from the Past and Present, T2104),

---

[13] Ono, *Shiryōhen*, 227. Some scholars argue that, immediately aupon Li Tai's death in 652, the Tang Dynasty government already established an unnamed monastery on the site of his residence, see Shi Hongshuai 史紅帥, "'Tang Liangjing Chengfang Kao' 'Ximingsi' Jiaowu 《唐兩京城坊考》'西明寺' 校誤," *Zhongguo lishi dili luncong* 中國歷史地理論叢 1 (1999): 184; Xu Song and Li Jianchao, Zengding *Tang Liangjing Chengfang kao*, 210.

[14] The novel was written by the British author Wilkie Collins (1824-1889), see Wilkie Collins and John Sutherland, *The Moonstone* (New York: Oxford University Press, 2008).

[15] As demonstrated on many occasions in his biography, Yang Su forced hundreds of soldiers to launch the first attack and ordered the execution of anyone who dared to return without defeating the enemies. See *Suishu*, 48.1281-296.

[16] *Bianzheng lun* 辯正論 (Discerning the Correct), T52, no. 2110, p. 519, c11-13; see also *Minggong faxi zhi* 名公法喜志, edited by Xia Shufang 夏樹芳, *XZJ* 150, p. 79, a17-18. The name of the monastery erected by Yang Su certainly reminds us of the literal meaning of "Ximing" (Western Brightness).

tells of the encounter of Yang Su with local Daoists residing at *Louguan tai* 樓觀台 (Platform of the Tiered Abbey), a celebrated Daoist Monastery at the foot of Mount Zhongnan 終南山 in the southern suburbs of Chang'an. In the story, they engaged in a debate on why Yin Xi 尹喜, who purportedly received the 5000-word teaching from Laozi, was depicted on the monastic fresco as a Buddhist ascetic (Ch. *Shamen* 沙门, Skt. *śramaṇa*) and transformed as Śākyamuni Buddha converting barbarians from Central Asia.[17] Obviously the scene contains allusion to the Buddhist refutation of the conversion of the barbarians by Laozi (*laozi huahu* 老子化胡), a topic provoking disparaging comments by Buddhists in medieval China. In Daoxuan's treatise, Yang Su told the local clergy that the metamorphosis of Yin Xi into the Gautama Buddha proves that the Buddhist way is superior to the Daoist path. The anecdote is passed down to us because both Daoxuan and Falin, in their canonical writings dated during the early Tang, cite the case of Yang Su as supporting evidence, probably used in court debate to gain imperial favor for the Buddhist religion.[18]

It is possible that the image of Yang Su in Buddhist literature circulated with Daoxuan's apologetic treatises, in which the author mentions the former a dozen times and praises him as a devout Buddhist. This is not a coincidence, considering the unique position of Ximingsi in the Buddho-Daoist debate in the early Tang. Another reason for the popularity of Yang Su, I suspect, lies in his fickle image as portrayed by popular literature and urban tales of Chang'an. Whether Yang Su was a true Buddhist is unknown to us, but the catastrophe of the Yang clan was well-known among the people of Chang'an, let alone the monastic community of Ximingsi.

The old houses scattered throughout Chang'an, like the ruins of antiquity, provided subject matter for both wandering minstrels and official writers. Among a cluster of medieval works capturing memories of Chang'an, *Liangjing xinji* 兩京新

---

[17] Yin Xi, also known as Wenshi zhenren 文始真人 in Daoist religion, was the gatekeeper of Hangu Guan 函穀關. His biography appears in a Taoist hagiography titled *Lishi zhenxian tidao tongjian* 曆世真仙體道通鑒 (or *Xianjian* 仙鑒), written by the Yuan Dynasty Daoist master Zhao Daoyi 趙道一. The story of Yin Xi's reception of the *Daodejing* is also recorded in the biography of Laozi (*Laizi Hanfeizi liezhuan* 老子韓非子列傳) in the *Records of the Grand Historian* (*Shiji* 史記); see Sima Qian 司馬遷, *Shiji* 史記 (Beijing: Zhonghuashuju, 1959), 2139-146.

[18] *Bianzheng lun*, T52, no. 2110, p. 522, b22-c12; *Ji gujin fodao lunheng* 集古今佛道論衡 (Collection of Critical Evaluations of Buddhism and Daoism from the Past and Present, abbreviated as *FDLH*), T 52, no. 2104, p. 378, c25-p. 379, a1. For a stimulating study of the text and the Buddo-Daoist court debate in early Tang, see Friederike Assandri, "Die Debatten zwischen Daoisten und Buddhisten in der frühen Tang-Zeit und die Chongxuan-Lehre des Daoismus" (PhD Dissertation, Heidelberg, 2002).

記 (New Record of the Two Capitals), preserves anecdotes and founding legends of residences that circulated in Chang'an during the eighth century. Written by the Tang historian Wei Shu 韋述 (8th c.) in the tenth year of Kaiyuan (722), only the third fascicle of *Liangjing xinji* survives today, as a manuscript preserved in the Kanazawa Bunko 金沢文庫 in Yokohama.[19] In his account of Ximingsi in the book, Wei Shu presents a household tale concerning Yang Su and his residence, an urban romance of a "broken mirror" (*pojing* 破鏡), a metaphor referring to the reunion of a couple parted in a chaotic time. In many extant texts, this annecdote becomes a famed motif representing people's imagination of Ximingsi.

According to *Liangjing xinji*, the last emperor of the Chen Dynasty (557-589) Chen Shubao 陳叔寶 (553-604) had a beautiful sister known as Princess Lechang (Lechang gongzhu 樂昌公主), who was originally married to Xu Deyan 徐德言, the retainer to the heir apparent of Chen. Just before the Chen Dynasty was crushed by Yang Su and his army, Xu Deyan realized that in this time of tumult his wife, owing to her beauty, would fall into the hands of the upper-class conquerors. He broke a mirror and told Princess Lechang to sell her half in the market of the Daxingcheng city on the fifteenth day of the first month so that he could follow this lead to find her. The couple was forced to endure a long separation, during which Princess Lechang, now known as Lady Chen, gained the favor of Yang Su and became one of his beloved concubines. After Chen was annexed by the Sui Empire, in the hope of finding his wife, Xu Deyan travelled to the far north and arrived in Daxingcheng. As hoped, one day he found the other half of the mirror, peddled by an old servant at an exorbitant price in the western market. On inquring about Chen's whereabouts and hearing of her marriage to Yang Su, he composed a poem on the surface of the mirror:

| 鏡與人俱去 | The mirror and person both departed, |
| 鏡歸人不歸 | The mirror returns but not the person. |

---

[19] This fragmentary manuscript, probably copied by Japanese monks, is preserved in the library of the Maeda clan (maedashi 前田氏) in the fief of Kaga (Kagahan 加賀藩). Titled "*Sonkeikaku zō Kanazawa Bunko bon* 尊經閣藏金澤文庫本," the manuscript was transmitted to Japan by the end of the Tang Dynasty. For an introduction of the text and its author, see Seo Tatsuhiko 妹尾達彦, "Wei Shu de 'Liangjing xinji yu bashiji qianye de Chang'an 韋述的《兩京新記》與八世紀前葉的長安," *Tang yanjiu* 9 (2003): 9-52; Rong Xinjiang, "Wei Shu jiqi 'Liangjing xinji' 韋述極其《兩京新記》," In *Sui Tang Chang'an: xingbie, jiyi ji qita* 隋唐長安：性別, 記憶及其他 (Shanghai: Fudan daxue chubanshe, 2010), 122-39.

無複恒娥影　　　Heng'e's image is no more;
空餘明月輝　　　Empty but for the moonlight.[20]

Touched by the love story of Lady Chen, Yang Su granted her freedom and reunited the couple. Fanciful though this imagined history may be, the tale took on a life of its own and survives even today in modern Chinese as a popular idiom called "a broken mirror made whole again (*pojing chongyuan* 破鏡重圓)."

The story circulated widely in Chinese and Japanese literature and left an indelible imprint in the succeeding dynasties. It is impossible to picture how the monks of Ximingsi retold the story in their casual talk, but the metaphor of the broken mirror formulated in the Tang dynasty as the story circulated is found in the Chan talks in the succeeding Five Dynasties (907-960). The *Jingde chuandeng lu* 景德傳燈錄 (Record of the Transmission of the Lamp Published in the Jingde Era [1004-1007], T2067), a representative collection of biographies of prominent Chan monks edited in 1004, documents a conversation between master Xiujing 休靜 and Zhuangzong 莊宗 (r. 923-926), the first emperor of the Later Tang Dynasty (923-936). Once in a dharma talk the emperor posed the question why the enlightened one (*Dawuderen* 大悟底人) has the possibility of backsliding into ignorance, Xiujing responded with a typical Chan rejoinder "a broken mirror doesn't reflect, as fallen blossom doesn't return to the branch".[21] Although the broken mirror in Zen Buddhism is about a cracked or shattered mirror in which the image is poorly reflected, the word "*pojing*" is understood as coming from the story of Yang Su.[22]

---

[20] Ono, *Shiryōhen*, 227-28; the story is also preserved in the Song Dynasty anecdotal anthology *Taiping guangji* 太平廣記 (Era of Great Peace, abbreviated as *TPGJ*), see *TPGJ* 166. 1212-213. Heng'e 姮娥, popularly known as Chang'e 嫦娥, is the Chinese moon goddess, whose story is available in the philosophical classic *Huainanzi* 淮南子 (Prince of Huainan). For a short English translation of the story of Xu Deyan, cf. Kang-i Sun Chang, Haun Saussy, and Charles Yim-tze Kwong, eds., *Women Writers of Traditional China: an Anthology of Poetry and Criticism* (Stanford: Stanford University Press, 1999), 133-34.

[21] The original text reads "破鏡不重照，落華難上枝", see *Jingde chuandeng lu* 景德傳燈錄 (Record of the Transmission of the Lamp Published in the Jingde Era [1004-1007]), T51, no. 2076, p. 338, a4-26. A disciple of the eminent Chan master Dongshan Liangjie 洞山良價 (807-869), Xiujing 休靜 officiated as the spiritual teacher of Emperor Zhuangzong. Xiujing was a monk registered at Huayan Monastery (Huayansi 華嚴寺) located in the southern suburbs of Chang'an. We can infer that he was familiar with the story of Xu Deyan since short novels and poetic renditions of the tale already spread widely in the capital after the eighth century.

[22] *Nihon kokugo daijiten*, s.v. *Hakyō futatabi tarasazu* はきょう再び照らさず; *Kōjien* 広辞苑, 6th ed.

At least after *Liangjin Xinji* and *Jingde chuandeng lu* were transmitted to Japan, the story of the *hakyō* 破鏡 (broken mirror), which was associated with Ximingsi, found many derivatives in Japanese language as "*Hakyō no nageki* 破鏡の嘆き" (the sigh for the broken mirror)", or as "*Hakyō futatabi tarasazu* 破鏡再び照らさず" (a broken mirror does not reflect), which is the direct translation of the Chan phrase in *Jingde chuandeng lu*.[23]

When the mansion was finally reconstructed as the newly-established Ximingsi, the vestige of Yang Su's residence, some of which was still preserved, must have reminded the monastics of the decline of the Yang Clan. Wei Shu had this to say regarding an old well left in the Cloister of Monk's Kitchen (*sengchuyuan* 僧厨院) in Ximingsi:

> There was an old well inside the monastery which once belonged to [the residence of] Yang Su. After Yang Xuangan was killed, his family [was forced to] cast gold into the well. Although residents of later time caught a glimpse of the gold in the water, they never succeeded in acquiring the gold. At that time the monks (of Ximing) called it a "mysterious well".

> 內有楊素舊井，玄感被誅，家人以金投井，後人雖能夠窺見，但鈎汲無所獲，當時寺衆稱此爲靈井.[24]

For people of traditional society, the very fact of living in Chang'an meant living in a world full of supernatural beings. As demonstrated by Yu Xin 余欣， in his research on what he called the "livelihood religions" (*Minsheng zongjiao* 民生宗教, or the religion of daily life) in Dunhuang, medieval citizens believed that an ominous mansion was besieged by homicidal demons and monsters of every conceivable variety. The long list of bogeys and specters that he enumerates explains why house-guarding rituals are so prevalent in Dunhuang manuscripts.[25] The case of the

---

(Tokyo: Iwanami shoten, 2008), s.v. *hakyō* 破鏡 (especially the example of *Hakyō futatabi tarasazu* 破鏡再び照らさず). The sixth edition of *Kōjien* is hereafter abbreviated as *Kōjien*.

[23] For some examples, see, *Kōjien*, s. v. *hakyō* 破鏡 and *rakka* 落花; See also *Zengaku daijiten* 禅学大辞典 (Tokyo: Taishūkan shoten, 1978), s.v. *Hakyō kasanete utsusazu* 破鏡不重照; hereafter abbreviated as *Zengaku daijiten*.

[24] Ono, *Shiryōhen*, 227.

[25] Yu Xin 余欣, *Shendao renxin: Tang Song zhiji dunhuang minsheng zongjiao shehuishi yanjiu* 神道人心: 唐宋之際敦煌民生宗教社會史研究 (Beijing: Zhonghua shuju, 2006), 196-239. The English title that Xu

mysterious well of Ximingsi reflects the fact that, as pointed out by Seo Tatsuhiko 妹尾達彦, by the eighth century, Chang'an had become the stage of innumerable poems, novels, tales and anecdotes, through which a common memory of the city was shared among its citizens.[26] At the same time, we may venture to say that the dark prehistory of Ximingsi was an edifying lesson to the monastic community —— as is well summarized by the vinaya master Chongye 崇業, who probably made the following comment in the early eighth century:

> The body [of the unenlightened worldling] is dependent on material things, but whatever is phenomenal is impermanent. I can not forget that time is passing by and there is no bubble that will not break in the end. If anyone wants to edify people by writing down the moral on the wall, please allow me to tell you a lesson based on what happened in the monastery. [Today] we can still find vestige of the old masters who had lived here. First we have Yang Su, the Duke of Yue and Director of the Department of State Affaires of the Sui Dynasty, and then he was followed by Li Tai, the Prince of Pu of our imperial dynasty. Then we know that if one's richness is not properly gained, his fortune will dry up. If one does not follow the virtue of thrift, what he acquires will be lost. [Therefore] not carrying something through to the end is different from the principle of cautious consideration at the beginning and complacency is not a means to maintain the achievements of one's predecessors.

此身有待, 諸行無常.[27] 欽不居之歲月, 無不滅之泡影. 樂化成而記壁者, 請因寺而言之.[28] 是則有隋尚書令越國公楊, 泊我濮王泰宅之舊區. 豈不當必蔀, 儉不師且奪. 終異謀始之則, 滿非守成之具.[29]

Xin used for his book is *Way of Gods, Life of Humans: Social History of the Livelihood Religions in Dunhuang during the Tang and Song Dynasties*.

[26] Seo Tatsuhiko, "Wei Shu de 'Liangjing xinji'yu bashiji qianye de Chang'an," 23-24.

[27] *Youdai* 有待 (relies on the power of another) is a special term used in the chapter of *Qiwulun* 齊物論 (Discussion of the Equality of All Things) in *Zhuangzi* 莊子. It also appears in the Daoist scripture *Zhen'gao* 真誥 (Declarations of the Perfected). In Buddhist parlance, it means that human body, which is dependent on material things, will decay. See *Mohe ziguan* 摩訶止觀, T46, no. 1911, p. 36, a1-3.

[28] The term *huacheng* 化成 (to receive virtuous influence and become a good person) is originally from section 32 of *Yijing* (Book of Changes): "聖人久於其道, 而天下化成."

[29] *Ximingsi tabei* 西明寺塔碑 (The Stūpa Tablet of Ximingsi), see *QTW* 257. 2597-598. The inscription is hereafter abbreviated as *TB*.

Chongye was a distinguished scholar of Ximingsi, who studied vinaya under the guidance of Wengang 文綱 (636-727), the disciple of the founding abbot Daoxuan.[30] His prose survived in *Tang Chang'an Ximingsi tabei* 唐長安西明寺塔碑 (The Stūpa Tablet of Ximingsi in Tang Chang'an), a stone inscription composed by the famous literatus Su Ting 蘇頲 (670-727) in 716 (Kaiyuan 4) to commemorate the establishment of a stūpa. Chongye considers the cases from General Yang Su to Prince Li Tai, treating them as an integral part of the history of Ximingsi. As a monk well versed in Buddhist doctrine, he realized that the monastery's past teaches us the Buddhist moral of impermanence (Skt. *anitya*, Ch. *wuchang* 無常), reminding the clergy that the monastery was erected on the ruins of a once bustling residence.[31]

Through the lens of history and imaginative literature, this short chapter examines the events preceding the founding of Ximingsi. The imposing residence that comprised the later Ximingsi was constructed somewhere between 584 and 599. From general Yang Su to Prince Li Tai, the residence was occupied and abandoned by some celebrated owners, who belonged to different generations but experienced the same vicissitudes that life had to offer. From the middle of the seventh century, for urban citizens living in the metropolis, the newly constructed Ximingsi became a numinous site alive with imagination and anecdotal history. The legends circulating on the streets of Chang'an open a window into the prehistory of Ximingsi. This is particularly evident in the case of Yang Su, whose image was recreated by the Ximingsi abbot Daoxuan and other Buddhist writers in the early Buddho-Daoist debates. Inspired by urban tales and founding myth, by the early eighth century, Wei Shu and other writers were entrusted with the duty of recording a city full of

---

[30] Chongye was quite active in the reign of Emperor Ruizong 睿宗 (r. 684-690) to whom he subsequently gave the bodhisattva precepts (Ch. *pusajie* 菩薩戒); see *SGSZ*, T50, no. 2061, p. 795, a15-25. For the dharma lineage transferred by Daoxuan, see *Mochizuki*, 3999.

[31] The maxim of "whatever is phenomenal is impermanent" (Ch. *zhuxing wuchang* 諸行無常, Skt: *sarva-saṃskārā anityāḥ*) as pervasively pointed out in all the major Buddhist canons, best describes the prehistory of Ximingsi. In the *Mahāparinirvāṇa Sūtra* (*Nirvāṇa Sūtra*, Ch. *Da banniepan jing* 大般涅槃經, T374), the Buddha further elaborates the superior truth in the famous gāthā that "All things Change, and this is the law of birth and death. When the birth and death is done away with, quietude is the bliss." See Kosho Yamamoto, *The Mahayana Mahaparinirvana sutra; a Complete Translation from the Classical Chinese Language in 3 volumes* (Ube: Karinbunko, 1973), 352-56. For the Chinese original (諸行無常, 是生滅法; 生滅滅已, 寂滅為樂), see *Da banniepan jing* 大般涅槃經 (Sūtra of the Great Decease), T12, no. 374, p. 450, a16-p. 451, b5.

anecdotes, unquiet ghosts and spiritual agencies. The localized stories, associated with celebrated residences and ranking temples, gave to Chang'an a sacred status unique among the cities of China. The story of the broken mirror, which was the most famous anecdote associated with Yang Su, eventually took on a life of its own. It not only became an exemplar of the public memory of Ximingsi in medieval China, but also found its derivatives in modern Chinese and Japanese. Other anecdotes of Yang Su, such as the eccentric story of the old well, were also widely known among the monastics of Ximingsi. The historic journey of the monastery was properly summarized by master Chongye as a lesson in the impermanence of life. For a millennium, these tales were seen as an integral part of the legacy of Ximingsi, imbuing it with a religious meaning that cannot be overlooked in any serious investigation of the monastery. But now, it is time to move from the prehistory of Ximingsi to its rich history and religious journey over the three hundred years of its heyday.

Chapter Three

For The Sage Kings: Ximingsi and the Early Tang Empire

Establishment of the Monastery

The English word "monastery," a word religious in its origins, is defined by Oxford English Dictionary as "a place of residence of a community of persons living secluded from the world under religious vows."[1] Likewise, the Buddhist monastery in ancient India, usually known as "vihāra" (Ch. *jingshe* 精舍), was an institution where the religious order can pray, meditate and practice their way to nirvāṇa.[2] For the Indian wanderers (Skt. *parivrājaka*) and the world-renouncing postulants, seclusion from mundane society was probably a prerequisite for the abodes of contemplatives.[3] *The Path of Purification* (Pali. *Visuddhimagga*), a Buddhist classic composed by the Theravada commentator Buddhaghosa (fl. 5th c.), contains a chapter titled "The Earth Kasina (Pali. *pathavī-kasiṇa-niddesa*)" in which the author argues that bhikkhu (Skt. *bhikṣu*) "should avoid a monastery unfavorable to the

---

[1] Originated from the Latin "monasterium," the word first appears in the manuscript of the *Rule of St. Benet* (1100–1450) as "Ofte-timis it happins þat be þe ordinance of þe prioresse greuus sklaunders rysis in monesterys." See monastery, n. Third edition, September 2002; online version September 2011. <http://www.oed.com/view/Entry/121112>; accessed 18 November 2011.

[2] There are other alternative terms used in Buddhist Sanskrit: e.g., *āvāsa* (Ch. *zhuchu* 住處), *ārāma* (Ch. *yuan* 圍); *saṃghārāma* (Ch. *sengqielan* 僧伽藍); *leṇa* (Ch. *sengyuan* 僧院); *guhā* (Ch. *kuyuan* 窟院), see *Iwanami Bukkyō jiten* 岩波佛教辭典 (Tokyo: Iwanami shoten, 2002), s.v. *jiin* 寺院; see also Gregory Schopen, *Buddhist Monks and Business Matters: Still More Papers on Monastic Buddhism in India* (Honolulu: University of Hawai'i Press, 2004), 76-77.

[3] For a discussion of the Indian monastery, see Sukumar Dutt, *Buddhist Monks and Monasteries of India: their History and their Contribution to Indian Culture* (London: Allen & Unwin, 1962); Dipak Kumar Barua, *Vihāras in Ancient India; a Survey of Buddhist Monasteries* (Calcutta: Indian Publications, 1969).

development of concentration and go to live in one that is favorable."[4] Buddhaghosa continues to enumerate the "eighteen faults of the monastery" and makes the further admonishment that one gone into the religious life (Skt. *pravrajita*) may not be able to concentrate on meditation in a monastery involved in worldly affairs. If a Buddhist institution has one or more of the eighteen faults listed by Buddhaghosa, then it is said to be unfavorable to the development of concentration and spiritual practice within the community.[5]

This idealistic view of early monasticism encountered problems when it came to spreading Buddhism in China. As Erik Zürcher (1928-2008) argues, the wandering Buddhist ascetics established residential monasteries near agricultural and commercial centers along trade and travel routes as a mode of "contact expansion."[6] In general terms, Buddhism in China was started more or less as an urban phenomenon. *The Path of Purification* might have had in mind a remote setting for meditation in ancient Sri Lanka when it listed among its eighteen faults"with nearby road" "with a nearby city," or "famous in the world"; but such faults were unavoidable for religious practitioners living in the urban monasteries in Chang'an. Indeed, the distraction of city life, at Ximingsi, was probably what forced Xuanzang to resign his abbotship in order to fulfill his task of translating the 600-fascicle *Mahāprajñāpāramitā-sūtra* (Ch. *Da bore jing* 大般若經, Great Scripture of the Perfection of Wisdom, T220). Xuanzang expressed this point clearly, in the winter of 663, after he completed the great job, "If I had stayed as before in the capital, where there were many miscellaneous affairs to distract my mind, how could I have finished the work in time?"[7] Given its special location closer to the heart of the Tang sovereign than most of the other giant monasteries dotting the landscape of Chang'an,

---

[4] Buddhaghosa, *The Path of Purification: Visuddhimagga*, trans. Ñāṇamoli (Seattle, WA: 1st BPE Pariyatti Editions, 1999), 118. In both China and Japan, the scripture is known as 清淨道論 *Qingjingdao lun* (Jap. *Shōjō dōron*).

[5] Buddhaghosa, *The Path of Purification*, 118-21.

[6] Erik Zürcher, "Han Buddhism and the Western Region," in *Thought and Law in Qin and Han China: Studies Dedicated to Anthony Hulsewe on the Occasion of His Eightieth Birthday*, ed. W. L. Idema and Erik Zurcher (Leiden: Brill, 1990), 169-71. For details of Buddhism and the trade networks in ancient South Asia, see Jason Emmanuel Neelis, *Early Buddhist Transmission and Trade Networks: Mobility and Exchange within and beyond the Northwestern Borderlands of South Asia* (Leiden; Boston: Brill, 2011), 183-216.

[7] Huili 慧立 and Yancong 彥悰, *A Biographyof the Tripiṭaka Master of the Great Ci'en Monastery of the Great Tang Dynasty*, trans. Li Rongxi 李榮熙 (Berkeley, Calif: Numata Center for Buddhist Translation and Research, 1995), 329; *Da Tang Da Ci'ensi Sanzang fashi zhuan* 大唐大慈恩寺三藏法師傳 (Biography of the Tripiṭaka Master of Da Ci'en Temple, abbreviated as SZFSZ), T50, no. 2053, p. 276, b8-14.

Ximingsi had to find a balance between survival as a state-sponsored monastery and its inherent duty as a religious institituon of Buddhist learning.

Among religions competing with one another for adherents in the capital, Buddhism became the obvious winner; the Buddhist community alone possessed more than 100 monasteries in Chang'an. Scholars specializing in Buddhist geography have reported that during the early Tang dynasty, Chang'an assembled about 124 monasteries in its metropolitan area, constituting, along with other twenty-one monasteries scattered in the nearby Zhongnan Mountain, nearly eighteen percent of all monasteries in the country.[8] By way of contrast, in spite of the obvious Daoist connection with dominant social groups, the number of Daoist monasteries had only increased to sixteen in urban Chang'an up until the Kaiyuan period (713-741).[9] Undoubtedly, except for the large undeveloped area in the scarcely populated southern part of the city, many of the urban monasteries in Chang'an were identifiable by huge temple complexes, towering pagodas, and the best scholar-monks of the country. Unlike the officially established monasteries (*guansi* 官寺) such as the Great Cloud Monastery (Dayunsi 大雲寺) or Dragon Ascending Monastery (Longxingsi 龍興寺), Ximingsi, along with the famous Ci'ensi, were great national monasteries enjoying superior privileges proffered by the state.[10] As indicated by Daoshi 道世 (d. 683), the eminent scholar in residence at Ximing, the celebration of great religious events like the ghost festival (Skt. *ullambana*, Ch. *yulanpenghui* 盂蘭盆會) at major temples in the capital was also sponsored by the

---

[8] Li Yinghui 李映輝, *Tangdai fojiao dili yanjiu* 唐代佛教地理研究 (Changsha: Hunan daxue chubanshe, 2004), 91.

[9] Fan Guangchun 樊光春, *Chang'an daojiao yu daoguan* 長安道教與道觀 (Xi'an: Xi'an chubanshe, 2002), 76. The author also informs us that the number of Daoist monasteries increased dramatically in the mid-Tang, amounting to nearly 60 in urban Chang'an.

[10] From 666 to 738, four Chinese imperial edicts were issued to authorize the establishment of state monasteries, such as Dayunsi 大雲寺, Zhong Dayunsi 中大雲寺, Zhongxingsi 中興寺, Longxingsi 龍興寺, and Kaiyuansi 開元寺. For discussion of the status of the "state monasteries" or "great monasteries," see Tsukamoto Zenryū 塚本善隆, "Kokubunji to Zui Tō no bukkyō seisaku narabini kanji 国分寺と隋唐の仏教政策並びに官寺," In *Tsukamoto Zenryū chosaku shū* 塚本善隆著作集, vol. 6 (Tokyo: Daitō shuppansha, 1974), 1-50; Antonino Forte, "Daiji 大寺 (Chine)," in *Hōbōgirin: dictionnaire encyclopédique du Bouddhisme d'après les sources Chinoises et Japonaises*, vol. 6 (Tokyo: Maison franco-japonaise, 1983), 682-704; James Robson, "Monastic Spaces and Sacred Traces: Facets of Chinese Buddhist Monastic Records," In *Buddhist Monasticism in East Asia: Places of Practice*, eds. James Benn, Lori Rachelle Meeks, and James Robson (New York: Routledge, 2010), 43-64.

government for the well-being of the empire.[11] The monks in residence were also a select elite class supplied by the government and schooled in the Buddhist classical tradition. Kenneth Chen describes it thusly:

> The national monasteries were accorded preeminent status in their respective communities; they were inhabited by highly educated monks, the elite in the monastic community; and they were supported by funds from the imperial treasury. We might say that the monks in these national monasteries were treated like members of the civil bureaucracy in having all their needs supplied by the state; they had no need to depend upon alms from ordinary laity for sustenance.[12]

Although a temple of Buddhism is supposed to be an abode away from the world, where monks can be free from secular burdens, the Buddhist churches in the Tang became increasingly secular and "unholy." Scholars believe that, by this time, Buddhism had already gained converts from all groups in Chinese society —— from the peasantry at the bottom, through the gentry and the educated, to the members of the imperial family at the top.[13] A great monastery like Ximingsi could thus play diversified roles in society, serving as a heaven for the literati, a spiritual arm for the imperial family, or a museum for the public. These prominent public roles were something of a mixed blessing for the institutions in question: on the on hand, the top-tier monasteries of the Sui-tang period, including the national monasteries and those huge "super monasteries" consisting of more than a dozen Buddhist cloisters, ushered in a "golden age" of Buddhism and enjoyed privileges comparable to the imperial ancestral shrine (*taimiao* 太廟); on the other hand, official documents demonstrate a continued alternation between the reverent and the regulatory in imperial attitudes toward the Buddhist saṃgha. For two and a half centuries, both Buddhist and Daoist temples were empowered to execute whatever they judged advantageous to the empire or agreeable to the royal family, serving as instruments for the Tang monarchs to cultivate merit for their control over the nation. To the

---

[11] Stephen F. Teiser, *The Ghost Festival in Medieval China* (Princeton, N.J.: Princeton University Press, 1988), 66. The ghost festival, also known as the Feast of Lanterns, took place around the fifteenth of July or August, depending on local customs.

[12] Kenneth Ch'en, "The Role of Buddhist Monasteries in T'ang Society," *History of Religions* 15, no. 3 (1976): 212.

[13] Ibid., 210.

imperial advantage, the Buddhist churches also created a unifying creed amid disparate peoples and cultures gathered in the capital.

One of the salient functions of religion for the imperial family was the purported effectiveness of healing through devotional activity. The Tang founding emperor Gaozu had figures of the Buddha created for the recuperation of his nine-year-old son Li Shimin. Later in 631 (Zhenguan 5), after Li Shimin became the emperor, he ordered the Daoist priest Qin Ying 秦英 to pray for the recovery of the crown prince Li Chengqian, a service rewarded by the founding of the Daoist monastery Xihua Guan 西華觀.[14]

The founding of Ximingsi is generally associated with the third monarch of the Tang dynasty, emperor Gaozong 高宗 (r. 649-683). In 656 (Xianqing 顯慶 1), Gaozong and his wife Wu Zetian 武則天 (623-705, or Empress Wu) had their four-year-old son Li Hong 李弘 (652-675) installed as heir apparent. The prince had just recovered from an illness that struck him in Luoyang. Impressed by the effectiveness of the Buddho-Daoist thaumaturgy employed in the cure, Gaozong decided to erect a Buddhist monastery to celebrate the occasion.[15]

At this time, the residence of the emperor's elder brother Li Tai had been confiscated for four years (652-656). Gaozong, by a decree of the throne, ordered that the abandoned residence be replaced by a Buddhist monastery and a Daoist institution. Xuanzang, the de facto Buddhist leader of Chang'an and the former spiritual mentor of the late Emperor Taizong, was appointed to inspect the site. The biography of Xuanzang, *Da Tang Da Ci'ensi Sanzang fashi zhuan* 大唐大慈恩寺三藏法師傳 (Biography of the Tripiṭaka Master at Ci'ensi of the Great Tang, T2053), has this to say regarding the occasion:

> In the first month of the third year of Xianqing (658), the emperor returned from the Eastern Metropolis to the Western Capital; and the Master also returned with him. In the seventh month, during the autumn, an edict was again issued, asking the Master to move his residence to Ximing Monastery. This monastery was constructed on the nineteenth day of the eighth month, in the autumn of the first year of Xianqing (656). A decree had previously been announced that one Taoist

---

[14] For the case of Li Shimin, see *Caotangsi weizi qiji shu* 草堂寺為子祈疾疏, *QTW* 3. 45. For the case of prince Li Chengqian, see *THY* 50.869.

[15] *TB*, 2597-598. Luo Xiaohong 羅小紅, "Tang Chang'an Ximingsi kao 唐長安西明寺考," *Kaogu yu wenwu* 考古與文物 2 (2006): 76.

temple and one Buddhist monastery should be built in the name of the Crown Prince at the site of the old house of the Prince of Pu on Yankang Street. The Master was asked to make a preliminary inspection of the place; and he reported after his inspection that the site was too narrow to contain two establishments. Thus the whole site was used for the construction of the Buddhist monastery, while the Taoist temple was separately built on Puning Street. The Buddhist monastery was built first; and the construction was completed in the sixth month, during the summer of the same [third] year.[16]

Xuanzang's objection to the original construction plan on the grounds that the Li Tai residence was not spacious enough to hold two institutions was only reasonable: The residence occupied only one fourth of the Yankang Ward —— in contrast, for example, to the enormous Da Xingshan Monastery (Daxingshansi 大興善寺), which had occupied the entire Jinshan Ward (Jingshan fang 靖善坊) since the Sui dynasty. The proposed Daoist monastery, later known as the Dongming (Eastern Brightness) Guan 東明觀, was therefore reassigned to the southeastern quadrant of the Puning Ward (Puning fang 普寧坊), which was adjacent to the northwestern city wall. Apparently the Dongming Guan was constructed for a sum equivalent to that of the architectural layout of Ximingsi. With long, enclosed corridors and ornate frescoes, Dongming Guan was unmatched for beauty among Daoist shrines in Chang'an.[17]

Xuanzang's biography, above, tells us that the foundations of Ximingsi were laid in the eighth month of 656, and the monastery was completed in the sixth month of 658 (Xianqing 3). To construct a monastery on the scale of Ximingsi was a daunting task in terms of both time and money. We know, for example, from an account of the Jing'ai Monastery (Monastery of Reverence and Benevolence), another great monastery concurrently built following the pattern and scale of Ximingsi in Luoyang, that the government had earmarked over 20,000 strings (*guan* 貫) of cash for the construction of such a monastery.[18] Nearly half of the Buddhist

---

[16] Li Rongxi, *Biography of the Tripiṭaka Master*, 325. *SZFSZ*, T50, no. 2053, p. 275, b22-27.

[17] Xu Song and Li Jianchao, *Zengding tang liangjing chengfang kao*, 244, see also, idem, *Da Tang gu Dongming guan Sun fashi mozhiming bing xu* 大唐故東明觀孫法師墓誌銘並序; *Xu gaoseng zhuan* 續高僧傳 (Further Biographies of Eminent Monks), T50, no. 2060, p. 547, c21-24.

[18] Wang Huimin 王惠民, "Tang dongdu Jing'aisi kao 唐東都敬愛寺考," *Tang yanjiu* 12 (2006): 366, Jing'ai Monastery was also known in the history of Tang Dynasty as the Foshoujisi 佛授記寺. In the wake of the construction of Ximingsi, Gaozong then continued to commission the construction of 20 additional monasteries in Chang'an for other princes and princesses, including Zijie 資戒, Chongjing 崇敬, Zhaofu

monasteries in Chang'an, however, were based on on private residences donated as temples by powerful dignitaries of the Sui-Tang ruling class,[19] and such a donation for the benefit of the imperial family would seem to be the rationale for the emperor's authorization of the use of his brother's residence for Ximingsi. This fact helps us to understand how such a grand monastery could have been completed in less than two years. Unfortunately, however, a paucity of textual records makes it almost impossible to get a clear sense of the original site plan of the residence or the details of its architecture and, hence, of the work needed to transform it into a magnificent monastery.

Less than two years, then, after the construction began on the monastery, Xuanzang returned from the eastern capital of Luoyang to Chang'an in the company of Gaozong. The emperor insisted on appointing him the first abbot of the newly completed Ximingsi. The grand opening ceremony of a great monastery like Ximingsi was certainly a public festival for the people of Chang'an. The opening day witnessed a formal celebration, lasting for the entire morning in which both lay and clergy assembled to witness the occasion. In response, the monastery provided free meals for the monks who swarmed in from all quarters. Xuanzang was invited to supervise the ordination ritual of selected postulants. There is a telling detail in the *Ji gujin fodao lunheng* recorded by Daoxuan:

Ximingsi was completed on the twelfth day of the sixth month in the third year of Xianqing. Both monks and lay people gathered on that occasion. Pennants and streamers assembled like clouds. The next morning was an auspicious day, [people] waited to enter the monastery. The sounds of flutes and drums were loud enough to shake the earth. Incense and flowers were thrown all over into the air. From the northern part of the city to the monastery in the south, the crowd filled the streets for more than ten *li*. In the early morning of the thirteenth day, Gazong stood on the lofty Anfu Gate with his dukes and bureaucrats lining up at the gate. The court bestowed upon the parade embroidered Buddha figures and big pennants of astonishing beauty.

招福 and Fushou 福壽; see *Fayuan zhulin* 法苑珠林 (The Pearl Grove of the Dharma Garden), T53, no. 2122, p. 1027, c4-6; see also *THY* 48.848.

[19] For some examples of the Buddhist and Daoist monasteries donated by the Chang'an celebrities, such as Chongshengsi 崇聖寺, Zhaofusi 招福寺, Haotianguan 昊天觀, Nüguanguan 女冠觀 and so forth, see Rong Xinjiang, *Sui Tang Chang'an: xingbie, jiyi ji qita*, 68-76.

顯慶三年六月十二日，西明寺成. 道俗雲合，幢蓋嚴華. 明晨良日，將欲入寺，簫鼓振地，香華亂空. 自北城之達南寺，十餘裡中，街衢闐闐. 至十三日清旦，帝禦安福門上，郡公僚佐備列於下. 內出繡像，長旛高廣，驚於視聽.[20]

One can imagine the procession, with loud music, banners and flowers, starting from the northern Anfu gate (Anfumen 安福門), situated between the imperial city (Huangcheng 皇城) and the palace city (Gongcheng 宮城). The parade then proceeded southward along the first major avenue on the west of the city for three miles to pass four residential wards before they finally reached the Yankang Ward. Again, Su Ting's stele has this to say about the celebration:

When the monastery was established, the imperial government bestowed a few hundred hectares of manors and lay servants; fifty carts, and 2000 bolts of silk (upon the monastery)…The procession congested the royal street leading to the celestial temple…The shade of banners and streamers encompassed forty *li*, the sound of the music shook the three thousand worlds [Skt. *trisāhasra mahāsāhasra-loka-dhātu*].

寺成之時，遂賜田園百頃，淨人百房. 車五十輛，絹布二千匹…導天衢，指天寺…幡幢之陰，週四十裡. 伎樂之響，震三千界.[21]

The music played on this occasion, as indicated many times in the textual record, was titled *jiubuyue* 九部樂 (nine section music), the court music of the Tang imperial government.[22] It is clear that the ceremonial procedure assigned to Ximingsi was

[20] *FDLH*, T52, no. 2104, p. 388, c24-p. 389, a1.

[21] *TB*, 2597-598.

[22] The nine-section music is still preserved in Japan as the *Tōgaku* (Ch. *tangyue* 唐樂) in the repertory of ceremonial imperial court music (Jap. *gagaku* 雅樂). For instance, titles of pieces performed in Tōdaiji in 752 are available in the epigraphic collection preserved in Shosoin 正倉院, the royal treasure house of Japan. For studies on Tang court music, see Kishibe Shigeo 岸辺成雄, *Tōdai ongaku no rekishiteki kenkyū* 唐代音樂の歴史的研究, vol. 2 (Tokyo: Tōkyō daigaku shuppankai, 1960), 21-81; Laurence Ernest Rowland Picken and R. F. Wolpert, *Music from the Tang Court* (London: Music Dept., Oxford University Press, 1981), 78-92; Geng Zhanjun 耿占軍, and Yang Wenxiu 楊文秀, *Han Tang Chang'an de yuewu yu baixi* 漢唐長安的樂舞與百戲 (Xi'an: Xi'an chubanshe, 2007), 80-101.

identical with that used at the inauguration of Da Ci'ensi 大慈恩寺 (Monastery of Great Compassion) and the reception for the imperial inscription (that is, *Da Tang sanzang shengjiao xu bei* 大唐三藏聖教序碑) composed by Emperor Taizong two years earlier.[23] In the early Tang, the nine section music was performed to amuse the diplomatic corps or to celebrate the emperor's birthday.[24] The inauguration of Ximingsi and Ci'ensi are the only cases found in Buddhist sources for which the nine section music was performed.

In addition to the pomp and ceremony, the Tang government appointed a coterie of eminent monk-scholars to administer the monastery, with numerous others ordained as their assistants. Furthermore, young *śramaṇeras* (novices) who excelled in Buddhist learning and morality were prepared to be ordained as clergymen. Again, Xuanzang's biographer, Huili, tells us:

> The Emperor had previously instructed the authorities to select fifty learned monks, each with an attendant. Later he also ordered that one hundred fifty youths who were practising moral deeds be chosen by examination to be ordained as monks. On the thirteenth day of that month [i.e., the sixth month of 658] a ceremony of ordination was performed in the monastery, and the Master [i.e., Xuanzang] was invited to supervise the ordination.[25]

Before 694, monastic affair were entrusted to the Court for State Ceremonials (*honglusi* 鴻臚寺), which was in charge of the appointment of monk-officials at Ximingsi.[26] As usual in the case of a national monastery, virtuous priests (Ch. *dade* 大德, Skt. *bhadanta*) were selected to officiate as administrators. As the founding abbot, Xuanzang was provided with one of the best rooms in Ximingsi. He also accepted ten newly ordained novices as disciples. Xuanzang's biography indicates that, in his short abbotship, the master received alms from palace messengers and courtiers, spenting them all for the construction of stūpas, or for copying scriptures

---

[23] *SZFSZ*, T50, no. 2053, p. 260, c20-29; see also *QTW* 742. 22. For a description of the inauguration of Ci'en Monastery, see *Fozu tongji* 佛祖統紀 (Complete Chronicle of the Buddha and Patriarchs), T49, no. 2035, p. 366, c7-11.

[24] Kishibe Shigeo, *Tōdai ongaku*, vol. 2, 21-30.

[25] Li Rongxi, *A Biography of the Tripiṭaka Master*, 326; *SZFSZ*, T50, no. 2053, p. 275, c5-7.

[26] *XTS* 48. 1252-53, Honglusi was known since 684 as the Court in Charge of Foreign Visitors (*sibinsi* 司賓寺), see also *Fozu tongji*, T49, no. 2035, p. 329, b22-25.

for the benefit of the country. "He made a vow to make ten *koṭis* [Ch. *juzhi* 俱胝) —— one koti being one million [sic] —— of images of the Buddha, which all were made."[27] We can infer that the "merit" that Xuanzang piled up during this period stayed with Ximingsi. In the tenth month of 659, Xuanzang left the monastery for the suburban Yuhua Palace (Yuhuagong 玉華宮), a palatial building that had been converted to a Buddhist monastery in 651.[28] As we have seen above, Xuanzang feared that if he stayed in Chang'an, where there were many distractions, he might not be able to devote his time to the highly esteemed *Mahāprajñāpāramitā-sūtra* (*Da bore boluomiduo jing* 大般若波羅蜜多經, T220).[29]

When Xuanzang stepped down at Ximingsi, leadership at the monastery passed into the capable hands of the famous monk Daoxuan (Figure. 4). Daoxuan, who studied under the eminent scholar Zhishou 智首 (567-635), had already been invited to serve as the superintendent (Ch. *shangzuo* 上座, Skt. *sthavira*) of the monastery. As early as 645, he had been one of two eminent scholars invited to assist Xuanzang with his translation.[30] Over the first few decades of the Tang dynasty few Buddhists had made such an impact on the revival of the ordination platform (Ch. *jietan* 戒壇) as Daoxuan. He composed numerous books and commentaries dealing with the spread of the *Four Division Vinaya* (Ch. *Sifenlü* 四分律, Skt. *Dharmagupta-vinaya*, T1428), while practicing meditation in monasteries on Mount Zhongnan. Through his writing and teaching, not to mention his role in the ordination movement for which he was the major promoter, he exerted profound influence over generations of Buddhist scholars. The choice of Daoxuan as the monastic supervisor was crucial to the success of Ximingsi: he was not only the leading figure at the monastery, esteemed by numerous Tang rulers, but he was the actual founder, who breathed life into the scholastic tradition that made the monastery so preeminent for three centuries.

---

[27] Li Rongxi, *A Biography of the Tripiṭaka Master*, 326-27.

[28] Fan Wenlan 范文瀾 and Zhang Zunliu 張遵驑, *Tangdai fojiao* 唐代佛教 (1979; repr., Chongqing: Chongqing chubanshe, 2008), 114.

[29] Ibid., 327.

[30] *SGSZ*, T50, no. 2061, p. 790, c22-25; *Fanyi mingyi ji* 翻譯名義集 (Compilation of Translated Buddhist Terms), T54, no. 2131, p. 1074, c15-20. Fan Wenlan, *Tangdai fojiao*, 111. During his early years, Daoxuan intended to practice meditation, but he then shifted his direction to the study of *vinaya*. He was ordained in 615 at the Dachandingsi 大禪定寺 by Zhishou. For studies on Daoxuan and his contribution to the ordination platform, see Fujiyoshi Masumi 藤善眞澄, *Dōsen den no kenkyū* 道宣伝の研究 (Kyoto: Kyōto daigakugakujutsu shuppankai, 2002), 150-55; Chen Huaiyu, *Revival of Buddhist Monasticism*, 93-131.

Figure. 4 The Portrait of Daoxuan (Ch. *Nanshan dashi Daoxuan xiang* 南山大師道宣像, Jap. *Nanzan daishi Dōsen zō*) at Sennyūji 泉湧寺 in Kyoto. Source: Itō Daisuke 伊藤大輔, *Shōzōga no jidai: chūsei keiseiki ni okeru kaiga no shisōteki shinsō* 肖像畫の時代: 中世形成期における絵畫の思想的深層, 263.

Among other talented monk-officials at Ximingsi, Master Shencha 神察 became the monastery chief (Ch. *sizhu* 寺主, Skt. *Vihārasvāmin*). Zhiyan 智衍 and Zili 子立 were appointed the rector (Skt. *karmadāna*, Ch. *weina* 維那), the third in command of a monastery.[31] This information comes to us from the stele by Su Ting, which introduces us to four other masters in the rank of top administrators: Yuanze 元則, who held the position of transmitter of learning (*chuanxue* 傳學);[32]

---

[31] In Tang Buddhist monasteries, the monastery chief (or temple head) was in charge of all practical and administrative affairs, such as supplies and finances, while the duty distributor (or rector) was charged with enforcing rules and maintaining discipline. Along with the superintendent, they constitute the three top officers (Ch. *sangang* 三綱) of a monastery. For a discussion of the position of karmadāna, see Jonathan Silk, *Managing Monks: Administrators and Administrative Roles in Indian Buddhist Monasticism* (New York: Oxford University Press, 2008), 127-35.

[32] The meaning of *chuanxue* is not clearly stated in Buddhist texts, but Huilin mentions *chuanxue fanseng* 傳學梵僧 (Indian monks responsible for the transmission of knowledge) in his magisterial lexicography compiled in Ximingsi, see *Yiqiejing yinyi* 一切經音義 (The Sounds and Meanings [of all the words in] the Scriptures), T54, no. 2128, p. 471, a2-3.

Jingding 靜定, who specialized in Chan meditation (*qichan* 棲禪); and two vinaya adepts, Daocheng 道成 and Huaisu 懷素 (624-697), who took up the position of observer of the discipline (*chilü* 持律).[33] In addition to executive positions, other eminent priests such as Daoshi, the author of several Buddhist encyclopedias, were summoned to join the community of scholars. The *Xu gaoseng zhuan* 續高僧傳 (Further Biographies of Eminent Monks, T2060) tells us that Ximingsi even assigned a separate *dhyāna* courtyard (*chanfu* 禪府) for a newly recruited Buddhist yogin Jingzhi 靜之, a pre-eminent ascetic skilled in Chan meditation.[34] The appointment of such elite priests marked the beginning of Ximingsi as a monastery of advanced Buddhist practice and a leading "Buddhist university" in the empire. Whether and in what senses we might think of the scholastic community of Ximingsi as a distinctive "school" of Buddhist thought remains an interesting question for further exploration.

What is Ximing (Western Brightness)?

The names attached to temples, residences, gates or other structures in ancient China could assume rich cultural and religious connotations that shaped public perception of the places. In the case of our monastery, the term *ximing* 西明, meaning "western brightness," while not a common compound in ordinary Chinese, evokes multiple associations in the Buddhist world.[35] In Chinese Buddhist terminology, the "west" commonly suggests the "the western regions" or the "western heavens" (*xitian* 西天; i.e., "Sindh in the west), expressions indicating especially the Indian subcontinent. Hence, the name Ximingsi could associate the monastery with the "illumination from the West" —— i.e., the wisdom of Buddhism brought from India. Horiike Shunpō 崛池春峰, has suggested that this association was intended in particular to link

---

[33] *Fozu tongji* T49, no. 2035, p. 367, a24-26; *TB*, 2598. The Huaisu of Ximingsi was not the well-known Tang monk-calligrapher, instead, he was the distinguished disciple of both Xuanzang and Daoxuan. He also authored the *Sifenlü kaizong ji* 四分律開宗記 (*XZJ* 735). For a brief account of his life, see *Mochizuki*, 743.

[34] *Xu gaoseng zhuan*, T50, no. 2060, p. 602, a19-24.

[35] Here I follow the translation given by Victor Xiong, see Xiong, *Sui-Tang Chang'an*, 263. There are certainly other options that we can choose, such as, "western illumination," "western clarity," "western light" or "western brilliance." However, the Japanese term *nishiakari* 西明り is a rather modern usage which means twilight or western evening sky. The two kanji characters, if pronounced as *saimyō* 西明, are identical to the Chinese counterpart suggesting western brightness. *Nishiakari* 西明り is alternatively simplified as "西明," see *Kōjien*, s.v. *nishiakari*.

Ximingsi with Ci'ensi, as the two monasteries most identified as centers of the new Buddhist learning brought back from the "West" by Xuanzang.[36] It is, perhaps, no mere coincidence that the old translation center of Kumārajīva, the most famous translator of Indic materials before Xuanzang, was called the Pavilion of Western Brightness (Ximingge 西明閣). Kumārajīva's monastery was located in the northern suburbs of the old Han Chang'an, facing the River Wei, not so very far from the site of Ximingsi in Tang Chang'an.[37]

A second obvious Buddhist connotation of "west" is the western pure land of the Buddha Amitābha (Ch. *amituofo* 阿彌陀佛). As the Japanese historian Ono Katsutoshi 小野勝年 (1905-1988) has pointed out, "western brightness" alludes to the infinite light emitted by this buddha of the western direction, whose name means Immeasurable Light (Ch. Wuliangguang 無量光).[38] The first and most important translation of the *Amitābha-sūtra* (*Foshuo Amituojing* 佛說阿彌陀經, T366), also known as the *Smaller Sukhāvatī-vyūha*, was accomplished by Kumārajīva. Xuanzang himself contributed a third translation of the Smaller *Sukhāvatī-vyūha* entitled *Chengzan jingtu fo sheshou jing* 稱讚净土仏摂受經 (Sūtra In Praise of the Pure Land, T367), it was finished at Ci'en Monastery in 650, eighteen years before the inauguration of Ximingsi.

While it could well be mere coincidence, we may also note the connection of Ximing with Daoxuan. Little is yet known of Daoxuan's involvement in the founding of the monastery, or whether he had discussed the temple name with Xuanzang or Gazong; but one is tempted to speculate on his involvement by the evidence

---

[36] Horiike Shunpō 堀池春峰, "Nittō ryūgakusō to Saimyōji 入唐留學僧と長安・西明寺," in *Nanto bukkyōshi no kenkyū. shoji hen* 南都仏教史の研究. 諸寺篇 (Kyoto: Hōzōkan, 2003), 253.

[37] *Zhaolu shu* 肇論疏 (Commentary on Zhaolun), T45, no. 1859, p. 177, a7-9.

[38] See *Mochizuki*, 2329, s.v. *jōni kōbutsu* 十二光佛 (Ch. *shier guangfo*). See also *Jiupin wangsheng Amituo sanmodi ji tuoluoni jing* 九品往生阿彌陀三摩地集陀羅尼經, T19, no. 933, p. 79, b21-c24. Ono also reminds us that the western gate of the Luoyang city in the Northern Wei dynasty was also named "Ximing" (Ximing men 西明門); see Ono, *Kaisetsuhen*, 148; see also Karasawa Shirō 唐澤至朗, "Muryō kōmyō kō —— kōmyō hyōgen to amidabutsu raigen no ninshiki 無量光明考 —— 光明表現と阿彌陀仏來現の認識," *Gumma kenritsu rekishi hakubutsukan kiyō* 群馬県立歴史博物館紀要 28 (2007): 73-92. Wulianguang 無量光, in Sanskrit, is *apramāṇābha* (infinite light or splendor). The Buddha of Great Light (Ch. *Damingfo* 大明佛, Skt. *Mahāraśmiprabha*) is also mentioned in the *Smaller Sukhāvatī-vyūha*, see *Foshuo amituo jing* 佛說阿彌陀經, T12, no. 366, p. 346, b28-c3. Separate English translations of Sanskrit and Chinese versions of the Larger and Smaller *Sukhāvatī Sūtras* are offered by Luis Gómez; see Luis Gomez, *The Land of Bliss: The Paradise of the Buddha of Measureless Light* (Honolulu: University of Hawai'i Press, 1996).

disclosed by *Shanxi tongzhi* 陝西通志 (Local Gazetteer of Shanxi), according to which a domestic shrine located in the residence of prince Yongxing (Yongxing wangfu 永興王府) was also called Ximingsi. The small private temple kept this name until the end of Zhenguan, when it was renamed Linggansi 靈感寺 (Monastery of Spirit Response). Daoxuan is said to have practiced meditation and established a pure land altar (*jingtutan* 淨土壇) at this place.[39] In short, that the name "Ximing" carries multiple connotations: closely associated with the immeasurable light of the Buddha, it could also imply a monastery of bright light situated in the western portion of Chang'an city. Moreover, if we consider it together withXiming's counterpart monastery the Daoist Dongming Guan (Monastery of Eastern Brightness), we can assume that "brightness" also becomes the very embodiment of Indian and Chinese "deities" (*shenming* 神明) respectively. In any case, the term "ximing" became a popular name for Buddhist temples, and, we can identify numerous examples of Ximingsi established across China in the succeeding dynasties; and, if we broaden our vision to investigate Japanese sources, we will find at least three "Ximingsi" monasteries ("Saimyōji" in Japanese). The first is a temple of the Shingon Sect, situated in Tochigi prefecture in the Kanto region and founded by the mendicant priest Gyōki 行基 (668-749). Later it was rebuilt by the regent of the Kamakura Shogunate Hōjō Tokiyori 北條時頼 (1227-63). The second, founded by the Shingon priest Sanshū 三修 (829-99), is a temple of Tendai Buddhism located in Shiga prefecture in the Kinki 近畿 area. The third is also a Shingon temple established by Kūkai's disciple Chisen 智泉 (789-825) in Kyoto in 832. Some of the Japanese Saimyōji founders can trace their dharma lineage back to masters in residence in the Tang-dynasty Ximingsi; however, the connection between them and their monasteries remains an open question that will need to be further explored.[40]

---

[39] Zhou Wenmin 周文敏, *Chang'an fosi* 長安佛寺 (Xi'an: Sanqin chubanshe, 2008), 37-38; *Shanxi tongzhi* 陝西通志, *SKQS* 552: 443 For information on the "pure land altar" in Chinese Buddhism, see *Xiuxi wenjian lu* 修西聞見錄, *XZJ* 135, p. 558, b2-4; *Fajie shengfan shuilu dazhai puli daochang xingxiang tonglun* 法界聖凡水陸大齋普利道場性相通論, *XZJ* 129, p. 610, b10-18. However, I suspect the altar might refer to a Buddhist ordination platform; see *Da Song sengshi lüe* 大宋僧史略 (Historical Digest of the Buddhist Order Compiled in the Great Song), T54, no. 2126, p. 238, b15-17.

[40] Dietrich Seckel already points out in his study of Japanese temple names (*Buddhistische Tempelnamen in Japan*) that many Japanese monasteries borrowed their names directly from their Chinese predecessors. See Dietrich Seckel, *Buddhistische Tempelnamen in Japan* (Stuttgart: F. Steiner Wiesbaden, 1985), 271-279.

For the Sage Kings

Debates at Court and the Sino-Indian Controversy

Situated in the vicinity of the Western Market, Ximingsi was just a few miles away for the imperial city, the nerve center of the Tang empire. From its inauguration, Ximingsi was embroiled in dramas of Chang'an's political life and resonated to the cultural reverberations of the capital city. Indeed, the monastery's founding ceremonies themselves put on ritual display the religious politics of the Tang court.

It happened that the inauguration day of Ximingsi was also Gaozong's birthday. Soon after the opening ceremony, at the behest of the emperor, a court debate was held in the magnificent Baifu Hall (Baifudian 百福殿), a place referred to as *yulunchang* 禦論場 (royal field of debate) by Daoxuan.[41] The custom of such debate started before the founding of the Tang dynasty, when the imperial court functioned as a forum where religious adherents could exchange views or debate about sensitive issues that affected society (Figure. 5). Two teams, of Buddhist monks and Daoist priests, were summoned to undertake inter-religious debate to celebrate the occasion. Not surprisingly, court debate was a central arena for political interplay and competition between the religious communities. As Friederike Assandri points out:

> One reason for the growing attraction of the imperial court for Buddhists and Daoists was certainly the increasing grip of the state on religious institutions. Intensified administrative control, but also generous imperial patronage ultimately led to close relationships between the leaders of the clergy of both religions in the capital and the secular powers. Buddhists and Daoists who were invited to debate at court were members of the intellectual, religious and social elite of their times, often well acquainted with eminent personalities or with the imperial family.[42]

---

[41] *FDLH*, T52, no. 2104, p. 388, c21-23. For the culture of *lunchang* 論場 (field of debate) in the Tang dynasty, see *Da Tang xiyu ji* 大唐西域記 (Record of Travels to Western Lands), T51, no. 2087, p. 914, a18-25; *SGSZ*, T50, no. 2061, p. 734, c10-14. For a study of *FDLH*, see Friederike Assandri, "Die Debatten zwischen Daoisten und Buddhisten in der frühen Tang-Zeit und die Chongxuan-Lehre des Daoismus" (PhD Dissertation, Heidelberg, 2002).

[42] Friederike Assandri and Dora Martins, eds., *From Early Tang Court Debates to China's Peaceful Rise* (Amsterdam: Amsterdam University Press, 2009), 16-23.

Table 1.1   *Inter-religious court debates of the Early Tang Dynasty reported in ! 2104, 4*

Date	Place	Occasion
Xianqing 3 (659), 4th month	Imperial Palace, Hebi hall	
Xianqing 3 (659), 6th month, 12th day	Imperial Palace, Linde hall	Emperor's birthday and inauguration of Ximing temple
Xianqing 3 (659), 11th month	Imperial Palace	Sacrifice to bring about snow
Xianqing 5 (661), 8th month, 18th day	Imperial Palace of Luoyang	
Longshuo 3 (664), 4th month, 14th day	Imperial Palace, Penglai hall	Note: Two days later, Gaozong issued the edict that the monks had to bow in front of their parents.
Longshuo 3 (664), 5th month, 16th day	Imperial Palace, Penglai hall	
Longshuo 3 (664) 6th month, 12th day	Imperial Palace, Penglai hall	Emperor's birthday

Figure.5 Inter-religious Court Debates of the Early Tang Dynasty. Source: Friederike Assandri and Dora Martins, eds., *From Early Tang Court Debates to China's Peaceful Rise*, 17.

Besides politics, entertainment and education were the principal purposes for this court debate. Each team, comprised of seven debaters led by leading scholars from Ximingsi and the Daoist Dongming Guan, engaged in "pure talk" to the amusement of Gaozong. Led by court officials, the panel of the Daoists was placed at a superior position in the west of the Baifu Hall, while the seven Buddhist scholars lined up in the east. As was customary, the teams took turns choosing a subject and posing questions to challenge each other. According to Daoxuan's *Ji guji fodao lunheng*, the Buddhist monks opened the debate with the "four kinds of fearlessness" (Ch. *siwuwei* 四無畏, Skt. *catvāri vaiśāradyāni*) and then proceeded to the "theory of the six caverns (*liudongyi* 六洞義)" proposed by their Daoist opponents.[43] Predictably, the debate ended with a victory of Buddhism in which the Buddhist scholar Zili defeated the Daoist master Li Rong 李榮. Zili is popularly known in Buddhist history as Huili 慧立 (615-?), a distinguished scholar of Buddhist logic and author of the Biography of Xuanzang.[44] At the time, Huili had already come to the service of Ci'en Monastery as the translation *bhadanta* (Ch. *fanjing dade* 翻經大德). Obviously his expertise in Buddhist logic won him the debate and the attention of emperor Gaozong. In view of his eloquence and erudition, Xuanzang

---

[43] *FDLH*, T52, no. 2104, p. 388, c21-p. 389, c19.

[44] By introducing the science of *hetuvidyā* (Ch. *yinming* 因明) to the gargantuan world of Chinese scriptures, Xuanzang made an indelible impression upon the field of Buddhist debate in the seventh century. Too deep and broad, the *yinming* logic was mastered by only a few of his disciples. Enumerated as one of the five studies (Skt. *pañcavidyā-sthānāni*, Ch. *wuming* 五明) of ancient India, this Indian logical reasoning had not only epistemological value, it was also a highly efficient weapon in debate. For a detailed scrutiny of the topic, see Fyodor Shcherbatskoĭ, *Buddhist Logic* (Osnabrück: Biblio Verlag, 1970).

recommended that Huili officiate as the rector of Ximingsi. In spite of the victory of the Buddhists, the priority of the Daoists at court continued until 674. In that year, under the influence of Empress Wu, Gaozong finally issused an edict putting Buddhists and Daoists once more on an equal footing.[45]

The *Ji gujin fodao lunheng*, authored by Daoxuan and presented to Gaozong, expressed not only the Buddo-Daoist competition in early Tang but also the intense Sino-Indian controversy over etiquette in Chinese society.[46] The gravity of this issue, difficult for us to imagine today, made it a subject of hot debate at the imperial court as well as among the upper-level circles of Tang society. The debate was kindled by the perennial argument over the balance between the notion of the Indian monastic order and the Chinese secular life.The event that put Ximingsi in the spotlight of the etiquette controversy was an imperial decree issued after Gaozong assumed the title of celestial emperor (*tianhuang* 天皇) under the reign title of Longshuo 龍朔 (661-663). The decree, titled *Shamen deng zhibai junqin chi* 沙門等致拜君親勅, orders both Buddhist and Daoist clerical communities to pay respect to the ruler and their parents (*junqin* 君親), like the populace at large.[47] This was a recurrent topic in the Buddho-Confucian debate of early Chinese history, in which the Buddhists claim that their treatment of filial piety is superior to that of Confucianism.[48] The conflict between the Chinese emphasis on filial piety in everyday life and Buddhist institution of a renunciate religious order became even more vexed during the Tang period.

---

[45] Helwig Schmidt-Glintzer, "Buddhism in the Tang Period," *Buddhist Studies Review* 16, no. 2 (1999): 195.

[46] For an introduction of the court debate, see Friederike Assandri, "Inter-religious Debate at the Court of the Early Tang: An Introduction to Daoxuan's *Ji gujin fodao lunheng*," In Assandri, *From Early Tang Court Debates*, 15-32..

[47] *Ji shamen buying baisu dengshi* 集沙門不應拜俗等事, T52, no. 2108, p. 455, a23-b4; see also *Guang hongming ji* 廣弘明集 (Extensive Texts to Propagate and Elucidate [Buddhist Doctrines]), T52, no. 2103, p. 284, a15-27.

[48] In 403, the eminent monk Huiyuan 慧遠 (334-416) had already written a series of five articles, entitled *Shamen bujing wangzhe lun* 沙門不敬王者論, to refute Huan Xuan 桓玄 (369-404), the ambitious politician of the Jin Dynasty (265-420); see *Guang hongming ji*, T52, no. 2103, p. 285, b26-c17. The question was again mooted in the Sui dynasty by Emperor Yang, who promulgated a similar edict on the occasion of paying homage to his ancestors in the southern suburbs of the Daxing cheng city. In contrast to the silence of the Daoists, a monk named Mingzhan 明瞻 remonstrated on the ground that if the great dharma is truly profound then this physical body under its *kaṣāya* (monastic robe) ought not to pay respect to anyone. See *Fozu lidai tongzai* 佛祖歷代通載 (A Comprehensive Registry of the Successive Ages of the Buddhas and the Patriarchs), T49, no. 2036, p. 562, a13-18; *Longxing biannian tonglun* 隆興編年通論, *XZJ* 130, p. 419, b18-p. 420. For detailed discussion of the controversy, See Guang Xing, "A Buddhist-Confucian Controversy on Filial Piety," *Journal of Chinese Philosophy* 37, no. 2 (June 2010): 248–60.

Preceding the final decision to implement the decree, a dispute over the matter arose among 900 ranking officials who were supposed to make a final vote.

The fickleness of the ruling class was definitely a devastating blow to the Buddhist community, which had recently seen enough good will from Gaozong. For them, the matter was grave enough to assemble a group of about 300 monks outside the Penglai Palace (Penglai gong 蓬萊宮). When they tried to submit a petition, the anxious monks were told by the Duke of Longxi (Longxiwang 隴西王) to wait until the decision was final. Headed by the Ximing abbot Daoxuan and Weixiu 威秀 from the Great Zhuangyan Monastery (Da Zhuangyansi 大莊嚴寺), the Buddhist delegation chose Ximingsi as a rendezvous point and swarmed in the courtyard of the monastery to plot the next step of remonstration.[49] Given the urgency of the matter, in addition to Weixiu's petition to Gaozong, they agreed to appeal to some high-ranking officials and dignitaries of the imperial family. Daoxuan, who was suffering the debility of old age, volunteered to compose an epistle to the second son of Wu Zetian, Prince Li Xian 李賢 (Zhanghuai Taizi 章懷太子, 651-684). Although a child, the young pro-Buddhist young prince had already obtained the nominal title *Yongzhoumu* 雍州牧 (governor of the Chang'an area). Daoxuan next sent a second petition to Madam Rongguo 榮國夫人 (579-670), the mother of the future Empress Wu.[50] Pressed by repeated petition from the saṃgha and more than 500 officials who voted in support of the Buddhist community, Gaozong was compelled to suspend the decree, though he continued to insist, in his *Ting shamen baijun zha*o 停沙門拜君詔, that the ordained monk should pay respect to their parents.[51] In the wake of this event, we can infer that the Confucian officials of the

---

[49] According to Daoxuan, about three hundred monks participated in the protest, including Linghui 靈會 from Ci'en Monastery, Huiyin 會隱 from Hongfu Monastery (Hongfusi 弘福寺) and, so forth; see *Guang hongming ji*, T52, no. 2103, p. 286, b24-c9.

[50] For the biography of Daoxuan and Weixiu, see *SGSZ*, T50, no. 2061, p. 790, b7-p. 791, and b26 & p. 812, b10-c2. The two letters written by Daoxuan are *Shang Yongzhoumu Peiwang Xian lun shamen buying bai sujia qi* 上雍州牧沛王賢論沙門不應拜俗家啓 and *Shang Rongguo furen Yangshi qinglun shamen buhe baisushi qi* 上榮國夫人楊氏請論沙門不合拜俗事啟; see *Ji shamen buying baishu dengshi*, T52, no. 2108, p. 455, c12-p. 456, a4.

[51] *Ji shamen buying baishu dengshi*, T52, no. 2108, p. 470, b26. Documents related to the saṃgha and the Tang government are also available in Daoxuan's *Guang hongmingji*. Xuanzang's disciple Yancong 彥悰 (627-49), who also submitted a memorial with Daoxuan, solicited imperial edicts and petitions related to the controversy from previous dynasties, compiling a *Summa Contra Gentiles* titled *Ji shamen buying baisu deng shi* (T2108); see *Kaiyuan shijiao lu* 開元釋教錄 (Record of Buddhist Teachings Compiled During the Kaiyuan Period), T55, no. 2154, p. 563, a2-9. In Chinese Buddhist history, Yancong is also credited with the

court, who expressed their opposition to Buddhism during the controversy, were not happy with the fact that a powerful monastery adjacent to the imperial palace was on the rise.[52] However, despite this short, unpleasant battle between the state and the Buddhist saṃgha, a number of events from this period still point to the eminence of Ximingsi under Gaozong's rule.

Prince Zhanghuai and the Bell Inscription

By the time the reign title of Longshuo was replaced by Linde 麟德 (664-665), Ximingsi had already established itself as a great center of Buddhist learning.[53] In the second year of Linde (665), the twelve-year-old prince Li Xian had a gigantic bronze bell, with a total weight of about 10,000 *jin* (five tons) cast for the monastery. The bell was intended to celebrate the morals and grace of his parents, who assumed the honorary title "two sages (*ersheng* 二聖)." The young prince also composed a laudatory inscription, titled *Jingshi Ximingsi zhongming* 京師西明寺鍾銘 (The Bell Inscription of Ximingsi in the Capital City), as a gesture cementing the imperial friendship with Daoxuan and his great monastery. Li Xian, or better known as the Crown Prince Zhanghuai 章懷 (lit. Cherishing literary talent), was a distinguished talent among the progeny of Gaozong and Wu Zetian.[54] In Paul Kroll's words, "He was the scholar among princes, perhaps best known for the commentrary he wrote on the *Hou Han shu* 後漢書 (History of the Latter Han), which is now normally printed with that text."[55] As we saw above, when Li Xian accepted Daoxuan's petition, he was only nine years old, but his precociousness and preference for Buddhism were already widely known. Within less than a decade, Ximingsi had developed a close rapport with two sons of Gaozong: the monastery had been

authorship of *Da Tang jingshi silu* 大唐京師寺錄 (Record of Monasteries of the Capital in the Great Tang), a book believed to contain the record of Ximingsi but unfortunately now lost to us.

[52] For detailed discussion of the issue, including Daoxuan's viewpoint; see Michihata Ryōshū 道端良秀, *Chugoku Bukkyōshi zenshū*. 中國佛教史全集, vol. 2, *Tōdai bukkyōshi no kenkyū* 唐代佛教史の研究 (Tokyo: Shoen, 1985),413-440.

[53] In 664, the Ximingsi abbot Daoxuan completed his magisterial Buddhist catalogue *Da Tang neidian lu* and submitted to the throne. It was an imperial project based on the rich collection in the library of Ximingsi.

[54] Li Xian became the real crown prince (*huang taizi* 皇太子) in 675 (Shangyuan 上元 2) after his older brother Li Hong's death. On that occasion, he also donated his residence as the Qianfu Monastery (Qianfusi 千福寺), a pilgrim site famous for the stūpa of the *Lotus Sūtra*.

[55] Paul W. Kroll, *Dharma Bell and Dhāraṇī Pillar: Li Po's Buddhist Inscriptions* (Kyoto: Scuola italiana di studi sull'Asia orientale, 2001), 18.

established in the name of the heir apparent Li Hong, and now it had accepted the bell offering of Li Xian, who will become the future crown prince. According to his inscription, the bell was made of secret metals from the mountain of Shu (*Shushan* 蜀山) using precious water ferried from the River Han.[56] The bell inscription is beautifully composed in the style of parallel prose in twenty tetrasyllabic lines:

The god of the East prays for us, and the cloud lit by the rising sun gives birth to a dragon horse. The whirlpool and river cultivate moral character, and flowers fall on the Jasper Ridge. The sound of the *lü* flute demonstrates the temperament of the prince; he pays respect to his parents to show loving-kindness. You speak of the good karma leading to the pure land and open for me the path to the Buddhist kingdom. [The bell] was cast by seven previous things and decorated with nine nipple-shaped motifs. The flying dragon was carved as if it was going to make a move. It is suspected that the supine beast may have been startled. The specification of the bell exceeds the standard set up by the Zhou Dynasty and the manufacturing skill surpasses the bells made in the Han Dynasty. The wind wafts [the bell's] echoes at morn, the frost carries its tolling at night. Above it engages august majesty, blow it guides the common folk. Its voice mounts up for a million kalpas, Felicity brimming over a thousands years.[57]

青祇薦祉, 黃離降精.[58] 渦川毓德, 瑤嶺飛英. 吹銅表性, 問寢登情.[59] 興言淨業, 載啟香城.[60] 七珍交鑄, 九乳圖形. 翔龍若動, 偃獸疑驚. 製陵周室,

---

[56] However, Fujiyoshi Masumi argues that Daoxuan might have written the inscription for Li Xian, see Fujiyoshi Masumi 藤善眞澄, "Yakushiji tōtō no satsumei to Saimyōji shōmei 薬師寺東塔の擦銘と西明寺鍾銘," *Ajia yūgaku* アジア遊學 (Tokushū: Nihon no kentōshi —— hatō banri・chōan o mezasu 特集: 日本の遣唐使 —— 波濤萬裏・長安を目指す) 4 (1999): 70-71.

[57] For the final six tetrasyllabic lines, starting from "The wind wafts [the bell's] echoes at morn," I use Paul Kroll's translation; see Kroll, *Dharma Bell and Dhāraṇī Pillar*, 19.

[58] *Qingqi* 青祇 also means the god of spring. In some Tang texts, *huangli* 黃離 assumps the connotation of prince; see *Guangzhou Baozhuangyansi sheli tabei* 廣州寶莊嚴寺舍利塔碑 (by the Tang poet Wang Bo 王勃, 650-76), *QTW* 184.1871.

[59] For an explanation of *chuitong* 吹銅, see and Dai De 戴德, *Da dai liji jinzhu jinyi* 大戴禮記今註今譯, trans. Gao Ming 高明 (Taipei: Taiwan shangwu yinshuguan, 1975), 126; see also *Ce sui wang wei huang taizi wen* 冊遂王爲皇太子文; in *QTW* 63.671.

[60] *Xiangcheng* 香城 refers to a Buddhist kingdom called All Fragrances, the abode of the preaching bodhisattva Dharmodgata, to which bodhisattva Sadāprarudita (the Ever-weeping, Ch. *Changti pusa* 常啼菩薩) makes his way at the cost of great effort, in order to hear the Dharma. Cf. the section of xiangcheng in

規踘漢庭. 風飄旦響, 霜傳夜鳴. 仰延皇祚, 俯導蒼生. 聲騰億劫, 慶溢千齡.[61]

The tradition of writing inscriptions for imperially-commissioned bells, known from Daoxuan's *Guang hongming ji*, started with the bell inscription for the two religions (Buddhism and Daoism) in the Northern Zhou (*Dazhou erjiao zhongming* 大周二教鍾銘) and continued with the bell inscription composed for the Great Xingshan Monastery (*Da Tang xingshansi zhongming* 大唐興善寺鍾銘).[62] It appears the panegyric by Li Xian was so well composed that Japanese scholars agree that it was brought back to Japan as a model essay for prose writing. The Buddhist history scholar Fujiyoshi Masumi 藤善真澄 found connections between Li Xian's prose and a succinct bell inscription engraved on a bronze pillar (*satsu* 擦) of a stūpa at Yakushiji 薬師寺 in Nara. The verse was composed elegantly in the Japanese *kanbun* 漢文 (classical Chinese) on the occasion of the construction of the East Stūpa (*tōtō* 東塔). The Yakushiji, commissioned by Emperor Tenmu 天武天皇 (r. 673-686) in 680 for the recovery of his queen (the later Empress Jitō 持統天皇, r. 690-697) from an illness, was accomplished around 698.[63] Some early Japanese envoys, probably student monks who had studied with Xuanzang, such as Dōshō 道昭 (629-700), must have made copies of Li Xian's inscription and taken it back to Japan.[64]

Mohe bore chanwen 摩訶般若懺文 (by Emperor Wu of the Liang dynasty, or Liang Wudi 梁武帝, 464-549); in *Guang hongming ji*, T52, no. 2103, p. 332, a29-b20.

[61] For the complete inscription, see *Guang hongming ji*, T52, no. 2103, p. 330, a23-b8. *QTW* 99.1019-20. For an introduction to the bell inscription, see Kroll, *Dharma Bell and Dhāraṇī Pillar*, 18-20.

[62] *Guang hongming ji*, T52, no. 2103, p. 329, c27-p. 330, a22.

[63] Fujiyoshi Masumi, "Yakushiji tōtō no satsumei," 66-80. For an explanation of the inscription, see *Kokushi daijiten* 國史大辭典 (Tokyo: Yoshikawa kōbunkan, 1979), s.v. Yakushiji. *Satsu* 擦 (or *setsu* 剎, Skt. *satchāya*) is a rare word in Japanese, interesting, for a detailed discussion, see Giuseppe Tucci, *Stupa: Art, Architectonics and Symbolism*, trans. Uma Marina Vesci (New Delhi: Aditya Prakashan, 1988), 53-57; Du Qi 杜齐 (Giuseppe Tucci), *Fantian fodi. diyi juan, xibei yindu he Xizang xibu de ta he caca* 梵天佛地. 第一卷, 西北印度和西藏西部的塔和擦擦, trans., Wei Zhengzhong 魏正中 and Saerji 萨尔吉 (Shanghai: Shanghai guji chubanshe, 2009), 32-35.

[64] For an literary account of Dōshō's visit to Chang'an, see Marian Ury, *Tales of Times Now Past: Sixty-Two Stories from a Medieval Japanese Collection* (Berkeley: University of California Press, 1979), 84-86. The exchange between the cultural circle of Ximingsi and some Japanese monasteries, Daianji in particular, is further explored by Kuranaka Shinobu 蔵中しのぶ, who traces the reception of Xuanzang's biography in the literary circles of Daianji. See Kuranaka Shinobu, "*Narachō kanshibun ni okeru Genjō sanzō den no juyō ni tsuite―― Chōan Saimyōji to kanbunden jussaku no ba ・ Daianji* 奈良朝漢詩文における玄奘三蔵

For the Sage Kings

In addition to the precious gift of the bell, it was incumbent upon the Tang government to provide supplies out of state coffers to Ximingsi for the celebration of the traditional ghost festival.[65] Daoshi's massive encyclopedia *Fayuan zhulin* 法苑 珠林 (The Pearl Grove of the Dharma Garden, T2122) records a memorandum of the occasion which probably took place around 668, a few years after the bell was cast:

> In the great national temples like Hsi-ming and Tz'u-en ssu in Ch'ang-an, there are endowed fields and gardens in addition to land distributed on the basis of population, and everything that is given [during the ghost festival] is considered to be a national offering. Now every year when people send bowls of offerings and all sorts of items, with musicians and the like carrying the bowls and with more than one government official bringing bowls...[66]

It is clearly indicated in Daoshi's record that, among the many kinds of Buddhist temples that graced Chang'an, the day-to-day administration of the national monasteries was supported by the landed endownments and a poll tax on the inhabitants of the Tang Empire. This government support for the elite Buddhist institutions tells us much about the social situation of monasticism at the beginning of the Tang period: unlike the mendicant monks in the countryside, the resident clerics at Ximingsi never knew the alms-bowl. As an important figure in the Buddhist establishment in Chang'an, Daoshi was called by Gaozong to take up a post at Ximingsi. Based on other pieces in the body of *Fayuan zhulin*, Teiser thinks that Daoshi himself wrote the entry. It is likely that the celebration of the festival continued as a routine in Ximingsi until the end of the Tang Dynasty. Yet, however much such public spectacles may have contributed to the monastery's profile in the city, Ximingsi's international reputation was also established through its role as

---

伝の受容について――長安西明寺と漢文伝述作の場・大安寺," *Tōyō kenkyū* 東洋研究 120 (1996): 31-48; idem., "Xuanzang zhuan dao Jianzhen zhuan ―― Chang'an Ximingsi yu Da'ansi wenhuaquan 從 玄奘傳到鑒真傳 ―― 長安西明寺與大安寺文化圈," *Yangzhou daxue xuebao (Renwen shehui kexue ban)* 揚州大學學報 (人文社會科學版) 2 (2010): 87-92.

[65] *Fayuan zhulin*, T53, no. 2122, p. 750, b10-13. For the establishment of state-sponsored monasteries (*kanji* 官寺) in the Tang, see Michihata Ryōshū, *Tōdai bukkyōshi no kenkyū*, 16-24. For detailed description of Daoshi's memorandum on offerings to the Buddha during the Ghost Festival in Chang'an, see Teiser, *Ghost Festival*, 66-71; Teiser thinks that the account was probably also based on Daoshi's own experience at Ximingsi.

[66] Teiser, *Ghost Festival*, 68.

51

academy of Buddhist learning. Let us turn, then, to a look at several of the Buddhist luminaries who graced the monastery in its early years.

Buddhapāla, Wŏn Chŭk and Fazang

From the reign of Gaozong and Empress Wu, until the end of the eighth century, Ximingsi was a leading institute for the translation of Buddhist texts. We could investigate the careers of the foreign translators and scholar-monks who worked on these translations and the value of scriptures that they translated, but instead of elaborating on Buddhist philosophy or being trapped in the complicated sectarian history of this era, my focus in this and the following chapter is the interaction between Ximingsi and the Tang government. For this, I will select a few prominent figures and representative scholars associated with Ximingsi who can serve to exemplify the theme of church and state. Much of the credit for the translation projects at Ximingsi must go to the staunch support of Gaozong and Empress Wu, who lavished wealth and honors on the national monasteries that they sponsored. Little is known about which scriptures were systematically rendered into Chinese at Ximingsi during the early years, for much of the Buddhist translation was accomplished at Ci'ensi, with which Xuanzang was somehow more closely associated. Indeed, Daoxuan himself, along with some other masters registered at Ximingsi were also invited to join Xuanzang's atelier as they endeavored to put into Chinese the Indian manuscripts preserved in the library of the Great Wild Goose Stūpa (Dayanta 大雁塔) at Ci'ensi.

As far as we know, one of the earliest Buddhist scriptures translated at Ximingsi was probably the *Foding zunsheng tuoluoni jing*. It was brought by the Kasmiri missionary and translator Buddhapāla (or Buddhapālita), one of the pioneers of esoteric Buddhism, who arrived in Ximingsi with the Sanskrit manuscript around the year 679.[67] The story of this manuscript went back to 676, when Buddhapāla visited Mount Wutai in the hope of having a vision of Mañjuśri. Instead, he was told by an old man that he could not see the Bodhisattva unless he brought back from India a

---

[67] *Foding zunshen tuoluoni jing* 佛頂尊勝陀羅尼經 (Dhāraṇī of the Jubilant Corona), T19, no. 967, p. 349, a2-p. 352, c22; *Mochizuki*, 3169-70. See also *Foding zunsheng tuoluoni jing shi* 佛頂尊勝陀羅尼經釋, *XZJ* 92, p. 146, a2-b9. For some Chinese commentaries, see Fachong 法崇's *Foding zunsheng tuoluoni jing jiaoji yiji* 佛頂尊勝陀羅尼經教跡義記 (Meanings of the Doctrinal Traces of Dhāraṇī of the Jubilant Buddha-Corona, T1803).

copy of the *Foding zunsheng tuoluoni*, an important tantric text believed to provide remission of karmically deserved rebirth in one of the evil destinies (Skt. *durgati*, Ch. *equ* 惡趣).[68] By evoking the power of the Uṣṇīṣavijayā (or *Tīkṣṇoṣṇīṣa*, Ch. Zunsheng foding 尊勝佛頂, figure.6), the practitioner who recites, copies or spreads the *dhāraṇī* can prolong his life and cultivate merits. The manuscript was first translated in the palace, and Gaozong wanted to keep the scripture in his private library. According to the preface attached to the *Foding zunsheng tuoluoni jing*, Buddhapāla tearfully appealed to the emperor:

> I risked my life and brought the scripture to China from afar, in the hope that it can give succor to all the living beings and rescue them from suffering. I am not concerned about monetary benefit nor do I care about fortune and reputation. I sincerely hope your majesty can release the manuscript and put it into circulation so that the sentient beings can derive benefit.

> 貧道捐軀委命, 遠取經來. 情望普濟群生, 救拔苦難. 不以財寶為念, 不以名利關懷. 請遷經本流行, 庶望含靈同益.[69]

Eventually, Gaozong acceded to his request, by keeping the translated copy in the palace and releasing the original Sanskrit copy to him for retranslation at Ximingsi. With the assistance of the Ximing scholar Shunzhen, one of the few monks of that time reputed to have some knowledge of Sanskrit, Buddhapāla's translation became the most influential editon of a series of translations of the same scripture.[70]

The period of Gaozong and Empress Wu witnessed a boom in the translation of Indian scriptures that opened up the esoteric Budhist teachings to the Chinese audience. The selection of scriptures to be translated seems quite arbitrary, apparently dependent simply on the itineraries of the Indian missionaries who brought the manuscripts. The enterprise of translation was a united effort involving international scholars and monks from diverse local monasteries. Upon imperial request and under the recommendation of their counterparts, the skilled clergymen either translated the

---

[68] For studies on Buddhapāla and the *dhāraṇī*, see Robert Gimello, "Changing Shang-Ying on Wu-T'ai Shan," in *Pilgrims and Sacred Sites in China*, ed. Susan Naquin and Yü Chün-Fang (Berkeley: University of California Press, 1992), 89-102; Liu Shufeng, *Miezui yu duwang*, 12.

[69] *Foding zunshen tuoluoni jing*, T19, no. 967, p. 349, b28-c1; see also *SGSZ*, T50, no.2061, p. 718, a2-10.

[70] For a detailed account of the story, see Kroll, *Dharma Bell and Dhāraṇī Pillar*, 40-44.

texts at their home monasteries or lodged in other monasteries as assistant members of the ateliers. In many cases it becomes impossible to distinguish between the contributions of the monks belonging to Ximingsi and other visiting monks —— a problem that poses a challenge for scholars seeking to treat the history and character of the monastery.

Figure. 6   Uṣṇīṣavijayā (Ch. Zunsheng foding 尊勝佛頂). Source: Yoritomi Motohiro 頼富本宏, ed., *Mikkyō butsuzō zuten: Indo to Nihon no hotoketachi* 密教仏像図典: インドと日本のほとけたち, 230.

One of the most well-known monk-scholars of Ximingsi is the Korean prince Wŏn Chŭk, the famous philosopher of *vijñapti-mātratā* (Ch. *weishi* 唯識). In the first year of Yonglong 永隆 (680), he collaborated with the Indian master Divākara (Ch. Dipoheluo 地婆呵羅 or Rizhao 日照, 613-688) at Hongfu Monastery (Hongfusi 弘福寺) to render the *Foshuo zaota gongde jing* 佛說造塔功德經 (Scripture of Merit for the Establishment of a Stūpa, T699) into Chinese.[71] We know that Wŏn Chŭk spent most of his time at Ximingsi doing exegetical work on Yogacara Buddhism —— work dramatically dissimilar to translation of the *Zaota gongde jing*, a concise text on stūpa worship. We should bear in mind, however,

---

[71] *Foshuo zaota gongde jing* 佛說造塔功德經 (Scripture on the Virtues of Making Stūpas), T16, no. 699, p. 801, a3-7

several points that make Wŏn Chŭk's summons to Hongfusi to work on this devotional text less surprising than it might initially seem.

First, scripture translation was an imperial mission requiring the participation of talented scholars selected from local temples. Wŏn Chŭk was certainly well qualified, he was even popularly known as Ximing fashi 西明法師, or the Master of Ximing, testifying to his reputation as a first-class expert on consciousnesses-only doctrine. He and Daoxuan are the only two exceptional scholars in the Buddhist history of Ximingsi who shared the honorific title "Ximing".[72] Also, it seems that, in addition to his exegetical work, Wŏn Chŭk was involved in other translation projects. As indicated in his biography, beginning from the latter days of Gaozong, he was summoned by the government to take up a post in the Institute of Scriptural Translation (Yijingguan 譯經館) at Ximingsi —— an establishment likely resembling the Cloister of Sutra-Translation (Fanjingyuan 翻經院) that Xuanzang had established at Ci'en Monastery.[73] Finally, we should not be surprised that a Buddhist scholar might also be interested in a devotional work. Just as scholars find it hard to accept Daoxuan's vision from a deity or the mysterious stories offered in his prolific works, the identity of Wŏn Chŭk as pious practitioner has been downplayed in the extensive scholarly study of his sophisticated commentaries. Modern scholars are mostly interested in doctrinal elaboration but and rarely seem to consider that both Daoxuan and Wŏn Chŭk, like their Indian colleague Buddhapāla, were monks of pious religious faith, whose Buddhism was far broader than their scholarly work. Without an adequate appreciation of this fact, it will be difficult properly to interpret their demeanor and the mentality manifest in their interactions with the Tang regime.

In addition to translation, the court had other interests in Ximingsi, as exemplified in an incident in the biography of the famous figure Fazang 法藏 (643-712, Figure. 7), the third patriarch of Huayan Buddhism, also cooperated with Wŏn Chŭk's and Divākara in the translation of the *Avataṃsaka sūtra* during his stay in Chang'an.[74] Fazang was most popularly known as the person who the expounded

---

[72] *Cheng weishi lun liaoyi deng* 成唯識論了義燈, T43, no. 1832, p. 687, c19-23; *Jingang ying juan shang* 金剛映卷上, T85, no. 2734, p. 59, b20-23; *Sifen lü shu shi zongyi ji* 四分律疏飾宗義記, XZJ 66, p. 101, b17-p. 102, a1.

[73] For the short biography of Wŏn Chŭk (*Tang Jingshi ximingsi yuance zhuan* 唐京師西明寺圓測傳) and his work at Ximingsi, see *SGSZ*, T50, no. 2061, p. 727, b4-14.

[74] *Tang Tae Ch' ŏnboksa kosaju pŏn'gyŏng taedŏk Pŏpjang hwasang chŏn* 唐大薦福寺故寺主翻經大德法

the *Chapter of the Golden Lion of the Avataṃsaka-sūtra* (*Huayan jin shizi zhang* 華嚴金獅子章, T1881) to Empress Wu.[75] He was one of the greatest Buddhist metaphysicians and practitioners of the *Avataṃsaka-sūtra* in medieval Asia.[76] Revered as a monk of great wisdom and passion, Fazang was a "visiting scholar" associated with Ximingsi, whose prestige was well-established by this time. In Chuigong 垂拱 3 (687), Fazang was lecturing on the *Avataṃsaka sūtra* at Ci'en Monastery when the capital area was threatened by severe drought. Fazang, famous for his magic power as well, was ordered by the state to establish an altar at Ximingsi and perform rain-prayer rituals. It was an official mission, as Zhang Luke 張魯克 (d. 687), the incumbent magistrate of the Chang'an Sub-prefecture, acted as the "host of prayers" (*qingzhu* 請主). After nearly seven days of fasting and observing precepts, the rain finally did come.[77]

Figure. 7 The Portrait of Fazang (643-712), 13th Century. Hanging Scroll, Color on Silk; 152 cm x 81.4 cm. Tōdaiji, Nara, Japan. Source: Chen Jinhua, *Philosopher, Practitioner, Politician: The Many Lives of Fazang*, cover.

藏和尚傳, T50, no. 2054, p. 282, a18-26.

[75] *Huayan jing jinshizi zhang zhu* 華嚴經金師子章註, T45, no. 1881, p. 668, a9-15. For an annotated edition of this commentary, see Fang Litian 方立天, *Huayan jing jinshizi zhang jiaoshi* 華嚴經金師子章校釋 (Beijing: Zhonghua shuju, 1983), 1-171.

[76] For a study of Fazang, see Chen Jinhua, *Philosopher, Practitioner, Politician: the Many Lives of Fazang* (Boston, E.J. Brill, 2007).

[77] Chen Jinhua, *Fazang*, 130; see also *Tang Tae Ch' ŏnboksa kosaju pŏn'gyŏng taedŏk Pŏpjang hwasang chŏn*, T50, no. 2054, p. 283, c7-9. For another example of the seven-day rain prayer in Chang'an, see *Daizongchao zheng sikong dabianzheng guangzhi sanzang heshang biaozhiji* 代宗朝贈司空大辨正廣智三藏和上表制集 (Collected Documents on Regulations Bestowed by the Court of Daizong on the Minister of Works, the Greatly Skillful and Upright Guangzhi, the Venerable Tripiṭaka Master, abbreviated as *BZJ*), T52, no. 2120, p. 841, a2-18.

Empress Wu and the Nepali Pearl

The good will of Gaozong and his family members towards Ximingsi reached its peak with the ascension of Wu Zetian as virtually the first female monarch in China. Under her reign, as many scholars have noted, Buddhism as well as the empire as a whole flourished in peace and prosperity. Born into a family with pronounced Buddhist sympathies, Empress Wu had been ordained as a nun after Emperor Taizong passed away in 649. It was therefore no surprise that she was an ardent supporter of Buddhism. Like the Japanese Prince Shōtoku 聖德太子 (574-622), who sponsored the prosperity of Asuka Buddhism, the Zhou Dynasty that Empress Wu established officially elevated the status of Buddhism. As Weinstein put it in his *Buddhism under the Tang*:

> In the fourth month of 691, an imperial edict formally ranked Buddhism above Taoism, thereby reversing the policy of the three preceding T'ang emperors, and ordered that henceforth Buddhist monks and nuns should take precedence over members of the Taoist clergy. This action was taken, in the words of Empress Wu, because 'Buddhism opened the way for changing the Mandate of Heaven.'[78]

Court Buddhism, represented by palace chapels (*nei daochang* 內道場) in both capitals, prospered in Empress Wu's palaces, since she realized that the Buddhist sūtras contained information that could be helpful for a woman sovereign.[79] Forte's research of the Dunhuang document S6502 shows that the two ideas of "Wu Chao Cakravartin" and "Wu Chao Bodhisattva" were associated with Buddhist texts such as the *Dayun jing* 大雲經 (a.k.a. *Da fangdeng wuxiang dayun jing* 大方等無想大雲經, Skt. *Mahāmegha-sūtra*, T387). The sacral political unity of the Son of Heaven is reconfirmed and re-inforced by means of the appeal to the figures of the Cakravartin and the Bodhisattva.[80] We should keep in mind that Empress Wu was the founding

---

[78] Weinstein, *Buddhism under the Tang*, 43. On Empress Wu and the Buddhist church, see R. W. L. Guisso, *Wu Tse-T'en and the Politics of Legitimation in T'ang China* (Bellingham, Wash: Western Washington, 1978), 26-50.

[79] Lewis, *China's Cosmopolitan Empire*, 10; for a study of the Palace Chapel in the Tang, see Chen Jinhua, "Tang Buddhist Palace Chapels," *Journal of Chinese Religions* 32 (2004): 101-73.

[80] Antonino Forte, *Political Propaganda and Ideology in China at the End of the Seventh Century: Inquiry*

patroness of Ximingsi and thereafter a generous donor to the monastery. According to *Guangyiji* 廣異記 (Great Book of Marvels), an early Tang anthology of fantastic tales, the empress had lavishly bestowed exotic gifts on Ximingsi. There is in particular an anecdote about a precious pearl imported from Nepal as tribute. The story has it that once an envoy from a country in Serindia submitted a jewel called the blue-mud pearl (*qingnizhu* 青泥珠), a mandible bone of a deity, and the tongue of a *pratyekabudha* to the Tang court. Ignorant of its true value, Empress Wu bequeathed the pearl to Ximingsi, which subsequently embedded it into the forehead of the statue of a vajra-warrior (Ch. *jingang lishi* 金剛力士). The story then becomes interesting:

> Afterward Ximingsi sponsored public lectures. Then a Hu came to hear the preaching.[81] When he caught a glimpse of the pearl, he looked at it with fixed eyes. For ten days, [whenever he arrived in Ximinigsi] he would walk near the figure of the vajra-warrior and stared at the pearl with utmost concentration, without paying any attention to the sermon. Realizing what was happening, a monk asked him whether he was interested in buying the pearl. The Hu answered: "If you are willing to sell, I will certainly offer a high price." At first the monk asked for one thousand strings of cash, then gradually raised the price to ten thousands; but the Hu made no response. Finally when the monk lifted the price to a hundred thousand strings, he sold it.

> 後有講席, 胡人來聽講.見珠縱視, 目不暫舍. 如是積十餘日, 但於珠下諦視, 而意不在講. 僧知其故, 因問故欲買珠耶? 胡雲, 必若見賣, 當致重價. 僧初索千貫, 漸至萬貫,胡悉不醻. 遂定至十萬貫, 賣之.[82]

---

into the Nature, Authors and Function of the Tunhuang Document S.6502, Followed by an Annotated Translation (Napoli: Istituto universitario orientale, Seminario di studi asiatici, 1976), 169.

[81] In medieval China, *Huren* 胡人 (*hu* person), sometimes translated as "tartars", refers to people of the Northern barbarian tribes including Huns (Ch. *Xiongnu* 匈奴); Khan (Ch. *Xianbei* 鮮卑), *Si* 氏, *Qiang* 羌, Tibet (Ch. *Tubo* 吐蕃), Türk (Ch. *Tujue* 突厥), Mongolia (Ch. *Menggu* 蒙古), Kitan (Ch. *Qidan* 契丹), Jurchen (Ch. *Nüzhen* 女真), etc. In the Tang dynasty, the *hu* person also refers to the Sogdian, Persian and other people of Iranian origin.

[82] The story is taken from *Guangyiji* 廣異記 (Great Book of Marvels), see *TPGJ* 402. 3237; Ono, *Shiryōhen*, 230. *Qingni* 青泥, according to Huilin's lexicography *Yiqiejing yinyi*, is the dirty blue mud at the bottom of water, see *Yiqiejing yinyi*, T54, no. 2128, p. 350, b7.

For the Sage Kings

The pearl proved to be a jewel purportedly treasured in the remote land of Nepal. It was said to have possessed the magic power to purify muddy water and reveal treasures buried at the bottom. The story of this fabulous pearl and its sale to the Hu buyer give us some insight into Ximingsi's place in the life of the capital. Note that the foreigner is coming to the monastery for a series of Buddhist lectures, which lasted for ten days and were apparently open to the public regardless of nation and race —— an event testifying to the distinct international atmosphere and confidence of the metropolitan intelligentsia.

The story reflects the role of Ximingsi as a leading scholarly institution and one of the cultural crucibles of Chang'an. As we noted in chapter 2, the monastery was situated near the West Market, which was reputed to have more exotic goods for sale than the East Market. Located near the western Golden Light Gate (Jinguang men 金光門) of Chang'an, the Western Market was an ideal lodging place for foreign merchants arriving from the Silk Road. The local citizens were quite familiar with popular stories of Buddhist monks, of rare treasures from exotic places, and of the Persian businessmen active in the market. Another story, for example, told by the Tang historian Duan Chengshi 段成式 (d. 863) in the ninth century, also mentions a treasure bone (*gubao* 骨寶) that sold in the market at the astronomical price of one million strings of cash. Here again, it was a monk, from Puti Monastery (Putisi 菩提寺), who sold it to a typical gem lover of the time, a *Hu* merchant in the West Market.[83] Speaking in particular of the Persian merchant and his gems, Edward

---

[83] See *Sita ji* 寺塔記 (Record of Monaseries and Stūpas), T51, no. 2093, p. 1023, b29-c12. According to Duan Chengshi, the story was told by Yuanjing 元竟, the abbot of Puti Monastery (Putisi 菩提寺), who knew a great many old stories about Buddhists. The English translation of the story is provided by Alexander Soper as follows:

He said that whenever Li Lin-fu had a birthday he would always invite the monks of this temple to his mansion for a maigre feast. To one priest, for chanting praises of the Buddha, he gave a saddle that when sold proved to be worth 70000 for the materials alone. There was also another priest, Kuang, a man famous for his fine voice, who had recited *sutras* for several years running, and on this occasion also praised the Buddha. For having called down blessings on the minister's works of piety, he hoped to reap a rich reward. When the celebration was over he was handed, from behind my lord's curtains, a silk-wrapped coffer tied with a scented gauze kerchief, which contained something like a rusty nail, several inches long. The priest went away disconsolate, but after several days of depression, decided that a great lord would be incapable of treating him so shabbily; and so took the object to the western market. When he showed it to a foreign trader the latter started and said, "How did your reverence get hold of this? You must sell it at its proper value." The priest tentatively asked for 100000, at which the foreigner laughed and said, "not yet." The other, screwing up his courage, pushed his figure to 500000. The

Schafer says, "'A poor Persian' was a laughable contradiction in terms, and the Iranian Magus stalks the pages of T'ang popular stories, invested with the glamour of the sorcery he was reputed to practice, and above all enriched by the magical gems he was believed to carry. The Persian gem dealer was considered the last word in connoisseurship, and at the same time a worshiper of valuable jewels."[84]

The opulence of the Tang Dynasty monastery, as well as its connection with the market place, is also illustrated by archeological discoveries carried out in China. The Chinese scholar Qi Dongfang 齊東方, who has examined the exotic artifacts excavated from the sites of medieval temples, argues that the almost all the Persian coins and exotic glassware are found in the ruins of Buddhist monasteries.[85] It is believed that a large proportion of the wealth of Ximingsi was dependent upon donations made by the imperial family and other generous donors like Empress Wu in particular. In contrast to the abundant *engi* 緣起 literature on the foundation of Japanese temples and shrines, the lack of monastic gazetteers in the medieval Chinese Buddhist corpus makes it difficult for us to capture a detailed picture of the richness of the saṃgha and its property at Ximingsi.[86] We can only infer from the offering catalogues attached to the Chinese Famen Monastery (Famensi 法門寺) and the Japanese Tōdaiji 東大寺 that the jewels, vessels, silverware and other gifts housed in Ximingsi must amount to a stunning number.[87]

---

foreigner answered, "This is worth a cool million", and gave it to him. The priest asked the thing's name, and was told it was a Treasure Bone."

Alexander C. Soper, "A Vacation Glimpse of the T'ang Temples of Ch'ang-an. The Ssu-t'a Chi by Tuan Ch'eng-shih," *Artibus Asiae* 23, no. 1 (1960): 29.

[84] Edward Schafer, *The Golden Peaches of Samarkand* (Berkeley: University of California Press, 1963), 223; for detailed discussion of jewels, metals and sacred objects in the material civilization of the Tang Dynasty, see idem, 222-68; for the Chinese translation, see Edward Schafer, *Tangdai de wailai wenming* 唐代的外來文明, trans. Wu Yugui 吳玉貴 (Xi'an: Shanxi shifan daxue chubanshe, 2005), 283-329.

[85] Qi Dongfang 齊東方, "Fosi yizhi chutuwenwu de jige wenti 佛寺遺址出土文物的幾個問題," in *Fojiao wuzhi wen hua: siyuan caifu yu shisu gongyang guoji xueshu yantaohui lunwenji* 佛教物質文化: 寺院財富與世俗供養國際學術研討會論文集, ed. Sarah Elizabeth Fraser (Shanghai: Shanghai shuhua chubanshe, 2003), 81-91.

[86] *Engi* 緣起 (or *jisha engi* 寺社緣起) is a genre of Japanese Buddhist literature used to record the history of the foundation of Buddhist temples or indigenous shrines. For some examples, see *Yishiyamadera engi* 石山寺緣起 (A History of the Yishiyama Monastery); *Shigisan engi* 信貴山緣起 (A History of Shigisan); *Shoji engi shō* 諸寺緣起集 (Histories of Monasteries in Nara), and so forth.

[87] The Japanese *kenmotsuchō* 献物帳 (catalogue of articles for presentation) catalogue is the "*Tenpyō shōhō yatose rokugatsu sanjūyichinichi kenmotsuchō* 天平勝寶八歲六月三十一日献物帳", which is dated

During the reign of the formidable Empress Wu, the expansion of the imperial bureaucracy and its supporting population required the government to move temporarily to Luoyang, where food supplies and other necessities were more accessible. However, Ximingsi retained its superior status as an ideal temple for Buddhist ordination. The fame and power of the great national monasteries like Ximing and Ci'en, both of which were responsible for the symbolic ordination of the imperial family and the translation of state-sanctioned scriptures, continued to attract new recruits from talented monk-scholars or respected Buddhist practitioners across the country.[88] As a result, Ximingsi emerged from its formative period in the seventh century as a key magnet attracting the power, the knowledge and the wealth of the nation.

Yijing and the Corrupted Abbot

Described by some apocryphal scriptures as a sage king (Ch. *Zhuanlun shengwang* 転輪聖王, Skt. *cakravatin* or *cakravarti-rājan*), Empress Wu was happy to sponsor some of her favorite monks and generously subsidize numerous translation institutes active in the two capitals.[89] During this period when the Buddhist dharma blossomed under the sovereignty of the "two sages," the great scholar and pilgrim Yijing 義淨 (635-713) was a conspicuous figure in residence at Ximingsi. Yijing had followed Xuanzang's footsteps to India, where he stayed for 20 years. After returning to China in 695 with hundreds of Sanskrit scrolls, he commuted between Luoyang and Chang'an as a renowned translator and advocate of Sarvāstivādin vinaya. For three

---

in 756 and preserved in Shosoin 正倉院. The Chinese *yiwuzhang* 衣物帳 (catalogue of clothing and other articles) catalogue is the "*Xiantong shiwunian Jiansong zhenshen shi sui zhenshen gongyang daoju ji enci jinguan yiwu zhang* 咸通十五年監送真身使隨真身供養道具及恩賜金觀衣物帳", which is dated in 874 and preserved in the Famensi Museum. Empress Wu is believed to have donated generously to Famen Monastery; see Han Jinke, "Das Buddhistische Kaiserreich: Die Epoche Der Kaiserin Wu Zetian Und Der Famen-Tempel," in *Unter Der Gelben Erde: Die Deutsch-Chinesische Zusammenarbeit Im Kulturgüterschutz Kongressbeiträge* (Bonn. Mainz: Verlag Philipp Von Zabern, 2007), 167-79.

[88] See, e.g., the case of the monk Shenkai, from Taiyuan, reported in the *Song gaoseng zhuan*: SGSZ, T50, no. 2061, p. 730, c14-16.

[89] For instance, she had sponsored the translation of *Lalitavistara* (*Fangguang da zhuangyan jing* 方廣大莊嚴經, T187) and the unfinished part of *Dabaoji jing* 大寶積經 (Skt. *Ratnakūṭa-sūtra*, T310). In 693, she called herself "Sagelike and Divine Sovereign of the Golden Wheel" (*Jinlun Shengshen huangdi* 金輪聖神皇帝); see the preface of the 80-juan *Avataṃsaka sūtra*, *Da fangguang fo huayan jing* 大方廣佛華嚴經 (Flower Ornament Sutra), T10, no. 279, p. 1, a3-17.

years, starting in 700 (Jiushi 久視 1), he rendered a group of major scriptures and *dhāraṇīs* into Chinese. He even established an official Institute for Translation (*yichang* 譯場) at Ximingsi. His remarkable work included a new translation of the *Suvarṇaprabhāsottama Sūtra* (Ch. *Jin guangming jing* 金光明經, T665), a Mahayana text stressing the merit of the confession ritual of the golden light (*Jinguangming chanfa* 金光明懺法) and state-protection by the four guardian gods (Ch. *Sitianwang* 四天王, Skt. *catur-mahā-rājajikā*). Not only sharing in fame with the classics *Manusmṛit* and *Śāntiparvan* in India, the *Suvarṇaprabhāsottama Sūtra* was also recognized in traditional Nepalese Buddhism as one of the nine dharma jewels.[90] The precision of Yijing's translation for which is historically renowned, and its majesty of style, have enabled that monumental version of *Suvarṇaprabhāsottama Sūtra* to become the mainspring of national protective Buddhism in East Asia.[91]

Yijing's sojourn in Chang'an, as attested to in several colophons to translations that he completed in 703 (Chang'an 3), was spent in collaboration with Fazang at Ximingsi. The projects included the newly translated *Avataṃsaka sūtra* and some minor Buddhist text, like *Raśmivimalaviśuddhaprabhādhāraṇī* (*Wugou jingguang da tuoluoni* 無垢淨光大陀羅尼, T1024).[92] Generally speaking, for twelve years from 700-712, when Yijing visited Chang'an, he was lodged at either Ximingsi or Jianfusi 薦福寺. The biography of Yijing and Zhisheng 智昇's illustrious catalogue *Kaiyuan shijiao lu* 開元釋教錄 (Record of Buddhist Teachings Compiled During the Kaiyuan Period, thus *Kaiyuan Catalogue*, T2154) confirm that some of the texts were translated consecutively in the Fuxiansi 福先寺 of Luoyang and Ximingsi.[93]

---

[90] See *Jin guangming chanfa buzhu yi* 金光明懺法補助儀, T46, no. 1945, p. 957, b2- p. 961, c15-17. For a list of the nine Sanskrit scriptures, see Akira Hirakawa, *A History of Indian Buddhism: from Śākyamuni to early Mahāyāna*, trans. Paul Groner (Honolulu: University of Hawai'i Press, 1990), 284-95.

[91] *Suvarṇaprabhāsottama Sūtra* is one of the most important Buddhist scriptures in Japan. For the sūtra-chanting (*dokyō* 読経) and rituals regarding the scripture, see Tamura Enchō 田村圓澄, *Kodai kokka to Bukkyō kyōten* 古代国家と仏教経典 (Tokyo: Yoshikawa kōbunkan, 2002), 259-71; Nakabayashi Takayuki 中林隆之, *Nihonkodai kokka no Bukkyō hensei* 日本古代国家の仏教編成 (Tokyo: Hanawa shobō, 2007), 132-45. For some studies on *Suvarṇaprabhāsottama sūtra* and the subsequent translations, see Johannes Nobel, *Suvarṇaprabhāsottamasūtra. Das Goldglanz-Sūtra; ein Sanskrittext des Mahāyāna Buddhismus* (Leiden: E.J. Brill, 1958); R. E. Emmerick, *The Sūtra of Golden Light: Being a Translation of the Suvarṇaprabhāsottamasūtra* (1970; repr., London Boston: Pali Text Society; Distributed by Routledge & K. Paul, 2001).

[92] Chen Jinhua, *Fazang*, 147-48. For the life of Yijing, see Wang Bangwei 王邦維, *Nanhai jigui neifa zhuan jiaozhu* 南海寄歸內法傳校注 (Beijing: Zhonghua shuju, 1995).

[93] The nine scriptures that were published at Ximingsi in 703 are:

We may recall that as early as 690, by means of an edict, Empress Wu had sought to establish her famous network of "Great Cloud" monasteries (Dayunsi) across the country, where the monks had to explain and illustrate the *Dayun jing*.[94] Empress Wu must have been pleased to see that more state-protection scriptures were being introduced at Ximingsi. As Weinstein has pointed out, there can be little doubt about the genuineness of Empress Wu's piety and determination to propagate the Buddhist faith, for she "not only provided the financial support for a number of able translators but also personally participated in their work much as the Buddhist rulers of the fifth and sixth centuries had done."[95] However, the picture is not always so bright; history shows us that the unrestrained power of a religious institution will breed corruption within the very community that fosters it. This was especially true during the second reign of the Emperor Zhongzong 中宗 (r. 683-684 and 705-710) —— the crown prince and ruler installed by Wu Zetian. The privileged position of Buddhism under the reign of Zhongzong is well-known, for he had donated his residence to the Buddhist community as the Jianfu Monastery and authorized the nation-wide establishment of the state-sponsored Longxing Monasteries in each prefecture across the country.[96] When medieval China was governed by Empress Wu and Zhongzong, the wealth and fame of Ximingsi reached its apex, but soon after its reputation was threatened by accusations of wanton corruption and embezzlement made against its abbot, the infamous monk Huifan 慧範 (or 惠範, d. 713). Given his position as the head master of Ximingsi, information

---

1. *Suvarṇaprabhāsottama-sūtra*
2. *Vajracchedikā-prajñāpāramitā* (Ch. *Nengduan Jingang bore boluomi jing* 能斷金剛般若波羅蜜多經, T239)
3. *Manshushili pusa zhouzang zhong yizi zhouwang jing* 曼殊室利菩薩呪藏中一字呪王經 (T1182)
4. *Hasta-vāla-prakaraṇa* (Ch. *Zhangzhong lun* 掌中論, T1578)
5. *Quyin jiashe lun* 取因假設論 (T1622)
6. *Liumen jiaoshou xiding lun* 六門教授習定論 (T1607)
7. *Mūla-sarvāstivāda-vinaya* (Ch. *Genben Shuoyiqieyoubu pi'naiye* 根本說一切有部毘奈耶, T1442)
8. *Mūla-sarvāstivāda nidāna-mātṛkā* (Ch. *Genben Shuoyiqieyoubu nituona mudejia* 根本說一切有部尼陀那目得迦, T1452)
9. *Genben Shuoyiqieyoubu baiyi jiemo* 根本說一切有部百一羯磨 (T1453)

See *Kaiyuan shijiao lu*, T55, no. 2154, p. 567, a19-p. 568, b3, see also Chen Jinhua, *Fazang*, 228

[94] Forte, *Political Propaganda and Ideology*, 8-9.

[95] Weinstein, *Buddhism under the Tang*, 44.

[96] On Emperor Zhongzong and Buddhism in Chang'an, see Sun Yinggang, "Chang'an yu Jingzhou zhijian: Tang Zhongzong yu fojiao 長安與荊州之間: 唐中宗與佛教," in *Tangdai zongjiao xinyang yu shehui* 唐代宗教信仰與社會, ed. Rong Xinjiang (Shanghai: Shanghai cishu chubanshe, 2003), 125-50.

regarding this man in the history of Chinese Buddhism is surprisingly sparse. No conspicuous Buddhist lineage lines active in Ximingsi can be linked to him. Both religious and secular sources indicate that he defied all laws and utilized nepotism to mastermind political vice. As Chen Jinhua has pointed out, "He provides an example of the tightly wound, intimate links between Buddhist (and other) clerics and the agitated goings-on of the Wu and Li families. He was deeply trusted by empress Wu, Zhongzong, and the latter's brother Ruizong 睿宗 (r. 684–690, 710–712), as well as by the powerful Zhang brothers, empress Wei, and princess Taiping."[97]

Therefore not surprisingly, around 706 or even early, Zhongzong appointed Huifan as the concurrent abbot of three major monasteries (*sansizhu* 三寺主): Ximingsi, Zhongtiansi 中天寺 and Shengshansi 聖善寺. But the *Zizhi tongjian* 資治通鑒 (Comprehensive Mirror for Aid in Government), a classic reference in Chinese historiography, reveals him as a "barbarian monk" who worked his magic to attract court officials.[98] Not satisfied with the luxurious Shengshan Monastery in Luoyang, Zhongzong also commissioned him to supervise the construction of a huge Buddha statue at Changle Slope (Changlepo 長樂坡) near Chang'an, a project that exhausted most of the cash in the imperial treasury. Having the royal family, especially the princess Taiping (Taiping gongzhu 太平公主) (663-713), at his back, Huifan's profligacy remained for a while beyond the law's reach, but in the first year of Jinglong 景龍 (707) he was sued for embezzling public funds. The court inspector Wei Chuangong 魏傳弓 seized evidence showing that the money Huifan embezzled exceeded 40,000 *liang*. Though pressured by the court inspector, Zhongzong was reluctant to degrade Huifan and place him in confinement.[99] Huifan's downfall finally came in 712, when he was accused of conspiring with princess Taiping to depose the new emperor Xuanzong —— a charge that inevitably led to his execution along with the other plotters.[100] It would be helpful for our

---

[97] For a detailed study of Huifan and Shengshan Monastery (Shengshansi 聖善寺), see Chen Jinhua, "The Statues and Monks of Shengshan Monastery: Money and Maitreyan Buddhism in Tang China," *Asia Major* (2006): 111-59. See also *Da Song sengshi lüe* , T54, no. 2126, p. 244, c24-26.

[98] Sima Guang 司馬光 and Hu Sanxing 胡三省, *Zizhi tongjian* 資治通鑑 (Beijing: Zhonghua shuju, 1956), 6585. The book is hereafter abbreviated as *ZZTJ*.

[99] Ibid., 6616; *Cefu yuangui* 冊府元龜 (Outstanding Models from the Storehouse of Literature, hereafter abbreviated as *CFYG*), *SKQS* 911: 89. See also the section of *wuxing zhi* 五行志 (Treatise of Five Phrases) in *JTS* 37. 1374.

[100] For a sweeping history of Xuanzong's reign, see Denis Twitchett, ed., *The Cambridge History of China*, vol.3, bk.1, *Sui and T'ang China, 589-906* (Cambridge: Cambridge University Press, 2008), 333-463.

understanding of the case if we were able to probe into the background details of this scandal and clarify Ximingsi's response during the crisis, but Chen Jinhua has pointed out the difficulty in this:

> After such disgrace, Huifan must have become an embarrassment to Buddhist monks of all traditions. This fact probably accounts for the paucity of neutral, objective accounts of his actions and influence. It has become difficult to create a clear picture of almost any of his activities and their complicated social and political background and implications.[101]

We cannot help wondering how such a dishonored monk could have taken up the abbacy of Ximingsi, and indeed historical sources fail to provide a convincing explanation. By virtue of his research on Shengshansi, Chen Jinhua concludes that the position that Huifan obtained and managed to maintain in the contemporaneous religious world and his outstanding clout as a power-broker show that he must have been a man of exceptional talent and one who should not be dismissed lightly. In the end, however, he was in fact a political loser who, following his execution by Xuanzong, became anathema in both official and private contexts.[102] Huifan's fraud also gave Tang officials, such as Yao Chong 姚崇 (650-721), another opportunity to take up the recurrent issue of curbing the privilege of the giant monasteries and applying severe measures to restrain the saṃgha.

Kaiyuan: Ximingsi in its Prime

Huifang's profligacy did not stop the empire from supplying cash to the state monasteries and feasting monks on special occasions, but the court did move to put some restrictions on the saṃgha. Emperor Ruizong, the monarch who ruled the empire a second time for only two years (710-712), was forced to issue a decree criticizing Buddhist monasteries and Taoist temples for occupying extensive tracts of land and operating water-mills.[103] Soon thereafter, his son, Xuanzong, ushered in the Kaiyuan (713-741), the most prosperous in the history of the Tang Dynasty. In the first few years in his reign, Xuanzong had demonstrated his resolve to tackle the

---

[101] Chen, Jinhua. "The Statues and Monks of Shengshan Monastery," 114.

[102] Ibid., 158.

[103] *QTW* 19.3; see also Weinstein, *Buddhism under the Tang*, 50.

Buddhist problem by adopting measures such as massive purging of the clergy and the banning of construction of all new monasteries. However, monks and nuns were still allowed to give lectures to the lay adherents on the condition that their discourses were restricted to those matters pertaining to the Buddhist vinaya.

Probably after 713 (Kaiyuan 1), Xuanzong chose the newly established Anguo Monastery (Anguosi 安國寺) along with Ximingsi to feast 300 monks in commemoration of the anniversary of the death of his father, Emperor Ruizong.[104] Such feasting was a tradition in the religious community that had been initiated by the founding emperor of the Sui Dynasty, Yang Jian. This hard-working ruler ordered national monasteries to hold grand feasts and to arrange for the Buddhist clergy to participate in ritual processions (xingdao 行道) on the occasion of national memorials for deceased royal ancestors (guojiri 國忌日). Xingdao, or making a procession around a Buddhist hall or figure, is well described by the pure land advocate Shandao 善導 (613-81) in his Zhuanjing xingdao yuan wangsheng jingtu fashi zan 轉經行道願往生淨土法事讚 (T1979).[105] In order to show respect for deities and ancestors, participants in these processions were required to observe the eight precepts (Ch. baguan zhaijie 八關齋戒, Skt. aṣṭāṅgasamanvāgatopavāsa) and make confessions in public.[106] The choice of Ximingsi and Anguosi as the temples responsible for these events may have reflected their status as centers of vinaya studies. Anguosi was inaugurated in the first year of Kaiyuan (713) to offer worship to the Buddha Maitreya. With the infusion of ordained masters from Ximingsi, it became a thriving institute devoted to vinaya scholarship. The next source about Ximingsi, dated around 716, brings us, finally, to the occasion of the construction of a stūpa, or even twin stūpas, at Ximingsi. As we have seen, to celebrate the establishment of a stūpa at Ximingsi, Su Ting wrote an inscription for the stūpa tablet, the Ximingsi tabei. The prose calls attention to some vinaya masters who were present on the occasion. As noted in chapter 2, the great vinaya scholar Chongye pointedly commented on the successful reincarnation of the former aristocratic

---

[104] Kui tan lu 愧郯錄, SKQS 865: 180; Duli tongkao 讀禮通考, SKQS 111: 782.

[105] This ritual manual offers systematic instruction on the practice of xingdao and zhuanjing 轉經 (scripture recitation) that involves a procedure of confession, sūtra chanting and sevenfold circumambulation held to be conducive to rebirth in Sukhāvatī pure land. See Zhuanjing xingdao yuan wangsheng jingtu fashi zan 轉經行道願往生淨土法事讚 (Liturgy for the Ceremony with Recital of Sūtra and Circumambulation in Quest for Rebirth in the Pure Land), T47, no. 1979, p. 437, b16-c1.

[106] Lidai sanbao ji, T49, no. 2034, p. 107, c13-16; Shishi jigu lüe 釋氏稽古略 (An Outline of Historical Researches into the Śākya Family Lineage), T49, no. 2037, p. 807, b21-22.

mansion of Li Tai as Ximingsi. As the discipline of Daoxuan's student Wen'gang, Chongye inherited the lineage passed down from the Nanshan school of Vinaya (Ch. Nanshanzong 南山宗,) and stood out as the leading scholar of vinaya studies among the Buddhist community in the early eighth-century Ximingsi. While looking into the local history of the monastery, he also shed light on the future of Ximingsi:

> The residence of Prince Liang declined into a site for visitors; the pond and pavilion of the Prime Minister [Tian Wen] lapsed into a waste land for shepherds. How can this fate compare with the fact of becoming purified and being donated to the saṃgha? It is unthinkable in terms of infinite time, and it will not be destroyed by the ashes of the kalpa. Now clean trenches and lines of green trees surrounded the monastery. The water is running through the empty old residence. Although the old flowers fell steadily, the new flowers blossom yet again after the fresh rain. How wonderful it is that the monastery will solidly remain in the world.

> 從梁邸第，寧復賓遊. 封薛池臺，果成童牧. 孰若變為嚴淨，歸入檀那. 匪化塵之可思，匪劫燼之能毀. 轉以清渠灑道，綠樹分行. 水流舊空，花落雨新. 殿邦而住世者，不亦大哉.[107]

This is a passage from Sui Ting's inscription of the stūpa tablet, which is very likely based on the speech that Chongye made on the occasion of the inauguration of the Ximingsi stūpa. We are told here that Chongye compared the luxuriant residence of Yang Su to famous private gardens that had been entirely wiped out by the passage of time. It is evident that the memory of Yang Su, which persisted a century after the death of Yang Xuangan, remained alive among the monastic residents of Ximingsi.

By the first score years of the eighth century, Tang Chang'an had occupied the fertile land of Guanzhong for nearly a century and was a fully mature urban center. The optimism expressed here by Chongye is prescient of the exceptionally lengthy reign of Xuanzong and the emergence during his reign of China as a preeminent

---

[107] *TB* 2597-2598. In Chongye's use of metaphors in this text, *Liangyuan* 梁園 (Garden of Liang) was the well-known bamboo garden belonging to prince Xiao of the Liang 梁孝王 (184-144 BCE). The word then became an ephithet attached to the private house of the imperial family. The state of Xue 薛 was the enfeoffment of Tian Wen 田文 (d. 279 BCE), popularly known as Mengchangjun 孟嘗君 (Lord Mengchang [of Qi]), in the Warring States period (403-221 BCE).

national power in multiple arenas. During the affluent period, known as the "Flourishing age of Kaiyuan (*kaiyuan shengshi* 開元盛世)," the Chinese influence on the Asian mainland was not only economic, but also political, social and intellectual. As I established in chapter 2, history left us descriptions of the *Liangjin xinji*, of which a surviving chapter in the Kanazawa bunko preserves the urban clamor and monastic tales of this period.[108]

Meanwhile, in the remote land of the Indian subcontinent, the rise of new feudal states brought with it the new movement of Buddhist tantra. Ronald Davidson describes it this way in his monumental *Indian Esoteric Buddhism*:

> Esoteric Buddhism coalesced in the special circumstances of the rise of samanta feudalism in the seventh century C.E., a rise that was eventually reflected in the new Buddhist terminology and ritual systems. The fact that the political environment providing the basic model for esoterism did not itself emerge until the late sixth to early seventh centuries assists the chronology of the mature esoteric movement. Reinforcing our temporal parameters are the appearances of Buddhists in non-Buddhist literature, the translation of esoteric works into Chinese, the testimony of Chinese monks, and the lack of any prior notice of the mature esoteric system before the seventh century. Thus the Buddhist tantric movement is a consequence of the new culture of military adventurism, which brought the apotheosis of kings and their mandalas of vassals, with the concomitant feudalization of all forms of Hindu divinities.[109]

It is, then, at this point, in the early eighth century, that Indian tantric masters take center stage in China. Emperor Xuanzong, in spite of his early antipathy toward Buddhism, expressed particular interest in the new trend of Buddhist tantrism because of his fascination with Daoism, which made use of similar ritual practices such as incantations, exorcism and astrology. However, the incorporation of the

---

[108] Kanazawa bunko is a rare book library established by Hōjō Sanetoki 北條実時 (1224-76) in the Kamakuara period in Japan (1185-1333). For the remaining manuscript from *Liangjing xinji*, see Fukuyama Toshio 福山敏男, "Kōchū Ryōkyō Shinki kan daisan oyobi sono kaisetsu 校注兩京新記卷第三及其解說," in *Chūgoku kenchiku to kinsekibun no kenkyū* 中國建築と金石文の研究 (Tokyo: Chūō kōron bijutsu shuppan, 1983), 105-184; Hiraoka Takeo 平岡武夫 and Imai Kiyoshi 今井清, eds., *Tangdai de Chang'an yu Luoyang* 唐代的長安與洛陽, trans. Li Qing 李慶 (Shanghai: Shanghai guji chubanshe, 1989), 179-214.

[109] Ronald Davidson, *Indian Esoteric Buddhism: a Social History of the Tantric Movement* (New York: Columbia University Press, 2002), 166-67.

newly imported Indian teachings presented a difficult challenge to the Chinese Buddhist comunity. The Buddhist siddhas in India "both developed radical meditative techniques not seen before in the Buddhist world and wrapped them in language that was simultaneously playful and ferocious, erotic and destructive."[110] This innovative knowledge of esoteric Buddhism thus forced the great Buddhist institutions like Ximingsi to grapple with new rituals, to deal with the unfamiliar role model of crazy yogin, to develop new forms of hermeneutics by composing sinitic commenteries, and to comprehend an entirely new set of canonical texts.

The Kaiyuan period witnessed the arrival of the most important Indian missionaries, who were assigned by imperial order to government monasteries in Chang'an. Any list of the influential figures from the first half of the eighth century in Chinese Buddhism would arguably have to begin with the names of the "three masters of Kaiyuan" (*Kaiyuan sandashi*): Śubhakarasiṃha (Figure. 8), Vajrabodhi (Ch. Jinggangzhi 金剛智, 671-741), and Amoghavajra (Bukong 不空, or Amuqubazheluo 阿目佉跋折羅, or Bukong jin'gang 不空金剛, 705-774). Among them the Indian guru Śubhakarasiṃha was clearly associated with Ximingsi. Educated at Nālandā, Śubhakarasiṃha came to Chang'an in 716 with a mission to disseminate the *Mahāvairocana-sūtra* (*Da piluzhena chengfo shenbian jiachijing* 大毘盧遮那成佛神変加持經, T848), a central scripture of middle-period tantrism in seventh-century India. Japanese Buddhists also revered Śubhakarasiṃha as the fifth patriarch of the Shingon sect of Buddhism (Jap. Shingonshū 真言宗), whose lineage they traced back to the celestial Buddha Mahāvairocana.[111]

---

[110] Ibid., 337.

[111] For a general history and transmission of the text, see Chikyō Yamamoto and International Academy of Indian Culture, trans., *Mahāvairocana-Sūtra: Translated into English from Ta-p'i lu che na ch'eng-fo shen-pien chia-ch'ih ching, the Chinese Version of Śubhākarasiṃha and I-hsing, A.D. 725* (New Delhi: International Academy of Indian Culture and Aditya Prakashan, 1990).

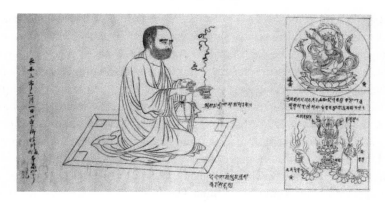

Figure. 8   The Portrait of Śubhakarasiṃha, from the Scroll of *Gobu shinkan* 五部心観 (Ch. *Wubu xinguan*, Essential Meditations on the Five Families). Source: Kyōto Kokuritsu Hakubutsukan 京都国立博物館, ed., *Kūkai to Kōyasan: Kōbō Daishi nittō 1200-nen kinen* 空海と高野山: 弘法大師入唐 1200 年記念, 183.

Figure. 9   Ākāśagarbha, the Principle Image of the gumonji Ritual (Kokuuzō gumonji honzon 虚空藏求聞持本尊), Dananji. Source: Nanto kokusai bukkyō bunka kenkyūjo 南都國際仏教文化研究所, Nanto daianji ronsō 南都大安寺論叢, fig. 1.

According to *Song gaoseng zhuan*, the Chinese story of Śubhakarasiṃha started with Xuanzong, who dreamed that he met an eminent monk of unusual appearance. The Emperor, applying the paint himself, portrayed the dream monk on the wall of his palace. When Śubhakarasiṃha arrived in the capital, he proved to be identical to the monk appearing in Xuanzong's dream.[112] At Chang'an, Śubhakarasiṃha was first stationed briefly in the southern quarter of the Xingfu Monastery (Xingfusi 興福寺) and soon after moved to Ximingsi. At the behest of Xuanzong, he quickly assembled a team of talented monks from Ximing and other major monasteries. Under his supervision, the temporary coalition of scholars started to work on tantric scriptures and exegeses in the Putiyuan 菩提院 (Bodhi Cloister), a famous manuscript library in Ximingsi.[113] Śubhakarasiṃha's first job was to render the *Xukongzang pusa nengman zhuyuan zuishengxin tuoluoni qiuwenchi fa* 虛空藏菩薩能滿諸願最勝心陀羅尼求聞持法 (Method for Reciting the Dhāraṇī of Bodhisattva Ākāśagarbha, Whose Unsurpassed Mind Can Fulfill All Requests, T1145) into Chinese. This was certainly a seminal scripture in the lineage of Chinese tantrism; in particular, it became central to the Japanese Tōmitsu 東密 (Eastern Esotericism) tradition. Centering on the major bodhisattva Ākāśagarbha (Jap. Kokuzō bosatsu 虛空藏菩薩, Ch. Xukongzang pusa, figure. 9) in the court of space in the *garbhadhātu* maṇḍala (Jap. *taizōkai mandara* 胎藏界曼荼羅) and the guardian of the treasury of all wisdom and achievement, the Japanese *gumonjihō* 求聞持法 (Ch. *qiuwenchifa*), a ritual derived from the scripture to strengthen the memory, was expounded in detail by Kūkai and other tantric masters in Japan.[114] Thus, the translation of the scripture

---

[112] For the biography of Śubhakarasiṃha, see Chou Yi-liang, "Tantrism in China," *Harvard Journal of Asiatic Studies* 8, no. 3/4 (1945): 251-71. For the Chinese translation of this article, see, Zhou Yiliang 周一良, *Tangdai mizong* 唐代密宗, trans. Qian Wenzhong 錢文忠 (Shanghai: Shanghai yuandong chubanshe, 1996), 3-121. The Japanese biography of Śubhakarasiṃha is preserved in the *Genkō shakusho* 元亨釈書 (History of Japanese Buddhism Compiled in the Gankō Era [1321-1323]). See also his funeral stele *Da Tang dongdu Dashenshansi gu tianzhuguo Shanwuwei sanzang heshang beiming bing xu* 大唐東都大聖善寺故中天竺國善無畏三藏和尚碑銘並序 (Inscription with Preface of the Late Tripiṭaka Upādhāya Śubhākarasiṃha from Central India, Who Died in the Great Shengshan Monastery in the Eastern Metropolis of the Great Tang).

[113] *SGSZ*, T50, no. 2061, p. 715, b8-12, see also Klaus Pinte, "Śubhākarasiṃha (637-735)," in *Esoteric Buddhism and the Tantras in East Asia*, eds., Charles Orzech, Henrik Sørensen and Richard Payne (Leiden, the Netherlands; Boston, Mass.: Brill, 2011), 340. The book is hereafter abbrevicated as *EBTEA*. For a detailed analysis of the Buddhist library at Ximingsi, see chapter 6, below.

[114] Detailed information regarding the ritual and practice of the *gumonjihō* are recorded in, for instance, Kūkai's *Sankyō shiki* 三教指帰 (Pointers to the Meaning of the Three Teachings, 797), Kōshū 光宗

detailing this ritual remains one of the greatest contributions of Ximingsi to East Asian Buddhism.

Chinese esoteric Buddhism probably began its transmission to Japan in the first years of the Kaiyuan era. From 702 (Daihō 大寶 2) to 718, the Japanese monk Dōji (Figure. 10) stayed at Ximingsi, making a round of calls on Buddhist pundits. He not only received the scholastic tradition passed down by the Ximing scholars, but was able to experience the monastery alive with the high culture of continental Buddhism.[115] In 718 (Yōrō 養老 2), he finished his study of the treatises of the *Mādhyamika* school at Ximingsi and returned to Japan with a wealth of information. The scripture he copied at Chang'an, included among others: *Ninnōhannyakyō* 仁王般若經, *Muryōjukyō* 無量壽經 (T360), and *Konkōmyōkyō* 金光明經. These are the three sūtras for the protection of the state (*Gokoku sambukkyō* 護國三佛經) that can be connected to literary activities at Ximingsi.[116] The *Konkōmyōkyō* circulated in Japan in 725 and inspired Emperor Shōmu to erect Tōdaiji and state monasteries dedicated to the scripture.[117] However, apart from *Konkōmyōkyō*, Dōji's other valuable acquisition at Ximingsi, I believe, was the manuscript of the *gumonjihō* ritual, which he transferred to Japan. This method was popular among Japanese ascetics from the 8th century onwards, and later was practiced by Kūkai.

During the forty-odd years of his reign, Xuanzong patronized all three of the famous tantric masters of Kaiyuan and received a high-level esoteric consecration from Amoghavajra, who studied tantric rituals under the tutelage of another great master Vajrabodhi.[118] Chiefly because the magical skills, incantation and divination,

---

(1276-1350)'s *Keiran shūyō shū* 溪嵐拾葉集 (Collection of Leaves Gathered in Tempestuous Brooks, T2410), or Jōnen 静然's *Gyōrin shō* 行林鈔 (or *Kaikōki* 戒光記).

[115] Marcus Bingenheimer, *A Biographical Dictionary of the Japanese Student-monks of the Seventh and Early Eighth Centuries: Their Travels to China and Their Role in the Transmission of Buddhism* (München: Iudicium, 2001), 85-97; *Mochizuki*, 3871-872; *Kokushi daijiten*, s.v. Dōji.

[116] Bingenheimer, *A Biographical Dictionary of the Japanese Student-monks*, 85-97. Among the three sūtras for the protection of the state, the *Muryōjukyō* (Skt. *Sukhāvatīvyūha sūtra*, T360) is alternatively replaced by *Hokekyō* 法華經. I will elaborate on Dōji's impression of Ximingsi in chapter 5, below.

[117] Abe Ryūichi, *The Weaving of Mantra: Kūkai and the Construction of Esoteric Buddhist Discourse* (New York: Columbia University Press, 1999), 116.

[118] Mark Lewis thinks that this thriving period of translation and learning was the second phase of the reign under Xuanzong which was marked by the resurgence at court of the great families of Guanzhong and the first appearance of specialist commissioners. Mark Lewis argues that the traditional Chinese two-part division of Xuanzong's reign is not the most analytically useful. Instead he proposed a more appropriate framework that divides the reign into three segments:

could fulfill secular purposes as well as provide a placebo in a life lived in uncertainty, esoteric Buddhism became widespread among major monasteries in Chang'an.

Figure. 10   The Portrait of Dōji (*Dōjizō* 道慈像) at Daiaiji. Source: Bessatsu Taiyō 別冊太陽, *Kūkai: Shingon Mikkyō no tobira o hiraita kessō* 空海: 真言密教の扉を開いた傑僧 (*Nihon no kokoro* 日本の こころ, 187), 31.

---

1.   The first period, from his accession in 712 until roughly 720, saw considerable continuity both in personnel and policies with the reign of Empress Wu.
2.   The next period, between 720 and 736, was marked by the resurgence at court of the great families of Guanzhong and the first appearance of specialist commissioners.
3.   In the final period, between 736 and the outbreak of the An Lushan rebellion in 756.
For the details of this classification, see Mark Lewis, *China's Cosmopolitan Empire: the Tang Dynasty* (Cambridge, Mass.: Belknap Press of Harvard University Press, 2009), 40.

Besides the activities of the tantric masters, there are a few other accounts pertaining to Ximingsi in the second half of the Kaiyuan period. We know that Xuanzong's imperial commentary on the *Diamond Sūtra* (*Jin'gang bore boluomi jing zhuxu [yuzhu bingxu]* 金剛般若波羅蜜經注序[御注并序]), along with a fresh exegesis by Daoyin 道氤 (668-740), the eminent scholar from Qinglong Monastery (Qinglongsi 青龍寺), was also preached at Ximingsi and other Buddhist establishments. *Song gaoseng zhuan* tells us that to celebrate the occasion, the lecture halls were constructed with fragrant mud, a precious building material in Buddhist circles. The solemnity of the sermon was unparalleled in Chang'an, which apparently attracted thousands of listeners, each of whom held a copy of the new commentary (i.e., *Yuzhu Jingang bore boluomi jing xuanyan* 御注金剛般若波羅蜜經宣演, T2733).[119] Ximingsi not only attracted the wider public to its open homily on Buddhist classics but also had its monastic plaque (*ximingsi'e* 西明寺額) rewritten under the patronage of Xuanzong. Probably in order to replace the old plaque which hung above the central gate for about three score years, Liu Zigao 劉子皋, the "Scholar of Nanxun Palace (*Nanxundian xueshi* 南薰殿學士)" was invited to undertake the calligraphic work.[120] The bestowal of a plaque (*ci'e* 賜額, or the conferral of tablets of official sanction) written by a prominent member of the national academy was symbolic of imperial trust and authorization. This acknowledgment was essential for a religious establishment on the highest level, attesting to the prominence and influence of Ximingsi in the early eighth century.

The paucity of extant sources makes it difficult for scholars interested in Chinese monasteries to provide a comprehensive case study of a giant monastery in the capital cities of the Tang dynasty. This chapter has traced the history of Ximingsi during the century that spans its foundation as a giant monastery in the middle seventh century to the introduction of esoteric Buddhism under the reign of Xuanzong. In the eyes of the Ximing scholar Daoshi, Ximingsi was an elite institution belonging to the category of "national giant monastery" (*guojia dasi* 國家

---

[119] *SGSZ*, T50, no. 2061, p. 735, a1-12. However, the Chinese *xiangni* 香泥 (Skt. *gomaya*) may also refer to the cow dung. For some examples of this usage in Daoxuan's writing, see *Shijia fangzhi* 釋迦方志 (Reports on the Spread of Buddhism in the Regions), T51, no. 2088, p. 962, b23-25; *Sifenlü shanfan buque xingshichao* 四分律刪繁補闕行事鈔, T40, no. 1804, p. 126, c20-23.

[120] Zhang Yanyuan 張彥遠, *Lidai minghua ji* 歷代名畫記 (Shanghai: Shanghai renmin meishu chubanshe, 1964), 68. For instances of the bestowal of monastic plaques in the Tang Dynasty, see Zhang Gong 張弓, *Han Tang fosi wenhua shi* 漢唐佛寺文化史 (Beijing: Zhongguo shehui kexue chuban she, 1997), 227-42.

大寺).[121] The difference between state monasteries and giant monasteries is that the latter are superior establishments, similar to later systems of the "five mountains and ten monasteries" (Ch. *wushan shicha* 五山十剎, Jap. *gozan jissatsu*) in both China and Japan, where a group of central Zen monasteries were honored with official status.[122] Antonino Forte thinks what sets the giant monasteries apart from the state monasteries is that the former were "private monasteries" donated by the emperor or his family. I think the word "private" fails to reflect the remarkable range of functions that a super monastery like Ximingsi can offer for the imperial goverment.[123]

The relationship between the priestly class at Ximingsi and royal class in Tang China was deep and complex. From the outset, the monastery was involved in a succession of controversial issues, like Buddho-Daoist debate or conflict between Indian renunciation and Chinese piety. Surprisingly, the power manifest in the "etiquette controversy" was not found, as might be expected, in the religious adherents, but in the voice of the majority of governmental officials in support of the saṃgha headed by Daoxuan and his colleagues in Ximingsi. In spite of imperial endorsement, the "petition" of the monastic community, submitted by Daoxuan and his fellow monks to the Tang dignitaries, revealed the lasting tension between the religious community and the Tang government. However, the succeeding monarchs, the formidable Empress Wu and the puppet emperors under her wing, paid plenty of attention to and demonstrated plenty of generosity towards Ximingsi. [124] In reciprocation, the resident clergy offered their energies for the translation of state-sanctioned scriptures and their thaumaturgic skills in the service of the country. One feature of the imperial-sponsored projects of scriptural translation in medieval China was the emphasis on the function of state-protection (*huguo* 護國). Xuanzang expressed it very well when he finished the translation of the *Mahāprajñāpāramitā*

---

[121] *Fayuan zhulin*, T53, no. 2122, p. 750, b10-12. For an early example of *guojia dasi* in the Northern Wei dynastery (386-534), see *Shishi jigu lüe*, T49, no. 2037, p. 799, c24-27. For the concept of *dasi* 大寺 (giant monastery, Jap. *daiji*), see Antonino Forte, "Daiji (Chine)," 682-704.

[122] For an introduction to the Chinese five-mountain system, see Martin Collcutt, *Five Mountains: The Rinzai Zen Monastic Institution in Medieval Japan* (Cambridge MA: Harvard University Press, 1981), 8-11.

[123] Antonio Forte, "Chinese State Monasteries in the Seventh and Eighth Centuries," In *Echō ō Gotenchikukoku den kenkyū* 慧超往五天竺国傳研究, ed. Kuwayama Shōshin 桑山正進 (Kyoto: Jinbun kagaku kenkyūjo, 1992), 216.

[124] Stanley Weinstein, "Imperial Patronage in the Formation of T'ang Buddhism," In *Perspectives on the T'ang*, ed. Arthur Wright and Denis Twichett (New Haven: Yale University Press, 1973), 265-30.

Sūtra, a philosophical scripture esteemed by the Japanese as a world of state protection as well. Xuanzang says:

> "It is with the spiritual assistance of the Buddhas and under the protection of the dragons and deities that I have completed the tasks. As this is a text that will guard the nation and a great treasure of men and heavenly beings, you all should rejoice and be glad at its completion."[125]

Thanks to the unremitting patronage of the Tang government, Ximingsi was transformed from an institution celebrated for eminent scholars in the seventh century to a state-protection monastery in the eighth century. It was not purely the success of monastic scholarship, for the ruling class used the entire Buddhist ideology and the practice of Buddhist rituals, the new teachings of esoteric Buddhism in particular, to secure their control and enhance their power. Following the Kaiyuan period, the history of Ximingsi went on as political infighting worsened in the middle of the eighth century, Ximingsi is drawn into the drama of national crisis; and, as we will see in chapter 4, the monastery's role of state-protection becomes more conspicuous in the Buddhist landscape of Chang'an now dominated by tantric Buddhism.

---

[125] Li Rongxi, *Biography of the Tripiṭaka Master*, 330; *SZFSZ*, T50, no. 2053, p. 276, b12-14.

Chapter Four

War, Renaissance and the Twilight of Ximingsi

Abandoned Shrine and Stolen Bell

The year 720, around the time that Chongye was celebrating the achievements of Ximingsi, marks the most flourishing phase of the monastery, when its influence extended well beyond the Tang Empire. It is from around this time that Dōji returned to Japan with a strong sense of Ximingsi's culture and traditions; as a result, Ximingsi's influence in Japan spread during the following ninth century and led to the arrival of a succession of Japanese student-monks at Ximingsi. This chapter concentrates on the history of Ximingsi's transition from a monastery serving to protect the state to an institution of interregional cultural exchange. That history begins at the end of the Kaiyuan era, continues through to the latter half of the Tang Dynasty, and finishes with the vestiges of the monastery that remained in the tenth century.

After the arrival of Śubhakarasiṃha, Ximingsi remained prosperous for another twenty years, until an insurrection broke out in Anxi 安西 in 742, marking the decline of Xuanzong's control over the nation. It was at this time that Xuanzong summoned the great Amoghavajra (Figure.11) to offer prayers for victory:

> Pu-k'ung chanted a sūtra dedicated to the protection of the empire and uttered mystical incantations while Hsüan-tsung held an incense burner. In due course the emperor saw an apparition of an army of heavenly beings who, Pu-k'ung asserted, would crush the rebels in An-his.[1]

---

[1] Weinstein, *Buddhism under the Tang*, 57.

Amoghavajra was more closely affiliated with another center of tantric learning, Da Xingshan Monastery, where he organized his translation bureau and built up the Wenshuge 文殊閣 (Mañjuśrī Pavilion), a Buddhist library rich in esoteric scriptures. Nevertheless, we should note that he had already selected some of his distinguished disciples from Ximingsi who were studying the maṇḍala rituals that he translated during this time. In this way, he spread the teachings and rites from the lineage of *Vajraśekhara Sūtra* (or *Sarvatathāgatatattvasaṃgraha tantra*, Ch. *Jin'gangding jing* 金剛頂經, T874) to Ximingsi.

Figure. 11   Amoghavajra, from *Shingon shichiso zō* 真言七祖像 (ca.800), by Li Zhen 李真 (7-8 cent.). Brought to Japan by Kūkai. Color and ink on silk; hanging scroll. Tōji 东寺 (Kyōōgokokuji 教王護国寺), Kyoto. National Treasure. Source: John Rosenfield, *Portraits of Chōgen: the Transformation of Buddhist Art in Early Medieval Japan*, 63.

This was the twilight of Xuanzong's reign, a time filled with internal crises and external troubles, a time serving as a kind of testimony to the central Buddhist truth that all things are impermanent. The final catastrophe that brought an end to Xuanzong's long reign and shook the very fabric of Tang society was the eight-year An-Shi Rebellion (*Anshi zhiluan* 安史之亂, 755-763). The seesaw battles in and around Chang'an and Luoyang wreaked havoc across the whole country and ushered in a period classed by historians and literary scholars as the Middle Tang (*zhongtang* 中唐, ca. 766-835). At the beginning of the rebellion, shortly after destroying the resistance of the Tang army before the Tong Pass (Tongguan 潼關), the rebel army entered Chang'an and occupied the great city for a year (756-757). Xuanzong's escape to Sichuan gave his third son, Li Xiang 李享 (711-762), a chance, certainly with the help of the eunuchs, to declare himself the next ruler, Emperor Suzong 肅宗 (r. 756-762). According to the third volume of the *Cambridge History of China*, after the death of the rebel An Lushan 安祿山 (703-757) and a number of encouraging victories, Suzong decided to prioritize the recovery of Chang'an. With the help of the Uighur Turkish cavalry from the northern steppe, Tang troops retook Chang'an in 757.[2] Like his father, the new emperor also authorized Amoghavajra to perform the esoteric *homa* (Ch. *humo* 護摩, burnt offering to the Buddha) rituals in the newly established palace chapel.[3]

However short-lived the sack of Chang'an may have been, it was a heavy blow to the monastic clergymen and wiped out many Buddhist establishments. Like many other temples in the city, Ximingsi was brought low by the chaotic invasion; many significant Buddhist writings in its libraries were destroyed by the rebel army and many of its halls were abandoned. The Buddhist priests and the community of believers at Ximingsi either fled for survival or ended up on the street, homeless. As a result, there is a paucity of extant sources from this period that has created a black hole in our knowledge of Ximingsi for a period of several years. One biographical account of Master Aitong 愛同 in *Song gaoseng zhuan* even suggests that the

---

[2] Twitchett, *The Cambridge History of China*, 565. For details of the rebellion, see Edwin Pulleyblank, *The Background of the Rebellion of An Lu-shan* (London: Oxford University Press, 1955), 61-74.

[3] Weinstein, *Buddhism under the Tang*, 58. Historians are of the opinion that the insurrection produced a religious frenzy at Suzong's court; Suzong had the famous finger-bone relic of the Buddha brought from Famen Monastery (Famensi 法門寺) in Fengxiang (today's Shanxi province) to the palace where people could worship it throughout the day.

monastery was later torched during the rebellion. According to Zanning 贊寧, the author of the book, Aitong had participated in the translation bureau that Yijing organized at Ximingsi along with other scholars in the second reign of Zhongzong (ca. 705-710):

> Promoted as *zhengyi* (man who confirms the interpretation), [Aitong] was involved in the project of the Institute of Sūtra Translation with Wen'gang and contributed to the scriptures Yijing translated. He composed a ten-fascicle commentary to the *Mahīśāsaka Vinaya*. On his deathbed he entrusted the task of revision to the vinaya master Xuantong from Ximingsi. Later the monastery was burned down in the tumult of the An-Shi Rebellion. Now the manuscript has been lost.

> 同與文綱等參預譯場, 推為證義. 義淨所出之經, 同有力焉. 著五分律疏十卷, 復遺囑西明寺玄通律師重施潤色. 後安史俶擾, 焚燎喪寺, 今無類矣.[4]

Other textual sources make clear that the spacious halls and cloisters of urban monasteries made these great institutions conspicuous targets for the rebel army and ideal places to station troops.[5] The account here of Aitong reveals the possibility that at least a part of Ximingsi was destroyed by fire. Additionally, even after Chang'an was retaken, Ximingsi remained abandoned or short-staffed for years. The Five-Dynasty fiction *Yutang xianhua* 玉堂閑話 (Casual Talks at the Jade Hall, ca. 948-950) contains a story of the monastic bell that clearly captures the desolate condition of Ximingsi:

> Concerning the bell at Ximingsi in Chang'an. After the rebellion, the monks departed and wandered afield, leaving the monastery deserted for years. A poor man planned to make a profit by selling the bronze the monastic bell was made

---

[4] For the biography of Aitong (*Tang Kaiyesi Aitong zhuan* 唐開業寺愛同傳), see *SGSZ*, T50, no. 2061, p. 796, a22-b4.

[5] For instance, the famous Tang poet Wang Wei 王維 (699-761), who held the position of *Shangshu youcheng* 尚書右丞 (assistant director of the right in the Department of State Affairs) during the An-Shi Rebellion, was captured by the rebel army stationed in the Cloister of Buddhist Scriptures (*jingzang yuan* 經藏院) in the Puti Monastery. For details, see Wang Xiang 王翔, "Beiye yu xiejing: Tang Chang'an de fojiao tushuguan 貝葉與寫經: 唐長安的佛教圖書館," *Tang yanjiu* 15 (2009): 503.

of. Hiding a chisel and a hammer in his sleeve, each day he sneaked into the monastery and drilled out three *jin* of bronze, selling them off on the market.

長安城西明寺鐘，寇亂之後，緇徒流離，闃其寺者數年．有貧民利其銅，袖鎚鑿往竊鑿之，日獲三斤，鬻於闤闠．[6]

The bell in question here may well have been the bronze bell cast at the behest of Prince Li Xian in 665, which in all likelihood was still preserved into the middle of the eighth century. The economic records in the *Old Book of Tang* (*Jiu tang shu* 舊唐書) provide some evidence that the story is reliable. The records are from some two years after Chang'an was retaken by the Tang army (759, Qianyuan 乾元 2). As a response to the inflation caused by the insurrection, the illicit production of coins became pervasive in Chang'an, forcing the mayor to enact severe measures. In the space of just a few months, 800 people were imprisoned and some of them were beaten to death.[7] Still, the strict prohibition and severe punishment failed to prevent people from stealing bells and bronze images from Buddhist and Daoist monasteries. They continued to melt down whatever metal they could find and privately mint currency. These accounts from historical sources give us some sense of the degree to which the mobs that took over the capital during the early years of the An-shi Rebellion must have torn the monastic community apart and forced the monks in residence to flee Ximingsi in the hope of finding refuge in the remote borderland of northwestern China.

Tankuang and His Refuge Writings on the Silk Road

We do not have sufficient records to trace the whereabouts of the Ximingsi saṃgha during the volatile An-shi Rebellion, but evidence shows that some monks went as far afield as the frontier provinces adjacent to Tibet. The vast majority of the empire was governed by the absolute power of the Tang government, excepting the boundary regions along the Silk Road (Figure.12). Among refugee monks who travelled to the western region of the empire, the case of Tankuang (c.700-788) and the extant

---

[6] The story in the *Yutang xianhua* 玉堂閑話 (Casual Talks at the Jade Hall) survives in *TPGJ* 116. 813; see also Zhao Xiaohuan, *Classical Chinese Supernatural Fiction: A Morphological History* (Lewiston, NY: E. Mellen Press, 2005), 401.

[7] *JTS* 48. 2100.

manuscripts of his authorship in particular has captured the attention of Buddhist Studies scholars. For instance, Ueyama Daishun has discussed Tankuang's life and his philosophical treatises, highlighting his influence on the minor Buddhist circles living in the garrison towns of the west during the Tang empire.

Figure. 12   Map of the Eastern Silk Road in Tang China, including Ganzhou 甘州, Suzhou 肅州 and Shazhou 沙洲. Source: Susan Whitfield, and Ursula Sims-Williams, eds., *The Silk Road: Trade, Travel, War and Faith*, 1.

Tankuang was an adherent of the Faxiang School (Faxiang zong 法相宗, the School of Consciousness Only) before he joined Ximingsi in 724. It is believed that among the coterie of scholars assembled at Ximingsi, Tankuang was not a prominent figure; information pertaining to his life exists only in his own writings, and these writings survive only thanks to the preservation of the Dunhuang manuscript cave. After studying *Vajracchedikā prajñāpāramitā* and *Awakening of Faith in the Mahayana* (*Dacheng qixinlun* 大乘起信論, T1667) at Ximingsi in the Tianbao 天寶 period (742-756), Tankuang escaped away from the imminent chaos of Chang'an and found his way to the desolate Hexi 河西 district (west of the Yellow River, modern Wuwei in Gansu Province). The whole of his reputation is associated with his commentaries and treatises on a few seminal scriptures on which he had labored in the capital city. His extant works were rediscovered among the Dunhuang manuscripts (S2690; P2690 and P2674) at the beginning of the twentieth century and subsequently included in the Japanese Taishō edition of the Chinese canon.[8]

---

[8] For a list of extant commentaries composed by Tankuang, see Ueyama Daishun, *Tonkō bukkyō no kenkyū,*

However, owing to his identity as a scholar from a prestigious Chang'an institution, the writings that he composed on his refugee voyage were widely recognized by the monastic community in the tiny garrison cities along the Silk Road. The powerful Tibetan army, under the sovereign Trisong Detsen, took Liangzhou 涼州 in 764 and sacked Ganzhou 甘州 and Suzhou 肅州, forcing the Hexi governor Yang Xiuming 楊休明 to hold his defensive line in Shazhou 沙洲 (Dunhuang district). In 774, the year that Tankuang arrived, the Tibetan advance besieged the Dunhuang garrison. That year, he wrote the following words in his preface to his *Dacheng baifa mingmenlun kaizong yijue* 大乘百法明門論開宗義決 (The Tenets of Setting Up a Teaching Tradition on *Mahāyāna śatadharma prakāśamukha śastra*, T2812, Figure.13):

This was a frivolous time and an age of arduousness. The dharma-seekers were preoccupied with [material needs like] food and clothing, those still under instruction toiled over paying respect to masters. While reading minor commentaries and scriptures, such people even hesitated as if they were facing a steep precipice, to say nothing of the major sūtras and commentaries which they all forsook the idea of mastering. They spent the whole of their lives ignorant of the three jewels (Ch. *sanbao* 三寶, Skt. *triratna*) and their mind had been obscured from knowing the four noble truths (Skt. *catur-ārya-satya*). Regretting that they squandered their time in vain and had long been confused, I hereby wrote an extended commentary either by filling the lacuna in the works of previous masters or by providing an epitomized synopsis by reducing the redundancy of the texts composed by ancient gurus.

當僥薄之時, 屬艱虞之代. 暮道者急急於衣食, 學者役役於參承.[9]小論小經, 尚起懸崖之想;[10] 大章大疏, 皆懷絕爾之心. 憒三寶於終身, 愚四諦於卒壽.

18-20. For studies of the library of Dunhuang, see Fujieda Akira, "Une Reconstruction de La 'Bibliotheque' de Touen-Houang," *Journal Asiatique* 269 (1981): 65-68. Rong Xinjiang, *Dunhuangxue shiba jiang* 敦煌學 十八講 (Beijing: Beijing daxue chubanshe, 2001), 75-90.

[9] Here the Chinese phrase *xuezhe* 學者 (person in training), used in contrast with *modaozhe* 暮道者 (religious investigator or seeker), means a student following the Buddhist path who has not yet reached the *arhat* position or achieved enlightenment.

[10] Robert Buswell, *The Korean Approach to Zen: the Collected Works of Chinul*, trans. Robert Buswell (Honolulu: University of Hawai'i Press, 1983), 144. The phrase *Xuanya zhixiang* 懸崖之想 (thoughts of precipice) also appears in the *Susim kyol* 修心訣 (Ch. *Xiuxingjue*, Secrets on Cultivating the Mind) written

餘慷茲虛度，慨彼長迷．或補前修之闕文足成廣釋，或削古德之繁猥裁就略章．[11]

Tankuang's comment accurately reflects Buddhism's decline in the wake of Xuanzong's prosperous reign and the deficiency of instruction in the Hexi district in particular. The experience of Ximingsi's Buddhist priests and their doctrinal writings are the topic of conceived future study, but it is worth noting here that Tankuang may not have been alone in spreading the Buddhist learning of Ximingsi to the western regions.

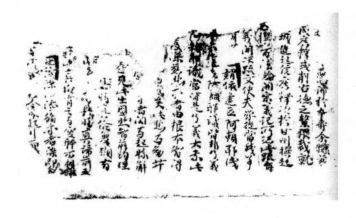

Figure. 13   Fragment of S. ch. 6219V: *Dacheng baifa mingmenlun kaizong yijue* 大乘百法明門論開宗義決． Source: Ueyama Daishun 上山大峻, *Tonkō bukkyō no kenkyū* 敦煌佛教の研究, I.

Okimoto Katsumi 沖本克己, for example, in tracing the doctrinal transmission at Ximingsi, connects the Buddhist revival in Tibet with the flourishing Vijñānavāda teaching at Chang'an monasteries. Further, Okimoto asserts that the champion of Zen

by the Korea Zen master Chinul (1158-1210); see *Goryeoguk Bojo seonsa Susimgyeol* 高麗國普照禪師修心訣 (The Secrets of Cultivating the Mind by the Korean Zen master Chinul), T48, no. 2020, p. 1006, b21-c8. See also Robert Buswell, *Tracing Back the Radiance: Chinul's Korean Way of Zen* (Honolulu: University of Hawai'i, 1991).

[11] *Dacheng baifa mingmen lun kaizong yijue* 大乘百法明門論開宗義決 (The Tenets of Setting Up a Teaching Tradition on *Mahāyāna śatadharma prakāśamukha śastra*), T85, no. 2812, p. 1068, a6-22. See also Ueyama Daishun, *Tonkō bukkyō no kenkyū*, 20-21.

Buddhism, the Chinese representative who articulated the "sudden enlightenment" teachings in the famed Sino-Tibetan debate at Bsam Yas around 781-782, was Moheyan 摩訶衍 (Mahāyāna, fl. 8th c.), a *bhadanta* from Ximingsi.[12] The evidence for this assertion is hardly definitive. It comes only from a memorial by Amoghavajra, submitted in the second year of Dali 大曆 (767), in which he mentions a "*bhadanta* Moheyan" from Ximingsi (*dade Moheyan* 大德摩訶衍, Figure.14). The occasion for the memorial was a Buddhist event (Ch. *foshi* 佛事, Skt. *buddha-kṛtya*) performed in the Hall of Ten Thousand Bodhisattvas (*wanpusa tang* 萬菩薩堂) in Huadu Monastery (Huadusi 化度寺), one of the five Sanjie-sect temples in the capital.[13] The memorial makes it clear that a group of more than thirty priests from major monasteries in Chang'an were invited to chant scriptures for the state during the three special months of abstinence. Among the selected monks well versed in mantra and vinaya, Moheyan was listed in parallel with Guangyan 光演, another Ximingsi master unknown to us.[14] We cannot pursue the question of whether this Ximingsi monk was the Moheyan who engaged in the crucial debate with Kamalaśīla (Ch. Lianhuajie 蓮花戒, 740-797) at Bsam Yas. Nor can we enter into consideration of Tankuang's complicated philosophical commentaries. However, it is worth pointing out here that the treatise composed by Tankuang in Dunhuang in response to the inquiries posed by the Tibetan king Trisong Detsen, titled *The Twenty-two Questions on Mahāyāna* (*Dacheng ershierwen* 大乘二十二問, T2818, Figure.15), was one of the most valuable doctrinal works reflecting the Sino-Tibetan cultural exchange in the eighth century.

---

[12] Okimoto Katsumi 沖本克己, "Saimyōji to toban bukkyō 西明寺と吐蕃仏教," *Zengaku Kenkyū* 禪學研究 71 (1993): 85-112. For a general study of the so-called Lhasa debate, see Paul Demiéville, *Le concile de Lhasa* (Paris, Impr. Nationale de France, 1952). For the Chinse edition, see Daimiwei 戴密微 (Paul Demiéville), *Tubo sengzheng ji* 吐蕃僧諍記 (Lanzhou: Gansu renmin chubanshe, 1984).

[13] Xinxing 信行 (540-94), the founder of the Three Stages Teaching (Sanjie jiao 三階教) movement, listed four other temples that belonged to the School: Guangmingsi 光明寺, Cimensi 慈門寺, Huirisi 慧日寺 and Hongshansi 弘善寺; see Jamie Hubbard, *Absolute Delusion, Perfect Buddhahood: the Rise and Fall of a Chinese Heresy* (Honolulu: University of Hawai'i Press, 2001), 15-16.

[14] In Buddhism, the first, fifth, and ninth months are known as the *zhaiyue* 齋月 (months of purification). Amoghavajra's memorial is entitled *Qing chou Huadusi wanpusa tang san changzhaiyue niansong seng zhi yishou* 請抽化度寺萬菩薩堂三長齋月念誦僧制一首; see *BZJ* T52, no. 2120, p. 834, c16-p. 835, a21.

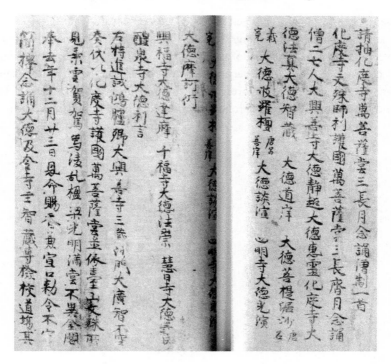

Figure. 14   Manuscript of *Qing chou Huadusi wanpusa tang san changzhaiyue niansong seng zhi yishou* 請抽化度寺萬菩薩堂三長齋月念誦僧制一首, from the Shōrenin 青蓮院 Edition of the *Daizongchao zeng sikong dabianzheng guangzhi sanzang heshang biaozhiji* 代宗朝贈司空大辨正廣智三藏和上表制集 (T2120, copied between 1087-1088). Source: Kyūsojin Hitaku 久曽神昇, Tsukishima Hiroshi 築島裕, and Nakamura Yūichi 中村裕一, ed., *Fukū Sanzō hyōseishū: hoka nishu* 不空三藏表制集: 他二種, 56-57.

According to Buddhist studies scholar Pachow, the *Twenty-two Questions* can be classified into seven categories, including topics on the unremitting practice of the bodhisattva (six questions); the practice of sentient beings (four questions); the differences of the three vehicles (four questions); the achievements of the Buddha (three questions); the categories of dharma-body (Ch. *fashen* 法身, Skt. *dharmakāya*, Tib. *chos kyi sku*) and nirvana (three questions); store consciousness (Ch. *alaiyeshi* 阿賴耶識, Skt. *ālaya-vijñāna*, Tib. *kun gzhi rnam shes pa*) and great wisdom (Ch. *da zhihui* 大智慧, Skt. *prajñā-jñāna*, Tib. *shes rab*), and lastly, the development of Buddhist sects (one question). Pachow argues that these questions are related to the unsolved debate of Lhasa.[15] Whether this is true or not, the surviving accounts at Dunhuang indicate that, as Ximingsi took its place as one of the central institutions of Chinese Buddhism that started to attract Indian masters in the eighth century, the monks closely tied to the monastery were extraordinarily influential in the spread of new knowledge to the western region. It is also possible that Ximingsi scholars played a crucial role in the the promulgation of Chinese Buddhism in Tibet, a topic worthy of future exploration.

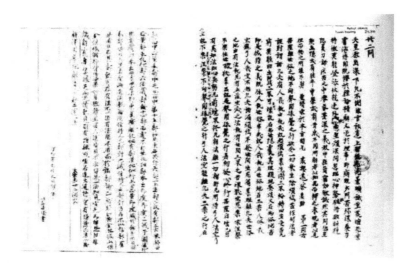

Figure. 15   Fragments of S. ch. 2674: *Dacheng ershier wen* 大乘二十二問. Source: Ueyama Daishun, *Tonkō bukkyō no kenkyū*, I.

---

[15] Ueyama Daishun, *Tonkō bukkyō no kenkyū*, 17-83. Yang Fuxue 楊富學 and Li Jihe 李吉和, *Dunhuang hanwen tubo shiliao jijiao* 敦煌漢文吐蕃史料輯校 (Lanzhou: Gansu renmin chubanshe, 1999), 24; Yoshimura Shūki 芳村修基, "Kaseisō Donkō no denreki 河西僧曇曠の伝歴," *IBK* 7, no. 1 (1958): 23-28. I intend to treat the doctrinal matters in detail in a subsequent study. For studies of the *Dacheng ershierwen*, see W. Pachow, "A study of the twenty-two dialogues on Mahayana Buddhism," *Chinese Culture* 20, no. 1 (1979): 35-110; W. Pachow (Bazhou 巴宙), "Dacheng ershierwen 大乘二十二問," *Zhonghua fojiao xuebao* 中華佛教學報 3 (1990): 83-116.

Scripture for Humane Kings and **Ximingsi**

When the new ruler, Daizong 代宗 (r. 762-779), succeeded his father to the throne, the victory the Tang army had won in the An-shi Rebellion was interrupted by the related problem of civil war. As the frontier crisis continued, this time the Tang government was locked in conflict with ambitious governors and competing powers entrenched on the border. To ensure that the grace of Buddhist deities was extended to the state, Ximingsi was pushed to the forefront of the national politics as a religious center providing state-protection and prayer for the safety of the imperial family. One major scripture with connections to Ximingsi that was sponsored by the imperial family was the creative redaction of the *Perfection of Wisdom Sūtra for Humane Kings Protecting Their Countries* (*Renwang huguo bore banluo miduo jing*, T246, abbreviated as *Scripture for Humane Kings*). Based on the "translation" of the first edition (*Renwang bore boluomi jing* 仁王般若波羅蜜經, T245) attributed to Kumārajīva, Amoghavajra rewrote this scripture in this time of national crisis. As one of the most influential of the Chinese apocrypha, or indigenous scriptures, it became a central canonical text for state protection sponsored by Chinese monarchies as early as the sixth century.[16] It was also one of the most important Buddhist texts elsewhere in East Asia. According to Charles Orzech, the *Scripture for Humane Kings* teaches inner and outer forms of protection in which an explicit analogy is drawn between kings and bodhisattvas, between the techniques used by kings and the protection of their states as the bodhisattvas promised.[17]

The rationale behind holding a grand ceremony at a national monastery on many occasions in the eighth century was to forestall the impending barbarian invasion, a menace the nation faced starting from the seventh century. Not surprisingly, the

---

[16] *Tang jingshi Da'an'guosi Zilin zhuan* 唐京師大安國寺子隣傳, *SGSZ*, T50, no. 2061, p. 722, a20-25. Vested with imperial honors, Amoghavajra also performed *abhiṣeka* ceremonies for Tang officials and military leaders, including the governor-general Geshu Han 哥舒翰 (d. 757) and his troops; see Martin Lehnert, "Amoghavajra: His Role in and Influence on the Development of Buddhism," In *EBTEA*, 351-59.

[17] According to the *Commentary on the Scripture for Humane Kings* (*Renwang huguo bore jingshu* 仁王護國般若經疏, T1705), the major portion of the text is divided into four: The earlier three narrative episodes (*pin* 品) explicate the inner protection, while the chapter on 'Protecting the State' explicates outer protection. The chapter on 'Offering Flowers' explicates the rewards of kindness and worship, and the chapter on 'Receiving the Keeping' explicates the scripture's overall import; see Charles Orzech, *Politics and Transcendent Wisdom: The Scripture for Humane Kings in the Creation of Chinese Buddhism* (University Park, Pa.: Pennsylvania State University Press, 1998), 70-71; *Renwang huguo bore jingshu*, T33, no. 1705, p. 280, a4-21.

Buddhist scholars clearly articulated the claim that Buddhist monasteries served as the spiritual arm and protecting force for the Tang sovereign. Firstly, this arrangement promoted the spiritual welfare and the well-being of the emperor; and secondly, it ensured that the protective influences of Buddhist deities would be extended to the imperial family and the empire.[18] During the early Tang, the ritual of *Scripture for Humane Kings* was performed on the basis of Kumārajīva's translation.[19] As early as the seventh century, the tradition of utilizing scriptures for state protection also traveled to Japan. By 676 (Tenmu 天武 5), the Japanese government stipulated that each province (*shokoku* 諸國) should sponsor a Buddhist service (*hōe* 法会, Skt. *dharma saṃgīti*) for ceremonial reading and discussion (*kōdoku* 講読) of the Ximingsi-translated *Scripture for Humane Kings* and *Golden Light Sūtra* (Figure. 16) to call for blessings for the imperial state.[20] It was not very long before the Japanese incorporated the *Lotus Sūtra* under the rubric of the so-called "three scriptures on state protection" (*gokoku sanbukyō* 護國三部經).

---

[18] Kenneth Chen, "The Role of Buddhist Monasteries in T'ang China," *History of Religions* 15, no. 3 (1976): 212. For instance, Taizong donated Taihe Palace (Taihegong 太和宮) to build Longtian Monastery (Longtiansi 龍田寺) as a merit transferred to his father Li Yuan in 627 (Zhenguan 1). In 629, Taizong also requested that monks and nuns from urban monasteries gather in the Longtian Monastery at Mount Zhongnan to make procession around the image of the Buddha and recite the *Scripture for Humane Kings* and *Mahāmegha-sūtra* (*Da fangdeng wuxiang dayun jing* 大方等無想大雲経, T387) on the fourteenth day of each month (*erqiri* 二七日, or days ending with the number two and seven in each month); see *Shishi jigu lüe*, T49, no. 2037, p. 813, b24-25.

[19] *Fayuan zhulin*, T53, no. 2122, p. 1027, a11-15. For details of the ritual, see *Zhiguan fuxing zhuan hong jue* 止觀輔行傳弘決 (Transmitting the Great Magnificent Determination Through Supplementing Discipline by Cessation of Contemplation and Examination), T46, no. 1912, p. 147, c17-18.

[20] First practiced in 559 in China, the Buddhist court ceremony of the *Scripture for Humane Kings* also became prominently integrated into Korean and Japanese traditions. Throughout East Asia, the ceremony is known as *ninnōe* 仁王會, offering to the humane king (Jap. *ninnōgu* 仁王供), or in Chinese, *renwang daochang* 仁王道場 (ceremony for recitation of the Sutra for Humane Kings). The two translations by Kumārajīva and Amogvajra are used respectively by the Japanese Shingon Esotericism (Tōmitsu 東密) and Tendai Esotericism (Taimitsu 台密).

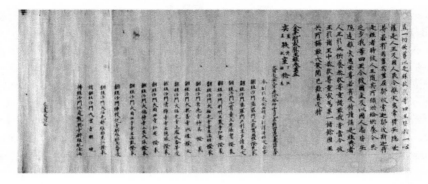

Figure. 16   The Tang Palace Copy of the *Jin guangming zuishengwang jing* 金光明最勝王經 (Skt. *Suvarṇaprabhāsottama sūtra*, Golden Light Scripture, T665). Dunhuang Manuscript, National Library of China. Source: Fan Jinshi 樊錦詩 and Luo Huaqing 羅華慶, eds., *Dunhuang shiku quanji: 20, Cangjingdong zhenpin juan* 敦煌石窟全集: 20, 藏經洞珍品卷, 28.

Apparently in 765 the threat of foreign invasion worsened.[21] The rise of independent military governors after the An-Shi Rebellion made the northeast a permanent center of resistance to the Tang court. The Tibetan army triggered the current crisis near Chang'an as early as 763, when they took most of the cities in the Hexi region and Longyou 隴右 (western part of Gansu), cutting off the Tang army's supply line. The Tibetan troops even occupied Chang'an for a short period of two weeks.[22] In the meantime, the Tang government was concurrently troubled by the union of the encroaching barbarian force and Pugu Huaien's 僕固懷恩 (d.765) insurrection. The name of this rebel general ironically suggests "feeling grateful to the royal benevolence."[23] It was he who launched an attack from three directions

---

[21] After Gaozong's death, the Tang literatus Chen Ziang 陳子昂 (661-702) dramatized the frontier crisis this way in an essay titled *Jian lingjia rujing shu* 諫靈駕入京書. The memorial was submitted to the throne: "The Yan and Dai regions are pressed by pending invasion of the Huns; Sichuan and Gansu districts suffered from the assault of the Tibetans. The old men of western Sichuan had to transport military provisions for a thousand *li*, while the young men of northern China are drafted by the garrison army when they were only fifteen." see Hu Yunyi 胡雲翼, *Tangwenxuan* 唐文選 (Shanghai: Zhonghua shuju, 1940), 138; Chen Yinke 陳寅恪, *Sui Tang zhidu yuanyuan lue lungao: Tangdai zhengzhishi shulun gao* 隋唐制度淵源略論稿: 唐代政治史述論稿 (Beijing: Shenghuo, tushu, xinzhi sanlian shudian, 2001), 149-53.

[22] Although the garrison army continued to defend the four military counties (*sizhen* 四鎮), they were not able to resume contact with the Tang government until 768 (Dali 大曆 3). See *Fozu tongji*, T49, no. 2035, p. 377, c26-p. 378, a1.

[23] A descendant from a Uighur tribe, Pugu Huaien started as a loyal minister instrumental to the final

allied with hundreds of thousands of Tibetans, Tanguts (*Qiang* 羌), Tuyuhun 吐穀渾 and Uighurs in an invasion directly against Chang'an. The whole country was shocked by the quick move of the rebel force, against which the armies of Guo Ziyi 郭子儀 (697-781) failed to reach the Guanzhong district in time and the Divine Strategy Army (*shence jun* 神策軍), the royal force responsible for the safety of Chang'an, was not readily mobilized to defend against attack. On behalf of the government, the celebrated eunuch Yu Chaoen 魚朝恩 (722-770) escorted the special palanquin that contained the *Scripture for Humane Kings* to the Buddha Hall of Ximingsi. He offered incense to the Buddha image and prayed through tears:

We offered incense in the ceremonial reading of the scripture on one hundred seats and the sky became clear. The sunny weather testified to the power of the scripture. Since the barbarian armies had encircled us from three directions and the official military force was late for the rescue, now we think that only the *Scripture for Humane Kings* will provide protection for the country. We pray that the autumn rain can fall down again from tomorrow to the twenty-fourth or twenty-fifth day of this month to stop the vile barbarians from advancing to the Hedong district. Let General Guo Linggong come to the rescue, and I hope he will prevent the city from falling into the hands of the enemy. This should be seen as the scriptural power of state-protection.

香從百座, 天極澄霽. 此之晴明, 表經威力. 今既蕃戎天下三面俱至, 國家兵馬又未相接, 仁王般若波羅蜜多實能護國者, 願從明日至二十四五日, 秋雨復下, 使其蕃醜不得進兵河東.[24] 令公複來至此, 容有准擬免其失守, 即是般若護國之力也.[25]

---

suppression of the An-Shi Rebellion but ended up, eight years later (764), as an enemy of the empire. In 756, Pugu Huaien went with Prince Li Chengcai 李承寀 (d.758) to the Uighur capital, where various marriages were arranged between the two states. See *Da Tang zhenyuan xu kaiyuan shijiao lu* 大唐貞元續開元釋教錄 (Continuation of the Kaiyuan Catalogue Compiled in the Zhenyuan Period of the Great Tang), T55, no. 2156, p. 752, b27-c19. For the rebellion of Pugu Huaien, see Hans Vande Ven, *Warfare in Chinese History* (Leiden: Brill, 2000), 142-49, Michael Weiers, *Geschichte Chinas: Grundzüge einer Politischen Landesgeschichte* (Stuttgart: Kohlhammer W., 2009), 85-86.

[24] Hedong 河東 refers to the east of the Yellow River.

[25] *Renwang jingshu faheng chao* 仁王經疏法衡鈔, *XZJ* 41, p. 227, a4-16. In the Tang period, General Guo Ziyi was also known as Guo Linggong 郭令公.

In the upcoming battle Ximingsi was expected to fend off the threat of Pugu Huaien'
and evoke divine intervention, a force that was believed to be effective in medieval
China.[26] In the ninth month of 765 (Yongtai 永泰 1), anticipating the pending
invasion, the Tang court set up elevated altars (or seats, Ch. *zuo* 座, Skt. *āsana*), or
one hundred lecture sites, at both Zishengsi 資聖寺 and Ximingsi, so that eminent
masters could lecture on the *Scripture for Humane Kings*. The two monasteries were
major Buddhist centers symmetrically located in the eastern and western parts of
Chang'an. Additionally, the Tang government had mobilized prelates from other
monasteries to join the ceremonial reading of scriptures and make a procession
around a Buddha image, but the ceremony was centered on Zishengsi and
Ximingsi.[27]

The sermon on the *Scripture for Humane Kings* was seen as a monastic tradition
to transmit merit and demolish potential invading troops. As described by the Song
Encyclopedia *Cefu yuangui* 冊府元龜 (Outstanding Models from the Storehouse of
Literature), the procession escorting the scriptural manuscript started with several
able-bodied servants dressed in golden armor. They shouldered two jeweled
palanquins (*baoyu* 寶輿), walking out from the imperial court. They adorned three
carts with bodhisattva festoons of the eight groups of demon-followers of the four
mahārājas (Ch. *babu guishen* 八部鬼神, Skt. *aṣṭa-gatyaḥ*).[28] To demonstrate
reverence on the occasion, government advisors and high officials from the two
councils (*liangsheng* 兩省), administrators above the four-class rank from the
Department of State Affairs (*shangshu sheng* 尚書省), and supervisors and head
officials from each bureau were required to participate in the ceremony and offer

---

[26] *Renwang jingshu faheng, XZJ* 41, p. 227, a1-5.

[27] *Da Tang zhenyuan xu kaiyuan shijiao lu*, T55, no. 2156, p. 752, b27-c5. For a study on the interaction
between this scripture and the Tang state, see Nakata Mie 中田美絵, "Tōchō seijishijō no 'Ninnōkyō'
hon'yaku to hōe: naitei seiryoku senken no katei to bukkyō 唐朝政治史上の『仁王経』翻訳と法会: 内廷
勢力専権の過程と仏教," *Shigaku zasshi* 史學雜誌 115, no. 3 (2006): 322-47. Xia Guangxing 夏廣興,
Mijiao chuanchi yu Tangdai shehui 密教傳持與唐代社會 (Shanghai: Shanghai renmin chubanshe, 2008),
182-95.

[28] *CFYG*, in *SKQS* 903.46. The three carts are the three vehicles in the *Lotus Sūtra*, namely, the goat carts
(Ch. *yangche* 羊車, Skt: *aja ratha*), deer carts (Ch. *luche* 鹿車, Skt: *mṛga ratha*) and bullock carts (Ch.
niuche 牛車, Skt: *go ratha*), representing practitioners at three levels: *śrāvakas*; *pratyeka-buddhas* and
bodhisattvas. The eight groups are half-ghost music masters (Skt. *gandharvas*); heavenly music masters who
are neither human nor not human (Skt. *kiṃnaras*); demigods of evil disposition (Skt. *asuras*); snake kings
(Skt. *nāgas*); snake spirits (Skt. *mahoraga*); golden-winged birds which eat dragons (Skt. *garuḍa*); spirits of
the dead who fly about in the night (Skt. *yakṣas*); and gods (Skt. *devas*). See also *Mochizuki*, 4223-224.

incense at Ximingsi. Typically the ritual process lasted for a whole day and was accompanied by official musicians.[29] A sense of the medieval ritual can be gleaned frome a variety of ceremonies and texts derived from the scripture, including *Instructions for the Rites, Chants, and Meditations of the Prajñāpāramitā Dhāraṇī Scripture for Humane Kings Who Wish to Protect Their States* (Ch. *Renwang huguo bore boluomiduo jing tuoluoni niansong yigui* 仁王護國般若波羅蜜多經陀羅尼念誦儀軌, T994). The narrative episode (*pin* 品) "Protecting the State" (*huguopin* 護國品) in Amoghavajra's *Scripture for Humane Kings* has this to say regarding the formal procedure:

> [Now], in all states, when [things are] on the brink of chaos and there are all [sorts of] disasters, difficulties, or bandits come to wreak havoc, you and the others and all kings should receive and hold, read and recite this *Prajñāpāramitā*. Sumptuously adorn a ritual arena and set up one hundred Buddha images, one hundred *bodhisattva* images, and one hundred seats for Buddhist masters, and invite one hundred masters of the Teaching to expound this scripture. Before all the seats light all kinds of lamps, and burn all kinds of incense, scatter various flowers and make vast and abundant offerings of clothing and utensils , drink and food, broth and medicines, places of shelter and repose, and all of the usual affairs of offering. Twice each day the Buddhist masters should lecture on and read this scripture. If the king, the great officers, *bhikṣus*, *bhikṣunī*s, *upāsaka*s, and *upāsika*s hear, receive, read, and recite it and practice it according to the prescribed method, the disorders and difficulties will forthwith be eradicated.[30]

It is not possible to ascertain whether the ritual in urban settings took place in the two monasteries and followed the procedures prescribed by the scripture, but scholars think that some Japanese manuals, *Bessonzakki* 別尊雑記 (Assorted Notes on Individual Divinities), *Kakuzenshō* 覚禅抄 (Excerpts of Kakuzen), or the

---

[29] *ZZTJ* 223.7176; Patricia Berger, "Preserving the Nation: The Political Uses of Tantric Art in China," In *Latter Days of the Law: Images of Chinese Buddhism, 850-1850*, ed. Marsha Weidner (Honolulu, Hawaii: Spencer Museum of Art University of Hawai'i Press, 1994), 92.

[30] Orzech, *Politics and Transcendent Wisdom*, 245-46. *Renwang huguo bore boluomiduo jing* 仁王護國般若波羅蜜多經 (Perfection of Wisdom Sūtra for Humane Kings Protecting Their Countries), T08, no. 246, p. 840, a10-19.

Byakuhōkushō 白寶口鈔 (Record of the Precious Spoken Tradition) in particular, may well shed light on how the actual procedure involving beneficent and wrathful forms takes place in the rituals performed at Ximingsi.[31]

Contrary to all expectations, Pugu Huaien suddenly fell ill and died in Lingzhou 靈州 (today's Lingwu city in Ningxia Autonomous Region,) in the middle of his campaign march to Chang'an. According the *Old Book of Tang*, on the day of Yinmao 辛卯 in the ninth month, "the planet Venus became visible in the broad daylight (*taibai jingtian* 太白經天), " a bad omen in the context of social astronomy in medieval China. A few days later, Pugu Huaien died on the day of Dingyou 丁酉, interpreted in Chinese celestial system as "fire overcomes gold."[32] The lecture on the *Scripture for Humane Kings* resumed in wintry October in Zisheng Monastery, where 100 monks from Ximingsi specializing in the sūtra also joined. Originally the incumbent emperor, Daizong, was a man who passionately offered sacrifices to the imperial ancestors, but he later proved himself to be one of the most devout Buddhists of all the Tang rulers. His Prime Minster, Wang Jin 王縉 (700-781), attributed Pugu Huaien's death and the retreat of the barbarian army to the chanting of the *The Scripture for Humane Kings* at Ximingsi. The Tang master Yurong 遇榮, author of the *Subcommentary on the Scripture for Humane Kings* (*Renwang jing shu faheng chao* 仁王經疏法衡鈔, T519), also confirmed that the armored deities scared away the Tibetan army when they appeared on the defensive ramparts.[33]

The esoteric ritual of the *Scripture for Humane Kings* staged at Ximingsi must have captured the attention of Yuanzhao, an eminent scholar-monk in residence there. We will elaborate on his contribution to the Buddhist bibliographical catalogues in chapter 6; but here we should note that he was recognized as one of the distinguished disciples of Amoghavajra and edited the lengthy *Daizong chao zeng sikong da*

---

[31] For instance, Charles Orzech offers one example of the ritual of Humane Kings as detailed in *Byakuhōkushō*; see Orzech, *Politics and Transcendent Wisdom*, 188-91.

[32] *JTS* 11. 279. The same astronomical phenomenon also occurred when Taizong killed his brother in the notorious Incident at Xuanwu Gate (*Xuanwumen zhibian* 玄武門之變) and restored the teaching of *Laozi*; see *Lidai shishi zijian* 歷朝釋氏資鑑, *XZJ* 132, p. 95, b9-11. 3.

[33] *Renwang jingshu faheng chao*, *XZJ* 41, p. 227, a10-16. Convinced by Wang Jin, Daizong then had no doubts about the Buddhist doctrine of cause and effect (Skt. *hetu-phala*, Ch. *yinguo* 因果). On many occasions, he generously bequeathed brocaded quilts and fine silk pennants to Amoghavajra and his entourage. See the biography of Wang Jin, *XTS* 145. 4715-717; *Fozu lidai tongzai*, T49, no. 2036, p. 600, a15-19; Tan Chung and Geng Yinzeng, *India and China: Twenty Centuries of Civilization Interaction and Vibrations* (New Delhi: Centre for Studies in Civilizations, 2005), 331. Wang Jin was the younger brother of the famous Tang poet Wang Wei.

bianzheng guangzhi sanzang heshang bianzhiji 代宗朝贈司空大辨正廣智三藏和上表制集 (T2120, Collected Documents on Regulations Bestowed by the Court of Daizong on the Minister of Works, the Greatly Skillful and Upright Guangzhi, the Venerable Tripiṭaka Master, abbreviated as *Collected Documents*), a collection of memorials, letters, official documents and biographical writings regarding Amoghavajra. [34] Orzech argues that the *Scripture for Humane Kings* figures prominently in the lineage of Amoghavajra's tantric teachings, which are mostly represented in Yuanzhao's catalogues edited at Ximingsi. In his words, the scripture "played a key role in the articulation of a comprehensive vision of polity in Pu-k'ung (Amoghavajra)'s lineage." *The Scripture for Humane Kings* and the documents Yuanzhao presented are the manifesto of East Asian Esoteric Buddhism and a paradigmatic portrait of the ideal religious polity as realized in joint rule by emperor and *ācārya* (spiritual teacher). [35]

By holding elaborate ceremonies that seemed to be effective for the state in crisis, Ximingsi reinforced its privileged status as a leading monastery in the matrix of Chang'an Buddhism and strengthened its relationship with the imperial court. In the net of the esoteric polity, rituals for state-protection also extended to other sacred sites outside the boundary of Chang'an. For instance, there must have been considerable communication between Chang'an and Mount Wutai in the eighth century, judging from materials found in Yuanzhao's *Collected Documents*. His writing contains the memorials by the Ximingsi master Huixiao 惠曉, a disciple of Amoghavajra who became a personal envoy for emperors Suzong and Daizong. Dispatched by Daizong on a religious mission, he was ordered to hold tantric ceremonies at major monasteries on Mount Wutai, the five sacred terraces devoted to the Bodhisattva Mañjuśrī (Ch. Wenshu 文殊).

Ximingsi and Mount Wutai

---

[34] The *Collected Documents* is an extremely useful source for the study of esoteric state polity modeled on the relationship between Amoghavajra and the Emperors Suzong and Daizong. By using the historical and autobiographical material under the editorship of Yuanzhao, Buddhist studies scholars have been able to examine the notion of esoteric policy and sketch an outline of the esoteric school through the second half of the eighth century. See Orzech, *Politics and Transcendent Wisdom*, 191-98.

[35] Orzech, *Politics and Transcendent Wisdom*, 198. The interpretive model proposed by Orzech in his study of the scripture is rather innovative; he put the relationships among transcendence, the world, and authority in the complex adaptive system of religion.

Mount Wutai (Five Terrace Mountain, Figure.17) is considered to be one of the most sacred mountains in Chinese Buddhism. Located in northeastern China in the Shanxi province, it is approximately 880 kilometers away from Chang'an. Tang records by Buddhist monks that mention Mount Wutai include works by Daoxuan and Fazang who, as we know, were associated with Ximingsi from the middle of the seventh century to the early eighth century.[36] If there is a special connection between Ximingsi and Mount Wutai, it likely started with Gaozong, who authorized the repairs of temples and stūpas on the mountain. When Buddhapāla finished his translation of the *Dhāraṇī of the Jubilant Corona*, he left Ximingsi and found refuge at Mount Wutai. Among a host of masters who lived on or visited this sacred mountain, Amoghavajra was largely responsible for the spread of the Mañjuśrī cult. Our earliest account after the seclusion of Buddhapāla begins shortly after the An-Shi Rebellion broke out, when Amoghavajra was urgently summoned back from Mount Wutai to the court at Chang'an to pray for the victory of the imperial forces, as he is said to have done once before in 742.[37] One of Suzong's favorite monks was Huixiao, the disciple of Amoghavajra and a clergyman registered at Ximingsi. When the rebels took Chang'an, Huixiao and Amoghavajra failed to flee with Suzong. Secretly, Huixiao continued to recite scriptures for the fortune of Suzong, who accordingly attributed the recovery of the lost capital in 757 to the power of the Buddha.

After the Tang army retook Chang'an, officials in charge of the goverment agency behind the Yintai Gate (*yintai menjia* 銀臺門家) of the imperial palace called upon four disciples of Amoghavajra, the four leading monks belonging to the generation of the dharma surname Hui 惠, to chant scriptures for the state in the palace chapels. The four priests, respectively Huixu 惠旴, Quna 瞿那, Huixiao and Huiyue 惠月, were accorded the privilege of riding on the "flying dragon horse (*feilongma* 飛龍馬)" raised in the royal stable.[38] As the Chinese poem runs, "a

---

[36] Mary Anne Cartelli, "The Poetry of Mount Wutai: Chinese Buddhist Verse from Dunhuang" (PhD diss., Columbia University, 1999), 18. The three books mentioned by Mary Anne Cartelli are *Ji shenzhou sanbao gantong lu* 集神州三寶感通錄 (Collected Records of the Three Jewel Miracles in China, T2106), *Daoxuan lüshi gantong lu* 道宣律師感通錄 (Record of Miracles Experienced by Vinaya Master Daoxuan, T2107), and *Huayanjing zhuanji* 華嚴經傳記 (Biograohies of the Flower Ornament Sūtra, T2073). For a general description of Mount Wutai in the Tang dynasty, see Ono Katsutoshi and Hibino Takeo 日比野丈夫, *Godaisan* 五臺山 (Tokyo: Zauhō kankōkai, 1942), 1-67.

[37] Weinstein, *Buddhism under the Tang*, 57.

[38] "Flying dragon horse" indicates selected steeds kept in the "Flying dragon stable" (*feilongjiu* 飛龍厩), one of the six royal stables in Tang China. The Tang tradition stipulates that intellectuals who ranked at the

minister's loyalty only manifests in the time of crisis" (*shiwei xian chengjie* 時危現臣節), the next ruler Daizong recognized Amoghavajra and Huixiao's allegiance and henceforth entrusted them with the duty of reciting scriptures at Mount Wutai.[39]

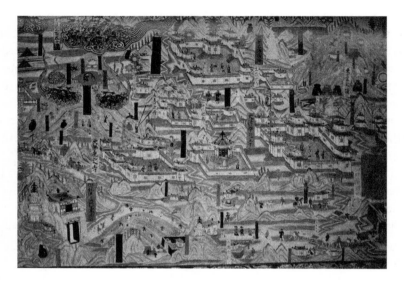

Figure. 17   Map of Pilgrimage Routes to Mount Wutai, Cave 61, Dunhuang. Source: Adriana Proser, ed., *Pilgrimage and Buddhist Art*, 28.

Although Amoghavajra spent most of his time in the Xingshan Monastery, Yuanzhao's *Collected Documents* shows that he had several disciples from Ximingsi. In 768 (Dali 3), three people were ordained on Daizong's birthday. At Amoghavajra's request, the thirty-year-old Tocharian Luo Wencheng 羅文成 was ordained as a disciple under his supervision. The man later joined Amoghavajra's entourage as Huihong 惠弘 and was assigned to take lodging at Ximingsi. However, Huihong qualified for ordination not only because of Amoghavajra's petition but also due to his ability to recite *Diamond Sūtra* (Skt. *Vajracchedikā prajñāpāramitā*), *Awakening of Faith* (Ch. *Dacheng qixin lun*, Skt. *Śraddhotpāda Śāstra,*) and *Bodhisattva-bhūmi*

---

top of the national examination have the privilege of riding the flying dragon horse. See *JTS* 170.4437.
[39] *BZJ*, T52, no. 2120, p. 858, b11-17.

(Ch. *Pusa jiejing* 菩薩戒經).[40] This testified to the fact that the standard for going forth into religious life in a premier monastery like Ximingsi remained strict even in the late eighth century when many of the monastic holdings disappeared in the wake of the An-shi Rebellion. In order to encourage and reward the Buddhist merit that Huixiao unremittingly generated in the Buddha halls at Ximingsi, Daizong issued an order to make sure that the government provided Huixiao's meals and carts.[41]

Huixiao's biographical account is absent from the works that fall under the rubric of monastic hagiographies (*sengzhuan* 僧傳). In his memorial, he tells us that he took the monastic vow in his twenties and studied with Amoghavajra for some thirteen years. Well versed in the mantras of the five classes (Ch. *wubu zhenyan* 五部真言) in *Vajraśekhara-sūtra* which Amoghavajra transmitted to Ximingsi through his disciples,[42] Huixiao and his fellow monks at Ximingsi and other monasteries were summoned to chant the *Scripture for Humane Kings*, *Ghana-vyūha Sūtra* (*Dacheng miyan jing* 大乘密嚴經, Great Vehicle Secret Adornment Sūtra, T682) or to perform *homa* rituals of esoteric Buddhism for the country in palace chapels such as Hanhui 含暉, Yanying 延英 and Changsheng 長生.[43]

Daizong's resolve to secure peace and safety never declined. Around 777 (Dali 12) he designated Huixiao as the Commissioner of Good Works for Mount Wutai

---

[40] *BZJ*, T52, no. 2120, p. 836, c27-28; *Mochizuki* 4661. Another monk named Huijun also registered at Ximingsi upon the request of Amoghavajra; see *Qing jiangdanri duseng wuren* 請降誕日度僧五人, *BZJ*, T52, no. 2120, p. 836, a1-2.

[41] *Enzhi ming Ximingsi gei zhoufan wanglai qicheng zhi* 恩旨命西明寺給粥飯往來騎乘制, *BZJ*, T52, no. 2120, p. 858, b18-23.

[42] The most popular Chinese edition of the *Vajraśekhara-sūtra* was made by Amoghavajra. Titled *Jin'gangding yiqie rulai zhenshi shedacheng xianzheng dajiaowang jing* 金剛頂一切如來真實攝大乘現證大教王經 (T865), it is one of the two main scriptures of esoteric Buddhism. The mantras of the five classes can be summarized as "a vam ram ham kham 阿鑁覽唅欠" in the Vajradhātu maṇḍala; see also *Sanzhong xidi podiyu zhuan yezhang chu sanjie mimi tuoluoni fa* 三種悉地破地獄轉業障出三界祕密陀羅尼法 (Secret Dhāraṇi Method of Three Attainments which Destroy Hell and Reverse Karmic Hindrances in the Three Worlds), T18, no. 905, p. 910, c2-17.

[43] The first few officials who were appointed as the Commissioner of Good Works, including Li Yuancong 李元琮, Huixiao and Li Xiancheng 李憲誠, had long and close association with Amoghavajra, who was held in high esteem by Xuanzong, Suzong and Daizong. *BZJ*, T52, no. 2120, p. 858, b4-10. Prefaced by Daizong, *Ghana-vyūha Sūtra* was also translated a second time by Amogavajra. For a study of the palace chapel in the age of Amoghavajra, see Iwasaki Hideo 岩崎日出男, "Fukū no jidai no naidōjō nit suite —— tokuni Daisō no jidai no naidōjō ni aterareta kyūchū shoden no kōsatsu o chūshin to shite 不空の時代の内道場について —— 特に代宗の時代の内道場に充てられた宮中諸殿の考察を中心として," *Kōyasan daigaku mikkyō bunka kenkyūjō kiyō* 高野山大学密教文化研究所紀要 (2000): 65-77.

(*wutaishan xiugongdeshi* 五臺山修功德使); his main responsibility was to propitiate the Bodhisattva Mañjuśrī and perform protective rituals at the five terraces for the welfare of Daizong. The Commissioner of Good Works was originally a post concerned with religious affairs established in the late 760s to supervise Buddhist monasteries in Chang'an. Another new office known as the Commissioner of Good Works for Buddhist Monasteries and Taoist Temples in the Capital (*jingcheng siguan xiugongdeshi* 京城寺觀修功德使) made its debut in 774 when Amoghavajra passed away.[44] It is presumed that Huixiao's position likewise required overseeing church affairs at Mount Wutai and ensuring that rituals were properly performed in the interest of the state.

The choice of the sacred Mount Wutai was no coincidence, since the mountain had been famous for its miracles. As early as Gaozong's reign, the emperor quickly dispatched monks from Chang'an to look into the matter. After Buddhapāla's legendary encounter with Mañjuśrī, both Amoghavajra and his disciple Hanguang 含光 (fl. 8th c.) lost no time promoting the cult of Mañjuśrī across the country. At Mount Wutai they proposed the construction of Jin'ge (Golden Pavilion) Monastery (Jin'gesi 金閣寺), a project initiated under Xuanzong's patronage.[45] Huixiao's memorial shows that he climbed to the southern terrace in the spring of 778 (Dali 13) to search for a ruby named *kiṃśuka* (Ch. *zhenshu jiabao* 甄叔迦寶 or *chibao* 赤寶), a precious red stone described in the *Lotus Sutra*.[46] He probably collected information about the *kiṃśuka* from the account of an anonymous Indian monk who was believed to be the secluded Buddhapāla. It is said that Huixiao acquired thirty pieces of *kiṃśuka* from a pond inside a small cave and presented them to emperor Daizong on the lunar New Year's Day.[47] In the same year he also performed a successful *homa* ritual in Jin'ge Monastery:

---

[44] For study of the Commissioner of Good Works, see Weinstein, *Buddhist under the Tang*, 84-85.

[45] *Liangbu dafa xiangcheng shizi fufa ji* 兩部大法相承師資付法記 (Record of Successive Masters Transmitting the Methods of the Great Dharma Characteristics of the Two Classes [of Maṇḍala]), T51, no. 2081, p. 784, a8-14. Tansen Sen, *Buddhism, Diplomacy, and Trade: the Realignment of Sino-Indian Relations, 600-1400* (Honolulu: University of Hawai'i Press, 2003), 83-84. At the behest of Daizong, Hanguang not only oversaw the construction of the esoteric Jin'ge Monastery, which was established at the bottom of Wutaishan, but also went on to inspect the Buddhist figures and mudrās. Daizong also entrusted him with the task of conducting *homa* rituals to end calamities (Skt. *śāntika*, Ch. *xizai* 息災) at other monasteries scattered across the five terraces.

[46] *Wang Wutaishan xiu gongde cixie sheng'en biao* 往五臺山修功德辭謝聖恩表, *BZJ*, T52, no. 2120, p. 858, b24-c14. *Kiṃśuka* is mentioned in the *Lotus Sūtra*, see *Miaofa lianhua jing*, T09, no. 262, p. 55, b21-24.

[47] *Yuanri xian zhenshujiabao biao* 元日獻甄叔迦寶表, *BZJ*, T52, no. 2120, p. 859, a7-20.

Receiving the longstanding vow of Mañjuśrī, I released the posthumous power of my deceased master. Vaguely the divine power descended to the altar. The color of the flame was forthwith rosy and cheerful and smoke failed to arise. Not like other days, the result of the ceremony indicates a pure and lucid sign, signifying the peacefulness of China and the sign of ceasefire.

陳文殊宿願, 啟先師冥力. 依僑有憑, 響像來應. 遂得火色鮮潤, 煙氣不起, 異於他日, 實表清時. 是華夏晏謐之徵, 兵塵止息之驗. [48]

Found across the tantric world in India, East Asia and Tibet, a *homa* ritual (Figure. 18) is a fire offering to the deities, so that Buddhas, Bodhisattvas or the esoteric messengers —— *vidyā-rājas* (Ch. *mingwang* 明王) —— and their retinues may be invoked against evil spirits. In the second half of the eighth century, Amoghavajra translated a *locus classicus* for the fivefold taxonomy of *homa*: *Regulations for Homa for Vajra Pinnacle Yoga* (*Jin'gangding yuqie humo yigui* 金剛頂瑜伽護摩儀軌, T908).[49] Under the tutelage of Amoghavajra, whom Daizong routinely called upon to execute similar rituals, Huixiao was well versed in esoteric ceremony. We can infer from the context that what he performed at Wutai was probably the *homa* of *śāntika*, in which the practitioner uses the magical formulae to prevent disasters and calamities. After the departure of Śubhakarasiṃha, Ximingsi probably relinquished its position as a center of tantric Budhism to Xingshansi, where Amoghavajra painstaking built up his tantric enterprise. However, Ximingsi remained an important link in the esoteric network Amoghavajra established. In addition to Huixiao, the prominent Yuanzhao, who also studied under the tutelage of Amoghavajra, was particularly influential under the reign of the next Tang emperor.

---

[48] *Jin Wutaishan xiu humo gongde biao* 進五臺山修護摩功德表, *BZJ*, T52, no. 2120, p. 859, b1-14.

[49] The fivefold *homa* rituals are called *wuzongfa* 五種法 (Jap. *goshuhō*): *Śāntika* is employed for protection; *pauṣṭika* (Ch. *zengyifa* 增益法, Jap. *sōyakuhō*) for prosperity; *ankuśa* (Ch. *gouzhaofa* 鉤召法, Jap. *kōchōhō*) for summoning and influencing the beneficent powers; *vaśīkaraṇa* (Ch. *jing'aifa* 敬愛法, Jap. *keiaihō*) for gaining love and respect; and *abhicāraka* (Ch. *tiaofufa* 調伏法, Jap. *jōbukuhō*) for subjugating adversaries. For studies of homa rituals, see Richard Payne and Charles Orzech, "Homa," in *EBTEA*, 133-40. For the six stages of the homa fire rite, especially those practiced in the Japanese Tendai tantric Buddhism; see Michael R. Saso, *Homa Rites and Mandala Meditation in Tendai Buddhism* (New Delhi: International Academy of Indian Culture and Aditya Prakashan, 1991), 24-102.

Figure. 18　　Homa (Jap. *goma* 護摩) Ritual, Okunoin 奥ノ院 (inner sanctuary) at Kōyasan 高野山. Source: Miyasaka Yūshō 宮坂宥勝, Kanaoka Shūyū 金岡秀友, and Manabe Shunshō 真鍋俊照, eds., *Mikkyō zuten* 密教図典, 87.

Emperor Dezong and Yuanzhao

The peace foretold by the *homa* ritual lasted for only three years. Shortly after Dezong 德宗 (r. 779-805) ascended the throne, the central authority of what was, by that time, the precarious Tang rule was confined to four regions: the capital province, the northwest frontier zone, the lower Yangtze, and the corridor of the Grand Canal.[50] In the fourth year of Jianzhong 建中 (783), the country was troubled again by the military insurrection led by Zhu Ci 朱泚 (742-784), a Chang'an general who staged a rebellion to avenge his brother.[51] The pressing situation in frontier cities like Youzhou 幽州, Jizhou 冀州 and the three regions around Chang'an (*sanfu* 三輔) compelled the Tang army to conscript more solders.[52]

As early as 780, the government had instituted a two-tax system (*liangshui fa* 兩稅法) that enabled the state to collect taxes more readily. With the outbreak of the rebellions in the northern provinces, the monopoly tax increased considerably between 782 and 784. In the north the rate under the direct control of the Public

---

[50] John Stewart Bowman, *Columbia Chronologies of Asian History and Culture* (New York: Columbia University Press, 2000), 25

[51] *Fengtian lu* 奉天錄 (Record of Fengtian), *Congshu jicheng chubian* 叢書集成初編, vol. 3834 (Shanghai: Shangwu yinshuguan, 1935), 1-2; *Fozu lidai tongzai*, T49, no. 2036, p. 605, c19-20.

[52] The bloody war and bitter hatred between contending troops were dramatized in the *Fengtian lu*, whose author tells us, "although the royal army reaped many victories, the enemy was not exhausted. Victory and defeat followed each other, while the casualties amount to tens of thousands." See *Fengtian lu*, 1-2.

Revenue department rose to 560 cash.[53] Under the belief that military expenditures added up to tremendous amounts, the assistant minister from the Ministry of Revenue (*hubu shilang* 戶部侍郎), Zhao Zan 趙贊, submitted a proposal to the throne, suggesting an imposed tax based on differing standards of residences (*jianjia* 間架) in the three regions around Chang'an. Moreover, Ximingsi and Ci'ensi had temporary cloisters set up to collect money from the rich merchants in the two markets of the capital.[54] As early as the An-shi Rebellion, when monks were scattered and the lines of doctrinal descent were frequently interrupted, Buddhist monasteries had helped the Tang government raise money in order to meet military expenses. As Schmidt-Glintzer describes it, "In 755 permits for monks' ordination were sold for the first time. This measure was very successful and, in 757, in the region of the capital Chang'an alone, more than 100,000 people applied for permits."[55]

When it became increasingly clear that Dezong faced a combination of a riotous mob and mutinous soldiers led by Zhu Ci, the emperor was forced to flee again and took refuge in the walled city of Fengtian (modern Qian County 乾縣 in Shanxi province) eighty miles away. Before Zhu Ci launched his attack on Fengtian, he seized a monk called Fajian 法堅 who was skilled in siege weaponry. According to *Taiping guangji* (Wide Gleanings from the Taiping Era), Fajian was registered at Ximingsi. Realizing that he would now have to mount a siege against Fengtian, Zhu Ci employed the service of Fajian, who demolished a nearby Buddhist temple in order to obtain timber to build a "cloud ladder" (*yunti* 雲梯) for scaling the city walls.[56] The only source for this account is a collection of unreliable stories compiled in the Song dynasty, but the precedents of two other Ximingsi monks, Tankuang and Huixiao, lead us to believe that the story is in a sense convincing: Fajian chose to flee from the war, and he was simply unfortunate to have been captured by the rebel army.

It is impossible to evaluate the damage Ximingsi incurred in the series of

---

[53] Denis Twitchett, *Financial Administration under the T'ang Dynasty* (Cambridge: Cambridge University Press, 1970), 55; Weinstein, *Buddhism under the Tang*, 93-94.

[54] *Fengtain lu*, 1-2; see also Michihata Ryōshū, *Tōdai Bukkyō shi no kenkyū*, 514-41.

[55] Schmidt-Glintzer, "Buddhism in the Tang Period," 197.

[56] *TPGJ* 76. 480-481; *ZZTJ* 228.7364. For an English account of the story, see Stephen Turnbull and Steve Noon, *Chinese Walled Cities 221 BC-AD 1644* (New York: Osprey, 2009), 52 ; see also Yihong Pan, *Son of Heaven and Heavenly Qaghan: Sui-Tang China and its Neighbors* (Bellingham, Wash.: Western Washington University, 1997), 162. The prolonged series of wars in late Tang was studied by Edwin G. Pulleyblank, "The An Lushan Rebellion and the origins of chronic militarism in late Tang China," in *Essays on T'ang Society*, ed. John Perry and Bardwell Smith (Leiden: Brill, 1976), 32-60.

prolonged insurrections beginning in 755 and lasting for thirty years, but Dezong finally restored order in Chang'an and met again with Yuanzhao, the most distinguished scholar from Ximingsi in the last half of the eighth century. Yuanzhao had assumed a position in many translation offices since the reign of Xuanzong and participated in the compilation of a definitive commentary on the vinaya that was begun the under imperial aegis of Daizong. In 780 when Yuanzhao presented the completed commentary to Dezong, the latter already responded graciously by awarding Yuanzhao a "purple robe" (*ziyi* 紫衣), the highest mark of distinction for a monk. However, it was after the unsuccessful wars against the military governors between 781 and 786 that Dezong eventually emerged as one of the most devout Buddhist rulers of the Tang dynasty.

As we have seen, Yuanzhao also faithfully preserved the correspondence between Amoghavajra, Huixiao and the Tang rulers in his *Collected Documents*. A specialist in Sarvāstivādin Vinaya, he was a scholiast and cataloger of the rich collection in the monastic library of Ximingsi. While Dezong was drawn to the new esoteric form of Buddhism, the urban Buddhist community seemed rejuvenated in the wake of a prolonged series of wars. The period of Zhenyuan 貞元 (785-805) was indeed a productive epoch for Buddhist scholarship at Ximingsi. As was the case with previous Tang rulers, Dezong was in rapport with Ximingsi. *Taiping guangji* even contains a story suggesting that Dezong discretely visited Ximingsi and had tea with a man by the name of Songwu 宋五, who was lodged in the special cloister reserved for examinees in preparation for the national examination.[57] One arm of Buddhist scholarship that Dezong sponsored at Ximingsi was the translation of the *Scripture of the Six Pāramitā of Mahāyāna* (Ch. *Dacheng liqu liu boluomiduo jing* 大乘理趣六波羅蜜多經, Skt. *Mahāyāna-naya-ṣaṭ-pāramitā-sūtra*, T261) and additional texts acquired by the Kashmir pundit Prajñā 般若 (Zhihui 智慧), who studied extensively at Nālandā and other eminent monastic universities in India.[58] He was probably the last prominent foreign translator who ever visited Ximingsi. Like many Indian monks, Prajñā arrived in Chang'an via the southern region of Guangzhou because of the far-reaching reputation of Mount Wutai. Soon after his arrival, he became the beneficiary of the Institute for the Translation of Buddhist Scriptures (Yijing yuan 譯經院) commissioned by Dezong at Ximingsi. In 788 (Zhenyuan 4),

---

[57] *TPGJ*, 180.1338-339.

[58] For the biography of Prajñā (*Tang Luojing zhihui zhuan* 唐洛京智慧傳), see *SGSZ*, T50, no. 2061, p. 716, b15-28.

under gracious imperial patronage, eight eminent scholars, including monks at Ximing such as Yuanzhao and Liangxiu 良秀, were instructed to reside at Ximingsi and take part in the translation of the *Scripture of the Six Pāramitā of Mahāyāna*. Yuanzhao shares his perspective as a participant in his *Da Tang zhenyuan xu kaiyuan shijiaolu* 大唐貞元續開元釋教錄 (Continuation of the Kaiyuan Catalogue Compiled in the Zhenyuan Period of the Great Tang, T2156); he says that the Sanskrit manuscripts of the scripture were taken out from the imperial library and escorted to Ximingsi by ranking officials in charge of Buddhist matters in Chang'an. Wang Xiqian 王希遷, the Commissioner of Good Works of the Right Half of Chang'an (*youjie gongdeshi* 右街功德使), and the great general of the Right Divine Strategy Army Wang Mengshe 王孟涉 led a procession accompanied by musicians and chariots. As usual, the spectacular procession looked like a grand music festival:

> The six pitches, five musical tones and the eight musical instruments conformed to the same rhythm. The musicians from the "four-part" assembled together, playing the Buddhist hymns that were clamoring with each another. The beautiful music of *xiaoshao* was so loud that it rocketed into the sky and the sounds of the drum and the bell shook the earth. [The scripture] was escorted out from the imperial palace and entered the city through the Fanglin Gate. The main avenue was filled with chariots and horses. The streets overflowed with men and women. The procession entered into Ximingsi to carry out the translation of the true canon. The same day the emperor provided one hundred strings of cash, thirty strings of tea, and a big box of incense as offering to the Institute for the Translation of Buddhist Scriptures.

六律五聲, 八音合韻.[59] 四部雲集, 歌唄交誼.[60] 簫韶沸天, 鼓鍾震地. 發彼禁闥, 出芳林門. 車騎滿於天衢, 士女溢於閭裡. 入西明寺, 翻譯真經. 同日恩賜錢一百千文, 茶三十釧, 香一大合, 以充譯經院供養.[61]

---

[59] In Chinese musicology, *liulü* 六律 (six bamboo pitches) are *huanzhong* 黃鐘, *dacu* 大蔟, *guxi* 姑洗, *ruibin* 蕤賓, *yize* 夷則 and *wushe* 無射. In this context, *Bayin* 八音 is not the eight tones of the Buddha's voice, but the eight instruments, namely, *jin* 金, *shi* 石, *si* 絲, *zhu* 竹, *pao* 匏, *tu* 土, *ge* 革, *mu* 木.

[60] The four-part music of the Tang was divided into *qiucibu* 龜茲部, *dagubu* 大鼓部, *hubu* 胡部 and *junyuebu* 軍樂部, see *XTS* 222. 6309.

[61] *Da Tang zhenyuan xu kaiyuan shijiaolu*, T55, no. 2156, p. 756, b6-24; *Dacheng liqu liu boluomiduo jing* 大乘理趣六波羅蜜多經 (Scripture of the Six Pāramitā of Mahāyāna), T08, no. 261, p. 865, b4-12.

This scripture enumerates the six perfections of Bodhisattava practice in the service of the state. Dezong praised the scripture in his preface to the new translation: "[The scripture] was protected by the dragon-god as if it was uttered from the golden mouth of the Buddha. Being held and supported by the monks, the sūtra is no different from the light emitted from the tuft in Buddha's forehead." [62] Dezong's death in 805, as Weinstein notes, marked the end of state-supported literary activities that were one of the hallmarks of Tang Buddhism.[63]

It is safe to assume that in the late eighth century, Buddhist Asia was under the supreme rule of two men, the Tibetan ruler Trisong Detsen and the Tang emperor Dezong. As we have seen, Trisong Detsen's inquiry brought about the twenty-two questions of Mahāyāna Buddhism solved by Tankuang, a scholar who had been well educated at Ximingsi. Dezong, for his part, was a patron of numerous Buddhist works edited by the Ximing scholar Yuanzhao.[64] The intentions of the two kings may have differed, but the two cases help us to see how the role of Ximingsi seems, as time passes, increasingly important in the Buddhist landscape of the eighth century.

Survival in the Suppression of Buddhism

Five Tang rulers ascended the throne within a short period between 805 and 840.[65] Despite the sporadic religious frenzy of the Buddha's relic sweeping the capital during these years, records of Ximingsi from this period are scant in both the

---

[62] The sentence reads: " 龍神翼衛如從金口之傳，梵眾護持無異毫光之現", see *Dacheng liqu liu boluomiduo jing*, T08, no. 261, p. 865, b12-13; see Wang Xiang, "Beiyu yu xiejing," 523; *Mochizuki*, 4260. Later Dezong even authorized the establishment of a special cloister called *Liu boluomi jingyuan* 六波羅蜜經院 (Cloister of the Six Pāramitā) at Liquan Monastery (Liquansi 醴泉寺) to publicize the scripture because it was valuable as a powerful synopsis of Mahayana teaching for beginners. The memorial is titled *Qing zhi liuboluomi jingyuan biao* 請置六波羅蜜經院表; see Chen Shangjun 陳尚君, ed., *Quan Tang wenbu bian* 全唐文補編 (Beijing: Zhonghua shuju, 2005), 645 .

[63] Weinstein, *Buddhism under the Tang*, 99.

[64] Only three of Yuanzhao's works survive in the Taisho canon; however, many of his books were very likely composed with imperial patronage, such as *Jingyun xiantian kaiyuan tianbao gaozhi* 景雲先天開元天寶誥制; *Bukong sanzang beibiao ji* 不空三藏碑表集; *Jianzhong Yuyuan Zhenyuan zhizhi shimen biaozou ji* 建中興元貞元制旨釋門表奏記; *Yuti Zhangxinsi shi taizi bailiao fenhe ji* 禦題章信寺詩太子百寮奉和集. For Yuanzhao's biographical sketch and a list of his works, see *SGSZ*, T50, no. 2061, p. 804, b17-p. 805, c20.

[65] The five Tang rulers during this period were Shunzong 順宗 (r. 805); Xianzong 憲宗 (r. 805-820); Muzong 穆宗 (r. 820-824) ; Jingzong 敬宗 (r. 824 and 826) and Wenzong 文宗 (r. 826-840).

biographical accounts and the national histories. *Song gaoseng zhuan* states that an eminent monk called Yunsui 雲邃 was in charge of Buddhist and Daoist affairs in the western half of Chang'an and concurrently held the *sthavira* position in Ximingsi and Qianfusi 千福寺 during the early years of Emperor Xianzong 憲宗 (r. 805-820).[66] In 815 (Yuanhe 元和 10) Ximingsi planned to move the image of the popular Buddhist guardian deity Vaiśravaṇa (Ch. Pishamentian 毘沙門天,) to Kaiyesi 開業寺. The reason for this is not recorded in extant sources. However, the incumbent Xianzong ordered that "the image first be lodged temporarily within his palace, to which it was carried in a spectacular procession replete with religious banners and canopies under escort of the imperial cavalry."[67] Meanwhile, probably by the middle of Yuanhe (806-820), the prominent Xuanchang, the future leader of Ximingsi, made his debut in Chang'an. After receiving complete Buddhist precepts at the ordination platform of *Tuṣita* (*doushuai jietan* 兜率戒壇) in Fuzhou, he arrived in Ximingsi to study with Vinaya Master Huizheng 惠正. What also drew him to the capital was the reputation of Daoxuan, who seems to have had remarkable influence upon the Buddhist community after he passed away.[68] It is notable that even the next ruler, Muzong 穆宗 (r. 820-824), who did not particularly concern himself with Buddhist affairs, composed a *Panegyric on Vinaya Master Daoxuan* (*Daoxuan lüshi zan* 道宣律師贊) by the end of his reign.[69]

As the ninth century moved into its second quarter, the Buddhist saṃgha was standing on the threshold of the radical change that was soon to follow. Ten years before the notorious Huichang 會昌 suppression (841-846), the young emperor Wenzong 文宗 (r. 826-840) had already received a memorial recommending the wholesale purge of the Buddhist and Daoist clergies. By that time, it seems that the Buddho-Daoist communities already lacked bureaucratic control, owing to Xianzong's order in 807, which, in effect, entrusted the maintenance of clerical registers to the eunuch Commissioners of Good Works instead of the officials in the Department of Sacrifices (*cibu* 祠部).[70] In 839, based on the memorial submitted by Cui Li 崔蠡, the Vice President of the Board of Rites (*Libu shilang* 禮部侍郎), Wenzong prohibited the long-standing tradition of feasting members of the Buddhist

---

[66] *Tang jingzhao Qianfusi Yunsui zhuan* 唐京兆千福寺雲邃傳, *SGSZ*, 735 T50, no. 2061, p. 894, a7-20.

[67] *CFYG*, see *SKQS* 903.49.

[68] *SGSZ*, T50, no. 2061, p. 818, a19-b19.

[69] *Nanshan lüshi zan* 南山律師贊, *QTW* 67. 712; *Fozhu tongji*, T49, no. 2035, p. 297, b2-5.

[70] Weinstein, *Buddhism under the Tang*, 108.

clergy in observance of memorial days for deceased emperors, a traditional practice that Ximingsi participated in for more than a century.[71] With this prohibition, the custom initiated during the reign of Taizong was brought to come to a halt at Ximingsi. As Weinstein states, by the time of Wenzong's death, "the stage had been set for the brutal suppression of Buddhism that was soon to follow."[72]

The new ruler, Wuzong 武宗 (r. 840-846), was the half-brother of Wenzong. Unlike his brother, Wuzong was fascinated by Daoism and keen to pursue the longevity propagated by Daoist priests during his short thirty-two-year-long life. Evidence shows that the Huichang suppression, initiated by Wuzong in 841, inflicted heavy losses upon Ximingsi, although its prominence and honored history of imperial patronage by previous rulers protected it from total destruction.[73] In the first few years of the persecution, Wuzong carried out a plan leading from the expulsion of unaffiliated monks to a general purge of the Buddhist clergy. By 843, the urban Buddhist communities were despondent, due to the succession of imperial decrees issued during the previous three years that were overtly hostile towards Buddhist churches. Xuanchang, the incumbent abbot of Ximingsi, remonstrated on behalf of the Buddhist circle, with several memorials describing the traditional pattern of imperial patronage in the preceding dynasties.[74] An account in *Song gaoseng zhuan* describes it this way:

> Meanwhile the Buddhist practitioners in the capital city were scared and helpless. The two recorders of the clergy Linyan and Bianzhang simultaneously chose Xuanchang as the leader to submit memorials [to the throne]. Then Xuanchang wrote a book titled *Record of Previous Emperors*, but Wuzong turned a deaf ear to his advice. As a result Xuanchang defrocked and temporarily gave up his high-minded principle.

---

[71] See *Da Song sengshi lüe*, T54, no. 2126, p. 241, c12-17, especially the twenty fifth section of *xingxiang changdao* 行香唱導 (walking meditation and preaching).

[72] Weinstein, *Buddhism under the Tang*, 114.

[73] For some scholastic investigations of the Huichang Persecution of Buddhism, see Weinstein, *Buddhist under the Tang*, 114-36; Kenneth Ch'en, "The Economic Background of the Hui-Ch'ang Suppression of Buddhism," *Harvard Journal of Asiatic Studies* 19, no. 1/2 (1956): 67-105; George A. Fisher, Jr., "The Huichang Cash of the Tang dynasty," *Journal of East Asian Numismatics* 1 (1995). 24-37.

[74] *SGSZ*, 430, T50, no. 2061, p. 818, a20-b19. For the biography of Xuanchang (*Tang jingzhao Fushousi Xuanchang zhuan* 唐京兆福壽寺玄暢傳), see *SGSZ*, T50, no. 2061, p. 818, a19-b19.

時京城法侶，頗甚徬徨．兩街僧錄靈宴，辯章同推暢為首，上表論諫．遂著
歷代帝王錄，奏而弗聽，由是例從俗服，寧弛道情．[75]

Xuanchang tactically returned to lay life as a compromise and waited for his
opportunity to return to Ximingsi. There is no need to recapitulate the unprecedented
assault on Buddhism across the country since many scholars have published
informative work on the topic. By far the best known description of the Huichang
suppression in Chang'an is given by Ennin in his diary *Nittō guhō junrei kōki* 入唐
求法巡禮行記 (The Record of a Pilgrimage to China in Search of the Law).
According to Ennin, in the third year of Huichang (843), the monks in Chang'an
were terrified because on one occasion 300 monks, whose names did not appear on
the clerical registers, were executed after they attempted to conceal their status by
disguising themselves. During the ghost festival of the next year (844), instead of
holding grand ceremonies, more than 300 small Buddhist shrines (*fotang* 佛堂) in
Chang'an were destroyed, many of which were on par with those of the great
monasteries in the provinces. In the ninth month, another thirty small monasteries
were dismantled and their images transferred to larger monasteries and turned over to
Daoist temples.[76]

After the laicization of monks and nuns in Chang'an in 845, the promulgation of
an imperial decree in the seventh month only allowed four monasteries to function in
the future. On the left (eastern) half of Chang'an, only Ci'ensi and Jianfusi were
permitted to remain; on the right (western) half, Ximingsi and Zhuangyansi 莊嚴寺
were preserved. However, the decree stipulates that the size of the clergy in each of
the monastery could not exceed thirty.[77] It is obvious that most of the clerics at
Ximingsi were expelled or forced to return to the laity as Xuanchang did. Meanwhile
a proposal submtted by the Secretariat Chancellery (*zhongshu* 中書) suggested a
wholesale destruction of Buddhist images, which were forcibly turned over to the

---

[75] Ibid., p. 818, a29-b4.

[76] *Nittō guhō junrei gyōki* 入唐求法巡禮行記, *DNBZ* 72.126. Ono Katsutoshi, Bai Huawen 白化文, Li
Dingxia 李鼎霞, and Xu Denan 許德楠, eds. and trans., *Rutang qiufa xunli xingji jiaozhu* 入唐求法巡禮
行記校注 (Shijiazhuang: Huashan wenyi chubanshe,1992), 445-46; Weinstein, *Buddhism under the Tang*,
122-26, see also *(Gujin tushu jicheng) Shijiaobuhui kao* (古今圖書集成) 釋教部彙考, *XZJ* 133, p. 333,
a16-b2. For an English translation and study of Ennin's travelogue, see Edwin Reischauer, *Ennin's Travels
in Tang China* (New York,: Ronald Press Company, 1955); and idem., *The Record of a Pilgrimage to China
in Search of the Law.* (New York: Ronald Press Co, 1955).

[77] *JTS* 18. 605;*THY* 48. 1361; *(Gujin tushu jicheng) Shijiaobuhui kao*, *XZJ* 133, p. 333, a16-b2.

Commissioner for Salt and Iron (*Yantieshi* 鹽鐵使) for use in the minting of coins. Even the four monasteries officially sanctioned could not possess any metal images or bronze bells. It was probably for fear of confiscation that the remaining monks from Ximingsi sank copper ware and Buddha images into some of their monastic wells. An excavation conducted in 1985 on the northeastern corner of Ximingsi, where one of the thirteen Buddhist cloisters was situated, has revealed traces of the panic. The Xi'an archaeological team discovered about 150 gold-plated bronze Buddha figures (*liujin tongzaoxiang* 鎏金銅造像) at the site of Ximingsi. An Jiayao 安家瑤, the Chinese scholar who participated in the excavation, reports that all the images, ranging from 5.5cm to 14.5 cm in height, were disinterred from the second well. It is believed that the monks deliberately dropped the Buddha figures down into the well in a hasty act of precaution against confiscation.[78] Luckily for the Buddhist clergy in Chang'an, in the latter half of 845, Wuzong was struck with an illness explained by the Daoists surrounding him as a sign that he was becoming an immortal. However, before he had reached his thirty-second birthday he died suddenly of carbuncles that erupted on his back in the third month of 846.

Fushousi and the Twilight of Ximingsi

Being a devout Buddhist, the new heir to the throne, Xuanzong 宣宗 (r. 846-859) must have been devastated to witness the dilapidation of the urban monasteries. He swiftly reappointed Yang Qinyi 楊欽義 as the new Commissioner of Good Works, a post abolished by Wuzong in 845. As a signal that he would restore the Buddhist church, he approved the memorial Yang Qinyi submitted, sanctioning the reopening of twelve monasteries in addition to the four major remaining monasteries in Chang'an. Although Ximingsi had continued to function during the destruction of monasteries and laicization of the clergy, like many other monasteries in the Buddhist revival, it was obliged to change its name to Fushousi 福壽寺 (Monastery for Fortune and Longevity).[79] Particular reasons for the change of names are not given

---

[78] An Jiayao, "Tang Chang'an Ximingsi yizhi fajue jianbao," 52-53.

[79] Weinstein, *Buddhism under the Tang*, 137-38. Kamata Shigeo 鎌田茂雄, *Chūgoku bukkyōshi. Zui Tō no bukkyō* 中國仏教史.隋唐の仏教 (Tokyo: Tōkyō daigaku shuppankai, 1994), 138-39. For instance, in the left half of Chang'an, Qinglongsi became Huguosi 護國寺 (Monastery of State Protection); Putisi turned to Baotangsi 保唐寺 (Monastery for Protecting the Tang). For the right half of Chang'an, Ximingsi was renamed Fushoushi; Zhuangyansi turned into Shengshousi 聖壽寺 (Monastery for Emperor's Longevity);

in Tang sources, but Weinstein argues that:

> Since most of the monasteries that had been closed in 845 had already been dismantled or destroyed, it was proposed, no doubt with a view to curbing expenditures, that only those monasteries that were in a repairable state should be selected for reopening. The inevitable result was that a curious medley of monasteries reappeared - some famous and others that were totally obscure, but had happened somehow to escape destruction. To reduce rivalry among the recommissioned monasteries, seventeen, including some of the best known, were required to drop their former names in favor of new ones, which stressed their mission of affording protection to the state.[80]

However, instead of losing its identity in the restoration, Fushousi maintained its full status as a reputable establishment of vinaya in the first few years of Dazhong 大中 period (847-859). In 848, the government authorized the establishment of a special 'penitential' Mahāyānist ordination platform (*xichan jietan* 洗懺戒壇) on which ex-members of the clergy had a chance to repent their transgressions of the vinaya committed during the Huichang persecution. Gaoxian 高閑, a priest who had studied vinaya and canonical exegesis at the former Ximingsi, was invited to hand down the precepts (Ch. *shoujie* 授戒, Skt. *upasaṃpad*) and was granted a purple robe.[81] To mark the occasion of his birthday, Xuanzong resumed the early tradition of inter-religious debate and invited some of the most prominent monks at the time, including Zhixuan 知玄 and Xuanchang, to participate in debates between representatives of Buddhism, Daoism and Confucianism on the emperor's birthday (*danchen tanlun* 誕辰談論). Xuanchang, the formal abbot of Ximingsi, seized his opportunity to win favour again from the two emperors who followed Wuzong. On many of his birthdays, Xuanzong happily summoned Xuanchang to the palace chapel to talk on scriptures, granting him a purple robe and the title of Great Ordination Master (*lintan dade* 臨壇大德).[82] The traditions of lecturing on Buddhist scriptures

---

see *JTS* 18. 615; *ZZTJ* 248. 8024; Michihata Ryōshū, *Chugoku bukkyō shi zenshū*. 中國佛教史全集, vol.2 (Tokyo: Shoen, 1985), 210.

[80] Weinstein, *Buddhism under the Tang*, 138.

[81] *Tang Tiantaishan Chanlinsi guangxiu zhuan (Gaoxian)* 唐天臺山禪林寺廣脩傳 (高閑), *SGSZ*, T50, no. 2061, p. 895, a15-b5.

[82] *SGSZ*, T50, no. 2061, p. 818, b4-19. For the biography of Zhixuan (*Tang Pengzhou Danjingshan Zhixuan*

and court debates continued until Xuanzong's last years on the throne. The Tang writer Li Dong 李洞, in a poem presented to a monk serving at the altar in the imperial palace (*neigongfeng* 內供奉) in 859 (Dazhong 13), reminds us that in addition to the scriptural talk at court, lectures on Buddhist scriptures were routinely sponsored by Ximingsi in the summer.[83]

The days after Xuanzong are seen as the decline of the Tang dynasty. However, Xuanzong's successor, Yizong 懿宗 (r. 860-873), turned his back on the vexatious world of politics and embraced the Buddhist faith with enthusiasm. Proving to be even more devout than his father, Yizong made frequent visits to urban monasteries and gave lavish gifts to the Buddhist communities.[84] By this time Fushousi had changed its title back to "Ximingsi," since Yizong had taken the unusual step of establishing a convent under the name Fushousi within the imperial palace to serve as a retreat for courtesans who went forth to a religious life. The ordained nuns registered in this monastery were ordered to copy the 5000-fascicle Buddhist tripiṭaka at Yizong's behest.[85] It would have been highly unlikely for Yizong to allow two Fushou Monasteries to coexist in urban Chang'an.

There is no denying that the Tang court remained engaged in monastic issues into the last 50 years of the empire, although the souces concerning Ximingsi's activities during this period remain spotty. In the fourth month of 862 (Xiantong 咸通 3), the capital streets were again filled with monks awaiting ordination because the four major monasteries, including Ximingsi, received an order to practice *vaipulya* penances (Ch. *fangdeng chanfa* 方等懺法) and construct platforms for ordinations for twenty one days.[86] *Vaipulya* penances are a confessional practice derived from the manual *Methods of Vaipulya Samādhi* (*Fangdeng sanmei xingfa* 方等三昧行法, T1940) written by the Tiantai Master Zhiyi 智顗 (538-598).[87] As we might imagine,

---

zhuan 唐彭州丹景山知玄傳), see *SGSZ*, T50, no. 2061, p. 744, a3-8.

[83] The poem by Li Dong is titled *Zeng runei gongfeng seng* 贈入內供奉僧, see *QTS* 723.8293, Zhou Zuzhuan 周祖譔, *Zhongguo wenxuejia dacidian. Tang Wudai juan* 中國文學家大辭典. 唐五代卷 (Beijing: Zhonghua shuju, 1992), 303. The monk in the poem was called Qibai 棲白. The bureaucratic position of *neigongfeng*, also known as *gongfeng* 供奉, was instituted in 756. The Ximingsi monk Yuanzhao also took the position in 780 (Jianzhong 建中 1); see *Fozu tongji*, T49, no. 2035, p. 379, a23-24.

[84] Weinstein, *Buddhism under the Tang*, 144.

[85] Ibid. 145, see also *Da Song sengshi lüe* , T54, no. 2126, p. 252, a29-b3; *Tang jingzhao Da'an'guosi Sengche zhuan* 唐京兆大安國寺僧徹傳, *SGSZ*, T50, no. 2061, p. 745, a4-7.

[86] *Fayuan zhulin*, T53, no. 2122, p. 381, a14-17; *Shishi jigu lüe*, T49, no. 2037, p. 840, b25-28; *SGSZ*, T50, no. 2061, p. 744, c15-p. 745, a6.

[87] See *Fangdeng sanmei xingfa* 方等三昧行法 (Method for Practicing the Vaipulya Samādhi), T46, no.

111

Ximingsi monks swarmed to the Mahayana altar, which was open to the public, in order to practice *vaipulya samādh* (Ch. *fangdeng sanmei* 方等三昧). Here they meditated and repented the hindrances caused by the six sense organs. Yizong regarded the widely acknowledged Ximing master Xuanchang with veneration; Xuanchang had served three Tang emperors in the last fifty years, and now took the new post of rector at Zongchi Monastery (Zongchisi 總持寺). Xuanchang deserves credit not only for lecturing on vinaya sixty times, but also for ordaining thousands of monks. One year after he entered into nirvana, Yizong posthumously honored Xuanchang with the title Fabao dashi 法寶大師 (Great Master who is a Dharma Treature).[88] Xuanchang not only did his utmost to maintain the scholastic tradition at Ximingsi, but he also proved to be the last prominent master associated with the Tang monarchs.

In spite of the inevitable downfall of the Tang dynasty, the brief revival of Ximingsi still attracted foreign monk-scholars, a tradition that continued for two centuries. For instance, according to a text in the *Liaohai congshu* 遼海叢書, a magician monk Saduoluo 薩多羅 from the northeastern State of Balhae (Bohaiguo 渤海國, figure.19) took up lodging in Ximingsi around 860.[89] Although most of those residing at Ximingsi had to acquire official permission in advance, probably only a few of the most prominent foreign visitors captured the attention of the Tang government. Among these latter was a line of Japanese monks who visited Ximingsi, including a monk of imperial background and exceptional passion who joined the scholarly community in the fifth year of Xiantong (864). In Japanese history, he is also commonly known by his popular name, Prince Takaoka (Takaoka shinnō 高岳親王, or Shinnyo Shino 真如親王, 799-865, Figure.20), third son of the Emperor Heizei (Heizei Tennō 平城天皇, r. 806-809, 774-824) who ruled only for a short time. His dharma name, Shinnyo 真如, implies unchanging reality (Skt. *Tathatā* or *bhūtatathatā*) as contrasted in Buddhist literature to form or phenomena. As one of the ten major disciples of Kūkai (or Kōbō Daishi 弘法大師, as he would come to be

---

1940, p. 943, a2-p. 949, a10. The manual is written according to the ritual prescribed in *Dafangdeng tuoluoni jing* 大方等陀羅尼經 (Skt. *Pratyutpannabuddhasaṃmukhāvasthitasamādhi sūtra*, T1339).

[88] *Da Song sengshi lüe*, T54, no. 2126, p. 249, a7-10; *Xinxiu kefen liuxue shengzhuan* 新修科分六學僧傳, XZJ 133, p. 843, a4-16.

[89] It is said that Saduoluo 薩多羅 was well versed in bird divination. In the account of Saduoluo, Ximingsi is known as *Ximing jingshe* 西明精舍; see Jin Yufu 金毓黻, ed., *Liaohai congshu* 遼海叢書 (Shenyang: LiaoShen shushe, 1985), 177.

known), Shinnyo must have been acquainted with the reputation of Ximingsi, where Kūkai had lived and acquired Sanskrit manuscripts from Prajñā. In the fifth month of 864, Prince Takaoka and his entourage entered Chang'an through the eastern Gate of Spring Luster (Chunming men 春明門). Ensai 円載 (d. 877), the Japanese monk who was copying bundles of scriptures and secular codices at Ximingsi, reported Shinnyo's arrival to Yizong. Ensai was the disciple of Saichō 最澄 (766-822), the distinguished Buddhist patriarch who founded the Tendai school in Japan. Emperor Xuanzong allowed him to study at Ximingsi. In this way the students of the two most prominent founders of Japanese Buddhism had their meeting at Ximingsi. The Japanese historian Saeki Arikiyo 佐伯有清 (1925-2005) argues that Yizong then invited Shinnyo to court and arranged a "debate" on the topic of Buddhist doctrine between the prince and the celebrated tantric *ācārya* Faquan 法全 from Qinglong Monastery, who espoused a somewhat different tantric tradition from that of the well-known Huiguo.[90] As expected, Shinnyo's eloquence and erudition impressed the Tang ruler. Shortly after Shinnyo and his retinue copied ritual manuals at Ximingsi, they left Chang'an for India, because Shinnyo had failed to find a qualified teacher to quench his intellectual thirst for authentic knowledge of esoteric Buddhism.[91]

In a long list of foreign visitors, Shinnyo and his entourage were perhaps the final generation of Japanese monks in residence at Ximingsi. His departure drew to a close the cultural exchange between Japanese dharma seekers and the great Ximingsi. Like some Chinese pilgrims who never returned to China, the Japanese Shinnyo died an untimely death, for reasons that still puzzle us, during his trip to India. His Ximingsi friend Ensai, who received the purple robe at Linde Palace, also lost his life in a storm on his way back to Japan.[92] The point here is that the tragic fate of these

---

[90] In Japanese history, Shinnyo is also known as Shinnyo Shino 真如親王. Regarding his trip to Tang China, see *Zudashinnō nittō ryakuki* 頭陀親王入唐略記 (A Brief Account of the Imperial Prince Zuda Who Visited China), witten by Ise Okifusa 伊勢興房 in 865. The text is included in *Nittō gokeden* 入唐五家傳 (Biographiese of Five Monks Who Visited China); see *DNBZ* 68. 162-63. For a study of Shinnyo's travel in the Tang, see Saeki Arikiyo 佐伯有清, *Takaoka Shinnō nittō ki: haitaishi to kogai densetsu no shinsō* 高丘親王入唐記: 廃太子と虎害伝説の真相 (Tokyo: Yoshikawa kōbunkan, 2002), 192-208.

[91] Shinnyo's death remains a mystery: after he departed from Guanzhou in 865, he was reported to have died in Luoyueguo 羅越國 (today's Laos); see Saeki Arikiyo, *Takaoka Shinnō nittō ki*, 208. For an original record of Shinnyo's death in Japanese official history, see Fujiwara Tokihira 藤原時平, *Nihon sandai jitsuroku* 日本三代実録, in *Kokushi taikei* 國史大系, no. 4, ed. Kuroita Katsumi 黒板勝美 (Tokyo: Yoshikawa kōbunkan, 1964), 570-71; see also *Mochizuki*, 2085-086.

[92] For evidence of Ensai's experience in Ximingsi, see *Da Song sengshi lüe*, T54, no. 2126, p. 249, a13-16;

two Japanese masters, like the decline of Tang China, foreshadowed the eclipse of Ximingsi in the last thirty years of the dynasty.

Figure. 19   Balhae (Ch. Bohaiguo 渤海國), an Ancient Korean Kingdom. Source: Sakayori Masashi 酒寄雅志, *Bokkaito kodai no Nihon* 渤海と古代の日本, 100.

Taijin liangjie xuemai 胎金兩界血脈 (The Lineage of the Two Realms of Garbhadhātu and Vajradhātu), *XZJ* 95, p. 993, a18; *Shin shosha shōrai hōmon tō mokuroku* 新書寫請來法門等目錄 (Catalogue of the Newly Copied Imported Doctrines and Other Goods), T55, no. 2174A, p. 1111, c1-6; Ono, *Kaisetsu hen*, 155.

Figure. 20   Shinnyo Shino 真如親王 (799-865), from *Sangoku soshi ei* 三国祖師影, Daigoji 醍醐寺.
Source: Saeki Arikiyo 佐伯有清, *Takaoka Shinnō nittō ki: haitaishi to kogai densetsu no shinsō* 高丘親王
入唐記: 廃太子と虎害伝説の真相, I (Fig.1).

The Last Years of Ximingsi

When Yizong's son Xizong 僖宗 (r. 873-888) succeeded to the throne, the Tang
state was already wracked by drought and plagued by independent local generals
disloyal to the central government. The last two Tang rulers —— Zhaozong 昭宗 (r.
888-904) and Aidi 哀帝 (r. 904-907) —— would inherit an empire that existed in
name only. For the last twenty years of the dynasty, Chang'an, along with other

115

major centers of Buddhist learning, such as Luoyang, Hangzhou and Taiyuan, became victims of prolonged civil wars among local generals.[93] The Buddhist church, still not fully recovered from the Huichang purge, had most of its libraries and buildings torched, a calamity very similar to what it had encountered in the An-shi Rebellion.

The historical trajectory of Ximingsi during this dark period of Buddhism remains obscure except for some fragmentary entries in *Song gaoseng zhuan*. The last identifiable record of monks ordained at Ximingsi is titled *Biography of Huize (and Yuanbiao) from Ximing monastery in the Capital City of Liang* (*Liang jingzhao ximingsi huize zhuan [Yuanbiao]* 梁京兆西明寺慧則傳[元表]). Among more than 600 monks listed in the *Song gaoseng zhuan*, Huize and Yuanbiao are the last ones whose biographies belong to the Tang-Five dynasty transitional period. The Chinese character "Liang 梁" in the title of the entry refers to the brief Later Liang (907-923) dynasty established right after the Tang by the provincial governor Zhu Quanzhong 朱全忠 (907-912). Huize left his hometown in Suzhou and became a monk in Ximingsi in the seventh year of Dazhong (853). With the guidance of Xuanchang, he grew up as a qualified priest lecturing on *Abhidharmakośabhāṣya* (Ch. *Apidamo jushe lun* 阿毘達磨俱舍論, T1558), a seminal treatise on human consciousness and its relationship to the environment. Xuanzang had rendered the second edition of this text shortly before Ximingsi was established. In 880 or thereabouts, Huize's scholarly life came to close, since the insurrection of Huang Chao 黃巢 (d. 884) forced him to leave Chang'an and find refugee in provincial monasteries near his hometown in southern China. While he stayed in the Monastery of Aśoka (Yuwangsi 育王寺), the Mingzhou 明州 (today's Ningbo) governor Huang Sheng 黃晟 (d. 909) received the eight precepts under his supervision.[94] Yuanbiao, the other scholar who studied vinaya with Xuanchang, left for the southern region of the Yangzte River and settled down at Dashan Monastery (Dashansi 大善寺) in Yuezhou 越州 (today's Shaoxin). As he lectured on the vinaya and subsequent commentaries transmitted in the

---

[93] A large part of Chang'an was virtually destroyed in the long series of wars between 883-904, see Liu Anqin 劉安琴, *Chang'an dizhi* 長安地志 (Xi'an: Xi'an chuban she, 2007), 111-13. For a vivid report of Chang'an from the ninth to tenth centuries; see Edward Schafer, "The Last Years of Chang'an," *Oriens Extremus* 10 (1963): 133-79; Arthur Wright, "Tch'ang-ngan, 583-904: Esquisse historique," in *Mélanges de sinologie offerts à M. P. Demiéville*, vol. 2, ed. Paul Demiéville (Paris: Presses universitaires de France, 1974), 348-50.

[94] *Liang jingzhao Ximingsi Huize zhuan (Yuanbiao)* 梁京兆西明寺慧則傳 (元表), *SGSZ*, T50, no. 2061, p. 809, a11-b10.

Nanshan School, scholars from nearby counties gathered to his dharma seat in crowds. In the chronicle of Ximingsi that we have thus far endeavored to reconstruct, he is probably the last monk on record whose literary activities were linked in various ways to the Buddhist lineage passed down from Daoxuan.

It is customary for scholars to assume that Ximingsi was destroyed in the calamities of the first decade of the tenth century, when the last emperor, Aidi, was compelled to move his court from Chang'an to Luoyang. In the second month of 904, Chang'an became earth-heaps and waste-land because, as Edward Schafer put it, "Palace buildings, public offices and private dwellings were dismantled, made into rafts on the Wei River, and floated down to Lo-yang."[95] However, a stele preserved in the Museum of the Western Market (*Da Tang xishi bowuguan* 大唐西市博物館) in modern Xi'an suggests that Ximingsi might have existed at least until the middle of the tenth century. The stele, titled *Ximingsi xilou bei* 西明寺戲樓碑 (Stone tablet for the opera tower at Ximingsi), was carved in the third year of Kaiyun 開運 (946), a reign title of Chudi 出帝 (r. 942-946) of the Later Jin Dynasty (936-946). A survey of the history of Chang'an in the brief Five Dynasties period reveals that the central part of the city was renamed *Da'anfu* 大安府 (907) in Later Liang and restored to its original *Jingzhaofu* 京兆府 —— by the sovereign of Later Tang (923-936) as a signal of legitimacy. By 938, Later Jin replaced *Jingzhaofu* with *Jinchangjun* 晉昌軍. In the following dynasties, when metropolitan monasteries no longer decorated the landscape of Chang'an, the city boundary simply shrank dramatically. As a fledgling military garrison in northwestern China, the old Chang'an city was now confined within what was once defined as the imperial city —— a fairly small part of metropolitan Tang Chang'an.[96] The inscription on the stone tablet, only partially legible, prolongs the history of Ximingsi to nearly three centuries, from 658 to somewhere approaching 950:

> In the newly established Ximingsi stood an opera tower, a front gate and a bell tower. Honored by time, they survived from Tang Dynasty to the present day. Weathered by wind and rain, the buildings somehow capsized and fell into disrepair. Now…seeing them in a state of dilapidation, …feel sad and made a

---

[95] For a very brief study of the history of Ximingsi, see Luo Xiaohong 羅小紅, "Tang Chang'an Ximingsi kao 唐長安西明寺考," *Kaogu yu wenwu* 考古與文物 2 (2006): 76-80. Edward Schafer tells us of the chaos of Chang'an in the tenth century; see Schafer, "The Last Years of Chang'an," 168.

[96] Liu Anqin, *Chang'an dizhi*, 113.

vow to repair…, however, it could not be achieved by us alone. The devotees of our society generously agreed to raise the funds. Now it already…perfect, Together…flourishing age, now the project was successfully accomplished…thus marking the immortal work.

創建西明寺內，有戲臺一座，以及大門，鐘樓．自唐及今，由來久矣．而風雨剝蝕，不無傾頹．今*等目睹心惻，發願補*，奈獨立難成．本社信士，慷慨應成…今已*贊成美，共*盛世，功成告竣…以志不朽雲爾．[97]

Indeed, if Ximingsi did survive in the wilds southwest of the ramparts of *Jinchangjun* city, then the inscription provides a window into a philanthropic project that aimed to restore the "immortality" of the monastery, as the vinaya master Chongye had expressed two centuries before, "Although the old flowers fell steadily, the new flowers blossom yet again after the fresh rain. How wonderful it is that the monastery will solidly remain in the world."[98] However, the vision of an immortal Ximingsi was destined to be an unrealized dream sealed in the cultural memory of medieval Tang China.

The preeminence of Ximingsi lasted from its inauguration in a period of great expansion for the Tang Empire in the middle of the seventh century to the chaotic tenth century when the grand kingdom itself became history. This chapter focuses especially on Ximingsi and its major heroes through the historical lens of both Buddhism and the Tang Empire after the height of the Kaiyuan era. Although the last days, especially concerning the destruction of Ximingsi, are among those as yet mostly hidden from our view, this chapter has portrayed Ximingisi as a prominent institution in shaping an extensive Buddhist network, extending from India and Tibet in the west to Japan and Korea in the east. If we return to previous chapters, we will see that many "histories" of Ximingsi, both real and imagined, as illustrated by the whole of chapters 2 through 4, are intriguing in their own right because they illustrate how larger social, economical and ideological trends worked themselves out at a local level in a place like Ximingsi.

On the surface, most of the significant religious activities of the monastery

---

[97] Hu Ji 胡戟, "Ximingsi xilou 西明寺戲樓," in *Shoujie Chang'an fojiao guoji xueshu yantaohui lunwenji disan juan* 首屆長安佛教國際學術研討會論文集第三卷, ed. Zengqin 增勤 (Xi'an: Shanxi shifan daxue chuban zongshe youxian gongsi, 2010), 450-51.

[98] *TB*, 2597-598. We have discussed Chongye's speech in chapter 3.

revolved around the central government. This reveals the fact that, as early as the eighth century, the monastery already defined itself as a shrine of state-protection, and this interdependent relationship of church and state continued through the end of the empire. However, scriptures that may have been produced for superficial political reasons actually found life and value among generations of Buddhist scholars and lay followers across East Asia, including contemporary adherents of Tantrism. In addition, the economic function of a major Tang monastery is also made evident through both the positive and the negative examples of the abbots of Ximingsi, as described in these chapters.

The ongoing transformations in the monastery typically mirrored all the conspicuous changes in the Tang's political and religious order. As a continuation of the monastic history, this chapter is a preliminary step toward understanding the sheer force that bound the monastery and state together. In short, by revealing the rich facts of Ximingsi during the reign of each of the Tang monarchs, for the first time, the fabric of the complete religo-political history of a major Buddhist monastery in Chang'an becomes clear. As a major Tang Buddhist institution that survived the vicissitudes of Chang'an history for nearly three centuries, an institution known for its echelon of eminent scholars and its magnificent building complex, Ximingsi must have a richer multi-faceted story to tell. For instance, the monastery's architectural beauty gave Japanese visitors the impetus to build Daianji; for a period of more than two centuries, the institution also earned a reputation as a site of one of the richest manuscript holdings of East Asian Buddhism. With the historical stage set in the first few chapters, the art-historical and bibliophile culture of Ximingsi will unfold in the following pages. In chapter 5, we will begin this journey by revisiting the artistic world and going further to explore the possibility of reconstructing the monastic plan of Ximingsi.

PART TWO

Art and Scholarship of Ximingsi

Figure. 21   Reconstruction of the Ximingsi Complex. Source: Heng Chye Kiang, *Tang Chang'an de shuma chongjian*, 63.

Chapter Five

A Tale of Three Monasteries: Jetavana, Ximingsi and Daianji

The Problem of Attempted Reconstruction

With the historical details explicated above, in the present chapter, we confine our investigation to the sacred space of Ximingsi, with a focus on the related visual, historical, archaeological and textual sources. The attempted reconstruction of Ximingsi, which will involve three interregional monasteries located in India, China and Japan, will help us understand the mystery of Chang'an monasteries. In retrospect, the on-site investigation of the Buddhist remains of Tang Chang'an, a project that attracted East Asian scholars to the northwestern inland of the Qing Empire (1616-1911), is comparable to the dominance of the Greco-Roman world over the intellectual mind of Europe. In the nineteenth century, endorsed by the burgeoning fields of classical archeology and art history, studies of classical capitals such as Rome and Athens accumulated in large numbers.[1] Like the western idealization of Greco-Roman culture, Oriental writers and scholars, especially those influenced by the long-standing Chinese tradition, indulged their romantic imagination in commemoration of the eternal city of Chang'an. The history of archeological exploration and art historical investigation of Chang'an is beyond the scope of this chapter. The current endeavor is a modest study of a major monastery at

---

[1] For instance, in Germany, since Johann Joachim Winckelmann (1717-68) published his *Geschichte der Kunst des Alterthums* (The History of Ancient Art among the Greeks) in 1764, the tyranny of Greece over Germany has been evident through iconographers, travelers, writers, philosophers and sentimental intellectuals in the last three centuries. See Eliza Butler, *The Tyranny of Greece over Germany* (London: Cambridge University Press, 1935); Fani-Maria Tsigakou, *The Rediscovery of Greece: Travellers and Painters of the Romantic Era* (New Rochelle, N.Y.: Caratzas Brothers, 1981).

a local level, which, it is hoped, can fit into a much broader project on the reconstruction of ancient Chang'an.

If the city of Chang'an enjoyed a reputation as a feast for eyes, it was as a consequence of the institutional success of the Buddhist churches and the magnificent buildings they presented to any visitor. Like other Chinese capitals built over the course of centuries, Chang'an, with thousands of houses dotted like pieces on a chess-board, also reflected a traditional architectural plan which embodied the politico-religious ideology of an orderly cosmos. Like other preindustrial cities that share many traits in the religious realm distinguishing them from industrial-urban centers, Chang'an was described as a "ritual city," for it had its cultural forms centered on the cult centers, temple complexes, tall stūpas, royal courts and rivers meandering throughout the urban jungles of residential wards and the lofty buildings of the imperial palace.[2] Buddhist monasteries, proud of their towering stūpas and multi-storied pavilions, numbering more than one hundred in their heyday, created the most prominent religious skyline of Chang'an city.

One facet of Chang'an's landscape relevant to the subject of the present chapter is the hermeneutics of religious space —— that is to say, interpretation of the sanctified space of Ximingsi in its historical development and stylistic contexts.[3] The unhappy truth is that the monastery itself no long exists, nor did it reincarnate in later dynasties, like a few other Tang counterparts such as the Great Ci'en Monastery or Xingshan Monastery. Reorganized around the grand Tang-period Great Wild Goose Pagoda (Dayanta, see Figure. 22), the Ci'en Monastery, most of which was rebuilt in the Ming Dynasty (1368-1644), was revived as the one of the most valuable cultural sites in modern Xi'an. It is true that any discussion of monastic architecture in classical Chang'an has to face the problem of the paucity of both visual and archaeological resources. Like other cultural sites in Chang'an that were destroyed, the construction and transformation of Ximingsi in its prime remain shrouded in mystery. However, our investigation of the visual culture of Ximingsi can be carried

---

[2] Gideon Sjoberg divides the world's urban centers into the preindustrial city and the industrial city. In preindustrial cities, religion pervades all facets of urban life, and religious ceremonies are crucial in integrating the individual into his community. See Gideon Sjoberg, *The Preindustrial City, Past and Present* (Glencoe, Ill: Free Press, 1960), 256-84.

[3] For some examples of contemporary art history scholarship on Buddhist monasteries, see Gregory Levine, *Daitokuji: the Visual Cultures of a Zen Monastery* (Seattle: University of Washington Press, 2005); Sherry Dianne Fowler, *Muroji: Rearranging Art and History at a Japanese Buddhist Temple* (Honolulu: University of Hawai'i Press, 2005).

out by bringing parallel examples into the discussion. For many years now, art historians of Tang architecture have adopted such a comparative method by looking to Japan for those prominent Buddhist wooden buildings that can aid in the reconstruction of Buddhist architecture in continental East Asia.[4]

Figure. 22   Reconstruction of the Great Wild Goose Pagoda (Dayanta 大雁塔).
Source: Heng Chye Kiang, *Tang Chang'an de shuma chongjian*, 67.

Undoubtedly, as a great monastery and seat of Buddhist learning, Ximingsi was one of the largest and most magnificent building complexes that Chang'an residents had ever seen. The story of the "broken mirror," related in chapter 2, had made the original site of Ximingsi known to both local citizens and foreign travelers. Once the site was designated for the monastery, what had been a closely guarded aristocratic mansion was transformed into the open public space of a religious institution. Due to its convenient proximity to the city market and its reputation as a scenic spot, Ximingsi also became a favorite site among lay visitors and men of letters. Thus it is that the Tang writers, in their texts and conversations, depicted the monastery as a botanical garden full of exotic flora. The monastic flowers, peony in particular, inspired literary pieces written by Bai Juyi, Yuan Zhen, Wen Tingyun and a host of other poets of stature, who wielded their brushes to describe their visits to the monastery. For instance, the late-Tang poet Gu Feixiong 顧非熊 (fl. 836) composed

---

[4] A good example, certainly, is the reconstruction of the Mizong hall of Qinglong Monastery in Xi'an; see Yang Hongxun 楊鴻勳, "Tang Chang'an Qinglongsi mizong diantang (yizhi 4) fuyuan yanjiu 唐長安青龍寺密宗殿堂 (遺址 4) 復原研究," *Kaogu xuebao* 考古學報 3 (1984): 383-401; Nancy Steinhardt, "The Mizong Hall of Qinglongsi: Space, Ritual, and Classicism in Tang Architecture." *Archives of Asian Art* (1991): 27-50.

a poem titled "*The Peony and Mimosa at Ximingsi* "(*Ximingsi hehuan mudan* 西明寺合歡牡丹) around 854, informing us that the beauty of the peony also won the favor of court ladies in the imperial harem.[5] In addition to its fame as a "park" for city-dwellers, Ximingsi boasted dazzling murals and inscriptions contributed by well-known literati and calligraphers of the day. In sum, the monastery served the medieval public as an epigraphic museum and "gallery of Buddhist art," remarkable for its visual splendor, architectural beauty, exquisite statues and a rich collection of steles and wall paintings.

One issue that has puzzled scholars is the original layout of Ximingsi and its likely relationship to other Buddhist shrines in India and Japan. Some sources indicate that the monastery was constructed in accordance with the legendary Jetavana Anāthapiṇḍadasyārāma in India, an exemplary temple held in esteem by the Ximing abbot Daoxuan. It is also believed that generations of Japanese monk-scholars, who observed the magnificence of Ximingsi, presented reports and illustrative records of this earthly paradise to their emperors; and it is suggested, mainly in Japanese sources, that Daianji Monastery, one of the four great temples (*shidaiji* 四大寺) in the Nara period, was modeled after Ximingsi. The ambiguous relationship among the three monasteries —— Jetavana, Ximingsi and Daianji —— will lead to the heart of our discussion. We will pay particular attention to three subjects: Daoxuan's vision of Jetavana as presented in his illustrated scriptures, the problem of Daianji and the mystery of a monastic diagram of doubtful provenance preserved in Hōryūji 法隆寺.

Prior to the middle of the twentieth century, the most significant find of medieval Chinese architecture was the main Buddha hall of Foguang Monastery (Foguangsi 佛光寺). In June 1937, shortly before the Battle of Shanghai, the building complex of Foguang Monastery was found silently situated in the forests of Shanxi province.[6] But one case of some surviving Buddha halls dated back to the Tang is not enough, as art historian Nancy Steinheart has noted, the link of

---

[5] Chen Shangjun, ed., *Quan Tang shi bubian* 全唐詩補編 (Beijing: Zhonghua shuju, 1992), 1109.

[6] When the Society for Research in Chinese Architecture (*Zhongguo yingzhao xueshe* 中國營造學社) was active in 1930s to 1940s, the Chinese architect Liang Sichen 梁思成 (1901-1972) and his research partners found four Tang wooden buildings in Shanxi province, but any attempt to locate more Tang architecture after 1949 inevitably failed. However, some Japanese cities, Nara and Nara prefecture in particular, have preserved about eleven examples of monastic architecture dated before the ninth century. See Liang Sicheng, "Women suo zhidao de Tangdai fosi yu gongdian 我們所知道的唐代佛寺與宮殿," *Zhongguo yingzao xueshe huikan* 中國營造學社彙刊 3, no.1 (1932): 15-46.

architectural genealogy between monasteries in the three East Asian kingdoms, namely, China, Korea and Japan, is broken. More importantly, she thinks that "Except for the east hall of Foguang Monastery, China's twenty earliest wooden buildings tell us mostly about Buddhist architecture in the countryside, and little about her great imperial urban monasteries or possible influences on Buddhist architecture farther east in East Asia."[7] We tend to agree with her that most extant Tang Buddhist buildings were merely architectural remains of small temples dotting the rural landscape. In terms of rank and quality, they were inferior to the grand monasteries in the two capitals, where, as we know from Ennin's diary, a single Buddhist cloister is equal to the entire temple compound of the small town. It was probably for this reason that Ennin and other pilgrims made no comment on the names of these rural buildings in their travelogues. In other words, in contrast to the comprehensive scholarship on medieval Japanese monasteries, the urban Buddhist monasteries of Tang China remain a virgin territory largely unknown to us. Present evidence and current scholarship are thus insufficient for scholars to reconstruct the architectural layout of the premier monasteries of the High Tang.

In spite of the difficulty, however, architectural historians have recently attempted to recapture the urban glory of Chang'an through three-dimensional models. For instance, enormous illuminated models of Tang Chang'an are on display in the local museums and theme parks in Modern Xi'an (Figure.23). In the dynamic field of Digital Humanities, the Singaporean scholar Heng Chye Kiang 王才強 also initiated a project titled "Digital Reconstruction of Chang'an." A small part of his project is devoted to monastic architectures; it relies heavily on the model of Foguang Monastery and images drawn from tomb paintings near Xi'an to partially rebuild what Heng perceived to be the major temples of Chang'an. In his book, which is full of software-generated images and three-dimensional simulations, only one picture refers to the imagined Ximingsi in its prime, which he considers one of the four greatest monasteries in terms of both size and religious significance (Figure.21).[8] He notes, "Modern archaeological excavation had been conducted on

---

[7] Nancy Steinhardt, "Seeing Hōryūji Through China," in *Hōryūji Reconsidered*, ed. Dorothy C Wong and Eric M. Field (Newcastle, UK: Cambridge Scholars Pub., 2008), 83.

[8] Heng Chye Kiang (*pinyin*: Wang Caiqiang 王才強), *Tang Chang'an de shuma chongjian* 唐長安的數碼 重建 (Beijing: Zhongguo jianzhu gongye chubanshe, 2006), 63. The CD-ROM attached to the book also provides a rich collection of pictures produced in the project. To compare digital Chang'an with the ongoing reconstruction of Nara city, see Tsuboi Kiyotari 坪井清足 and Tanaka Migaku 田中琢, *The Historic City*

the site of a side hall of Ximing Monastery. The findings help us to have a better understanding of the layout and magnitude of this important religious complex."[9]

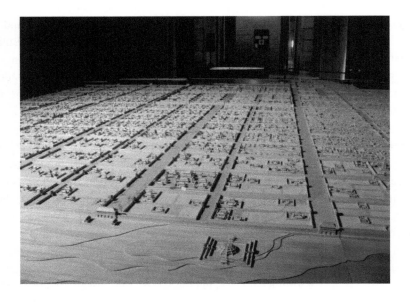

Figure. 23   Wooden Model of Tang Chang'an, Xi'an Museum (Xi'an Bowuyuan 西安博物院). Source: Photo by Wang Xiang, 2008

For our purpose in the present chapter, while historical facts extracted from Buddhist texts are helpful, they are hardly sufficient to solve the mystery of Ximingsi. Hence, in my inquiry into the plan of the monastery, I am more interested in moving from texts to a variety of visual records concerning Ximingsi. While even a discussion combining textual and visual sources is still deficient, it does offer hope of limited progress. In particular, I want to bring into the discussion sources, like the Illustrated Scriptures of Daoxuan, well known to Buddhist art historians but often ignored by religious studies scholars. Thus, with a part of the Ximingsi site now having been excavated in the last century and with some illustrative record now disclosed, I seek in this chapter tentatively to reconstruct as far as currently possible

---

of Nara: An Archaeological Approach (Tokyo: Centre for East Asian Cultural Studies, 1991).
[9] Heng Chye Kiang, *Tang Chang'an de shuma chongjian*, 62.

the temple complex in the tangled cultural sources of the three kingdoms of Buddhist Asia: India, China and Japan.

Geomancy and the Sacred Realm of Ximingsi

Before we cast our gaze on the architectural space of Ximingsi itself, we would do well to attend to the context of the monastery in its environs and the broader cosmological design of Chang'an, since the positioning of the monastery within the city carries a meaning of its own. With this view, we should recall the construction of Sui-Tang Chang'an, for which Chinese cosmological concern was crucial in the overall city plan. As introduced in chapter 1, the canonical paradigm established by *Records for the Scrutiny of Crafts* and the *Book of Changes* provides rough prescriptions for the contour of the city, the number and location of its gates, the road network, and the position of ritual centers, palaces, and markets.[10] We can imagine that a visitor to Chang'an might well be struck with awe while walking along the city's broad thoroughfares. He could hardly miss a gorgeous monastery located between two ridge areas in the nearby Yankang Ward, a district renowned for the palatial residences of the ruling elite.[11] *Chang'an zhi* 長安志 (Record of Chang'an), by Song Mingqiu 宋敏求 (1019-1079) and *Tang Liangjing Chengfang kao* 唐両京城坊考 (Investigation of the Two Tang Capitals and Their Wards) by Xu Song 徐松 (1781-1848) clearly indicate that Yankang Ward was situated to the west of the second street on the western side of Vermilion Street (Figure. 24). In the late 1950s and early 1960s, the Chang'an archaeological team found that the area of Yankang Ward measures 520 meters by 1020 meters. The two streets that flanked Yankang

---

[10] The *Yuanhe junxian tuzhi* 元和郡縣圖志 (An Illustrated Gazetteer of Prefectures and Counties During the Yuanhe Period) is the earliest extant primary source connecting the plan of Chang'an with the two classics. It is believed that Yuwen Kai 宇文愷 (555-612) fully considered geomantic and numerological ingredients in his design of the city. He managed the art of divination as a convenient instrument of policy and acknowledged the general advantages of religion. For detailed analysis of the city plan of Chang'an, see Xiong, *Sui-Tang Chang'an*, 31-54; Seo Tatsuhiko, *Chōan no toshi keikaku* 長安の都市計畫 (Tokyo: Kōdansha, 2001), 86-152.

[11] Seo Tatsuhiko, "The Urban Systems of Chang'an in the Sui and Tang Dynasties A.D.583-907," in *Historic Cities of Asia: An Introduction to Asian Cities from Antiquity to Pre-modern Times*, ed. Muhammad Abdul Jabbar Beg (Kuala Lumpur, Malaysia: Percetakan Ban Huat Seng, 1986), 159-200. Victor Cunrui Xiong thinks the most noticeable development in Yankang Ward after the High Tang was the establishment of new quarters for the Administrative Office of Princes (*zhuwangfu* 諸王府). The new office served as a base for the staff of the princes when they were on duty at the capital; see Xiong, *Sui -Tang Chang'an*, 231.

were each about forty meters wide.[12]

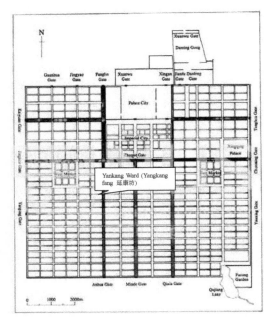

Figure. 24 Chang'an and Its "Six Avenues" (*liujie* 六街)." Source: Heng Chye Kiang, *Tang Chang'an de shuma chongjian*, 21.

It is assumed that the terrain of Chang'an was divided into six ridge areas running from northeast to southwest (Figure.25). Yuwen Kai, the vice director-general of the project, then matched the ridges with the diagram *qian* 乾, the only hexagram composed of six solid lines in the *Book of Changes*. It is believed that no other hexagram is as fraught with royal symbolism of the entrepreneurial spirit as *qian,* the quintessential graph of Heaven. Due to its celestial signification, this diagram came to be closely identified with the court and its sovereign, and also with the "superior man" or *junzi* 君子, a figure held up as the paragon of virtue. Ximingsi, contextualized in Yankang Ward, was situated between the third and the fourth ridges, a place explained by the *Book of Changes* and its commentary as nonroyal yet

---

[12] An Jiayao, "Tang Chang'an Ximingsi yizi de kaogu faxian," 338. We should give credit to Hiraoka Takeo 平岡武夫 (1909-95) for his meticulous work on the map of Chang'an; see Takeo Hiraoka and Imai Kiyoshi 今井清, *Tōdai no Chōan to Rakuyō* 唐代の長安と洛陽 (Kyoto: Dōhōsha, 1977); idem., *Tang dai de Chang'an he Luoyang ditu* 唐代的長安與洛陽地圖 (Shanghai: Shanghai guji Chubanshe, 1991).

containing favorable locations for living quarters and markets.[13] The monastery was also interconnected with the main waterway of the western half of Chang'an, the River of Jiao (Jiaoqu 交渠, Figure.1), a city canal established in the Sui Dynasty. Fed from the suburban Xiangji Monastery (Xiangjisi 香積寺), the river went on to flow towards the northwestern region of Chang'an. Before the river found its confluence in the West Market —— the "downtown area" of the city —— it passed through the western walls of six consecutive residential wards including Yankang.[14]

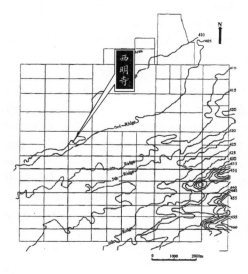

Figure. 25   The Six Ridges (liupo 六坡) of Chang'an. Source: Xiong, Sui-Tang Chang'an, xxiii (Illustration 2.3. Topography of Chang'an).

Among some one hundred odd residential wards in Chang'an, those adjacent to the imperial palaces were regularly adorned with one to two monasteries; but it is not easy to discern the motives behind the construction of Ximingsi in this location. It is possible that Gaozong had consulted with Xuanzang on the matter before he issued

---

[13] See Xiong, Sui-Tang Chang'an, 45-46; Thomas Thilo, Chang'an: Teil 1, 23-40; For an explanation of the eight trigrams (bagua 八卦) used in Taoist cosmology, see Daeyeol Kim, "Bagua," in Encyclopedia of Taoism, ed. Fabrizio Pregadio (London; New York: Routledge, 2008), 201-03.

[14] Xu Song and Li Jianchao, Zengding Tang liangjing chengfangkao, 233. As Heng Chye Kiang says, "At least seven major canals were built during the Sui and Tang periods to help improve transportation and ensure the provision of the city needs which came largely from the Lower Yangzi region. The many private gardens beyond the earthen walls of the enclosed wards also depended on the excellent irrigation system of the city both within and beyond the wards. The banks of the canals were lined with trees and became the subject of some memorable Tang poems." See Heng Chye Kiang, Tang Chang'an de shuma chongjian, 26.

the imperial edict, but locating one of the most important national monasteries in the southwestern quadrant of Yankang must have other considerations. It is worth noticing in this regard that other geomantic factors played a role in the deployment of Buddhist and Daoist monasteries in Chang'an. Victor Cunrui Xiong summarizes the theory this way:

> By far the most common location for Buddhist and Daoist structures was in the southwest quadrant of a ward. It was standard practice in Sui-Tang Chang'an to locate religious institutions in problem areas to suppress their evil influences, and the southwestern locations of important religious institutions indicate the widespread awareness of geomantic theory among patrons.[15]

Therefore the question becomes, "was the southwestern corner of Yankang Ward a problem area in the early Tang?" As discussed in chapter 2, the dark prehistory of Ximingsi does suggest that such a problem already existed in the Sui dynasty, a few decades predating the founding of the monastery: the tragedy of Yang Xuangan followed by the exile of Prince Li Tai, both of which were known stories that had became the subject matter of tavern yarns. It was shortly after the demise of Li Tai, that the Tang government reclaimed the property and erected a monastery. What had befallen the aristocratic mansion no doubt made the city inhabitants believe that the residence was charged with an enervating force that required expulsion.

Exactly what Xuanzang had in mind when he was commissioned to examine the abandoned residence is unknown to us, but the traditional procedure of inspecting a site, sometimes called geomantic siting (*xiangzhai* 相宅, see Figure.26), has to take into consideration a variety of elements. Steinhardt points out:

> Siting describes the belief that natural phenomena, mountains, wind, water must be harmoniously interrelated at a site in order to ensure auspicious human existence. The practice of divination for the purpose of determining a positive balance of natural forces before selecting a site is often called *fengshui* or *kanyu*, both sometimes translated as Chinese geomancy.[16]

---

[15] Xiong, *Sui-Tang Chang'an*, 48-49.

[16] One pictorial record of the practice of siting is a Qing-Dynasty illustration titled "*The Diviner Inspects [a Site] for a Dwelling (Taibao xiangzhai tu* 太保相宅圖, Figure.26)," see Steinhardt, *Chinese Imperial City Planning*, 12; cf. Ronald G. Knapp, *China's Living Houses: Folk Beliefs, Symbols,*

Figure. 26   The Diviner Inspects [a Site] for a Dwelling (*Taibao xiangzhai tu* 太保相宅圖). Source: Thomas Thilo, *Klassische chinesische Baukunst: strukturprinzipien und soziale Funktion*, 222.

The application of *fengshui* 風水 (geomancy, lit. wind and water) and *kanyu* 堪輿 (topomancy, lit. heaven and earth) are similar concepts practices derived from traditional Chinese cosmology, including the five elements and the divination system contained in such works as the *Book of Changes* and *Fengsu tongyi* 風俗通義 (The Comprehensive Meaning of Customs). This geomantic siting technique was not only applied in grand city planning but also widely used for selecting sites for individual residences and religious compounds. As James Robson points out, the role of siting for Chinese Buddhist monasteries, which is downplayed by many scholars, is actually a necessary step to convert the monastery into a sacred site.[17] Thanks to Su Ting,

---

and *Household Ornamentation* (Honolulu: University of Hawai'i Press, 1999), 29-39.

[17] Holmes Welch, in his *The Practice of Chinese Buddhism, 1900-1950* (Cambridge: Harvard University Press, 1968), gives us another example of siting a Buddhist monastery by the eminent maser Xuyun 虛雲 (1840-1959). However, Welch thinks Xuyun's suggestion as heretical. James Robson argues against him, saying that one of the main elements found in the monastic records in medieval China was a treatment of the special qualities, or anomalous elements of the natural setting; see Benn, Meeks, and Robson, *Buddhist Monasticism in East Asia*, 59.

whose inscription on Ximingsi is imbued with rich detail, we have a glimpse of the procedures that Xuanzang took:

> At first, [Xuanzang] was dispatched [by the emperor] to inspect the length and area of the residence. He [had people] measure the land with rope and ink markers. Then [the emperor] appointed two junior judges, Wu Xing and Shen Qianzhi, as his assistants. They exhausted tax revenues and the State coffers to establish the monastery. [First of all they] made a miniature model on the basis of the monastery. The process of making the blueprint had used carpentry's square. They drew water from the northern hills and cut timber from the southern mountains…it adhered to the balance of Yin and Yang elements and was situated evenly along the meridional line.

> 首命視延袤廣輪, 往以繩度, 還而墨順. 次命少監吳興, 沈謙之, 傾水衡之藏. 徹河宗之府.[18] 制而縮版, 參以懸槼; 鉤北阜之舄, 伐南山之枚…揆陰陽之中, 居子午之直.[19]

The prose brings to life the preparatory work prior to construction ——measurement and creation of building plans. Whether the latter was simply a site plan or a scale model is unclear, but the inscription offers clues as to the instruments that were used in the process. Scholars have tended to measure the achievement of pre-modern Chinese cartography in terms of its application of numerical technique and specialized tools. In this case, it is believed that a group of carpenters and cartographers, equipped with compasses, graduated rods (*guiju* 規矩) and plumb lines (*shengmo* 繩墨), were involved in the initial inspection superintended by Xuanzang (Figure. 27). Together these tools could be used to measure the size of the residence, so that the cartographer could then draw up a blueprint.[20] It is suspected

---

[18] In different editions of the *TB*, there are alternative characters used in the same paragraph. Here I compare the *Quan Tang wen* 全唐文 (The Complete Prose of the Tang, 1814) edition of the *TB* with the *Wenyuan yinghua* 文苑英華 (Finest Blossoms in the Garden of Literature, 987) edition, an anthology of poetry, odes, songs and writings from the Liang Dynasty to the Five Dynasties era (abbreviated as *Wenyuan yinghua*). See Li Fang 李昉, *Wenyuan yinhua* (Beijing: Zhonghua shuju, 1966), 4517. Su Ting also composed the *Stone Tablet for longxingsi in Shanzhou* (*Shanzhou longxingsi bei* 陝州龍興寺碑).

[19] *TB* 2597; *Wenyuan yinghua*, 4517; Zhou Shaoliang 周紹良, ed., *Quantangwen xinbian* 全唐文新編, vol. 2 (Changchun: Jilin wenshi cubanshe, 2000), 2873.

[20] Cordell Yee shows that by the Song dynasty, if not before, the Chinese already possessed the means to

that in the case of Ximingsi, *suoban* 縮版, or a "blueprint", suggests that such conventional carpentry and workmanship were already widely used in the construction of religious establishments in Tang China.[21] German art historian Lothar Ledderose points out that the traditional modular system (*mojian* 模建), elaborated in the architectural canon *Yingzao fashi* 營造法式 (Treatise on Architectural Methods or State Building Standards), runs through Chinese art and architecture. Certainly, the modular pattern would have been quite efficient in the mass production of building materials required for a grand project like Ximingsi.[22] Ledderose uses the Tang-dynasty Foguang Monastery as an example:

> The main hall of Foguangsi is a fine specimen in the pervasive and all-encompassing system of Chinese post and beam architecture. The system comprises several levels of increasing complexity. One can distinguish the five levels of bracketing, bays, buildings, courtyards, and cities, each of which merits a closer look at its technical aspects as well as some economic and social implications.[23]

Figure. 27 Calculation of Distance Using a Sighting Board, Water Level, and Graduated Rod (from the *Siku quanshu* 四庫全書 edition of the *Wujing zongyao* 武經總要). Source: J. B. Harley and David Woodward, ed., *The History of Cartography*, vol. 2, bk. 2, *Cartography in the Traditional East and Southeast Asian Societies*, 117.

---

produce maps based on direct and indirect measurements. Such techniques are often used to justify claims of a distinct quantitative tradition of Chinese cartography. See Cordell Yee, "Taking the World's Measure: Chinese Maps between Observation and Text," in *The History of Cartography*, vol. 2, bk. 2, *Cartography in the Traditional East and Southeast Asian Societies*, eds. J. B. Harley and David Woodward (Chicago: University of Chicago Press, 1994), 116.

[21] Here *suoban* could refer to "miniature model," but the word also means "binding wallboards with ropes," a building technology used in ancient China; cf. *Hanyu da cidian*, s.v. *suoban*; *Kōjien*, s.v. *shukuban*.

[22] The modular system is also known as *moshu* 模數 (mode number) or *caifenzhi* 材份制 (system of material and part). On the conception of module in Chinese art and architecture, see Lothar Ledderose, *Ten Thousand Things: Module and Mass Production in Chinese Art* (Princeton, NJ: Princeton University Press, 2000), 103-20; On the scale and standard of Tang-Song architecture, see Xiao Min 肖旻, *Tang Song gujianzhu chidu guilü yanjiu* 唐宋古建築尺度規律研究 (Nanjing: Dongnan daxue chuban she, 2006).

[23] Ledderose, *Ten Thousand Things*, 107.

134

The making of the mock-up of Ximingsi was a necessary procedure so that the timber-framed modules could be applied accordingly. Then, using all the science and art technologies available, the builders and carpenters would be entrusted to execute the project according to their skills. The existence of a miniature model or blueprint of Ximingsi also agrees with the boom of "illustrated canon" (*tujing* 圖經) in the early Tang. We can infer that such a site plan and model, in all likelihood preserved in the Ximingsi collection, might have inspired Dōji to sketch out his own copy of Ximingsi.

Another factor that we should consider here is the popular practice of conversion of Chinese-style residence into Buddhist monastery in medieval China. After the victory of the imperial Li Clan, donating private houses to serve as monasteries became prevalent among the rich upper class, a trend prominent in the two capitals of the empire. As a result of their generosity, buildings imbued with distinctive Chinese aesthetic principles shaped the monastic landscape in Chang'an. Local carpenters and workers might have found themselves accustomed to the exponential growth of commissions to convert traditional Chinese secular architecture to Buddhist monasteries. The way they built the monasteries was understandably in accordance with traditional Chinese geomantic ideas. That is to say, if according to Su Ting's inscription, Ximingsi was coherent with "the balance of the Yin-Yang elements and situated along the meridional line," then it must, like many other solemn structures in urban Chang'an, open its main gate to the south, facing the grand forty-meter wide street dividing Yankang and Chongxian Wards (Chongxian fang 崇賢坊).[24]

Also worthy of note is that it took less than two years for the grand project of Ximingsi to be completed, in the sixth month of 658 (Xianqin 3). Given the location of the residence and the monastery's rank on the social ladder, the construction timeline must have been greatly shortened. Apparently, the former residential chambers of Li Tai and Yang Su were incorporated into the new architectural layout so as to shorten the construction time. Compared with the construction of its Japanese

---

[24] Intertestingly, *Essays in Idleness* (*Tsurezuregusa* 徒然草, 1331), a collection of Japanese essays written by the Buddhist monk Yoshida Kenkō 吉田兼好 (1283-1350), says that "The Hsi-ming Temple in China of course faces north [Jap. *Tōdo no Saimyōji wa kitamuki no mochiron nari* 唐土の西明寺は北向きの勿論なり]." See Yoshida Kenkō, *Essays in Idleness: The Tsurezuregusa of Kenko*, trans. Donald Keene (New York: Columbian University Press, 1967), 155.

twin, Daianji, which took some fourteen years to complete, the two-year deadline must have allowed little room to drastically alter the existing architectural structure as the finished complex involved thousands of rooms and more than a dozen huge Buddhist cloisters. Still, we may infer that a considerable number of new monastic elements, such as stūpa, sūtra-repository, bell tower, and ordination platform, filled the grounds of the former residence and that the entire complex was newly decorated with Buddhist elements. Again, Huili tells us of a chain of events that took place in 658:

> This monastery was constructed on the nineteenth day of the eighth month, in the autumn of the first year of Xianqing (656)…The Buddhist monastery was built first; and the construction was completed in the sixth month, during-the summer of the same [third] year…On the thirteenth day of that month a ceremony of ordination was performed in the monastery, and the Master was invited to supervise the ordination. On the fourteenth day of the seventh month, in the autumn, the monks were welcomed into the monastery…[25]

A careful reading of the text reveals a curious interval of about one month between the inauguration of the monastery and the formal date of opening. We may well wonder what the monks accomplish during this period besides performing the ordination ceremony.

While of course we cannot give a definitive answer to this question, it is not unreasonable to imagine that, especially given the troubled history of the site, it was necessary to perform a ritual of exorcism to dispel evil forces prior to the official entry ceremony. According to medieval sources, in addition to selecting an auspicious day to enter the house, the new owner of a house should invite religious adepts to perform an entry ritual titled "procedure of entering a house (*ruzhaifa* 入宅法)."[26]

---

[25] Li Rongxi, *Biography of the Tripiṭaka Master*, 325-26.

[26] For instance, *wuxing zhaijing* 五姓宅經 (P. 3281V), a Dunhuang manuscript dated in the Tang period, prescribes a ceremony containing seven steps leading to the official opening of a new house, which usually lasted for several days. Comparing it with the tantric ritual prescribed in the *Dhāraṇī Collection Scripture* (*Tuoluoni jijing* 陀羅尼集經, T885), Yu Xin points out that the similarity between the two texts is no coincidence, since the tantric text concerned with apotropaic rituals spread widely in Dunhuang and could have easily found expression in the secular ceremony of house-entering. see Yu Xin, *Shendao renxin*, 187-88. The "five surnames" (*wuxing* 五姓) refers to the five elements in Chinese geomancy, namely, *gong* 宮, *shang* 商, *jiao* 角, *zhi* 微 and *yu* 羽; see also *Zongjing lu* 宗鏡錄 (Record of the Axiom Mirror), T48, no.

Buddhist Studies scholars will immediately recognize that the Dunhuang document *Wuxing zhaijing* 五姓宅經 (P. 3281V, Book of the Dwelling of the Five Surnames), as well as the basic ideology of exorcism, prescribe the process of establishing an apotropaic realm called *jiejie* 結界 (Skt. *sīmābandha*; Jap. *kekkai*). *Jiejie* is a sacred place typically established through consecration rituals or sūtra-chanting. Imperceptible though it may, the sacred space created is capable of covering an entire monastery, a specified ritual zone or even a whole mountain (Figure.28). The space is then endowed with the power to eliminate the influences of vice and expel evil deities, so that it transformed into a purified place suitable for Buddhist practice.[27]

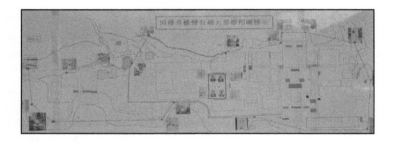

Figure. 28   The Map of *jiejie* 結界 (Skt. *sīmābandha*) at Biechuansi 別傳寺 (*Biechuansi sheseng youchang dajie biaoxiangtu bangshi* 別傳寺攝僧有場大界標相圖榜示), Mount Danxia (Danxiashan 丹霞 山), Guangdong Province. Source: Photo by Wang Xiang, 2011.

2016, p. 554, c1-20. However, other tantric scriptures such as the *Scripture of Pacifying the House* (*Foshuo anzhai shenzhou jing* 佛說安宅神咒經, T1394) might also apply in this case. French scholars are particularly interested in medieval Chinese divination and geomancy, see Chi Hsiao and Marc Kalinowski, *Cosmologie et divination dans la Chine ancienne: le compendium des cinq agents* (Paris: Ecole française d'Extrême Orient: Adrien-Maisonneuve, 1991); Marc Kalinowski, ed., *Divination et société dans la Chine médiévale: étude des manuscrits de Dunhuang de la bibliothèque nationale de France et de la british library* (Paris: Bibliothèque nationale de France, 2003).

[27] *Tuoluoni jijing*, T18, no. 0, p. 885, b20-p. 897, b18, For the *kekkai* drawn on the map of Shōmyōji 稱名 寺 (Monastery of Chanting the Holy Invocation), a monastery belonging to the Japanese Shingon Vinaya Sect (Shingon risshū 真言律宗), see Matsubara Seiji 松原誠司 and Yoshida Toshihiro 吉田敏弘, "Shōmyōji ezu to kekkaiki —— sono shiryō hihan no kokoromi (okushū: Shōmyōji ezu) 称名寺絵図と結 界記 —— その史料批判の試み (特集: 称名寺絵図)," *Kanazawa Bunko kenkyū* 金沢文庫研究 (1997): 3-24 .

It would require hard evidence to determine whether the practice of establishing *sīmābandha* to inaugurate a monastery was common in the early Tang; but given the increasing influence of tantrism and the promotion of apotropaic rituals in secular texts of the time, this would hardly be surprising. And, considering the dark prehistory of the residence, a major Buddhist institution like Ximingsi would certainly have had reason to adopt precautionary measures and rites of purification.[28] Prescriptions for *sīmābandha* were available in the translated vinaya canon and tantric scriptures current in the Tang Dynasty. The Ximing Abbot, Daoxuan, was a savant of vinaya studies and is well-known in Buddhist history as an "India" enthusiast. Given that establishing a *jiejie* was a crucial step in sacralizing a monastery, it would have been impossible for him to bypass the necessary procedures prescribed in scripture. As declared many times in the *Dhāraṇī Collection Scripture* (*Tuoluoni jijing* 陀羅尼集經, T885), an esoteric text translated by Atigupta (Ch. Adijueduo 阿地瞿多) in 654, a purified realm with *sīmābandha* is seen as the supreme location in which to erect a Buddha hall.[29] Atigupta had arrived in Chang'an in 651 and was installed at Ci'en Monastery; there he became acquainted with the head of Ximingsi, Xuanzang, and Xuanzang's biographer Yancong 彥悰 (627-649). These circumstances gave both Xuanzang and Daoxuan, who was assisting the former in his atelier, the opportunity to be acquainted with the procedures of establishing a variety of *jiejie* described in the *Dhāraṇī Collection Scripture*.[30] There are grounds, then, to speculate that, during the month between the completion of the monastery and the admission of the monks, Xuanzang and Daoxuan were engaged in rites to appease the local spirits, evoke protector deities, and convert Ximingsi from a haunted aristocratic mansion to an idealized Buddhist paradise.

---

[28] Establishing a *jiejie* within or outside a monastery was practiced in Chinese monasteries for more than a thousand years. It is required especially during the summer retreat. The practice has revived among monasteries which strictly follow the vinaya tradition. For instance, in today's Guangdong province, if visitors go to the Beichuan Monastery (Biechuansi 別傳寺) located at Mount Danxia (Danxiashan 丹霞山), they will find an illustrated *jiejie* map defining a major territory of Beichuan Monastery (*Biechuansi sheseng youchang dajie biaoxiangtu bangshi* 別傳寺攝僧有場大界標相圖榜示, figure.28).

[29] For instance, see *Tuoluoni jijing*, T18, no. 901, p. 813, c26-p. 814, a23.

[30] *Tuoluoni jijing*, T18, no. 901, p. 886, c22-24. For Daoxuan's remark on the purification of a Buddha Hall, see *Sifenlü shanfan buque xingshichao* 四分律刪繁補闕行事鈔, T40, no. 1804, p. 134, c20-21.

Buddhist Cloisters as Revealed Through Textual Sources

In the seventh month of 658, as we have seen, the specially selected Buddhist community of Ximingsi settled down in the newly established sacred realm of the monastery. Only some thirty years later did the Ximing rector Huili provide his first-hand description of the architecture and environment within the monastic walls. He and Yancong, the two authors of Xuanzang's biography, are believed to have personally witnessed the growth of the monastery. The *Biography of Xuanzang*, edited by Huili before 688 (Chuigong 垂拱 4), predated Su Ting's inscription for the monastery by three decades. According to the biography:

> The Monastery was 350 *bu* on each side, with a circumference of several *li*.[31] On both the left and right sides there were thoroughfares, while in the front and at the back there were markets and hamlets. Green locust trees were planted in rows outside the buildings, and a brook of limpid water flowed through the compound. With many imposing and spacious buildings constructed exquisitely, this was the most magnificent Buddhist monastery in the capital. The corridors, halls, storeyed houses, and terraces were so tall that they would frighten flying birds and touch the Galaxy. The gilded door knockers and the beams painted in colors were as dazzling as the glow of sunlight. There were ten courtyards with more than four thousand rooms. The whole establishment was so splendidly decorated that neither Tongtai Monastery of the Liang dynasty nor Yongning Monastery of the Wei dynasty could surpass it.[32]

The matching of textual sources and archaeological discovery makes the literary texts Huili and Su Ting provide credible sources. First of all, Huili's account tells us, from east to west, the monastery measured 350 paces (*bu* 步). According to the calculation of the Chinese archaeologist An Jiayao, in Tang China, 350 paces equal 514.5 meters, very close to the 500 meters measured in the first excavation of Ximingsi (Figure.29).[33] Secondly, in chapter 3, we saw that Master Chongye commented on

---

[31] The original text for this sentence reads: "其寺面三百五十步,周圍数里" (*SZFSZ*, T50, no. 2053, p. 275, b27-28). I think Li Rongxi's translation should be modified, as the character *mian* 面, refers to the façade of Ximingsi, not "each side" of the monastery.

[32] Li Rongxi, *A Biography of the Tripitaka Master*, 325-26. *SZFSZ*, T50, no. 2053, p. 275, b21-c4.

[33] An Jiayao, "Tang Chang'an Ximingsi yizi de kaogu faxian," 341.

the reincarnation of the ruined building complex as the newly erected monastery. His speech also shed light on the environment of Ximingsi. Su Ting's inscription of Chongye's account, carved on the stūpa tablet, informs us that clear channels (*qingqu* 清渠) lined the monastic roads, with green trees planted in rows, thus suggesting that a small stream ran through the monastery.[34] It testifies to our understanding that the River Jiao, a canal built in the Sui Dynasty, meandered through the western part of Yankang Ward, probably also cleaving Yang Su's residence in halves. In a city dominated by wooden buildings, running water, ponds and brooks were favorable factors that the designers of Ximingsi had to consider in its overall plan.

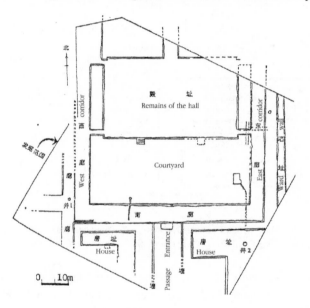

Figure. 29   1985 Archaeological Map of Ximingsi (First Excavation). Source: Ho Puay-Peng, "The Ideal Monastery: Daoxuan's Description of the Central Indian Jetavana Vihara," 9.

To picture the setting of Ximingsi in the southwest quadrant of Yankang Ward, we must remember that it was located within a castle-like walled residential ward with a central gate on each of the four sides. The Yangang Ward was divided into four equal quadrants by broad avenues, fifteen meters wide. Each of the huge rectangular

---

[34] *TB*, 2597-598

living zones (quadrants) was identical in area with Ximingsi itself (Figure.30). With the northern and eastern walls of Ximingsi built in parallel with the two internal, central avenues of the ward, four lengthy streets encircled the monastery, making its gates on all four sides of its walls open onto major thoroughfares.

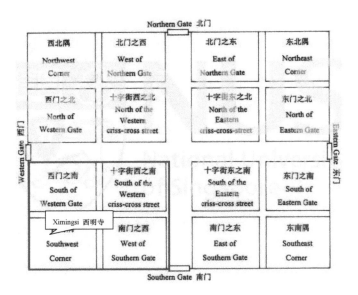

Figure. 30   Layout of a Residential Ward (e.g. Yankang fang) in Chang'an.
Source: Heng Chye Kiang, *Tang Chang'an de shuma chongjian*, 49.

We may get some sense of the grand scale and magnificence of Ximingsi through descriptions of comparable monasteries established in Chang'an and Luoyang. One of them was Jing'aisi, or the Monastery of Reverence and Love. Located in Luoyang, Jing'aisi was sponsored by the young prince Li Hong to repay the kindness of his parents. Under imperial auspices, this monastery produced two major catalogues of the Buddhist canon. The scale and expenditure of Jing'aisi were consistent with that of Ximingsi, costing about 200,000 in cash. "The splendor of its precincts, halls, sacred images, pennants, and furnishings match the celestial order. The ingenuity of the workmanship equals the work of spirits and demons."[35] Another

---

[35] Eugene Yuejin Wang, *Shaping the Lotus Sutra: Buddhist Visual Culture in Medieval China* (Seattle,

141

religious institution modeled after Ximingsi was the Daoist Dongming Guan, located in the southeastern quadrant of Puning Ward in Chang'an. As we have seen in chapter 3, the Yankang site was originally supposed to house both Ximingsi and a Daoist temple; but after inspection of the site, Xuanzang had concluded that it was too narrow to situate two religious establishments, and as a result Dongming Guan was separately constructed in Puning Ward. According to Xu Song's *Tang liangjing chengfang kao*, Dongming Guan's display of beauty was unmatched among Daoist monasteries, for it had long corridors and vast halls elaborately decorated with wall paintings and figurative images.[36] The literary works in which these accounts of Ximingsi and other monasteries are found may not be entirely trustworthy as historical records, but they are rich social documents that suggest how these institutions were experienced by contemporary commentators.

In their essays edited or composed between the late seventh and early eighth century, both Huili and Su Ting provide a rough number of the cloisters (*yuan* 院) within Ximingsi, a factor central to any reconstruction of the monastery in its prime. During the course of over three centuries disrupted by rebellion and war, the number of cloisters might well have changed somewhat but probably not dramatically. Unfortunately, while showing some relation to each other, the extant sources are not entirely consistent on the number of cloisters at Ximingsi. According to Huili, the monastery consisted of ten cloisters with more than 4000 rooms.[37] Su Ting, who wrote his text about twenty-eight years later, put the number of cloisters at twelve.[38] To make the matter more complicated, *Fozu tongji* 佛祖統紀 (A Chronicle of Buddhism in China, T2035), a thirteenth-century history of Chinese Tiantai Buddhism, claims that Ximingsi possessed of thirteen great halls and 4000 pavilions, towers, verandas and corridors.[39] Regardless of the slight difference; these records

---

Wash.: University of Washington Press, 2005), 132; Wang Huimin 王惠民, "Tang dongdu Jing'aisi kao 唐東都敬愛寺考," *Tang yanjiu* 12 (2006): 357-77; Zhang Yanyuan also offers a detailed account of the statues and wall paintings at Jing'aisi, which helps us imagine the artistic world of Ximingsi. For an English translation and analysis of the account of Jing'aisi written by Zhang Yanyuan, see Eugene Wang, "Pictorial Program in the Making of Monastic Space: From Jing'aisi of Luoyang to Cave 217 at Dunhuang," In *Buddhist Monasticism in East Asia: Places of Practice*, ed. James Benn, Lori Meeks and James Robson (New York: Routledge, 2010), 68.

[36] Xu Song and Li Jianchao, *Zengding Tang liangjing chengfang kao*, 244.

[37] Li Rongxi, *A Biography of the Tripitaka Master*, 325-26. The original text is a rare account of the scale of Buddhist cloisters at Ximingsi; it reads, "有十院，屋四千餘間," see *SZFSZ*, T50, no. 2053, p. 275, b21-c4.

[38] The original reads: "凡十有二所，每動微風，滴細霤." See *TB*, 2597; *Wenyuan yinghua*, 4517.

[39] The original reads: "大殿十三所，樓臺廊廡四千區." See *Fozu tongji*, T49, no. 2035, p. 367, a24-26.

agree that, from the middle of the seventh century to the early eighth century, Ximingsi had already been reincarnated from an abandoned residence to a sacred realm of ten to thirteen monastic courtyards, each of which was surrounded by long corridors, and contained 300 to 400 rooms.

Other reliable sources, especially the "art historical" texts rich in facts concerning wall paintings and statues, offer clue to the layout and art space of Ximingsi in the ninth century. According to existing evidence, it is believed that at least sixty-four urban monasteries in Chang'an had their walls painted by sixty-six painters.[40] Among these monasteries, Ximingsi was not only a famous sight-seeing spot but also a "museum" renowned for paintings and calligraphic works. Tang poet Wen Tingyun praised the monastery in his *Ti Ximingsi sengyuan* 題西明寺僧院 (Poem Written on the Wall of the Buddhist Cloister of Ximingsi): "I came here to the monks' cloister to look for famous paintings; while visiting a person at leisure I had the opportunity to watch them play *weiqi* [the game of go, Jap. *igo* 囲碁]."[41]

Zhang Yanyuan 張彥遠 (815-874), in his *A Record of the Famous Painters of All the Dynasties* (*Lidai minghuaji* 歷代名畫記), provides a brief report on the wall paintings of Ximingsi:

[*There is a frontal plaque written by Liu Tze-kao who was a Literatus of the Nan-hsün palace during the reign of the Emperor Hsüan Tsung (712-755)*]. The wall to the south as you enter the west gate has two paintings of divinities by Yang T'ing-kuang. They have been spoiled by being finished in colours. On the east side of the east cloister corridor in the first wall section are Transmitters of the Dharma (patriarchs) with a eulogy in the handwriting of Ch'u Sui-liang. In the third wall section (is the painting of) Li Fang and others. [42] In the fourth wall sections is (a portrait of) T'an-k'o-chia-lo with (an inscription in) the handwriting of Ou-yang T'ung. To the east of this temple on of the tiles (?) of the wall of Ch'ung-fu-sze are landscapes by Ch'en Chi-shan. In the Cloister of

---

[40] Wei Yanjian 魏嚴堅, "Tangdai chang'an siyuan de bihua yu huajia 唐代長安寺院的壁畫與畫家," *Guoli Taizhong jishu xueyuan renwen shehui xuebao* 國立臺中技術學院人文社會學報 3 (2004): 59-78. Bi Fei 畢斐 thinks the number of monasteries that had wall paintings should be forty-five, see Bi Fei, *Lidai minghua ji lungao* 歷代名畫記論稿 (Hangzhou: Zhongguo meishu xueyuan chubanshe, 2008), 165-67.

[41] The original reads "為尋名畫來過院, 困訪閒人得看棋." See *QTS* 578.16.

[42] According to Daoshi's account, Lifang 利防 was a foreign monk who brought Buddhist scriptures to China during the period of Qin Shihuang 秦始皇 (r. 221-210 BCE), the first Emperor of China; see *Fayuan zhulin*, T53, no. 2122, p. 379, a6-9.

the Three Phases are paintings by Ts'ai Chin-kangand Fan Ch'ang-shou.[43]

The record is dated in the ninth century, somewhere between 847 and 854; however, it contains information regarding the artwork produced since the founding of Ximingsi. In the seventh century, a fascination with a utopian India in Buddhist circles had prompted leading monasteries to commission painters and calligraphers to render the images of eminent foreign translators on their monastic walls.[44] It is clear that Ci'en Monastery had its Hall for Translating the Sūtras (Fanjingtang 翻經堂) decorated with portraits of past translators, and Ximingsi probably followed suit.

Chu Suiliang 褚遂良 (596-658), mentioned in our passage as having left his handwriting on the *Illustrated Eulogy of the Transmitters of the Dharma* (*Chuanfazhe tuzan* 傳法者圖贊), was one of the four great calligraphers of the early Tang period; he was active between 636 and 658 and died the year that Ximingsi was founded.[45] Thus, if Zhang Yanyuan's report is to be believed, the *Illustrated Eulogy of the Transmitters of the Dharma* in the first wall section of the east cloister corridor must have been the earliest wall paintings of Ximingsi, with the other paintings and calligraphic works added later. The calligrapher Ouyang Tong 歐陽通 (d. 691), who authored the inscription for the portrait of Dharmakala (Tankejialuo 曇柯迦羅, 3th c.), was considerably younger than Chu Suiliang and officiated as Minister of Defense in the latter half of the seventh century.

Zhang Yanyuan's report also informs us of the existence of a West Gate (*ximen* 西門) opening out, presumably, to the street between Yankang and Huaiyuan Wards (Huaiyuan fang 懷遠坊).[46] It is not clear whether the East Corridor (*donglang* 東廊) mentioned here belongs to the central Buddhist cloister or refers to the eastern-most corridor of the monastery. I presume it refers to the elongated central cloister of Ximingsi, which would have served as the main area for ritual activity and public

---

[43] William Reynolds Beal Acker, *Some T'ang and Pre-T'ang Texts on Chinese Painting, Translated and Annotated* (Leiden: E.J. Brill, 1954), 293-94; Zhang Yanyuan, *Lidai minghua ji*, 68.

[44] *Kaiyuan shijiao lu*, T55, no. 2154, p. 562, b2-8.

[45] The other three early Tang calligraphers celebrated with Chu Suiliang are Ouyang Xun 歐陽詢 (557-641), Yu Shinan 虞世南 (558−638) and Xue Ji 薛稷 (649-713).

[46] Based on my impressions after reading many sources, I suspect that the Cloister of Three Stages (Sanjieyuan 三階院, translated above as "Cloister of the Three Phases") and Chongfu Monastery (I think the character *si* 寺 ["monastery"] should be *yuan* 院 ["cloister"]) in Zhang Yanyuan's account were names of other Buddhist courtyards situated in Ximingsi. For one reference to the Sanjieyuan, see *Kaiyuan shijiao lu*, T55, no. 2154, p. 679, a16-17.

festivals. It is also suggested in the text that the cloister had East-West corridors, each of which consisted of at least four rooms in a row. Typically this foremost courtyard would be situated in the central area of a giant monastery, understood as the axis and convergent point of a huge rectangular establishment like Ximingsi.

Other sources supplement Zhang Yanyuan's art historical sketch. It seems in the ninth century, the famous calligrapher Liu Gongquan 柳公權 (778-865) became a patron of Ximingsi and was invited several times to transcribe literary pieces for the monastery. In 841, shortly before the Huichang suppression of Buddhism, Liu wrote an inscription for a stone tablet erected in the Vinaya Cloister of Daoxuan (*Ximingsi xuangong lüyuan jie* 西明寺宣公律院碣).[47] About eighteen years later (859), Emperor Wenzong ordered Liu Gongquan to copy the *Diamond Sūtra* on the walls of Ximingsi. At that time, the temple already featured the copies of the same scripture by six famous calligraphers, but the emperor is said to have praised Liu's writing above all the others.[48] The *Guangchuan shuba* 廣川書跋 (Colophon to Paintings of Canton and Sichuan) has this to say:

> The sūtra was originally written at Ximing Temple, but it has been often changed afterward. The stones of the sutra have fortunately been preserved, and were not destroyed during the war.[49]

A stone rubbing from the Pelliot Collection of Dunhuang manuscripts, P4503 (Figure.31), is thought to be a copy of the *Diamond Sūtra* written by Liu Gongquan. Completed in 824 for the monk-official Lingzhun 靈准, the calligraphy was then mounted and preserved at Ximingsi.[50] Shi Yongyou thinks that P4503 is likely one of

---

[47] Cheng Longhai 陳龍海, "Liu Gongquan shubei xi'nian kao 柳公權書碑系年考," *Huazhong shifan daxue xuebao (Renwen shehui kexue ban)* 華中師範大學學報 (人文社會科學版) 2 (2000):116.

[48] Shi Yongyou, *The Diamond Sutra in Chinese Culture* (Los Angeles: Buddha's Light Pub, 2010), 63; I think Shi Yongyou's intepretaton might have a minor problem. It is possible that, instead of having multiple copies of the *Diamond Sūtra* written by six famous calligraphers, Ximingsi had a *Diamond Sūtra* by Liu Gongquan, which contained styles of the six famous calligraphers. For the original record, see *JTS* 165. 4311; *XTS* 163. 5029; Jin Wenming 金文明, *Jinshi lu jiaozheng* 金石錄校證 (Guilin: Guangxi shifan daxue chubanshe, 2005), 185. For a study of the twenty extant calligraphy works by Liu Gongquan, including the Ximingsi edition of the *Diamond Sūtra*; see Cheng Longhai, "Liu Gongquan shubei xinian kao,"114-20.

[49] Shi Yongyou, *Diamond Sutra in Chinese Culture*, 64. The original text from *Guangchuan shuba* is cited in *Liuyi zhiyi lu* 六藝之一錄; see *SKQS* 831: 713.

[50] Zhu Guantian 朱關田, *Zhongguo shufa shi. Sui Tang Wudai juan* 中國書法史. 隋唐五代卷 (Nanjing: Jiangsu jiaoyu chubanshe, 1999), 176-77.

the earliest stone rubbings of Liu's *Diamond Sūtra* and that Ximingsi might have preserved two engraved *Diamond Sūtra* copies by Liu Gongquan.[51]

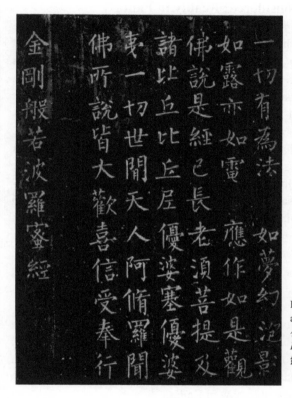

Figure. 31   P4503: The *Diamond Sūtra* at Ximingsi, Copied by Liu Gongquan 柳公權 (778-865). Source: Liu Gongquan, *Liu Gongquan Jingang jing* 柳公權金剛經, 58.

Our consideration of the art and architecture of Ximingsi cannot be confined solely to the world of the Chinese literati but must be extended to the monastery's interregional connections with two other famed religious intuitions of Asia. When we introduce new materials from archives in Japan, the topic becomes truly international, obliging us to explore the interconnections of monasteries among three Buddhist countries in medieval Asia. On the surface, Ximingsi's association with India and

---

[51] Shi Yongyou, *Diamond Sutra in Chinese Culture*, 65. For the manuscript of P4503, see Liu Gongquan 柳公權, *Liu Gongquan Jingang jing* 柳公權金剛經, ed. Shanghai shuhua chubanshe (Shanghai: Shanghai shuhua chubanshe, 2001).

A Tale of Three Monasteries

Japan may seem fanciful, but it does reflect explicit sentiments about the monastery as a profound source of religious charisma.

Jetavana Reconsidered: Reality in Fantasy

Early sources on Ximingsi give the impression that the monastery had something of an Indian color, praised in Su Ting's epigraphical essay as "a solemnity was unprecedented in China."[52] Impressed by the exotic accounts of travelers, Daoxuan felt it was his responsibility to gain an intimate knowledge of the Indian monastic system. He is described by Su Ting as so fascinated by Śrāvastī that he was "unmoving like Mount Meru (*xumi* 須彌)."[53] The mention of Śrāvastī (Ch. Sheweicheng 舍衛城, Jap. Shaejō) in the inscription is no coincidence. Located near today's Sahet-Mahet, Śrāvastī was one of the six largest cities in ancient India during the Buddha's lifetime. More pertinent to our subject, it was the seat of the legendary Jetavana Monastery, an Indian sacred site that has been cited in connection with Ximingsi in many sources. In Chinese Buddhist texts, the monastery, associated with the well-known story of the lay disciple Anāthapiṇḍika, was one of the five celebrated Buddhist monasteries in India.[54] Indian philosopher-poet Aśvaghoṣa (Ch. Maming 馬鳴, 1-2th cent.), in his epic poem *Buddhacarita*, tells us something about Buddha's encounter with Jetavana:

The Buddha, having had compassion on the great multitude in Kapilavastu, set forth with a mighty following for the city guarded by the arm of Prasenajit. Then he arrived at the glorious Jetavana, brilliant with the outspread bloom of its aśoka trees, resonant with the voices of intoxicated cuckoos, and having a row of lofty dwellings, white as the snow of Kailāsa.[55]

---

[52] *TB*, 2598; *Wenyuanyinghua*, 4517.

[53] The original text reads "法師舍衛是求, 須彌不動." See *TB*, 2598; *Wenyuanyinghua*, 4517. For the metaphor of one's body as Mount Meru; see *Gengbenshuo yiqieyoubu pinaiye yaoshi* 根本說一切有部毘奈耶藥事, T24, no. 1448, p. 64, b12-16.

[54] According to *Da Ming sanzang fashu* 大明三藏法數 (Categories of the Tripiṭaka of the Great Ming), the five Indic monasteries (*wu jingshe* 五精舍) are Jetavana; Vulture Peak (Ch. Jiuling 鷲嶺; Skt. Gṛdhrakūṭa-parvata); Vaiśālī (Ch. Mihoujiang 獼猴江); Amrapālī-ārāma (Ch. Anluoshuyuan 菴羅樹園); Venuvana vihāra (Ch. Zhulin jingshe 竹林精舍); see Yiru 一如, *Da Ming sanzang fashu: 50 juan* 大明三藏法數 50 卷 (Taipei: Fojiao chubanshe, 1975), 1155-157.

[55] Edward Hamilton Johnston, trans., *Aśvaghoṣa's Buddhacarita, or, Acts of the Buddha*, bk.3 (Delhi:

147

Later the famed Buddhist garden at Jetavana also became a stage for the story of the *Smaller Sukhāvatī-vyūha* (Ch. *Amituo jing* 阿彌陀経, T366) and many other classic works before it retreated into obscurity in India. John McRae shows that Daoxuan wrote of his awareness that Jetavana had been the Buddha's residence where he preached many of his scriptures, specifically the four noble truths, the eightfold path, and the four Āgamas —— a fact had lead Daoxuan to search widely through Buddhist literature to learn more about it.[56] From Nālandā to Turfan, from Chang'an to Nara, the legend of Jetavana is repeated everywhere, carved on stone tablets, committed to illustrated manuscripts and recorded in notable writings.

From ancient times, it is assumed, at least in Japanese literature, that Ximingsi can be traced back to the legendary Jetavana, and even further, to the mythological Tuṣita heaven. *The Foundation of Daianji* (*Daianji enki* 大安寺縁起) put it this way:

> The Jetavana Vihara, located in Śrāvastī of Central India, was modeled on the palace of Maitreya (Skt. *tuṣita-bhavana*; Ch. *doushuaitian* 兜率天). The Ximingsi in the Great Tang was built after the Jetavana Vihara. Then the Daianji in our country was constructed on the model of Ximingsi.

> 中天竺舍卫国祇園精舍，以兜率宫为规模焉，大唐西明寺以彼祇園精舍为规模焉.[57]

Tuṣita heaven is a place where the future Maitreya Buddha teaches, practices and awaits his entry into the physical world. A lifetime in Tuṣita is said to be 4,000 years, with each morning and evening being equivalent to 400 years in earth-time. It is said

---

Motilal Banarsidass, 1984), 49.

[56] John McRae, "Daoxuan's Vision of Jetavana: The Ordination Platform Movement in Medieval Chinese Buddhism," in *Going Forth: Visions of Buddhist Vinaya: Essays Presented in Honor of Professor Stanley Weinstein*, ed. Stanley Weinstein and William Bodiford (Honolulu: University of Hawai'i Press, 2005), 72.

[57] Fujita Tsuneyo 藤田經世, *Kōkan bijutsu shiryō. Jiin hen* 校刊美術史料. 寺院篇 (Tokyo: Chūō kōron bijutsu shuppan, 1972), 84. Interestingly, the Japanese scholar Itō Chūta 伊東忠太 (1867-1954) mentions that, it is known among the circle of Japanese artisans that the famous White Horse Monastery (Bamasi 白馬寺), located in Luoyang, was also built after Jetavana; see Itō Chūta, "Gionshōja zu to Ankōru Watto 祇園精舍図とアンコールワット," *Tōyō kenchiku no kenkyū* 東洋建築の研究 (Tokyo: Hara shobū, 1982), 368.

that the Buddha Maitreya resides in the inner palace of the Tuṣita heaven, a pure land situated in the fourth heaven in the realm of desire (Ch. *yujie* 欲界; Skt. *kāma-dhātu*). Kūkai reinforced the soteriological aspiration for the Tuṣita pure land in his will (*Shūso Kōbō Daishi oyuigō* 宗祖弘法大師禦遺告) drafted in 835 (Jōwa 承和 2); in it he says that the building complex of Daianji was taken from the Palace of Maitreya and Jetavana.[58] However, scholarly opinion holds that the mysterious relation between Ximingsi and Jetavana is a fantasy, in which Daoxuan's creative misreading of things Indian has wholly triumphed. Yijing stated that "the Jetavana illustration circulating in the capital is a false one, merely a broad outline, no more than a rough sketch based on strange hearsay."[59]

Daoxuan, who should have heard Xuanzang's personal account of Jetavana, successfully transformed the institution from a remote historical site into a blueprint for the ideal monastery in China.[60] In the preface to the Illustrated Scriptures, Daoxuan states that many great events took place in Jetavana; therefore he intended to search the literature for descriptions of the monastery in order to compile a detailed account of it.[61] Beyond that, Ximingsi presented a unique opportunity in which Daoxuan might have expected to see some of his ideas become reality. Stephen Teiser argues that "Buddhist temples, in the eyes of Daoxuan, are not based on human blueprints. Rather, they are manifestations of the Buddha's compassionate urge to incarnate himself in forms that have an effect on people."[62] Fantasy though this may be, the illustrations that Daoxuan envisioned took inspiration from the tales of India he heard and from his experience of the ornate architecture in Chang'an,

---

[58] For Kūkai's will (*Shūso Kōbō Daishi oyuigō* 宗祖弘法大師禦遺告), see Daianji shi henshū iinkai 大安寺史編集委員會, *Daianji shi · shiryō* 大安寺史 · 史料 (Tokyo: Hatsubaijo meicho shuppan, 1984), 5.

[59] Tan Zhihui, "Daoxuan's Vision of Jetavana: Imagining a Utopian Monastery in Early Tang" (PhD diss., University of Arizona, 2002), 229. Yijing expressed it in detail in his *Da Tang xiyu qiufa gaoseng zhuan* 大唐西域求法高僧傳 (Great Tang Chronicle of Eminent Monks Who Traveled to the West Seeking the Dharma, T2066); see *Da Tang xiyu qiufa gaoseng zhuan*, T51, no. 2066, p. 6, a13-16. John McRae, on the other hand, focused on the ordination platform Daoxuan envisioned and reminded us that Daoxuan established a real platform at Jingye Monastery (Jingyesi 淨業寺) in 667; see McRae, "Daoxuan's Vision of Jetavana," 68-100.

[60] After Xuanzang's trip to Kausambi, he had travelled to Śrāvastī; see Sally Hovey Wriggins, *Xuanzang: A Buddhist Pilgrim on the Silk Road* (Boulder, Colo: Westview Press, 1996), 94-95.

[61] Ho Puay-Peng, "The Ideal Monastery: Daoxuan's Description of the Central Indian Jetavana Vihara," *East Asian History* 10 (1995): 2.

[62] Stephen F. Teiser, *Reinventing the Wheel: Paintings of Rebirth in Medieval Buddhist Temples* (Seattle: University of Washington Press, 2006), 136-37.

presenting to us a marvelous and magical representation of the Buddhist paradise.

Daoxuan meticulously expressed his vision of Jevavana in two texts: *Zhong tianzhu sheweiguo qihuansi tujing* (Illustrated Scripture of Jetavana Monastery of Śrāvastī Kingdom in Central India, hereafter abbreviated as *Illustrated Scripture of Jetavana*) and another text containing the diagram of Jetavana titled *Guanzhong chuangli jietan tujing* 關中創立戒壇圖經, (T1892, Illustrated Scripture of the Ordination Platform Established in Guanzhong, hereafter abbreviated as *Illustrated Scripture of the Ordination Platform*). Tai Zhihui studied the *Illustrated Scripture of Jetavana* and its relationship with the *Illustrated Scripture of the Ordination Platform*. He reports a scholarly consensus that the diagram (Figure. 32) found in the *Illustrated Scripture of the Ordination Platform*, attached in the *Illustrated Scripture of the Ordination Platform* of the *Taishō shinshū daizō kyō* 大正新脩大蔵経 (Taishō tripiṭaka), is the illustration that at one point accompanied, or was intended to accompany, the *Illustrated Scripture of Jetavana*. He further argues that the cloisters Daoxuan suggested in his illustration may also have impacted the construction of Chinese monasteries and illustrations found in Dunhuang.[63]

A detailed investigation of the monastic diagram of Jetavana, is beyond the scope of this chapter.[64] Many scholars and reference works use this diagram affiliated in the Taishō tripiṭaka to reflect the realities of medieval Chinese monasteries without carefully considering its provenance; but we must keep in mind that the diagram, originally titled *Gikkodokuonzu* 給孤獨園圖 (Ch. *Geiguduyuan tu*, The Illustration of Anāthapiṇḍika [Jetavana], Figure.33), was printed much later than Daoxuan's day, in the Song Dynasty (1153, Shaoxing 紹興 22). In fact, the Taishō illustration does not adequately match the description provided by both the *Illustrated Scripture of the Ordination Platform* and the *Illustrated Scripture of Jetavana*.[65] Recent scholarship on Sui-Tang architecture has produced two reconstructed

---

[63] Ibid., 11. Tan Zhihui, "Daoxuan's Vision," 11. For instance, he also suggests that Daoxuan's placement of the Cloister for King Mahābrahmā (*Dafan tianwang zhiyuan* 大梵天王之院) and the Cloister for the Dragon King (*Longwang zhiyuan* 龍王之院), may have impacted the construction of Chinese monasteries after his time; see ibid., 230.

[64] For the two illustrations, see *Guanzhong chuangli jietan tujing* 關中創立戒壇圖經 (Illustrated Scripture of the Ordination Platform Established in Guanzhong), T45, no. 1892, p. 812 -13.

[65] Itō Chūta, "Gionshōjato to Ankōru Watto 祇園精舎図とアンコールワット," in *Tōyō kenchiku no kenkyū* 東洋建築の研究, vol. 2 (Tokyo: Hara shobū, 1982), 376-78. However, we should also be aware that the *Gikkodōkuonzu* provided by Itō Chūta was a manuscript printed in 1315 (Yanyou 延祐 2) in Hangzhou.

diagrams precisely drawn in accordance with Daoxuan's description (Figures. 34 and 35).[66] It is clear that the layout of the imagined Jetavana revolves around a central cloister containing three main Buddha halls and other traditional Buddhist architecture, situated in the upper half of the diagram.

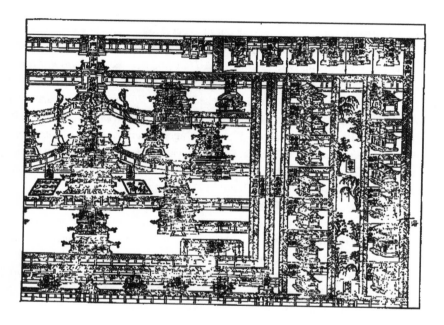

Figure.32   Diagram of Jetavana from *Guanzhong chuangli jietan tujing* 關中創立戒壇圖經 (T1892).
Source: T45, no. 1892, p. 812.

---

[66] Pan Guxi 潘谷西 and Guo Daiheng 郭黛姮, *Zhongguo gudai jianzhushi* 中國古代建築史, vol. 2 (Beijing: Zhongguo jianzhu gongye chubanshe, 2001), 478-79. Ho Puay-Peng also provides a schematic plan of Jetavana Monastery based on Daoxuan's vision; see Ho Puay-Peng, "The Ideal Monastery," 6 (fig.2).

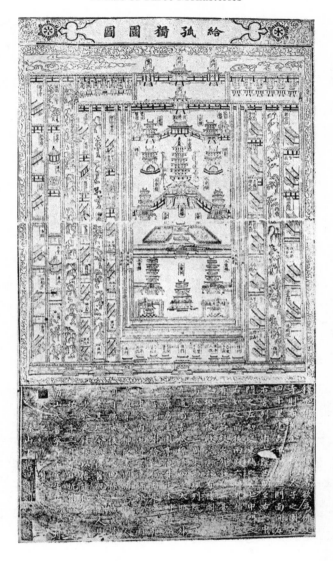

Figure. 33   *Gikkodokuonzu* 給孤獨園圖 (The Illustration of Anāthapiṇḍika [Jetavana]). Source: Itō Chūta 伊東忠太, *Tōyō kenchiku no kenkyū* 東洋建築の研究, vol. 2, figure. 998.

A Tale of Three Monasteries

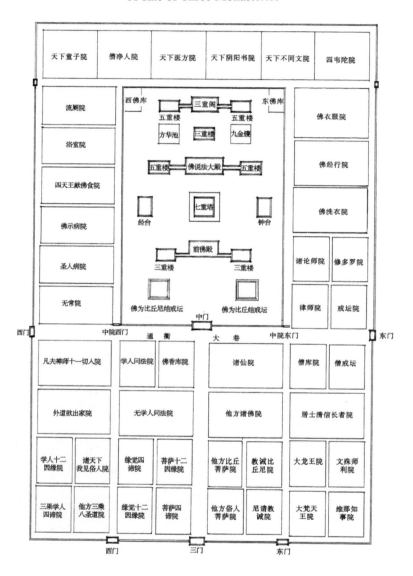

Figure. 34   Sketch Map from the *Illustrated Scripture of Ordination Platform*. Source: Pan Guxi 潘谷西 and Guo Daiheng 郭黛姮, *Zhongguo guodai jianzhushi* 中國古代建築史, vol. 2, 479.

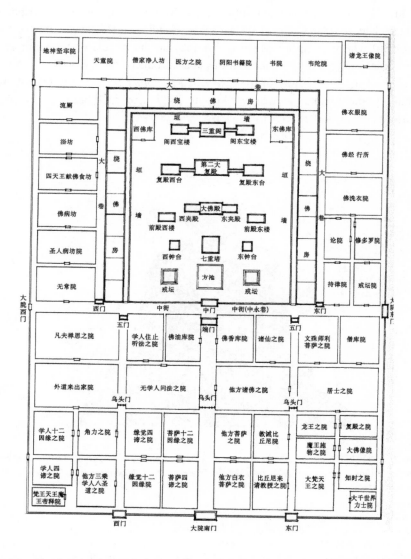

Figure. 35   Sketch Map from the *Illustrated Scripture of Jetavana*. Source: Pan Guxi and Guo Daiheng, *Zhongguo guodai jianzushi*, vol. 2, 478.

In addition to their potential influence on Ximingsi, the illustrated scriptures by Daoxuan had profound impact on Japanese Buddhist architecture. It was Enchin (Figure.36) who took up residence in Ximingsi in the middle of the ninth century, made copies of these illustrated scriptures and introduced them to Japan.[67] Antonino Forte points out that a copy of the *Illustrated Scripture of Jetavana* was offered to Enchin by the meditation master Zhanyu 湛譽 and had been copied from a manuscript dated in 807.[68]

Figure. 36   Enchin. Dated to ca. 891. Bundled Woodblock Construction. Lacquer, Onjōji 園城寺, Shiga Prefecture. National Treasure. *Source: John Rosenfield, Portraits of Chōgen: the Transformation of Buddhist Art in Early Medieval Japan,* 72.

---

[67] We will discuss the case of Enchin in chapter 6. Daoxuan's two illustrated scriptures are listed in *Tōiki dentō mokuroku* 東域傳燈目録 (The Buddhist Catalogue of Transmitting Lamp in the Eastern Region, T2183), a crucial Japanese Buddhist catalogue edited by Eichō 永超 (1014-95) in the late Heian period (1094).

[68] Antonino Forte, *Mingtang and Buddhist Utopias in the History of the Astronomical Clock: The Tower, Statue and Armillary Sphere Constructed by Empress Wu* (Paris: Istituto italiano per il Medio ed Estremo Oriente; Ecole française d'Extrême Orient, 1988), 51.

The cult of Jetavana is clear throughout Japanese history, as reflected in the famous opening lines of the *Tale of the Heike* (*Heike monogatari* 平家物語):

The bells of the Gion monastery in India echo with the warning that all things are impermanent. The blossoms of the sala trees teach us through their hues that what flourishes must fade. The proud do not prevail for long but vanish like a spring night's dream. In time the mighty, too, succumb: all are dust before the wind.[69]

The Japanese fascination with Jetavana, a tradition that can trace one of its links to Daianji and Ximingsi, continued into the seventeenth century. During the reign of the Bakufu government, the third shogun Tokugawa Iemitsu 德川家光 (1604-1651) even dispatched a Dutch-language translator, Shimano Kenryō 島野兼了, to organize an expedition to investigate the site of Jetavana. Shimano brought back a rough sketch, known as the *mitozu* 見取図 (A Rough Sketch), of what he claimed was the monastery. In 1715, the prefect of Nagasaki, Fujiwara no Tadachūgi 藤原忠義, copied the sketch and renamed it the *Illustration of Jetavana Vihāra* (*Gionshojiazu* 祇園精舍図). Shimano Kenryō's account of Jetavana, however, was proved by the Japanese scholar Itō Chūta 伊東忠太 (1867-1954) to be scandal: instead of going to Northern India, he had gone to Cambodia, where he mistook Angkor Wat for Jetavana.[70]

Like the fate of many Chinese Buddhist manuscripts, Daoxuan's two illustrated scriptures disappeared in the eleventh century, only to be recovered in the early Edo period (1681) in the Shinto Shrine of Iwashimizu (Iwashimizu jingū 石清水神宮) in Kyoto. On this occasion, the Shingon monk Sōkaku 宗覺 (1639-1720) was invited to write an introduction to the reprinted manuscript, in which he highly praised its contribution, saying that the manuscript had brought to life the holy monasteries of India in the latter days of the dharma. He further states that the illustration was invaluable as a model for the construction of monasteries and pagodas in Japan, as

---

[69] Burton Watson and Haruo Shirane, trans., *The Tales of the Heike* (New York: Columbia University Press, 2006), 8.

[70] At the end of the Meiji period, the Japanese scholar Itō Chūta studied the four illustrations of Jetavana circulating in Japanese history; see Itō Chūta, "Gionshōjazu to Ankōru Watto," 367-406.

the art of monastery building had long been lost.[71] The mystery of Jetavana was partially disclosed in the nineteenth century, when it became a notable excavation site visited by western explorers. The total excavation area of Jetavana is about 32 acres.[72] Between 1986 and 1989, with the joint efforts of the Archaeological Survey of India and Kansai University (Kansai Daigaku 關西大學) of Japan, a three-year excavation project at Saheth was organized (Figure. 37 and 38).[73]

Figure.37

Map of Archaeological Excavations of Jetavana (1986-1988). Source: Ryūkoku Daigaku sanbyaku gojū shūnen kinen gakujutsu kikaku shuppan henshū iinkai 龍谷大学三五〇周年記念學術企畫出版編集委員會, *Bukkyō tōzen: Gion Shōja kara Asuka made* 佛教東漸: 祇園精舍から飛鳥まで, 36.

---

[71] *Zhongtianzhu Sheweiguo Qihuansi tujing*, T45, no. 1899, p. 882, b28-c2. See also Ho Puay-Peng, "The Ideal Monastery," 4.

[72] The following is a brief early history of the archaeology of Jetavana. The British archaeologist Alexander Cunningham (1814-1893) first identified the site of Jetavana and carried out excavations in 1863. Following his footsteps the high-ranking Indian official W. Hoey carried out smaller scale excavations at both Saheth and Maheth. Subsequent excavations conducted by Jean P. Vogel and his entourage from 1907 to 1908 provided detailed measurements of the site and records of unearthed artifacts. Then, Sir John Marshall (1876-1958), the director-general of the Archaeological Survey of India and discover of Mohenjodaro, uncovered the surrounding areas of the remains in 1910 and offered a historical and archaeological analysis of Jetavana (*Annual Report of Archaeological Survey of India*, 1910-1911, Reprint 2002). For details, see Tan Zhihui, "Daoxuan's Vision," 84-86; D. C. Ahir, *Sravasti, Where the Buddha Spent 25 Retreats* (New Delhi: Buddhist World Press, 2009), 61-84.

[73] For the excavation of Jetavana, see Akanuma Chizen 赤沼智善, "Shaeijō oyobi Gion Shōja no kenkyū 舍衛城及ひ祇園精舍の研究," *Bukkyō kenkyū* 仏教研究 1, no. 1 (1920): 1-44; Aboshi Yoshinori 網幹善教, "Shaeijō to Gion Shōja (Oboegaki 1) 舍衛城と祇園精舍覺書一," *Kansai Daigaku kōkogaku tō shiryōshitsu kiyō* 關西大學考古學等資料室記要 4 (1987): 1-13.

Figure. 38   The First Excavation of Jetavana. Sponsored by Kansai University (Kansai Daigaku 關西大學). Source: Nanto kokusai bukkyō bunka kenkyūjo 南都國際仏教文化研究所, *Nanto daianji ronsō henshū* 南都大安寺論叢, 459.

The site of Jetavana, as the several excavations have revealed, proves to be a typical Indian monastery, square in plan and consisting of different cells. At the ground level of the monastery an entrance with wooden doors is clearly indicated. Above the main cell, a railed gallery juts out, from which the upper part of the temple rises; this part of the temple, consists of two stories, each with a small window and crowned by a four-angled dome. Today, the remains of Jetavana Monastery have more than twenty-five temples and stūpas in the monastic complex, including ruins of double stūpas (Pakki Kuti and Kacchi Kuti).[74]

We might be forced to conclude that Jetavana's ground plan has no connection with the layout of Ximingsi, although most of our knowledge of the latter is limited to plausible hypothesis. Still, as Antonino Forte says, "At the origin of any creation or invention lie the imagination and the ability to dream;" and, in fact, some researchers, many East Asian scholars in particular, suggest that certain salient features of the

---

[74] Ryūkoku Daigaku sanbyaku gojū shūnen kinen gakujutsu kikaku shuppan henshū iinkai 龍谷大学三五〇周年記念學術企畫出版編集委員會, ed., *Bukkyō tōzen: Gion Shōja kara Asuka made* 佛教東漸: 祇園精舍から飛鳥まで (Kyoto: Shibun kaku shuppan), 32-45. D. C. Ahir also provides a report on today's Jetavana, see Ahir, *Sravasti*, 85-95. For an early description of Jetavana, see Ananda Coomaraswamy, "Sculptures from Mathurā," *Bulletin of the Museum of Fine Arts* 25, no. 150 (1927): 50-54.

Jetavana envisioned by Daoxuan are reflected at Ximingsi.[75] The vision presented in the *Illustrated Scripture of Jetavana*, finished in 667, about nine years after the founding of Ximingsi, represents Daoxuan's transcription of information learned from a god named Huang Qiong 黃瓊.[76] Theoretically it is possible that Daoxuan had enough time to implement the inspiration he acquired from the writing of the Sui vinaya monk Lingyou 靈祐, who talked about the construction of Jetavana, as well as the exotic Indian tales that were widely circulated in the early Tang.[77] Other scholars, such as Tan Zhihui and Ho Puay-peng, argue against this viewpoint. As Tan Zhihui says:

> The spatial complex and architectural design of the monastery visibly appropriates the symmetrical structure of the Chang'an City. The monastic compound is spatially organized into specialized cloisters and halls for the Buddha, the various ranks of Buddhist saints, the immortals and heavenly beings, the different commoners and laity who are visiting or living in the monastery. The text interfuses fact and fantasy, historical reality and religious vision; its description of extraordinary artifacts, divine creatures, and plants certainly mirror the Buddhist paradisal representations in texts and art. It is equally important to realize that such imagery is also derived in part from the exotic products, cultural curiosities, fantastical creatures imported from foreign lands that pervaded the markets of the cosmopolitan Chang'an in the Tang.[78]

Thus immediate connection between the gorgeous Ximingsi, which reflected the free spirit of the Tang, and the visionary Jetavana of Daoxuan, may seem to be ambiguous, but our investigation of Daoxuan's reading of Jetavana may as well reveal more connections between the legendary monastery and Ximingsi. Shortly after completing

---

[75] Forte, *Mingtang and Buddhist Utopias*, 45-50. On the traditional view of the relationship between the diagram of Jetavana and Ximingsi, see *Mochizuki* 1428.

[76] McRae, "Daoxuan's Vision of Jetavana," 73.

[77] For some examples of the tales and some Indian messengers active in Chang'an, see Kuwayama Shōshin 桑山正進, "How Xuanzang learned about Nalanda," in *Tang China and Beyond: Studies on East Asia from the Seventh to the Tenth Century*, ed. Antonino Forte (Kyoto: Istituto italiano di cultura, Scuola di studi sull'Asia orientale, 1988), 1-33.

[78] Tan Zhihui, "Daoxuan's Vision," 7; cf. Ho Puay-peng, "The Ideal Monastery," 1-18. Add to this is the fact that Ximingsi was constructed upon the remains of a princely residence, whose style of "Chinese courtyard" was common throughout the whole of Chang'an city.

the two illustrated scriptures, Daoxuan passed away and "entered the inner court of the Tuṣita heaven," although the authority of his reputation remained at Ximingsi through the latter half of the seventh century. To some extent one may suspect that Daoxuan's vision of the Buddhist monastery, whatever its connection with Jetavana, could have been reflected in the real layout of Ximingsi. For instance, in the second month of 667, Daoxuan actually celebrated the establishment of a stone ordination platform (Figure.39) at Jingye Monastery (Jingyesi 淨業寺) near Chang'an, where he bestowed Buddhist precepts on twenty-seven monks.[79] The ordination platform he envisioned and the inscription composed for the ordination ritual held at Jingye Monastery are also present in the *Illustrated Scripture of the Ordination Platform*.[80]

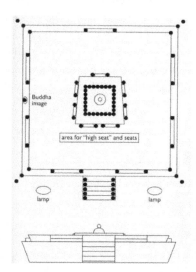

Figure. 39 Schematic Representations of Daoxuan's Ordination Platform. Drawing by John R. McRae. Source: John McRae, "Daoxuan's Vision of Jetavana: The Ordination Platform Movement in Medieval Chinese Buddhism," in *Going Forth: Visions of Buddhist Vinaya: Essays Presented in Honor of Professor Stanley Weinstein*, ed. Stanley Weinstein and William Bodiford, 72.

Another example of evidence in support of speculation linking the illustrated scriptures with Ximingsi is Daoxuan's frequent reference to Lingyou, known for his instructions on building a monastery in his *Temples Revelations* (*Sigao* 寺誥), a text now lost but partially preserved in Daoxuan's commentary literature. Daoxuan seems

---

[79] *Fozu tongji*, T49, no. 2035, p. 367, c18-20; for details of this event and the comparison between Daoxuan's vision of the ordination platform and the Japanese diagram of Daoxuan's platform, see McRae, "Daoxuan's Vision of Jetavana," 78-84.

[80] *Da Tang Yongzhou Chang'an xian qingguan xiang Jingyesi jietan zhi ming* 大唐雍州長安縣清官鄉淨業寺戒壇之銘, see *Guanzhong chuangli jietan tujing*, T45, no. 1892, p. 818, a19-b14.

to have been quite familiar with *Sigao*, as he reports that the text consists of ten essays on differing topics, such as siting and construction of a monastery. I suspect the original manuscripts of the illustrated scriptures probably also contained what Daoxuan called the "sketch of Jetavana (*qihuan tuyang* 祇桓圖樣)" in Linyou's work, for Linyou alluded to the existence of such a map in his writing. The only problem with Linyou's sketch of Jetavana is, given the limit of his sources, Lingyou failed to present a more accurate description, a task Daoxuan inherited and brought to partial completion in his illustrated scriptures.[81] Indeed Daoxuan cites the writings of Lingyou so many times that we have reason to believe that the construction and renovation of Ximingsi, or at least a part of its layout (such as the central cloister), might have relied on Lingyou's instructions during or even before Daoxuan's abbotship. I think Ho Puey-Peng is right to claim, above, that although Daoxuan's description may be heavily grounded in earthly architectural design, it is nevertheless an extravagant 'heavenly' model. However, as I have pointed out above, some architectural elements, such as the central cloister, the ordination platform and the sūtra repository, are testified to by additional illustrations and archaeological discoveries ignored by Ho Puey-Peng.

Figure. 40   Aerial   Photo   of   the Ximingsi Site (First Excavation, 1985). Source: Ono Katsutoshi 小野勝年, *Chuūgoku Zui Tō Chōan jiin shiryō shūsei* 中國隋唐長安寺院史料集成 (*Shiryō hen* 史料篇), figure.11.

---

[81] *Sifenlü shanfan buque xingshichao*, T40, no. 1804, p. 134, c17-19; *Zhongtianzhu Sheweiguo Qihuansi tujing*, T45, no. 1899, p. 883, a7-9. *Sifenlü xingshichao jianzheng ji*, 四分律行事鈔簡正記, XZJ 68, p. 987, a10-15.

Archaeological Excavation and the Case Study of the Sūtra Repository

This line of inquiry leads us to consider the two reconstructed diagrams of Daoxuan's Jetavana along with a variety of other visual and archaeological sources related to Ximingsi. Obviously, to unravel of the mystery of Ximingsi, nothing is more revealing than the archaeological excavation carried out on the monastic site in the last century. However, the buried ruins of Ximingsi, located somewhere near today's Baimiaocun 白廟村 area, currently overlaps with the modern living quarters of Xi'an city, making an overall excavation unpractical. Although large scale archaeological excavation of Tang Chang'an started after 1949, the site of Ximingsi was only modestly excavated twice, in 1985 and 1992 (Figure. 29, 40 and 41).[82] The excavation only brought to light the remains of a subsidiary building complex, which is believed to be one of the thirteen monastic cloisters of Ximingsi. However, the compound of Ximingsi, which occupied a quadrant of a residential ward in the Tang, was at that time 400 times larger than a normal house for Chang'an commoners.[83] The excavation of 1985 revealed for the first time an area of 7500 square meters, adjacent to the original exterior wall in the east, which occupies about 1/15 of the entire monastic foundation. The site was then identified by Chinese archaeologists as a branch temple complex, or a sub-cloister located in the middle of the eastern precinct of the monastery. It includes the remains of the east wall of the monastery and an east corridor associated with the revealed courtyard.

The second excavation, resumed in 1992 to continue the exploration in the north of the previously discovered site, found an extended part of the easternmost cloister, composed of three sub-courtyards centering on three main halls. According to An Jiayao's unofficial report, the excavated site is the central hall (*zhongdian* 中殿)

---

[82] For a brief report of the excavations of Ximingsi, see An Jiayao, "Tang Chang'an Ximingsi yizhi fajue jianbao," 45-55; idem., "Tang Chang'an Ximingsi yizi de kaogu faxian," 37-52. In contrast, palatical buildings of the Tang dynasty have received more scholarly attention; see Zhongguo shehui kexueyuan, and Xi'an Shi Daming gong yizhi qu gaizaobaohu lingdao xiaozu 中国社会科学院, 西安市大明宫遗址区改造保护领导小组, *Tang Daming gong yizhi kaogu faxian yu ya jiu* 唐大明宫遗址考古发现与研究 (Beijing: Wenwu chubanshe, 2007).

[83] For a comparison of of Ximingsi with that of other residential buildings in Chang'an, see Wang Guixiang 王貴祥, *Zhongguo gudai jianzhu jizhi guimo yanjiu* 中國古代建築基址規模研究 (Beijing: Zhongguo jianzhu gongye chubanshe, 2008), 42-63.

connected with another southern hall through a central corridor (*zhonglang* 中廊).[84] The two excavations validate the textual evidence that Ximingsi had a rectangular shape with a size of 500m by 250m, or 125,000 square meters in total area. Although the two archaeological investigations were "salvage excavations" —— like many other sites in modern Xi'an —— the artifacts unearthed already suggest that the full extent of the Ximingsi site is worth unearthing. Chinese archeologists found more than one hundred bronze Buddha icons, stele fragments, glassware and a number of terracotta pieces and eaves tiles (*wadang* 瓦当, Figure.42).[85] It is believed that these artifacts are still preserved in the depots of the Chang'an archaeological team, situated in both Beijing and Xi'an, making them inaccessible to scholars outside the circle of Chinese archaeology.[86] Ever since the publication of the brief report on Ximingsi (*Tang Chang'an Ximingsi yizhi fajue jianbao* 唐長安西明寺遺址發掘簡報) in 1990, scholars have anticipated the release of a full-fledged archaeological report, which is purportedly still under preparation.[87] Given the unsatisfactory quality of the published archaeological illustrations and limited information available to us, I will not here go fully into the excavated items from the Ximingsi site. A detailed art-historical report and a scrutiny of the inventory of excavated items will be the subject of new articles in my research in the future.

---

[84] An Jiayao, "Tang Chang'an Ximingsi yizhi de kaogu faxian," 350.

[85] An Jiayao, "Tang Chang'an Ximingsi yizhi fajue jianbao," 45-55.

[86] The eaves tiles excavated at Ximingsi are preserved in the Xi'an study room (Xi'an yanjiushi 西安研究室) of the Institute of Archaeology in the Chinese Academy of Social Sciences (Zhongguo shehui kexueyuan kaogusuo 中國社會科學院考古所); see Wang Shichang 王世昌, *Shanxi gudai zhuanwa tudian* 陝西古代磚瓦圖典 (Xi'an: Sanqin chubanshe, 2004), 434-35.

[87] For the brief archaeological report of Ximingsi; see An Jiayao, "Tang Chang'an Ximingsi yizhi fajue jianbao," 45-55.

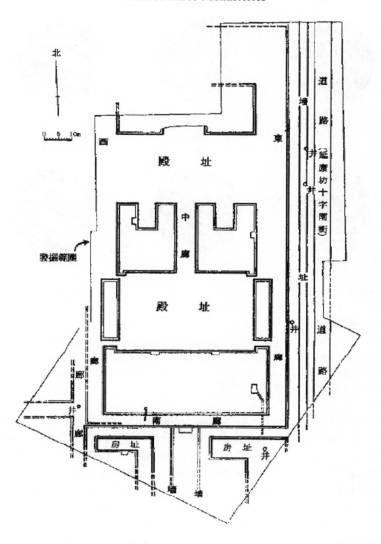

Figure. 41   The Second Excavation of Ximingsi (1992). Source: An Jiayao 安家瑤, "Tang Chang'an Ximingsi yizhi de kaogu faxian 唐長安西明寺遺址的考古發現," *Tang yanjiu* 唐研究 6 (2000): 350.

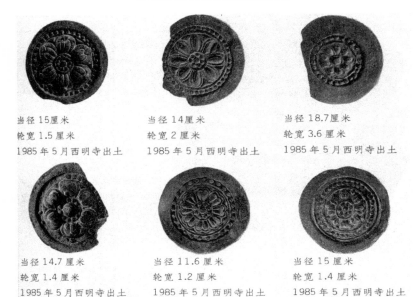

当径 15 厘米
轮宽 1.5 厘米
1985 年 5 月西明寺出土

当径 14 厘米
轮宽 2 厘米
1985 年 5 月西明寺出土

当径 18.7厘米
轮宽 3.6 厘米
1985 年 5 月西明寺出土

当径 14.7 厘米
轮宽 1.4 厘米
1985 年 5 月西明寺出土

当径 11.6 厘米
轮宽 1.2 厘米
1985 年 5 月西明寺出土

当径 15 厘米
轮宽 1.4 厘米
1985 年 5 月西明寺出土

Figure. 42   Eaves Tiles (*wadang* 瓦当) Excavated at Ximingsi (1985). Preserved in the Xi'an Study Room (Xi'an yanjiushi 西安研究室) of the Institute of Archaeology in the Chinese Academy of Social Sciences (Zhongguo shehui kexueyuan kaogusuo 中國社會科學院考古所). Source: Wang Shichang 王世昌, *Shanxi gudai zhuanwa tudian* 陝西古代磚瓦圖典, 434.

Both An Jiayao and her colleague Gong Guoqiang point out that one of the intriguing features of the second excavation is the discovery of two square-shaped symmetrical foundations associated with the central hall. Each of the structures is about 10.5m by 6.9m, stretching southward from both the east and the west parts of the central hall.[88] Based on my research on monastic libraries in medieval China and the evidence of the *Illustrated Scripture of Ordination Platform*, it is clear that they are the remains of two symmetrical elements of a medieval monastery: the bell tower and "sūtra platform." The discovery of the vestiges of a sūtra repository in a Chinese Buddhist monastery is significant but its location here is confusing, since it is known that the sūtra repositories and bell towers are ritual buildings typically found

---

[88] An Jiayao, "Tang Chang'an Ximingsi yizi de kaogu faxian," 343; Gong Guoqiang 龔國強, *Sui Tang Chang'an cheng fosi yanjiu* 隋唐長安城佛寺研究 (Beijing: wenwu chubanshe, 2006), 175-76.

(especially in Japan) in the central Buddhist cloister of a monastery. Extrapolating from the dimensions of the excavated cloisters, the 500-meter length of Ximingsi from east to west allows for five to six such cloisters side by side in parallel; while the 250-meter width north to south can contain two to three cloisters. Among the dozen such huge cloisters at Ximingsi, it is still unclear why the sūtra repository and bell tower are found in a marginal sub-cloister adjacent to the eastern wall of the monastery. In any case, the discovery of the foundations of the sūtra-repository at Ximingsi enables us to pursue a case study to test the possible links between the illustrations attached to Daoxuan's scriptures and the architectural reality in Ximingsi.[89]

In Buddhist book culture, the term "sūtra-repository" refers to a Buddhist library set apart to collect Buddhist scriptures, secular texts and ritual utensils. Such an institution is usually called *jingzang* 經藏 in early medieval China, literally "sūtra repository" or "treasure of scriptures." After the Song Dynasty, for reasons so far unknown to us, reference to the sūtra repository from Buddhist writings and evidence of the actual structures fade away as well. The monastic library had metamorphosed into the "tower of Buddhist scripture" (*zangjinglou* 藏經樓), a building well-known to modern readers and tourists to Buddhist sites. What little evidence there is for sūtra repositories in China comes largely from Tang or pre-Tang sources. In my opinion, the sūtra repository was once prevalent throughout the Tang Empire, from Longxing Monastery in Dunhuang to Qinglong Monastery in Chang'an. Some scholars drawn to this topic suspect that one common feature of major Tang-Dynasty monasteries was a central bibliotheca, with several secondary libraries for extra copies.[90] There is some disagreement as to whether it was common before the Song Dynasty, in the front patio of a monastery, to see the symmetrical arrangement of bell tower and sūtra repository in the front courtyard of a monastery.[91] When the Tang literatus Duan Chengshi visited Puti Monastery in the ninth century (853), he remarked that "In the usual plan of a temple the bell-tower stands on the east. Here alone it is on the west, because in the beginning the eastern site was occupied by the mansion of Li Lin-fu

---

[89] For more cases of Buddhist libraries in Chang'an, see Wang Xiang, "Beiye yu xiejing," 494-514. The problem of the sūtra repository is also discussed in detail in chapter 6.

[90] Wang Xiang, "Beiye yu xiejing," 518.

[91] In many other texts, the sūtra repository is also called sūtra tower (*jinglou* 經樓) or sutra platform (*jingtai* 經台).

when he was appointed as the Junior Councillor."[92] Since the symmetrical structure at many Buddhist monasteries in medieval China was called "bell left and library right" (*zuozhong youzang* 左鐘右藏), it was very likely that Puti Monastery had a sūtra repository as well, the difference was it was built in the east. The presence of sūtra repository at Puti Monastery, Ximingsi and other major monasteries suggests that the sūtra repository might in fact have been a standard element in numerous Buddhist establishments in Tang Chang'an.

So far there has been no research revealing the origin of the Chinese sūtra repository, nor can we find extant examples of such a structure in China.[93] It is against this background that we should reconsider the material related to Ximingsi. On the diagram attached to *Illustrated Scripture of Ordination Platform*, we can identify a sūtra platform near the central seven-storied stūpa (*qichongta* 七重塔, Figure.32).[94] Based on the illustrated manuscript and the existing structure at Foguang Monastery, Heng Chye Kiang presents a reconstructed picture of Ximingsi in his digital Chang'an project. Instead of providing a complete bird's-eye view, the picture gives us a snapshot of the main courtyard as seen from the south-west (see Figure.21). It appears from this that the central tower, in the form of a five-storied pagoda (Ch. *wuchongta* 五重塔, Jap. *gojūnotō*), was flanked by two symmetrical terraces. Using Danxuan's term, they are respectively *jingtai* 經台 (sūtra platform, Figure. 21 and 32) and *zhongtai* 鐘台 (bell tower), located in the central cloister at the heart of his envisioned Jetavana. It is likely that this arrangement reflected the presence of such structures at Ximingsi between 658 and 667. The pattern of the sūtra platform in the Taishō diagram seems to resemble sketches from Dunhuang murals and the gate-style architecture on the wall paintings in the tomb of prince Li Chongrun 李重潤 (682-701).[95] Today, it is noticeable that the two-storied terrace

---

[92] Alexander Soper, "A Vacation Glimpse of the T'ang Temples of Ch'ang-an," 28. See *Sitaji* 寺塔記 (Record of Monasteries and Stūpas), T51 no. 2093, p. 1023, b29-c1. The original text reads: "寺之制度，鐘樓在東，唯此寺緣李右座林甫宅在東，故建鐘樓於西."

[93] In considering the symmetry of the bell tower and sūtra repository in the architectural layout, circumstantial evidence is available at Kaiyuan Monastery (Kaiyuansi 開元寺) in Zhengding (Hebei province), where we can investigate a two-storied bell tower built in the late Tang as a point of reference.

[94] The history of East Asian Buddhist architecture shows the existence of several types of multi-storied stūpas, starting from three stories (Ch. *sanchongta* 三重塔, Jap. *sanjūnotō*); five stories (Ch. *wuchongta* 五重塔, Jap. *gojūnotō*); and going up to fifteen stories (Ch. *shiwuchongta* 十五重塔, Jap. *jūgojūnotō*). In many cases, the tower is situated in front of the main Buddha hall.

[95] *Guangzhong zhuangli jietan tujing*, T45, no. 1892, p.811a. The reconstruction of sūtra platform is available in Heng Chye Kiang, *Tang Chang'an de shuma chongjian*, 63; see also Xiao Mo 蕭默, *Dunhuang*

structures of bell tower and sūtra repository also find their modern replicas erected at some tourist sites, representing the modern presence of "Tang culture" in Shanxi province. For instance, in an effort to rebuild Famensi, another well-known Tang-Dynasty monastery near Xi'an, the designer applied the exact pattern found among the Tang tomb paintings to the newly erected bell tower.

The absence of an extant sūtra repository from medieval China compels us to cast our sight to the East, where we can get some help in understanding the significance of the sūtra repository at Ximingsi. As it turns out, in Japan, the sūtra repository (kyōzō 経蔵) was quite common during the Nara period (710-784) and was known as one of the seven standard buildings of a Buddhist temple complex.[96] The symmetrical placement of the belfry and sūtra tower is typical in monastic institutions of the period, including Daianji (8th cent.), Yakushiji (late 7th c.) and Hōryūji (7th cent. Figure.43). For instance, the two-storied sūtra repository at Hōryūji, standing on the western side of the belfry (shōrō 鐘楼), demonstrates a close approximation to Daoxuan's sūtra tower in his ideal plan of the "sinicized Jetavana."[97] The court scholar Ōmi no Mifune 淡海三船 (722-785) remarked upon the sūtra repository and bell tower at Daianji in his Daianji hibun 大安寺碑文 (Inscription of Daianji), composed in the sixth year of Hōki 寶亀 (775); and, as we will see in the following pages, from the early eighth century, Daianji became the primary model for the Japanese imagination of Ximingsi. A preliminary perusal of other temple gazetteers, such as the Shoji engishū 諸寺緣起集 (Histories of the Foundations of Monasteries in Nara), or entries in a variety of monastic schedules of property (shizaichō 資財帳), also reveals the presence of sūtra repositories in contemporaneous Japan.[98]

---

jianzhu yanjiu 敦煌建築研究 (Beijing: Wenwu chu banshe, 1980), 191-96; Su Zhenshen 蘇振申, ed., Zhongguo lishi tushuo 7: Sui Tang wudai 中國歷史圖說 7: 隋唐五代 (Taipei: Xinxin wenhua chubanshe, 1978-1980), 303.

[96] The seven buildings are known as the shichidō garan 七堂伽藍, or "seven-hall temple," in the Japanese Buddhist nomenclature. The seven halls generally include the golden hall (kondō 金堂), pagoda (tō 塔), lecture hall (kōdō 講堂), bell tower (shōrō 鐘樓), sūtra repository, monks' dormitories (sōbō 僧坊), and refectory (shokudō 食堂). See Mochizuki, 1910. See also Collcutt, Five Mountains, 171-220; Bernard Faure, Visions of Power: Imagining Medieval Japanese Buddhism (Princeton, N.J.: Princeton University Press, 1996), 194-95; Mae Hisao 前久夫, Jisha kenchiku no rekishi zuten 寺社建築の歴史図典 (Tokyo: Tōkyō bijutsu, 2002), 12-13.

[97] Guanzhong chuangli jietan tujing, T45, no. 1892, p. 811, a16-19.

[98] Tsuji Norio 辻憲男, "Daianji hibun o yomu 大安寺碑文を読む," Shinwa kokubun 親和國文 32 (1997): 15. For two editions of the Shoji engishū 諸寺緣起集 (Histories of the Foundations of Monasteries

Figure. 43   Sūtra Tower (*kyōrō* 経楼), Western Cloister (*saiin* 西院), Hōryūji. Source: Ōoka Minoru 大岡實, *Nanto shichidaiji no kenkyū* 南都七大寺の研究, 284.

Daoxuan seems to have used alternative terms in his vision of Jetavana to represent his experience of Buddhist libraries at Ximingsi. One such term, for example, was *jingfang* 經坊 (scripture cell). He makes mention of such a building in one of his most important commentaries on *Dharmagupta-vinaya*, known in Chinese as the *Sifenlü shanfan buque xingshichao* 四分律刪繁補闕行事鈔 (T1804). In Daoxuan's words, *jingfang* literally means temple or scripture cell in particular. He may be using it as alternative to "sutra platform" in his discussion of Lingyou's *Temples Revelations*:

> I hereby briefly cite the official ways to put up a monastery. First the choice of the location [for the monastery] must be made to avoid business activity and distracting interference, so the site should keep a distance from the nunnery and the city market. One should make the Buddha Hall and Scripture Cell as clean as possible.

> 略引宗科造寺一法，謂處所須避譏涉，當離於尼寺及市傍府側等，佛殿經坊，極令清素.[99]

---

in Nara), namely, the *gokokujihon* 護國寺本 and *gankehon* 菅家本; see Fujita Tsuneyo, *Kōkan bijutsu shiryō*, 257-584. The relationship between Daianji and Ximingsi is well known among Japanese scholars; see Hattori Masanobu 服部匡延, "Daianji wa Saimyōji no moken to iu setsu ni tsuite 大安寺は西明寺の模建という説について," *Nanto bukkyō* 34 (1975): 24-39; Kuranaka Shinobu 蔵中しのぶ, *Narachō kanshibun no hikaku bungaku teki kenkyū* 奈良朝漢詩文の比較文學的研究 (Tokyo: Kanrin shobō, 2003), 357-427.
[99] *Sifenlü shanfan buque xingshicha*, T40, no. 1804, p. 134, c19-21.

Indeed the "purity" of the temple complex was a matter of careful attention for Daoxuan and his followers, as they endeavored to restore Buddhist precepts by promoting ordination platforms and establishing standard Buddhist libraries with rich collections of vinaya studies at Chang'an monasteries.[100]

It is hard to determine to what extent Daoxuan's literary imagination reflects or conceals the truth of Ximingsi. Consider, for example, this account, for which there is no corroborating evidence, of a Cloister for Books (*shuyuan* 書院) in his *Illustrated Scripture of Jetavana*:

> Then, the second cloister on the west is called Cloister for Books. Various books from all over the great chiliocosm are collected in this place. There is a two-storied pavilion for keeping these books. The Buddha founded [the cloister for monks] to read [books], not [so much] to follow their views [but to read them] for the sake of subjugating the secular. In the middle is a small silver drum placed on the head of a stone man. If [a monk] wishes to enter this cloister, the stone man raises his hand and strikes the drum; a man of the *saṅghārāma* immediately comes and opens the door. The sound of its drum is like the sound of a human lute. When a monk reads the books, the sound of the drum continues, and the monk naturally resolves and understands [the books]. The drum was made by King Wushi 無施王 of the Videha Continent 弗波提州.[101]

However fanciful the account here of Jetavana may be, the importance placed on the book repository is at least suggestive of the reality of Ximingsi; for, we will see in chapter 6, the monastery possessed a highly reputed library of thousands of manuscripts that Daoxuan had seen in 664. Although we know of the existence of

---

[100] The Song vinaya master Yuanzhao 元照 (1048-1116), who studied under Daoxuan's lineage of the Nanshan 南山 Sect, expounds in his scholarly annotation on the *Sifenlü shanfan buque xingshichao* (T1804) that the scripture cell was the sūtra repository current in the Song Dynasty; see *Sifulü xingshichao zichiji* 四分律行事鈔資持記, T40, no. 1805, p. 399, b4-7. See also Wang Xiang, "Buddhist Manuscript Culture in Medieval China: *Neidian Catalogue* and Monastic Bibliotheca in Early Tang," in *2010 nian foxue yanjiu lunwenji: Diyijie guoji fojiao dacang jing xueshu yantao hui* 2010 年佛教研究論文集: 第一屆國際佛教大藏經學術研討會, ed. Li Jixiang 李紀祥 (Kao Hsiung: F.G.S. Foundation for Buddhist Culture and Education, 2011), 229-54.

[101] Tan Zhihui, "Daoxuan's Vision," 334. *Zhongtianzhu Sheweiguo Qihuansi tujing*, T45, no. 1899, p. 893, b5-11.

such a library from a substantial body of Buddhist texts, we have no record of the specifics of the bibliotheca. Still, it would seem safe to assume that at least in the first century of the monastery's history, the "sūtra tower" that Duanxuan envisioned in his writings is best understood as a real sūtra repository constructed at Ximingsi. If an imagined Indian monastery still served as an ideal model for Ximingsi in the seventh century, then by the eighth century the reputation of Ximingsi was such that its role had shifted from the inheritor of Buddhism from the West to the purveyor of Buddhism to the East. The progression of this intriguing cultural exchange within the pan-Asian Buddhist network eventually brings us to Japan, which we turn now for a brief discussion of the issue of Daianji as well as an illustrative record of Ximingsi.

Daianji and the Secret of *Saimyōjizu*

Over the period of more than a millennium, the reputation of Ximingsi in Japan was more far-reaching than we might expect. Although Ximingsi was probably destroyed in the latter half of the tenth century, its impact remained profound in the Buddhist circles of Japan. Japanese historian Kimiya Yasuhiko 木宮泰彦 (1887-1969) expressed in his *Nisshi kōtsūshi* 日支交通史 (History of Transport and Communications Between Japan and China) that Ximingsi was the most important among the Chinese monasteries connected with Japanese scholar-monks (*gakumonsō* 學問僧). Kimiya may have overstated the case, but in the past few decades, Japanese Buddhist delegations on pilgrimage to Xi'an often inquired about the whereabouts of Ximingsi.[102]

As we have seen, *The Foundation of Daianji* expressly states that Daianji was proud to trace its pedigree to the early Indian Jetavana Vihara through the Chinese Ximingsi. Similarly, a story from the famous *Konjaku monogatarishū* 今昔物語集 (Tales of Times Now Past), the thirty-one-volume collection of stories written during the late Heian period, also tells us that the Chinese Ximingsi modeled itself on Jetavana, while the architectural lineage was again transmitted to the Japanese Daianji.[103] This felt need to trace the temple genealogy through China to India

---

[102] Chen Jing 陳靜, *Tang Chang'an Ximingsi gouchen* 唐長安西明寺勾沉, in *Zongjiao yanjiu lunji* 宗教研究論集, ed. Bai Ming 柏明 (Xi'an: Shanxi renmin chubanshe, 1994), 368-73; Kimiya Yasuhiko 木宮泰彦, *Nisshi kōtsūshi* 日支交通史, vol.1 (Tokyo: Kinshi hōryūdō, 1926), 266; idem., *Rizhong wenhua jiaoliu shi* 日中文化交流史, trans. Hu Xinian 胡錫年 (Beijing: Shangwu yinshuguan, 1980), 163.

[103] The original text reads: "震旦の西明寺は祇薗精舎を移し造れり，本朝の大安寺は西明寺を移せる

---

reflects the traditional Japanese Buddhist geography of "the three kingdoms," seen in such Japanese works as the *Sangoku buppō denzū engi* 三國佛法傳通緣起 (The History of Buddhist Transmission in Three Countries) of 1311. In order to establish Japanese monasteries as the legitimate inheritor of the Buddhist dharma, the temples never failed to demonstrate their impressive linage somehow linking them back to mythical monasteries such as Baimasi 白馬寺 (White Horse Monastery), Ximingsi, Qinglongsi or Jetavana.

We know that the Tang capital Chang'an was the source of the city plans of the ancient Japanese capitals (Heijōkyō and Heiankyō 平安京) of the Nara and Heian periods.[104] In many of the Japanese accounts that we have not had occasion to mention in the present study, Ximingsi is cited along with Qinglongsi as an ideal Buddhist institution in Chang'an. Donald McCallum posits the question as to whether Japanese city planners might have considered the geographical relationship between Ximingsi and Qinglongsi in their relocation of monasteries to Fujiwarakyō:

In comparing the plans of Fujiwarakyō and Heijōkyō, we note a rather surprising feature; in both cases, Monmu Daikandaiji and Daianji are sited well to the east and slightly to the south in relationship to respective locations of the first and second Yakushiji. Perhaps this is a coincidence, but given the seriousness of city planning at the time, casual placement does not seem very plausible: could it reflect the placement in Tang Chang'an of Ximingsi and Qinglongsi?[105]

なり." See *Konjaku monogatarishū* 今昔物語集, vol. 1, in *Tōyō bunko* 東洋文庫, vol. 80 (Tokyo: Kadokawa shoten, 1959), 63.

[104] Nancy Steinhardt, "The Tang Architectural Icon and the Politics of Chinese Architectural History," *The Art Bulletin* 86, no. 2 (2004): 228-54.

[105] Donald McCallum, *The Four Great Temples: Buddhist Archaeology, Architecture, and Icons of Seventh-Century Japan* (Honolulu: University of Hawai'i Press, 2008), 253.

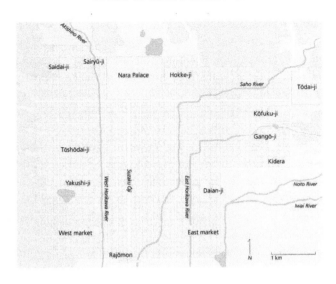

Figure. 44   Buddhist Monasteries in Fujiwarakyō 藤原京. Source: Michael Cunningham, John Rosenfield, and Mimi Hall Yiengpruksawan, eds., *Buddhist Treasures from Nara*, 2.

It is striking to note from the map of Tang Chang'an, that Ximingsi was constructed to the north and slightly to the west in relationship to Qinglongsi (Figure.2); and Kūkai, with his friends from Ximingsi, would have had to traverse half of Chang'an city to reach Qinglongsi. Therefore the relocation of Daianji in Fujiwarakyō seems to reflect the position of Qinglongsi in Chang'an (Figure.44). Nevertheless, there is no doubt that Daianji, one of the four great temples in Nara Japan, is the most important Japanese Buddhist institution associated with Ximingsi.

Japanese scholars like Ono Katsutoshi and Horiike Shunpō have contributed much to our understanding of monks from Japan who took up residence or studied at Ximingsi.[106] Among these, surely the most important for our purposes here was the monk Dōji, whose biography in the *Biographies of Eminent Monks in Our Country* (*Honchō Kōsō den* 本朝高僧傳), records the story of his role in the design of

---

[106] See Ono Katsutoshi, "Chōan no Saimyōji to nittō guhōsō," 65-86; Horiike Shunpō, "Nittō ryūgakusō to Saimyōji," 245-76. The stories of Japanese monks who studied at Ximingsi become the subject of popular literature concerned with Chang'an imaginaire in Japan; for instance, see Yamasaki Hisao 山崎久雄, *Chōan gensō to shiruku rōdo no tabi* 長安幻想とシルクロードの旅 (Tokyo: Bungeisha, 2002), 242-63.

Daianji. In the ninth year of Tenpyō (727), Emperor Shōmu 聖武天皇 (r. 724-749), by imperial command, authorized the search for a monastic pattern after which the reconstruction of the official Daianji could be carried out.[107] Dōji, who had returned from Ximingsi nine years before, presented a memorial expressing his hope to build a grand monastery modeled after Ximingsi. He said:

When I sojourned in China, I saw Ximingsi. I had the idea that once I returned to Japan, and if opportunity allowed, I should build a monastery modeled after it. Then I copied the pattern of numerous Buddhist halls that I saw and secretly tucked them into my bookcase. Now the inquiry of your majesty happens to match the view I have. So I have hereby presented the illustration [of Ximingsi] to your majesty.

臣僧在中華時，見西明寺，似念異日歸國，苟逢盛緣，當以此為則，寫諸堂之規，襲藏巾笥，今陛下聖問，實臣僧之先抱也，以圖上進.[108]

The impression we obtain from this account is that Dōji had secretly drawn a site map of Ximingsi. We know that a tradition of the transmission of monastic ground plans from China to Japan was common throughout the history of Sino-Japanese cultural exchange. For instance, when Japanese masters Eisai 栄西 (1141-1215), Dōgen 道元 (1200-1253) and Enni 円爾 (1202-1280) were enrolled in Chinese monasteries in the Song Dynasty, they took an active, observant interest in Chan monastic buildings, their furnishing and use. Some of their disciples did make detailed drawings of Song monastic buildings and their furnishings.[109] The account of Dōji's submission of the Ximingsi site map, found already in the classical *Continuation of Chronicles of Japan* (*Shokunihongi* 続日本紀), was apparently rehashed in slightly different ways in numerous sources, such as *Fusō ryakki* 扶桑略記 (A Short History of Japan), *Tōdaiji yōroku* 東大寺要録 (The Tōdaiji Temple

---

[107] The history of the construction and relocation of Daianji and its predecessors —— Kudara Ōdera 百済大寺 (639) and Daikandaiji 大官大寺 (673) —— is extremely complicated; see McCallum, *The Four Great Temples*, 83-154; Ōta Hirotarō 太田博太郎, *Nanto shichidaiji no rekishi to nenpyō* 南都七大寺の歴史と年表 (Tokyo: Iwanami shoten, 1979),77-85.

[108] *Honchō Kōsōden* 本朝高僧傳 (Biographies of Eminent Monks in Our Country), *DNBZ* 63: 40; Daianji Shi Henshū Iinkai, *Daianji shi shiryō*, 25. For a brief discussion of Dōji's experience at Ximingsi, see Chapter 2.

[109] Collcutt, *Five Mountains*, 172-74.

Records), and *Genkō shakusho* 元亨釈書 (History of Japanese Buddhism Compiled in the Genkō Era [1321-1323]).[110]

Since no pictorial evidence of Ximingsi, it seems, any longer exists in China, an early illustrated manuscript would of course be a crucial piece of evidence on the monastic layout of the monastery. In fact, though we cannot establish its provenance with certainty, we do have evidence of such a manuscript. According to *Kōbō Daishi nenpu* 弘法大師年譜 (Chronological Record of Kōbō Daishi), a text edited by Master Tokunin 得仁 (1771-1843) from Kōyasan 高野山, a manuscript titled *Saimyōjizu* 西明寺圖 (Illustration of Ximingsi, Figure.45) was preserved at Hōryūji. Hōryūji also collects many other illustrated site maps of ancient monasteries, and there is no need, in my opinion, to imagine that someone would have bothered to forge a manuscript of a Chinese monastery long gone in history. As we have seen, sketches and drawings of the ground plans of monasteries in Song China survive elsewhere in the libraries of Japanese monasteries —— the most comprehensive, known as *Gozan jissatsu zu* 五山十刹圖 (Illustrations of the Five Mountains and Ten Temples) is owned by Daijōji 大乗寺 in Kanazawa 金沢.[111] Fortunately, though we cannot be sure of its relationship to the Hōryūji manuscript, Tokunin attaches the *Saimyōjizu* in the format of a folded illustration as an appendix to the *Kōbō Daishi nenpu*. The explanatory notes in the modern printing of Tokunin's work do not discuss the provenance of the manuscript but do indicate the printing block for the long illustration of *Saimyōjizu* preserved in the Muryōjuin 無量寿院 (Cloister of Infinite Life) at Kōyasan.[112] Tokunin's narrative in the *Kōbō Daishi nenpu* shows that the illustration is about Ximingsi:

> Under the Tenpyō (710-794) era, on the occasion of establishing Daikanji 大官寺,[113] the vinaya master Dōji copied the floor plan of Ximingsi by imperial

---

[110] Daianji Shi Henshū Iinkai, *Daianji shi shiryō*, 25.

[111] Collcutt, *Five Mountains*, 74-77; Zhang Shiqing 张十庆, *Wushanshichatu yu Nan Song jiangnan chansi* 五山十刹图与南宋江南禅寺 (Nanjing: Dongnan daxue chubanshe, 2000), 6-12; and *Mochizuki*, addendum 2, 115.

[112] See *Kaidai* 解題, *Shingonshū zensho* 真言宗全書 vol. 43 (Koyasan: Shingonshū zensho kankōkai, 1933), 266. The series was compiled in Kōyasan 高野山 and Kongōbuji 金剛峰寺.

113 Located in Nara prefecture, Daikandaiji 大官大寺 predated Daianji (716) by 40 years. In the reign of emperor Monmu, the Daikandaiji possessed a series of building complex and Buddhist property, including a bell, a nine-storied stūpa (*kujōnotō* 九重塔), the main Buddha hall (*kondō*) and a sixteen-foot Buddha (*jōrokubutsu* 丈六仏).

command and submitted it to the court. Now the manuscript is preserved in the sūtra repository of Hōryūji.

天平中，因大官寺營構之事，道慈律師奉敕摸唐西明寺圖，以進呈之，其稿本現存法隆寺藏中.[114]

Japanese monks of the Heian period must have had the opportunity to peruse other manuscripts relevant to Ximingsi, for a scroll titled *Illustrated Eulogy on Ximingsi* (*Ximingsi tuzan* 西明寺圖贊) is listed as one of the thirty-seven works in the section of land (*tochika* 土地家) of the *Nihonkoku genzaisho mokuroku* 日本国見在書目録, a complete catalogue of existing Chinese books edited in 891 (Kanpyō 寛平 3).[115] Unfortunately, the *Ximingsi tuzan*, along with descriptions of Chang'an monasteries in their prime in the seventh century, such as Yancong's *Da Tang jingshi silu* 大唐京師寺録 (Record of Monasteries of the Capital in the Great Tang), are lost in both China and Japan.

---

[114] See Takaoka Ryūshin 高岡隆心, *Kōbō Daishi nenpu* 弘法大師年譜, in *Shingonshū zensho*, vol. 3, 42. The kanji "*mo* 摸" here refers to *moxie* 摸寫 (or 模寫), in Japanese it means *moshasuru* 模寫する (copy out); see *Nihon kokugo daijiten*, s.v. *mosha* 模寫.

[115] See Fujiwara Sukeyo 藤原佐世, *Nihonkoku genzaisho mokuroku* 日本國見在書目録 (Taipei: Guangwen shuju, 1972), 42; Beijingshi Zhongri wenhua jiaoliushi yanjiuhui 北京市中日文化交流史研究會, *Zhongri wenhua jiaoliushi lunwenji* 中日文化交流史論文集 (Beijing: Renmin chuban she,1982), 95.

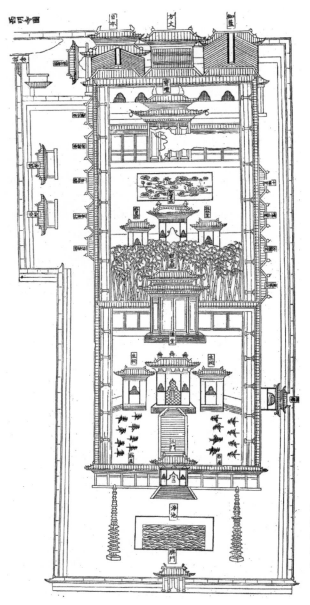

Figure. 45 *Saimyōjizu* 西明寺圖
(Illustration of Ximingsi). Hōryūji.
Source: Takaoka Ryūshin 高岡隆心,
Kōbō Daishi nenpu 弘法大師年譜,
appendix.

The layout of the Daianji complex is well known in Japanese architectural history as the *Daianjishiki garan* 大安寺式伽藍 (Daianji system). The distinguishing feature of this monastic pattern is the use of twin pagodas, known as East and West Pagodas, erected to the south of the central cloister containing the kondō 金堂 (Golden Hall), the main hall of a Buddhist temple.[116] The Daianji system was followed by many official temples of Japan, including Tōdaiji (Figure.46), Saidaiji 西大寺, Hokkeji 法華寺, Akishinotera 秋篠寺 and so forth. The layout of twin stūpa in the front courtyard of a monastery, as suggested by scholars such as Lee Heungbum 李興範, is associated with the notion of state-protecting.[117] I suspect that this particular pattern of Daianjin might have been derived from the ground plan of Ximingsi, which, as we have seen in chapter 3, had firmly established itself as a state-protecting monastery in the eighth century. The stone inscription of the Ximingsi stūpa also testifies to the possible presence of twin stūpas in the eighth century, and the pattern of the symmetrical East and West Stūpas was found at other contemporaneous monasteries in Chang'an. Starting from the latter half of the seventh century, the Buddhist ideology of "keeping the country tranquil" (Ch. *zhenhu guojia* 镇护国家, Jap. *chingo kokka*) was prevalent among East Asian countries. Many Korean monasteries also furnish us with cases of two stūpas, a pattern adopted from the *Lotus Sūtra*, another state-protection classic.[118] The bas relief of the humane kings, carved on some Korean stūpas, makes it clear that the design also took its idea from the *Scripture for Humane Kings*, an essential state-protecting canon that found favor in Korea as well.

---

[116] Mori Ikuo 森郁夫, *Nihon kodai jiin zōei no kenkyū* 日本古代寺院造営の研究 (Tokyo: Hōsei daigaku shuppankyoku, 1998), 100. For the case of the twin stūpas of Tōdaiji in the eighth century; see John Rosenfield, *Portraits of Chōgen: the Transformation of Buddhist Art in Early Medieval Japan* (Leiden, the Netherlands: Brill, 2011), 119.

[117] See Lee Heungbum 李興範, "Sui Tang shidai de Zhongguo pingdi qielan xingshi yu sixiang 隋唐時代的中國平地伽藍形式與思想," in *Di'er jie Tongchuan Xuanzang guoji xueshu yantaohui lunwen ji, Xuanzang yanjiu* 第二屆銅川玄奘國際學術研討會文集, 玄奘研究, ed. Huang Xinchuan 黃心川 (Xi'an: Shanxi shifan daxuechubanshe, 1999), 713.

[118] There are many notable cases in Korea, such as Sach'ŏnwang-sa 四天王寺 (679) and Bulguksa 佛國寺 (751). See Lee Heungbum, "Sui Tang shidai de Zhongguo pingdi qielan xingshi yu sixiang," 713. On the reception of the *Lotus Sūtra* and its influence on Buddhist architecture in real life; see Tamura Enchō, *Kodai Higashi Ajia no kokka to Bukkyō* 古代東アジアの国家と仏教 (Tokyo: Yoshikawa kōbunkan, 2002), 90-100

Figure. 46   The East and West Pagodas (F) of Tōdaiji in the Eighth Century. Source: John Rosenfield, *Portraits of Chōgen: the Transformation of Buddhist Art in Early Medieval Japan*, 119.

A central monastery in Nara, Daianji was also closely associated with the imperial family, and, hence, might well have been based on the model of a state-protecting monastery. Bingenheimer thinks that all sources show that Dōji, famed for his preaching of the *Golden Light Scripture* (Jap. *Konkōmyōkyō*) at Daigokuden 大極殿 (Council Hall in the Imperial Palace) in 739 (Tenpyō 9), was in charge of the temple's reconstruction, as the early *Continuation of Chronicles of Japan* says:

> When the Daianji was to be moved and rebuilt in Nara, Master Dōji was put in charge of the matter. The Master was a superb craftsman. And in construction and design everybody followed his guidelines. All workmen praised and admired him. [119]

---

[119]   Bingenheimer, *Biographical Dictionary of the Japanese Student-Monks*, 93.

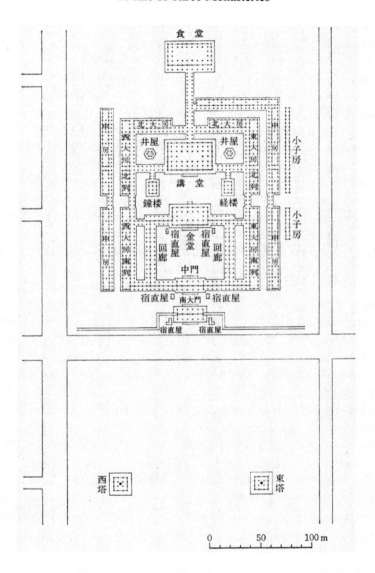

Figure. 47   Ground Plan of the Reconstructed Daianji Complex (*Daianji garan gukugen heimenzu* 大安寺伽藍復原平面圖). Source: Ōoka Minoru, *Nanto shichidaiji no kenkyū*, 159.

Yet scholars have differing opinions as to the architectural relationship between Ximingsi and Daianiji. Chinese scholars believe that Dōji, who also introduced the state-protecting *Konkōmyōkyō* and its relevant rituals to Japan, had ample reasons to build Daianji after Ximingsi, following its layout as well as its function. In contrast, Bingenheimer cautiously points out that neither *Continuation of Chronicles of Japan* or *Kaifūsō* 懷風藻 (Fond Recollection of Poetry), the oldest collection of Chinese poetry written by Japanese poets, mentions that the construction work was done according to the layout of Ximingsi. Horiike Shunpō also argues that the tale of Dōji modeling Daianji after his former residence in Chang'an developed only in the late ninth to early tenth centuries and is slightly flawed.[120]

The bewildering array of arguments regarding Daianji is beyond the scope of our current investigation. However, any serious study of the Ximingsi-Daianji relationship requires a careful reading of the *Saimyōjizu* presented by Dōji. Interpreting the purported map of a monastery lost to history is like cracking a criminal case. So far scholars, whether they relied on or denied the value of *Saimyōjizu*, have failed to provide a thorough analysis of the manuscript. As the sole potentially reliable visual source concerning Ximingsi, it is necessary to read it carefully in relation to the other extant sources relevant to the monastery. However, a close examination of the more than thirty Buddha halls listed on the site map would also require the space of a separate paper, a task that I hope to undertake in the future.

Dōji was not a professional architect; his diagram contains some confusing names of Buddha halls that cannot be found anywhere else in either Chinese or Japanese sources. Unlike the exact architectural drawing of the Chinese *jiehua* 界畫 (ruled-line painting), *Saimyōjizu* does not necessarily represent what Dōji might have seen at Ximingsi. It is very likely that at best it preserves the outline of the central Buddhist cloister of Ximingsi, something similar to the main body of the central section of the reconstructed Daianji complex (*Daianji garan gukugen heimenzu* 大安寺伽藍復原平面圖, figure.47) The following explication of some unique buildings on the illustration suggests some major elements that might capture our attention.

---

[120] Ibid. See also Horiike Shunpō, "Nittō ryūgakusō to Chōan Saimyōji,"123. Masanobu Hattori holds the same opinion, but his argument, based on a rich array of Japanese sources, is also extremely complicated; see Masanobu Hattori, "Daianji wa Saimyōji no moken to iu setsu nitsuite," 24-39.

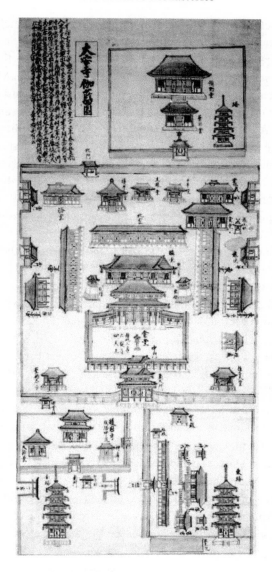

Figure. 48   The Ancient Map of Daianji Complex (*Daianji garan kozu* 大安寺伽藍古圖). Source: Daianji shi henshū iinkai 大安寺史編集委員會, *Daianji shi · shiryō* 大安寺史・史料, figure. 2.

- **The central cloister**: A glance at the *Saimyōjizu* immediately reveals a huge central cloister dominating the illustration, a feature found in both the *Daianji kogaranzu* 大安寺古伽藍圖 (ancient map of Daianji, figure.48) and the *Gikkodokuonzu* affiliated with Daoxuan's illustrated scripture. More than a simple site map, Daoxuan's Jetavana displays a huge central courtyard encircled by a set of minor cloisters. I suspect the layout accurately reflects the architectural reality of Ximingsi. As mentioned above, an estimate based on the Buddhist cloister revealed in the archaeological excavation of Ximingsi suggests that the east-west length of the monastery is enough to contain five similar cloisters parallel to each other, while the north-south width of the monastery has enough space to hold two to three cloisters. In sum, the central cloister depicted on all the manuscripts is probably the pictorial representation of the major courtyard situated in the central position of Ximingsi.

- **The plate door** (Ch. *paimen* 牌門, Jap. *haimon*): This is the main gate of the monastery, which opens in the middle of the southern wall. This might be a large wooden archway covered with tiles, which functions as a visual signal, symbolizing the passage from the profane Chang'an streets to the sacred monastic compound. However, on the diagram the traditional threefold gate (or gatehouse, Ch. *sanmen* 三門; Skt. *trividha-dvāra*, Jap. *sanmon*) is placed behind a "pure pond" (Ch. *jingchi* 淨池, Jap. *Jōchū*), which I suspect corresponds to the "pond for releasing living beings" (Ch. *fangshengchi* 放生池, Jap. *hōjōchū*) on the Daianji map.[121] Given the fact that Ximingsi was a typical case of residential conversion, it must have retained unique features of aristocratic residential landscaping prevalent in the early Tang. In Chang'an, placing an open space, usually in the form of a square between the outside and the interior gates, was a common feature found in noble residences. The space was seen as an elongated path used by visitors' carts and horses, leading up to the threefold gate.[122] The open space created by the distance between the two gates could be used for rituals. This theory explains why there is a passageway connecting the two gates and why the two stūpas, flanking the clean pond on the map, are constructed outside the

---

[121] In Chang'an, the West Market was also graced by the presence of *fangshengchi* in which people released fish, turtles or other animals to gain religious merit. In both the city market and monastery, the ponds were a welcome source of water in fighting the devastating fires that frequently raged in medieval China. See Heng Chye Kiang, *Tang Chang'an de shuma chongjian*, 44.

[122] Wang Guixiang, *Zhongguo gudai jianzhu jizhi guimo yanjiu*, 52.

confines of the main Buddha cloister.

- **Lifetime temple** (Ch. *shengci* 生祠, Jap. *seishi*): The strange combination of two lifetime temples (i.e., temples honoring someone during his lifetime) standing on both sides of the preaching hall (Ch. *jiangtang* 講堂, Jap: *kōdō*) in the first sub-courtyard of the main cloister also reflects the fact that the monastery once belonged to a high-ranking nobleman, who might be honored by such monuments. The Tang code, enhanced with a commentary in 653 (*Tanglü shuyi* 唐律疏議, The Annotation of the Law of the Tang Dynasty), stipulates strict punishment for any official who erects unauthorized *shengci* not matching his achievement and performance during his incumbency.[123] Li Tai was a prince very close to the throne; it makes sense for him to establish *shengci* temples in his own residence. Again, along the central axis in the third courtyard of the huge central cloister, a lifetime temple for the manor (Ch. *zhuangtian shengci* 莊田生祠, Jap. *shōden seishi*) stands next to a hall for the ordination platform.[124] This structure may corroborate our impression from the writing of the Ximing scholar Daoshi, who claims that great monasteries like Ximingsi or Ci'ensi possessed country estates (*tianzhuang* 田莊) provided by the government.[125]

- **Ordination Platform**: The *Saimyōjizu* also has clear signs belonging to a vinaya monastery, as it contains at least one major Buddhist hall by the unusual name of *dengtan jujie* 登壇具戒 (Jap. *tōdan gukai*, ascends to the ordination platform and receives the full set of precepts). It is very likely that the hall has an ordination platform erected inside, like the one Daoxuan envisioned. Three other minor buildings lining the eastern cloisteral wall —— the hall of ten preceptors (Ch. *shishi tang* 十師堂, Jap. *jisshidō*),[126] the hall of śrāmaṇera (Ch. *shamitang* 沙彌堂, Jap. *shamido*) and the hall of ten preceptors outside the ordination platform (Ch. *tanxia shishitang* 壇下十師堂, Jap. *danka jisshidō*) —— were explicitly associated with the ritual ceremony required for Buddhist ordination.

Thus, even a preliminary examination of the illustration already tells us that there are

---

[123] Zhangsun Wuji 長孫無忌, *Tanglü shuyi* 唐律疏議 (Taipei: Hongwen guan chubanshe, 1986), 217.

[124] *JTS* 18. 624.

[125] We have discussed the fact on the occasion of the ghost festival at Ximingsi in chapter 3; see also *Fayuan zhulin*, T53, no. 2122, p. 750, b10-12.

[126] The ten preceptors are the three leaders and seven witnesses (Ch. *sanshi qizheng* 三師七證, Jap. *sanshi shichishō*) required when a bhikṣu or bhikṣunī takes the precepts to enter the Buddhist saṃgha. One example of the hall of ten preceptors is recorded in a Yuan-dynasty manual, written for monks belonging to the Vinaya School; see *Lüyuan shigui* 律苑事規 (Regulations in the Grove of Vinaya), *XZJ* 106, p. 13, a9-10.

a number of references testifying to Ximingsi's conversion from a royal residence to a sacred vinaya monastery in the seventh century. Many historical facts are appropriately reflected in the layout of the shrines and Buddhist halls manifest on the *Saimyōjizu*. The rich array of illustrations in the present study shows that explicit correlations were drawn between the reconstruction map of Daianji and *Saimyōjizu*. Authenticating *Saimyōjizu* and its relationship with relevant monasteries across East Asia requires extensive further research and a comparison of architectural nomenclature among an overabundance of sources —— certainly a daunting job. In spite of its discrepancies with existing sources, the *Saimyōjizu* should be used as the starting point for future efforts to reconstruct the monastery. As I have argued, on the future reconstructed diagram of Ximingsi, the rich content of the central Buddhist cloister revealed by *Saimyōjizu* should constitute the heart of Ximingsi, encircled by ten to twelve smaller cloisters.

Bernard Faure thinks a Buddhist monastery is a total representation of the cosmos which becomes by extension the ritual area to which descends the sacred, the divine.[127] Expressing a realm of the Buddhist divinity in this mundane world is not without its precedents in both China and Japan. For instance, it is believed that the famous Phoenix Hall (Jap. Hōō-dō 鳳凰堂), constructed around 1053 at Byōdōin 平等院, established the locus of Amida Buddha's salvation in the unique space that the architecture itself had created.[128] Likewise, Ximingsi was a monastery imbued with sacredness far superior to that of the existing countryside temple Foguangsi. The present chapter contains a range of materials devoted to the preliminary steps towards the reconstruction of a medieval Buddhist paradise as such. The illustrative record of Daoxuan, *Saimyōjizu* and the Japanese Daianji, along with the foundational base revealed through the two limited but fruitful excavations, may also help us partially to restore a model of Ximingsi in its prime, or at least, to understand how its dozen cloisters spread to create the figure of the monastery in the Tang Dynasty.

Like the design of Chang'an, the creation of the sacred space of a religious institution like Ximingsi —— as well as the felt need to convert the inauspicious terrain of a former residence into the auspicious grounds of a holy Buddhist site —— no doubt reflects traditional Chinese concerns for geomantic forces and environmental features. When we move beyond such broad considerations to more

---

[127] Faure, *Visions of Power*, 194.

[128] Tomishima Yoshiyuki 冨島義幸, *Byōdōin Hōōdō: gense to jōdo no aida* 平等院鳳凰堂: 現世と浄土のあいだ (Tokyo: Yoshikawa kōbunkan, 2010), 15-24.

specific issues, as in sections 3 and 4 above in particular, the discussion becomes more speculative: if there is reality in Daoxuan's illustrated scriptures, where would such things have been found? The spatial program of the monastery introduces the problem of "Indian tyranny" over Chinese Buddhism in the seventh century, when Daoxuan was eager to materialize his vision of Jetavana by establishing a pure land at Ximingsi. Our focal point lingers in the late seventh to early eighth century, trying to find balance between Daoxuan's fantasy and other plausible historical facts. Some of the concepts he expressed in the two illustrated scriptures, such as the ordination platform and sūtra tower, become the subjects of our investigation.

The most important and confusing discovery of the Ximingsi excavation, as we have seen, is the foundations of the sūtra repository and bell tower. A case study of the sūtra repository at Ximingsi, verified by archaeological as well as pictorial evidence, adds to the credibility of the illustrated scriptures. On the basis of what we have examined, the "sūtra tower" that Daoxuan envisioned refers to a sūtra repository, where a complete set of the tripiṭaka could be preserved for the merit of the state.[129] To imagine the artistic world of Ximingsi in the latter half of its history, we have to rely on scant art historical sources, which picture Ximingsi as public space and popular museum with famous wall paintings and an epigraphic collection.[130]

In the eighth century, the rising power of the Tang Empire and the unremitting effort of Chinese Buddhist scholarship also give Ximingsi the authority to go beyond the confines of Chinese Buddhism and assert itself in Japan. Ximingsi's reputation as an sacred monastery is evident both in the careful planning of its cloisters, and in the underlying notion of state protection expressed by the lofty architectural elements such as stūpas. This is what Dōji witnessed and remembered of Chang'an. The 8intriguing relationship among Jetavana, Ximingsi and Daianji led us to probe Dōji's experience, the construction of Daianji, and the visible evidence of several illustrated manuscripts concerning the three monasteries.

The illustrated manuscript of *Saimyōjizu*, recovered in the nineteenth century by the priests from Kōyasan, may shed new light on the interior space of the Ximingsi complex but raise questions of authenticity as well. I tend to argue that a preliminary survey of *Saimyōjizu* tallies with the facts pertaining to Daoxuan and the dark prehistory of Ximingsi that we have examined in chapter 2. It may also reflect certain

---

[129] Gong Guoqiang, *Sui Tang Chang'an cheng fosi yanjiu*, 175-76.

[130] Rong Xinjiang, *Dushi kongjian yu wenhua: Sui Tang Chang'an yanjiu de xin shiye* 都市空間與文化: 隋唐長安研究的新視野, *Guangming ribao* 光明日報, October 2, 2010, 12.

actual features of the central cloister of the monastery in the early days of the eighth century. What the illustrative evidence ultimately suggests is that the central cloister, revealed through the *Saimyōjizu*, was the largest courtyard surrounded by a set of ten to twelve minor Buddhist cloisters. The major part of one of these inferior cloisters, located in the northeastern corner of Ximingsi, has already been revealed to us as the result of the two excavations conducted at the Ximingsi site. Ultimately, the present chapter affirms the fact that the architectural reconstruction of the sacred Ximingsi is such a topic of such interest and complexity that it calls for interdisciplinary as well international cooperation among art historians, Buddhist Studies scholars, archaeologists and historians.

Chapter Six

Bibliothecas and Catalogues: Ximingsi's Buddhist Collection

Realizing the Buddha nature, you may abandon the pattra sūtras.
Bodhi is nowhere to dwell, words are merely empty.
Seeing the finger is not viewing the moon, forgetting the trap is getting the fish.
I heard you had embarked on the other shore, how about letting go the raft?
——Bai Juyi (772-846)[1]

The So-Called "Ximing Tripiṭaka

Many sources tell us that one salient feature of Ximingsi was its renowned libraries and Buddhist bibliographical catalogues. In medieval Chang'an, the people who care to walk into a Buddhist library probably believed in the Buddhist teachings that the secular world was likened to a curtain of māyā (delusion), where the ultimate truth is veiled by the three basic afflictions of life (Skt. *tri-viṣa*, Ch. *sandu* 三毒): craving; anger and nescience. One happy way to find deliverance from this collective insanity is perhaps the perusal of Buddhist scriptures in the library. Ximingsi offered an ideal place for such perusal. Like a magnet, the wide-ranging collections at Ximingsi, made accessible by authoritative catalogues, attracted Buddhist scholars as well as the general public.[2]

When the subject of the Buddhist library is discussed in general terms, it is often

---

[1] *He Li Lizhou ti Wei Kaizhou jingzang shi* 和李澧州題韋開州經藏詩, see Bai Juyi 白居易, *Baishi changqing ji* 白氏長慶集 (Beijing: Wenxue guji kanxingshe, 1955), 452.

[2] For a brief discussion of the Buddhist collection at Ximingsi, see Wang Xiang, "Jiqie yu jiezang: Tang Ximingsi jingzangqun chutan 集篋與結藏: 唐西明寺經藏群初探," in *Shoujie Chang'an fojiao guoji xueshu yantaohui lunwenji disan juan* 首屆長安佛教國際學術研討會論文集第三卷, ed. Zengqin 增勤 (Xi'an: Shanxi shifan daxue chuban zongshe youxian gongsi, 2010), 432-44; Xu Shiyi 徐時儀, "Chang'an Ximingsi yu ximingzang kaotan 長安西明寺與西明藏考探," in idem., 123-31.

situated within a comparative context alongside that of the bibliophile culture of medieval China. Over the course of the first millennium, massive numbers of Buddhist scriptures were seamlessly woven into the Chinese book cult. The fact that sūtras rendered in Chinese were so widely circulated and were regarded as authoritative replacements for the Sanskrit originals indicates the degree to which the Buddhist sutras were integrated into the Chinese literary context. The Ming scholar and bibliophile Hu Yinglin 胡應麟 (1551-1602), after inspecting the sūtra collections of previous dynasties, noted in his *Shaoshi shanfang bicong* 少室山房筆叢 (Notes from the Study of Shaoshi Mountain): "Generally speaking, [the collection of the] Buddhist scriptures started from the Han dynasty, flourished in the Liang dynasty (502-557) and reached its peak in the Sui and Tang dynasties."[3] Indeed, starting from the seventh century, the need to reproduce Buddhist texts in large quantities for recitation not only made scripture-copying a profession but also gave rise to the first printing in human history.[4]

Like other manuscript centers in antiquity, Tang Chang'an was also renowned for its notable libraries, religious scriptoria and book collectors. In the earlier seventh century (626), the magnificent collection of the Institute for the Advancement of Literature (*hongwenguan* 弘文館) was reputed to have comprised more than 200,000 fascicles (scrolls) of hand-copied books.[5] However, the best sūtra collections in the city were assembled under official auspices of the Sui government and catalogued at some noteworthy monasteries as the model copies for replication.[6]

---

[3] Fu Xuancong 傅璇琮, *Zhongguo cangshu tongshi* 中國藏書通史 (Ningbo: Ningbo chubanshe, 2000), 249.

[4] Before the emergence of the Chinese *Kaibao Tripiṭaka* (*Kaibaozang* 開寶藏, 983) and the German Gutenberg bible (Die Gutenberg-Bibel, 1455), the classical world was known as the golden age of manuscripts when religious bibliothecas and scriptoria flourished in great cities such as Egyptian Alexandria, Byzantine Constantinople and Israeli Jerusalem. See James Westfall Thompson, *Ancient libraries* (Berkeley: University of California Press, 1940), 315. Lionel Casson, *Libraries in the Ancient World* (New Haven: Yale University Press, 2001).

[5] *THY*, 64. 1114. However, by the end of the ninth century (888), the Palace Library (*mishusheng* 秘書省) reported that they possessed 70,000 scrolls of manuscripts; see *JTS* 46. 1961. For a brief introduction of the book culture in the Tang, see Schafer, *The Golden Peaches of Samarkand*, 269-277.

[6] As indicated in the *Suishu jingjizhi* 隋書經籍志 (Book of Sui, Treatise of Classics):

> Official copies of the Buddhist canon were to be made and installed in monasteries in large metropolitan regions such as the capital, Bingzhou, Xiangzhou, and Luozhou. In addition a special copy was to be kept in the imperial library. All in the empire submitted to these orders, competing with one another in the expression of veneration. Buddhist scriptures among the population outnumber the Six Classics by

According to Daoxuan's *Shijia fangzhi* 釋迦方志 (Reports on the Spread of Buddhism in the Regions, T2088), the Sui government had generated forty-six sets of the tripiṭaka (*Dazangjing* 大藏經) in the form of hand-copied texts (Ch. *xiejing* 寫 經) amounting to 132,086 fascicles (*juan*), thus laying a solid foundation for the bibliographical enterprise in Chang'an under the Tang.[7]

Located as it was in Chang'an, Ximingsi appears in history as a site clearly steeped in the rich book culture of its time and place. To be sure, for the serious Buddhist practitioner, realizing one's inherent Buddha nature might be more significant than possessing an enormous collection of scriptures. Hence, Daoxuan, who as abbot of Ximingsi himself presided over the monastery's enormous collection of scriptures, reminds us, in his *Liangchu qingzhong yi* 量處輕重儀 (Method for the Allocation of "Light and Heavy" Objects, T1895), that the value of the Buddha dharma lies in practicing the teaching, not merely reading or reciting more scriptures, but the mass of the reading public of that age only cared about collecting texts.[8] The abbot's lament here reflects the fact that the Sui-Tang period in which he lived is remembered as the pinnacle of Buddhist literary culture, when Chinese Buddhists not only introduced new knowledge from India but also produced indigenous works that shaped the religion for future generations.

Among of the major Buddhist collections in medieval China, the Chinese scholar Tang Yongtong 湯用彤 (1893-1964) enumerated four famed sūtra repositories (Ch. *jingzang* 經藏) of the Sui-Tang period, they are:

---

thousands of times!

John Kieschnick, *The Impact of Buddhism on Chinese Material Culture* (Princeton: Princeton University Press, 2003), 177. For the original text, see *Suishu* 35. 1099. The passage is translated by John Kieschnick from Jean Drège's French edition; see Jean Pierre Drège, *Les bibliothèques en Chine au temps des manuscrits: Jusqu'au xe siècle* (Paris: Ecole française d'Extrême-Orient, 1991), 196.

[7] *Shijia fangzhi*, T51, no.2088, p. 974c. The word for standard Buddhist canon, "*Dazangjing* 大藏經 (great tripiṭaka)," appeared initially in a supplementary biography of the Sui Tiantai master Zhiyi, in which his disciple Guanding 灌頂 (561-632) mentions that the master had made "fifteen copies of the *Dazangjing*". The original reads: "造寺三十六所, 大藏經十五藏." See *Sui tiantai zhizhe dashi biezhuan* 隋天臺智者大師別傳 (Anecdotes of the Great Master Zhizhe of Tiantai Buddhism in the Sui Dynasty), T50, no. 2050, p. 197, c26-27.

[8] *Liangchu qingzhong yi* 量處輕重儀 (Method for the Allocation of "Light and Heavy" Objects), T45, no. 1895, p. 842, b19-27. As indicated in the text, Daoxuan must have paraphrased a sentence originally appeared in *Pinimu jing* 毘尼母經 (*Pinimu lun* 毘尼母論, Skt. *Vinaya mātṛkā-śāstra*, T1463), one of the four comprehensive vinayas and the five śāstras (Ch. *silü wulun* 四律五論) in the Chinese vinaya collection.

1. The jewel-terrace (*baotai* 寶台) repository of Jiangdu 江都 (today's Yangzhou). The library was built in the Sui Dynasty. It features Buddhist manuscripts collected from the south of the lower reaches of the Yangtze River and commentaries composed in the Six Dynasties (222-589).

2. The sūtra (or scripture) repository of the Buddhist Cave Monastery (Fokusi 佛窟寺) at Ox-head Mountain (Niutoushan 牛頭山) in Danyang 丹陽. It is traditionally considered consisting of seven-treasure scriptures (*qizang jinghua* 七藏經畫).[9] Unfortunately the library was torched in the early Tang (645).

3. The Buddhist library of Ximingsi, commissioned by the imperial government during the early years of Xianqin (656-661).

4. The Buddhist collection preserved at the Eastern Grove Monastery (Donglinsi 東林寺) at Mount Lu (Lushan 廬山).[10]

5.

Among these four great collections, the jewel-terrace repository and the collection of the Buddhist Cave Monastery vanished before the eighth century, while the other two libraries survived the infamous Huichang Buddhist persecution in the ninth century. As we know, Ximingsi probably fell into disuse by the Later Tang Dynasty, and the Eastern Grove Monastery flourished into the succeeding Song Dynasty and was reincarnated under the reign of Emperor Shenzong 宋神宗 (r. 1067-1085) as a Chan monastery by the name of Donglin Taiping Xingguo Chanyuan 東林太平興國禪院.

The monastic collections of Ximingsi, commonly referred to as the "*ximingzang* 西明藏 (Ximing Tripiṭaka)," represented the highest standard of the national Buddhist collections in the Tang Dynasty.[11] In sources from the eighth through the ninth centuries, some of the imposing cloisters at Ximingsi are vividly depicted as thriving manuscript centers that attracted aspiring pilgrims and travelling scholars from disparate Buddhist traditions. Many of the foreign missionary monks, upon their arrival, donated manuscripts written in Sanskrit and other languages, thus further enhancing the monastic libraries.[12] Although the monastery has long

---

[9] *Xu Gaoseng zhuan*, T50, no. 2060, p. 604, b3-6.

[10] Tang Yongtong 湯用彤, *Sui Tang fojiao shigao* 隋唐佛教史稿 (Beijing: Zhonghua shuju, 1982), 102-03.

[11] *SGSZ*, T50, no. 2061, p. 738, a22-b5.

[12] For detailed study of Buddhist libraries in Tang Chang'an, see Wang Xiang, "Beiye yu xiejing," 483-529.

vanished and is now buried one and a half meter deep under the modern city of Xi'an, some of the Buddhist scriptures edited or translated at Ximingsi remain central to East Asian Buddhist communities.

Scholars may disagree on the provenance of the word "Ximing," but their scholarship has unveiled a monastic world alive with great masters and scholars of international origin. Over three centuries, the elite scholastic community of Ximingsi, representing a rich array of Buddhist lineages, outshone their counterparts in other monasteries. Among the eminent scholar clerics, we have found followers of the Consciousness Only school (Ch. *Weishizong* 唯識宗, Skt. *Vijñāna-vāda*), headed by the Silla prince Wŏn Chŭk, and monks who specialized in vinaya studies such as Daoxuan, Yuanzhao and Xuanchang. Displaying the highest level of Buddhist scholarship, the monks affiliated with Ximingsi fully deserve the honorific titles "dharma generals" or "dragon elephants."[13] Articulated in a series of doctrinal treatises and translations, the scholarly community gathered about it a "Ximing School," whose influence spread rapidly throughout the Buddhist world of East Asia. Thus, we compare the monastery to a top tier university, like the Nālandā Monastery in India, whose notable libraries and manuscript collections are well worthy of our attention here.

Neidian Catalogue and Library Culture

Before we probe into the Buddhist collection of Ximingsi, it may be helpful to clarify the concept of "Buddhist library" in its Chinese context. A Buddhist library can be defined as a place set apart to collect Buddhist texts and artifacts. The usual term for such an institution, *jingzang*, literally means "sūtra repository (or scripture repository)". However, as was pointed out by Chengguan 澄觀 (737-838), the fourth patriarch of the Huayan School, *jingzang* is also the translation of the Sanskrit term sūtra (Ch. *xiudulu* 修妒路 or *sudalan* 素怛纜) and in many instances, refers to the tripiṭaka —— the tripartite division of the Buddhist literature.[14] This stock phrase

---

[13] In Chinese, "dharma generals" and "dragon elephants are, respectively, *fajiang* 法將 and *longxiang* 龍象. These are titles given to monks of high character and leadership. Daoxuan had used such terms in his works, such as the *Xu gaoseng zhuan*; see *Xu gaoseng zhuan*, T50, no. 2060, p. 551, c3-5 and p. 498, c6-8.

[14] *Dafangguang fo huayanjing shu* 大方廣佛華嚴經疏, T35, no.1735, p. 506, c28-p. 507, a3. As more tantric texts surfaced in Chinese history, the meaning of *jingzang* expanded from the traditional three piṭakas (i.e., Skt. *sūtra*, *vinaya* and *abhidharma*) to incorporate a wide range of *dhāraṇī* scriptures (Ch. *tuoluonizang*

had been used as well to signify scripture repository itself, and to that extent it jibed well with the long-standing bibliophile tradition in China.

Throughout the extensive territory of the Tang Empire, from Dunhuang's Longxingsi to Chang'an's Qinglongsi, it was common for major monasteries to rely on the service of a central bibliotheca and make use of numerous smaller libraries to house extra copies. In some instances, the central bibliotheca was utilized as a space reserved for the ritual tripiṭaka, while the minor ones were probably more often used as circulation libraries.[15] I intend to prove the likelihood that Ximingsi also possessed several libraries used for different purposes. On the basis of what we have seen in chapter 5, it seems clear that the "two-storied pavilion" and "sūtra platform" mentioned by Daoxuan accurately describes the standard sūtra repository located in the central cloister, used probably as a ritual library for the national tripiṭaka copied shortly after the construction of Ximingsi. I suspect that before Daoxuan took up the abbotship, Xuanzang, his predecessor, also had many scriptures copied with of the abundant alms offered to him at different times. Indeed, Xuanzang's biography reports that he spent at least some of the alms for "copying scriptures or making images of the Buddha for the benefit of the country."[16]

The Ximing library dates from the middle of the seventh century, by which time the new empire had enjoyed peaceful development for almost forty years; in Daoxuan's words, now the four seas had been purified and Buddhist monasteries emerged everywhere in large numbers.[17] In order to manage the ever-increasing number of texts, the monastic institutions in the capital brought in talented bibliographers to produce catalogues based on current collections. The Buddhist texts introduced to China were far more complicated than the Confucian or Daoist scriptures in the variety and profoundity of their teachings. During the first centuries of Chinese Buddhism, the lack of guidance to a path through the labyrinth of philosophical doctrines had been a problem even for those Buddhists who had the opportunity to study in a rich library. Particularly in an age of manuscripts, when many texts were available only in such a library, the library catalogue was both an essential tool of the scholar in search of formal Buddhist knowledge and an important

---

陀羅尼藏); see *Da Tang xiyu ji*, T51, no. 2087, p. 887, a7-9; *SGSZ*, T50, no.2061, p. 714, c13-15. See Oda, 1182; *Dacheng liqu liu boluomiduo jing*, T08, no. 261, p. 868, b26-c1.

[15] Wang Xiang, "Beiye yu xiejing," 518.

[16] Huili and Li Rongxi, *Biography of the Tripiṭaka Master*, 326.

[17] *NDL* T55, no. 2149, p. 280, b20-21.

advertisement for the collection that could attract erudite scholars from all directions.[18] the eminent Zhisheng, expressed his motive to compile the classical *Kaiyuan Catalogue* this way:

> Now as far as the inception of catalogues is concerned, they were intended to distinguish the genuine from the spurious, clarify what is authentic and unauthentic, record the period of the translation, indicate the number of sections and chüan, add what was omitted, and eliminate what was superfluous. They sought to make [Buddhist literature in China] correspond to the principles of the orthodox teaching and golden speech of the Buddha, and bring forward the essentials [of these texts] so that they would be readily observable [through the textual classifications used in the catalogues].[19]

Among seventy-six known Buddhist catalogues in Chinese history, including extant and nonextant compilations, some fifty-nine date from the Tang dynasty or earlier.[20] The continuing demand for new catalogues during this period was a function, not only of the monastic libraries themselves, but also of the steady growth of the Chinese Buddhist canon: as new texts were translated and composed, the need was felt both by Buddhists and the imperial government to control the definition of the canon through the compilation of scripture catalogues (Ch. *jinglu* 經錄).[21] The contents of the old monastic libraries in Chang'an whose catalogues are no longer

---

[18] For instance, during the period of Carolingian Renaissance (8-9 cent.), the English scholar Alcuin of York composed *Versus De Cuculo*, a famous classical poem written in Latin, and more importantly, a monastic catalogue based on books available at York Cathedral School in the eighth century. See J. D. A. Ogilvy, *Books Known to Anglo-Latin Writers from Aldhelm to Alcuin* (Cambridge, Mass: The Mediaeval Academy of America, 1936), 1-90.

[19] Tokuno Kyoko, "The Evaluation of Indigenous Scriptures in Chinese Buddhist Bibliographical Catalogues," In *Chinese Buddhist Apocrypha*, ed. Robert Buswell (Honolulu: University of Hawai'i Press, 1990), 32.

[20] Ibid., 31. The Japanese scholar Kawaguchi Yoshiteru 川口義照 argues that among the sixteen monastic catalogues produced in the Tang, about ten survived; whereas the Chinese scholar Feng Guodong 馮國棟 provides a list of ten more catalogues compiled in Chang'an and Mount Wutai. Kawaguchi Yoshiteru 川口義照, *Chūgoku bukkyō ni okeru kyōroku kenkyū* 中國仏教における経錄研究 (Kyoto: Hōzōkan, 2000), 39-43; Feng Guodong 馮國棟, "Tang Song wangyi fojiao jinglu congkao 唐宋亡佚佛教經錄叢考," *Zhejiang daxue xuebao (renwen shehui kexue ban)* 浙江大學學報（人文社會科學版）5 (2008): 52-60.

[21] *Mochizuki*, 3313.

extant are beyond retrieval, as they are only briefly addressed by bibliographers.[22] If we restrict our view simply to extant Buddhist catalogues edited in the Tang dynasty, we will find eleven major works produced in Chang'an and Luoyang.[23] Among these, nine were compiled in four different monasteries in Chang'an: the institutions Ximingsi, Xichongfu Monastery, Ci'en Monastery, and the suburban temple Huayan Monastery.[24] The other two catalogues —— one produced during the early stages of

---

[22] For instance, *Dazhou lu* 大周錄 (Great Zhou Catalogue, T2153) informs us of the existence of bibliothecas in Zhenjisi 真寂寺 (619-95); Xuanfasi 玄法寺; Fulinsi 福林寺 (672-95) and Yishansi 義善寺 (645). See *Dazhou kanding zhongjing mulu* 大週刊定衆經目錄 (Catalogue of the Buddhist Scriptures Collated and Sanctioned under the Great Zhou Dynasty), T55, no. 2153, p. 388, b23-24. The *Kaiyuan Catalogue* also provides a listing of thirty-one ancient catalogues (*gulu* 古錄); see *Kaiyuan shijiao lu*, T55, no. 2154, p. 574, b1-5. For a detailed discussion of the lost catalogues, see Fang Guangchang, *Zhongguo xieben dazang jing yanjiu*, 53-57.

[23] The eleven catalogues are:
1. *Da Tang dongjing da'jing'aisi Yiqie jinglu mulu* 大唐東京大敬愛寺一切經論目錄 (*Zongjing mulu*, Catalogue of Buddhist Scriptures and Commentaries at the Great Jing'aisi in the Eastern Capital of the Great Tang, 663-665)
2. *Da Tang neidian lu* (664)
3. *Gujin yijing tuji* 古今譯經圖記 (Illustrated Record of Translated Scriptures Past and Present, after 664, T2151)
4. *Da Zhou kanding zhongjing mulu* (T2153)
5. *Xu Da Tang neidian lu* 續大唐內典錄 (Continuation to the *Neidian Catalogue*, T2150)
6. *Xu gujin yijing tuji* 續古今譯經圖記 (Continuation to the *Illustrated Record of Translated Scriptures Past and Present*, 730)
7. *Kaiyuan shijiao lu* (730)
8. *Kaiyuan shijiao lu Lüechu* 開元釋教錄略出 (Abridged Catalogue from the Kaiyuan Catalogue, 730)
9. *Da Tang kaiyuan shijiao guangpin Lizhan* 大唐開元釋教廣品曆章 (Corrigendum to the Kaiyuan Catalogue in the Great Tang)
10. *Da Tang zhenyuan xu kaiyuan shijiao lu* 大唐貞元續開元釋教錄 (Addendum to *Kaiyuan Catalogue* Compiled in the Reign-era of Zhenyuan in the Great Tang, 794)
11. *Zhenyuan xinding shijiao mulu* 貞元新定釋教目錄 (A Catalogue of [the Texts about] Buddhist Teachings, Newly Collated in the Zhenyuan Era, 800)

Looking back at Chang'an in the Sui period, a time of significant doctrinal shifts in Buddhist scholasticism, we find several Buddhist bibliographies, among which three catalogues surfaced before the seventh century: *Dasui zhongjing mulu* 大隋衆經目錄 (Catalog of Scriptures in the Great Sui Period, T2146); *Zhongjing mulu* 衆經目錄 (Catalog of Scriptures, T2147); and *Lidai sanbao ji*. For a general introduction to Buddhist catalogues in ancient China, see Feng Chengjun 馮承均, *Lidai qiufa fanjing lu* 歷代求法翻經錄 (Shanghai: Shangwu yinshuguan, 1934).

[24] For a brief introduction of the catalogues compiled in the Tang dynasty, see Kamata Shigeo 鎌田茂雄, *Daizōkyō zenkaisetsu daijiten* 大蔵経全解說大事典 (Tokyo: Yūzankaku shuppan, 1998), 630-34. One catalogue compiled in Chang'an, the *Tang Kaiyuan shijiao guangping li zhang*, has received much scholarly attention; see Tejima Isshin 手島一真, "'Dai Tō kaigen shakkyō kōhin rekishō ni tsuite: Tōdai no kyōroku

Tang Buddhism, the other concluded during the interregnum of Empress Wu ——
were compiled in the eastern capital of Luoyang.

In a milieu favorable for the advancement of Buddhist scholarship, Ximingsi
built up a magnificent collection containing thousands of scriptures and manuscripts
important both for the quality of its contents and for the copious annotations that
Chinese monks added to their books. The monastery's collection enabled Daoxuan to
produce his monumental bibliography: *Da Tang neidian lu* (abbreviated as *Neidian
Catalogue*). In the ninth chapter of the catalogue, Daoxuan informs us that he edited
another ten-fascicle bibliography entitled *Da Tang zongjing lu* 大唐眾經録, or *Da
Tang neidian zongjing lu* 大唐內典衆經録, in the second year of Longshuo 龍朔
(662). Compiled just two years before the *Neidian Catalogue*, this might very well be
a draft prepared on the basis of the *Ximingsi lu* 西明寺録 (Catalogue of Ximingsi),
the inventory of books and the imperial tripiṭaka held by the Ximing community
during 656-661.[25] Like other Buddhist works composed in this period, the title of the
catalogue bears the prefix the "Great Tang (*Da Tang* 大唐)", expressing a pride not
only in the empire's territorial expansion but also in its regal literary culture.[26] The
traditional division of "internal" and "external" in Buddhist collections, respectively
neidian 內典 (Buddhist canonical scriptures) and *waidian* 外典 (non-Buddhist
scriptures), is also evident in the title.[27] In fact, the complete collection at Ximingsi
included not only all sorts of sūtra material, but also any indigenous works that
accorded with the taste of the emperor. At Ximingsi, the books accepted as canon and
circulated in public had to be approved by the government.

Since cataloguing in most cases was based on what the cataloguers could find in
the monastic libraries, analyzing the classification schema of Daoxuan's *Neidian
Catalogue* may give us a sense of how the core collection at Ximingsi were actually

---

to zōkyō ni kansuru ichi kōsatsu 大唐開元釈教広品歴章について: 唐代の経録と蔵経に関する一考
察," *Hokke bunka kenkyū* 法華文化研究 29 (2003): 24-38.

[25] *NDL*, T55, no. 2149, p. 325, c28-p. 326, a5.

[26] For instances, see *SZFSZ*; *Da Tang xiyu ji*; *Da Tang gu sanzang xuanzang fashi xingzhuang* 大唐故三藏
玄奘法師行狀 (T2052); *Da Tang xiyu qiufa gaoseng zhuan*. Likewise, when Japan rose to power after the
victorious Russo-Japanese War, the title *Dainippon* (Great Japan) was prevalent among many of the huge
series published since the end of the nineteenth century, including *Dainippon teikoku kenbō* 大日本帝国憲
法 (1889), *Dainippon zokuzōkyō* 大日本続蔵経 (1905), *Dainippon bukkyō zensho* 大日本仏教全書
(1922), *Dainippon kokiroku* 大日本古記録 (1952), etc.

[27] Another example is the *Naiten jinroshō* 內典塵露章 written by Gyōnen 凝然 (1240-1321), the
Japanese monk from Tōdaiji. The division also applies to *neijiao* 內教 (Buddhist canonical teachings), as
distinguished from *waijiao* 外教 (non-Buddhist teachings, or other religions).

organized. Drawing on materials from earlier catalogues, the *Neidian Catalogue* introduces 2,487 Buddhist scriptures that were translated into Chinese by 220 scholars. However, the Ximing tripiṭaka represents, not all these titles, but works available at the monastery in the early Tang. Like many other official monastic bibliographies edited in Chang'an, the *Neidian Catalogue* was compiled in accordance with the imperial order of Gaozong. To display the religious confidence of the rising empire, the purpose of the catalogue was to establish a standard Tang tripiṭaka by incorporating all sanctioned canonical writings. Daoxuan makes mention of the national tripiṭaka of 664 in his preface to the *Neidian Catalogue*, reporting that there were 3361 fascicles of canonical literature, plus a variety of classical and indigenous writings.[28]

The eighth chapter, titled *Lidai zhongjing zongcuo ruzang lu* 歷代眾經總撮入藏錄, enumerates the translated scriptures contained in the standard tripiṭaka —— the cream of the Buddhist collection at Ximingsi. This listing retains some elements initiated by the Sui cataloguers, such as Fei Changfang, who pioneered in his creation of the *Ruzangmu* 入藏目 (or *Ruzang lu* 入藏錄), a roster of selected scriptures included in the canon.[29] However, in the affixed prologue to the *Neidian Catalogue*, Daoxuan claims that his task was also to correct the errors of Fei Changfang, who mixed spurious sūtras with authentic ones. The entire list of Daoxuan's *Ruzang lu* chapter includes a set of 800 translated texts, the true canon of Buddhism in the early Tang. The manuscripts were copied on 56,000 sheets of paper and contained in 316 sutra cases (*jingzhi* 經帙). Since most Tang cataloguers relied on scriptures contained in their own monasteries, the contents of their versions of a *Ruzang lu* comes close to a de facto inventory of their monastic library. The contents of Daoxuan's version, the Ximing Tripiṭaka, as revealed in the eighth chapter of his catalogue, are listed as follows:

---

[28] *NDL*, T55, no.2149, p. 302, c1-2.

[29] One year after Daoxuan was born (597), the skilled translator Fei Changfang completed the monumental *Lidai sanbao ji* based on existing catalogues lost to us. Although he did not undertake a critical approach in dealing with his materials, his contribution to Buddhist bibliography is still laudable. For an encyclopedic study of Buddhist bibliographical catalogues compiled before the Tang Dynasty, see Hayashiya Tomojiro 林屋友次郎, *Kyōroku kenkyū* 経録研究 (Tokyo: Iwanami shoten, 1991).

Bibliothecas and Catalogues

Da Tang neidian lu

Year of compilation:	664 (Lingde 1)
Number of scrolls:	3361 fascicles
Existing collection:	800 scriptures

Neidian Catalogue	number	scroll	paper	book case
Mahāyāna scriptures that have one translation (*Dacheng jing yiyi* 大乘經一譯)	204	685	11042	66
The retranslated Mahāyāna scriptures (*Dachengjing chongfan* 大乘經重翻)	202	497	7290	49
Hīnayāna scriptures that have one translation (*Xiaochengjing yiyi* 小乘經一譯)	108	435	6690	39
The retranslated Hīnayāna scriptures (*Xiaochengjing chongfan* 小乘經重翻)	96	114	977	6
Hīnayāna vinaya (*Xiaocheng lü* 小乘律)	35	270	5813	28
Mahāyāna abhidharma (*Dacheng lun* 大乘論)	74	520	9130	52
Hīnayāna abhidharma (*Xiaocheng lun* 小乘論)	33	676	12177	68
Hagiography (*Xiansheng jizhuan* 賢聖集傳)	49	184	2808	18
total	800	3361	56,170	326

Table 1. *Lidai zhongjing jian ruzang lu* 歷代眾經見入藏錄, from *Neidian Catalogue*[30]

No doubt this is the most important sub-catalogue in Daoxuan's bibliography and gives us an impression of the scale of the state-sanctioned tripiṭaka during the early Xianqin era (656-661). Daoxuan divided the catalogue according to the recognized dichotomy of the Greater and Lesser vehicles, further categorized on the basis of single or multiple translations. The division between sūtra, vinaya, *abhidharma* and

---

[30] *NDL*, T55, no. 2149, p. 302, c22-p. 303, a5. *Fayuan zhulin*, T53, no. 2122, p. 1020, b4-14.

198

hagiographies is clear-cut. For scholars interested in Buddhist material culture, Daoxuan's account also offers a glimpse into the prototype of bibliotheca and book culture in medieval China. The scriptures enumerated in this particular catalogue were probably contained in an enormous sūtra cabinet in the Ximingsi bibliotheca. *Neidian Catalogue* shows that it contained 326 scriptural cases within which 3,361 fascicles of manuscripts were preserved. Daoxuan described the arrangement in this way:

> The scriptures are incorporated on the basis of their categories. They support each other in shelves and cabinets. The manuscripts are clearly distinguished by using book cases, the scroll shaft, sticks and tablets. If need be one can draw a book out accurately without messing up the collection.

依別入藏, 架閣相持. 帙軸籤牓, 標顯名目. 須便抽撿, 絕於紛亂.[31]

Daoxuan refers here to the internal arrangement of the sūtra repository at Ximingsi in 664. The shelves and cases are adjacent to one another. Labels of wood fiber were applied to the bookcases and scrolls to indicate the titles.[32] In some cases, the manuscript scrolls were "maintained on sandalwood rollers with crystal knobs, and colored ivory labels."[33] In the field of library history, we have very little knowledge of the details of shelving in monastic bibliothecas, although in this case we may attempt to generate a picture of the sūtra repository from Daoxuan's description —— three bookshelves, each of which contains eight to nine layers (or separators, *ge* 隔), holding 326 cases of books.

Daoxuan stressed in *Guang hongming ji* 廣弘明集 (An Extended Collection [of Documents] for Propagating Enlightenment, T2103) that a sūtra cabinet was also used to hold Buddha figures, saying five to ten figures are contained in one cabinet.[34]

---

[31] *NDL*, T55, no. 2149, p. 302, b25-29.

[32] Ibid., 302, b27-28.

[33] Edward Schafer, *The Golden Peaches of Samarkand*, 269; see also *XTS* 57.1421.

[34] The original text reads: "或十尊五聖, 共處一廚. 或大士如來, 俱藏一櫃." See *Guang hongmingji*, T52, no. 2103, p. 210, b5-10. On "table (*an* 案)" and "cabinet (*chu* 櫥)" in the Tang dynasty, see Han Jizhong 韓繼中, "Tangdai jiaju de chubu yanjiu 唐代傢具的初步研究," *Wenbo* 文博 2 (1985): 47-51. An excerpt from Enchin's (814-91) travel record, *Gyōrekishō* 行歷抄 (Selection of Travelling Experience), reveals that Buddhist texts might have been housed in a sūtra cabinet located in halls for tantric rituals. When Enchin visited the tantric guru Faquan 法全 at Qinglong Monastery, the famous master went to the *abhiṣeka* hall

So far only Dunhuang frescos or some ancient paintings provide reliable images of sūtra cabinets of the Tang period. But we believe such furniture was imported into Japan and somehow became *zushi* 廚子, a feretory with the appearance of a small shrine.[35]   Of course it is problematic to use a term that is specific in one historical context to describe the state of affairs in a different setting. However, we might use the Japanese *zushi* to help us imagine the sūtra cabinets of medieval Chinese libraries. Typically, certain multivolume scriptures in the Buddhist canon, such as the *Mahāratnakūṭa* (Ch. *Dabaoji jing* 大寶積經, T310) or *Mahā-prajñāpāramitā-sūtra*, could be treated as a single piṭaka: e.g., the "sūtra treasures of *Mahāratnakūṭa* (*Dabaoji jingzang* 大寶積經藏)" or "sūtra treasures of *Mahā-prajñāpāramitā-sūtra* (*Da banruo jingzang* 大般若經藏)." Thus, for instance, Tōdaiji (Eastern Great Temple), the headquarters of Kegon Buddhism in Nara, preserves a *Daihannyakyō zushi* 大般若經廚子 (Figure.49) made in the Kamakura period to contain the entire 600 fascicles of the *Mahā-prajñāpāramitā-sūtra*, which can fill up fifteen sūtra cases. This compact *zushi* has five layers, each separated by three caches.[36] In contrast, the sūtra cabinet at Ximingsi must have been enormous, large enough to be filled with 326 sūtra cases. Anyone who has seen the revolving bookcase in Hebei's Longxing Monastery or the long sūtra cabinets in Shanxi's Chongshan Monastery (Chongshansi 崇善寺) will be impressed by their size. On the basis of textual sources in *Neidian Catalogue*, both Jean Pierre Drège and Fang Guangchang 方廣錩 propose simplified illustrations in their separate studies to depict the arrangement of scriptures in the cabinet (Figure.50).[37] In sum, Buddhist bibliography can no longer be understood as a domain in which philology plays independently. Collaboration with other fields such as material culture may effectively contextualize the

---

(*guanding daochang* 灌頂道場) and took out a ritual manual from a sūtra cabinet; see Bai Huawen 白化文 and Li Dingxia 李鼎霞, *Xinglichao jiaozhu* 行歷抄校注 (Shijiazhuang: Huashan wenyi chubanshe, 2004), 42.

[35] The Japanese cabinet, which underwent constant change, was used for keeping Buddhist icons, relics, or scriptures. *Zushi* 廚子 are frequently listed among *shizaichō* (schedule of property) in ancient Japanese monasteries; many of them, such as the *tamamushi zushi* 玉蟲廚子 (buprestid cabinet) and *Tachibana funin zushi* 橘夫人廚子 (cabinet of Madame Tachibana), survive as national treasures. For details, see Ishida Mosaku 石田茂作, *Bukkyō kōkogaku ronkō 5. butsuguhen* 仏教考古學論考 5 仏具編 (Kyoto: Shibunkaku shuppan, 1977), 15-21; Okazaki Jōji 岡崎讓治, *Butsugu daijidten* 仏具大事典 (Tokyo: Kamakura shinsho, 1982). 56-59.

[36] *Kaiyuan shijiao lu*, T55, no.2154, p.698a; Okazaki Jōji, *Butsugu daijiten*, 59.

[37] See Drège, *Les bibliothèques en Chine*, 214; Fang Guangchang 方廣錩, *Zhongguo xieben dazang jing yanjiu* 中國寫本大藏經研究 (Shanghai: Shanghai guji chubanshe, 2006), 437.

manuscripts together with the bibliothecas back into their medieval milieu, helping us reconstruct the configuration of the Buddhist bibliotheca and understand the details of the medieval catalogue.

Figure. 49   *Daihannyakyō zushi* 大般若經厨子, Tōdaiji, Kamakura Period. Source: Okazaki Jōji 岡崎譲治, *Butsugu daijiden* 仏具大事典, 59.

Neidian Catalogue and Monastic Scholarship

Although with the effort of Japanese and Chinese scholars, the field of "Buddhist bibliography" has made rapid progress, the reconstruction of a complete Buddhist library in medieval China and its implications for monastic education still calls for further investigation. With this in mind, this section seeks to offer a sketch of the indigenous writings and monastic education as seen from the evidence of the *Neidian Catalouge*. By the middle of the seventh century, it was the attraction of the "real tripiṭaka" that put many religious seekers, including the first Ximingsi abbot, Xuanzang, on their dangerous journeys to the alien world of *Tianzhu* 天竺 (Skt. Sindhu, India). When Daoxuan composed his *Neidian Catalogue*, he was already about seventy years old. Although he had never been to India, his admiration for the Indian tripiṭaka, much like his passion for Jetavana, is explicit in his preface to the ninth chapter of the *Neidian Catalogue*:

Have you not heard that the catalogue in the dragon palace contains enormous number of scriptures that one cannot gather them all after searching thoroughly in China. Billions of elephants are not able to bear on their backs the scriptures contained in Mount Cakravāla. The cliff cave at Karghalik possessed the twelve divisions of the Mahāyāna canon (Skt. *dvādaśāṅgadharmapravacana*). The quiet temple at Nāga is home to tens of thousands of saints.

豈不聞龍海藏錄，竟夏尋而不周.[38] 鐵圍結法，億象負之莫盡.[39] 沮渠岩窟，恒鎮十二寶乘. 那伽幽寺，常住億千聖範.[40]

表二十九：西明寺經橱復原圖

左　　間		中　　間	右　　間	
一隔	大乘經重翻之一，8 袟	大乘經一譯之一，6 袟	大乘論之一，10 袟	
二隔	大乘經重翻之二，14 袟	大乘經一譯之二，14 袟	大乘論之二，25 袟	
三隔	小乘經一譯之一，12 袟	大乘經一譯之三，11 袟	大乘論之三，16 袟	
四隔	小乘經一譯之二，11 袟	大乘經一譯之四，13 袟	小乘論之一，46 袟	
五隔	小乘經一譯之三，13 袟	大乘經一譯之五，12 袟	小乘論之二，12 袟	
六隔	小乘經一譯之四，3 袟 小乘經重翻 6 袟	大乘經一譯之六，10 袟	小乘論之三，9 袟	
七隔	小乘律之一，10 袟	大乘經重翻之三，12 袟	賢聖集傳之一，10 袟	
八隔	小乘律之二，11 袟	大乘經重翻之四，12 袟	賢聖集傳之二，8 袟	
九隔	小乘律之三，7 袟			

Figure. 50　Reconstruction Diagram of the Scripture Cabinet of Ximingsi (*Ximingsi jingchu* 西明寺经橱复原图). Source: Fang Guangchang 方廣錩, *Zhongguo xieben dazang jing yanjiu* 中國寫本大藏經研究, 437.

---

[38] This is about the the tale of "dragon treasury (Ch. *longzang* 龍藏)" in Buddhist history. According to the biography of Nāgājurna 龍樹 (*Longshu pusa zhuan* 龍樹菩薩傳, T2047a), the Dragon King Anavatapta (Ch. Aruda 阿耨達) boasted that his seven-jewel collections (*qibao zang* 七寶藏), inherited from the past seven Buddhas, were infinite in this athenaeum. The story was so widely circulated in ancient China that the phrase *longzang* became a euphemism for Buddhist collection; see *Longshu pusa zhuan*, T50, no. 2047a, p. 184, c6-17.

[39] The Iron Enclosing Mountains (Skt. *cakra-vāḍa-parvata*, Ch. *Tieweishan* 鐵圍山) is supposed to encircle the earth, forming the periphery of the present world. According to *Da zhidu lun* 大智度論 (Commentary on the *Mahā-prajñāpāramitā-sūtra*, T1509), the Buddhist council at Cakravāla was organized by Mañjuśrī and Maitreya.

[40] *NDL*, T55, no. 2149, p. 313, a16-18.

As we have seen in chapter 5, Daoxuan had heard tales of Buddhist libraries in India and Central Asia. The so-called cave temples of Juqu (*juqu yanku* 沮渠巖窟) here probably refers to the site containing a scriptural collection near today's Yarkand (shache 莎车, a county in Xinjiang Uyghur Autonomous Region).[41] Throughout his writing, Daoxuan took Indian scriptures as more authoritative and belittled Chinese indigenous writings, although his Ximingsi colleague Daoshi, in his *Fayuan zhulin*, points out that the amount of local writings was tremendous in Chang'an.[42]

We must keep in mind that when Daoxuan left Ximingsi, the monastery had already built up a magnificent manuscript collection, amounting to several times the number of scriptures contained in the *Ruzang lu* bibliography in the *Neidian Catalogue*. Many of the indigenous works excluded from the *Ruzang lu* were commentaries derived from notes and doctrinal debates based on public lectures sponsored by major monasteries. In seventh-century Chang'an, it is necessary to clarify difficult theological points in an effort to understand the new teachings transmitted from the West, such as yogācāra (Ch. *yuqiexing* 瑜伽行 or *yujiaxing*), the practice of the view of all experience occurs through cognition only; or *daśabhūmi* (Ch. *shidi* 十地, ten stages), the ten grounds of bodhisattva practice in Mahāyāna Buddhism. Many other texts were composed by monks or even lay adherents in the course of philosophical debate. If we recall the Buddhist sectarian lineages passed down at Ximingsi, we can identify several doctrinal lines, including Vinaya, Zen, *Vijñapti-mātratā* and Tantrism.[43] Although the official *Ruzang lu* excluded most of them, the large corpus of commentarial literature dealing with such sectarian material also found it place on the library shelves at Ximingsi, although the official *Ruzang lu* excluded most of them. Daoxuan's distinction between the Buddhist philosophical texts and non-Buddhist secular writings also gives us space to discuss the contents of additional libraries other than the central one reserved for the sanctioned tripiṭaka.

---

[41] *Mochizuki*, 2143. In the sixth century, the Indic monk Jñānagupta (Ch. Shenajueduo 闍那崛多, 523-600), who was the leading translator of Daxingshan Monastery, told the local priests that a devout ruler from Karghalik (Ch. Zhejujia 遮拘迦) possessed a sizable collection of Mahāyānist sūtras in his palace. See *Lidai sanbao ji*, T49, no. 2034, p.103, a13-27. See also *Mochizuki*, 597.

[42] *Fayuan zhulin*, T53, no. 2122, p. 1020, b16-25.

[43] Ono Katsutoshi had enumerated the basic lines of doctrinal transmission at Ximing; see Ono Katsutoshi, "Chōan no saimyōji to nittō guhōsō," 74-80.

Even among the thousands of indigenous works available at Ximingsi, Daoxuan had to make his choice of which to include in the *Neidian Catalogue*. For instance, the prelate Huijing 慧淨 received his ordination at Jiguo Monastery (Jiguosi 紀國 寺) and served as the abbot of Puguang Monastery (Puguangsi 普光寺). As an eminent scholar of Chang'an, he had composed more than 100 fascicles of commentaries and treatises on scriptures such as *Mahāyānasūtrā-laṃkāra-ṭīkā* (Ch. *Dacheng zhuangyanjing lun* 大乘莊嚴經論, T1604), *Saṃyuktabhidharmā-hṛdaya śāstra* (Ch. *Za apitan xinlun* 雜阿毘曇心論, T1552) and *Abhidharmakośabhāṣya* (Ch. *Jushelun* 俱舍論, T1558).[44] Among these writings, in his sub-catalogue devoted to the monastic scholarship current in his own dynasty, Daoxuan selected *Shiyi lun* 釋疑論 (Expounding Doubts), *Neidian shi yinghua* 內典詩英華 (Selected Poems in Buddhist Scriptures) and two others.[45]

Erik Zürcher (1928-2008) made the point that, "the *sangha* by the beginning of the T'ang had already developed into a large and diversified group of literate and sometimes highly cultivated specialists. Within Chinese culture a body of a completely new type had come into being: the *sangha* had become a *secondary elite*."[46] As a highly literate community, the Buddhist saṃgha created monastic schools (*sixue* 寺學), offering two tracks of education —— one to provide instruction or promote scriptures to the laity; the other to disseminate knowledge to the clerics. Two seventh-century manuscripts excavated from Turfan testify to the fact that monks living in this peripheral zone of the empire in the seventh century were required to recite the *Saddharmapuṇḍrīka-sūtra* (Sutra on the Lotus of the Wonderful Law, Ch. *Miaofa lianhua jing* 妙法蓮華經, T262); *Yaoshi rulai benyuanjing* 藥師如來本願經 (Original Vow of Bhaiṣajyaguruvaiḍūryaprabha, T449) and *Foshuo foming jing* 佛說佛名經 (Scripture of Buddha's Names, T440). In addition to these demanding requirements, senior prelates were also expected to be well versed in *Dazhidu lun* 大智度論 (Commentary on the *Mahā-prajñāpāramitā sūtra*, T1509), a bulky commentary ascribed to Nāgārjuna on the voluminous *Mahā-prajñāpāramitā-sūtra*.[47] It is natural to assume that the literary bar for the elite

---

[44] *Mochizuchi*, 3274 and 3028.

[45] Titled *Huangchao zhuanyi fojing lu* 皇朝傳譯佛經錄, the section is listed under the rubric of *Lidai zhong jing zhuan yi suo cong lu* 歷代眾經傳譯所從錄; see *NDL*, T55, no. 2149, p.281, c9-25.

[46] Erik Zürcher, "Buddhism and Education in T'ang Times," 21-56.

[47] Meng Xianshi 孟憲實, "Tulufan xin faxian de'Tang longshuo ernian Xizhou Gaochang xian Si'en si seng ji' 吐魯番新發現的〈唐龍朔二年西州高昌縣思恩寺僧籍〉," *Wenwu* 文物 2 (2007): 50-55. The two

monks who resided at Ximingsi would have been at least as high if not higher.

In the *Neidian Catalogue*, Daoxuan praised master Zhenyi 真懿, a vinaya specialist at Ximingsi, for his contribution to helping postulants find their way in the Buddhist canon. For the convenience of beginners, Zhenyi created a selected bibliography titled *Lidai zhongjing juyao zhuandu lu* 歷代眾經舉要轉讀錄 (Catalogue Summarizing the Essential Points of Scriptures from Different Dynasties) that incorporated seminal texts central to the Buddhist teaching. Daoxuan's catalogue reveals that Zhenyi's catalogue lists only 337 texts, comprising scriptures, vinayas and treatises from the Greater Vehicles.[48] Not surprisingly, the list includes the above-mentioned four scriptures required of clerics.[49] Like a collection of "primers" of the sort contained in the bibliography, the monastic bibliotheca of Ximingsi possessed copies of basic textbooks, so that novice monks would have ready access to suitable reading materials in an age when printed books were not yet available. For instance, a manuscript of the *Shizhong   dacheng lun* 十種大乘論 (On Ten Categories of Mahāyāna), a treatise composed by Sengcan 僧粲 (529-613), was available in the library.[50] Noted for his eloquence and erudition, Sengcan was celebrated as the best Mahāyāna scholar among the twenty-five Buddhist communities (*ershiwuzhong diyi moheyanjiang* 二十五眾第一摩訶衍匠). His treatise was highly valued by both Fei Changfang and Daoxuan as a useful handbook for beginners.[51]

It is clear that Daoxuan aimed at raising the standards of Buddhist bibliography developed in the Sui dynasty, but he chose to retain the practice of listing indigenous works separately from Indian texts, in a sub-catalogue of the tenth chapter.[52] The

---

manuscripts are "*Tang longshuo ernian (662) Xizhou Gaochang xian Si'en si seng ji*" and "*Wuzhou zhengseng yuannian (695) wuyue xizhou gaocangxian congfusi zhuanjingli* 武周證聖元年 (695) 五月西州高昌縣崇福寺轉經歷."

[48] *NDL*, T55, no. 2149, p. 313, a29-b5.

[49] *Lidai sanbao ji*, T49, no. 2034, p. 106, a20-29; *NDL*, T55, no. 2149, p.312-313.

[50] The ten categories of Mahāyāna, according to *Neidian Catalogue*, are: *wu zhangai* 無障礙 (free from obscurations, Skt. *anāvaraṇa*); *pingdeng* 平等 (equality, Skt. *sama*); *ni* 逆 (disagreeable, Skt. *vāma*); *shun* 順 (go with the flow of saṃsāra); *jie* 接 (join); *cuo* 挫 (obstruction); *mi* 迷 (perplexity); *meng* 夢 (dream); *xiangji* 相即 (identification); *zhongdao* 中道 (middle way), see *NDL*, T55, no. 2149, p. 278, b26-c6.

[51] *NDL*, T55, no. 2149, p.278b-c; Kieschnick, *The Impact of Buddhism on Chinese Material Culture*, 164-84. On the twenty-five Buddhist communities (*ershiwuzhong* 二十五眾), see Yamazaki Hiroshi 山崎宏, *Shina chūsei bukkyō no tenkai* 支那中世佛教の展開 (Tokyo: Shimizu shoten, 1942), 298-309.

[52] *NDL*, T55, no. 2149, p.302c1-2. For a brief introduction of the *Neidian Catalogue*, see Kawaguchi

bibliography, titled *Lidai daosu shuzuo zhujielu* 歷代道俗述作注解錄 (Explanatory Catalogue of the Works by Monks and Laymen from Previous Dynasties), devoted to assemble indigenous Buddhist works from the fourth to the seventh century.[53] Titles of compositions by Chinese monk-scholars were also collected elsewhere in the three-fascicle *Ximingsi lu*, compiled in 659 to reflect the a wider variety of books housed in the bibliotheca of the monastery. This catalogue does not survive today, but it is thought that the most important titles are preserved in the *Neidian Catalogue*. A well-known feature of the *Ximingsi lu* is the collection of miscellaneous canon (Ch. *zazang* 雜藏, Skt. *saṃyuktapiṭaka*), which includes genres such as encyclopedia, doctrinal treatise, hagiography and Buddhist history.[54]

Space does not permit here detailed discussion of other titles; but any estimate of the extent and content of the Ximing collection in the seventh century should not overlook the evidence of the *Fayuan zhulin*, the 100-fascicle encyclopedia by Daoshi, which cite a rich variety of scriptures readily accessible in the Ximing library. Kawaguchi Yoshiteru has points out that, among the more than 400 Buddhist scriptures quoted in *Fayuan zhulin*, many are not listed in the current Taishō canon. He identifies about 121 texts belonging to the category of *isonkyō* 逸存經, scriptures lost but partially extant in other sources. It is possible that the Ximing library of the middle seventh century contained such eccentric texts as *Xiao wuzhuo jing* 小五濁經 (Small Scripture of Five Turbidities) or *Wumeng jing* 五夢經 (Scripture of Five Dreams).[55] The *Neidian Catalogue* was more than a guide to Ximing's library; it was a resource for libraries everywhere, and its reputation quickly spread to the national level. Adopted by many monasteries across the country as the model for sūtra-collection, it became the benchmark catalogue that stood the test of time. The present modest introduction to the work is just an invitation to further critical research on this subject.

Yoshiteru, *Chūgoku bukkyō ni okeru kyōroku kenkyū*, 111-27; Ono Genmyō 小野玄妙, *Bukkyō kyōten sōron* 佛教經典總論 (Tokyo: Daitō shuppansha, 1978), 502-09.

[53] *NDL*, T55, no. 2149, p.338a -0326c.

[54] Tang Yongtong, *Sui-Tang fojiao shigao*, 100; Feng Guodong, "Tang Song wangyi fojiao jinglu congkao," 54; see also *Zongjing mulu*, T55, no. 2148, p. 181, a1-5.

[55] Kawaguchi Yoshiteru, *Chūgoku Bukkyō ni okeru kyōroku kenkyū* , 172-95. For an introduction of the two encyclopedias compiled by Daoshi, *Fayuan zhulin* and *Zhujing yaoji* 諸經要集 (Collected Essential Phrases from All the Scriptures, T2123); see Stephen Teiser, "T'ang Buddhist Encyclopedias: An Introduction to Fa-yüan Chu-lin and Chu-ching Yao-chi," *Tang Studies* 3 (1985): 109-28.

The Putiyuan Library in the Eighth Century

If the *Neidian Catalogue* opens the curtain on Ximing library in the seventh century, it is the Putiyuan cloister that is considered the real bibliotheca at Ximingsi in many sources. Horiike Shunpō, a scholar specializing in Buddhist history of Nara, even argues that the national tripiṭaka on which Daoxuan reported was well preserved in Putiyuan.[56] However, the first mention of Putiyuan in Buddhist sources, as we have seen in chapter 3, is associated with the Institute of Translation superintended by Śubhakarasiṃha, who arrived in Chang'an in 716. Shortly after he arrived at Ximingsi, he established the institute in the Putiyuan cloister. The Chinese character *yuan* 院 (cloister, Skt. *ārāma*) means in this case a enclosed courtyard on temple grounds, consisting of a major Buddha hall and numerous subordinate rooms. The Putiyuan at Ximingsi was likely one of the thirteen huge Buddhist cloisters mentioned by Tang writers. The title "*puti* (bodhi)" was not unique for another major monastery located in Pingkang Ward (Pingkang fang 平康坊) in Chang'an was known as Puti (Bodhi) Monastery . Yijing also informs us that Saṃghavarman 僧伽跋摩, a monk from Samarkand, had carved out a figure of Avalokiteśvara under the *aśoka* tree (Ch. *wuyoushu* 無憂樹) in a "Bodhi Cloister" at Dajue Monastery (Dajuesi 大覺寺) located in the western region.[57]

The extant accounts concerning the Putiyuan at Ximingsi are centered on Śubhakarasiṃha, who brought loads of Sanskrit manuscripts to Chang'an and was first housed in Xingfu Monastery. He soon moved to Ximingsi and proposed to Xuanzong that eminent scholars be invited to take positions in his translation office situated in Putiyuan. It was customary for Chang'an monks to attach a library to the numerous Institutes for the Translation of Scriptures so that books of diverse editions and manuscripts written in foreign languages became accessible to translators, scholars, their assistants and visitors from other monasteries. Moreover, scribes could efficiently transcribe new translations and return the original texts in the library holdings. However, like Buddhapāla, Śubhakarasiṃha was not able to keep his Sanskrit manuscripts in the Putiyuan library, as he was ordered to tender the original

---

[56] Horiike Shunpō, "Nittō ryūgakusō to Saimyōji," 245-76. A foreign example of a Bodhi Cloister (Jap. Bodaiin) was found at the famous Japanese Monastery Kōfukuji 興福寺, located in Nara city; see *Mochizuki*, 1082. See also the postscript to the *Dacheng fayuan yilin zhang* 大乘法苑義林章 (T1861); *Dacheng fayuan yilin zhang*, no. 1861, p. 343, a27-b9.

[57] *Da Tang xiyu qiufa gaoseng zhuan*, T51, no. 2066, p. 4, c15-24.

manuscripts to the imperial library, which, like the national monasteries, was considered an important repository for Buddhist scriptures.[58] The fragmentary sources from the eighth century, however, are not sufficient to prove that Putiyuan was the same monastic library that was earlier used by Daoxuan and Daoshi; it is possible that the Putiyuan collection associated with Śubhakarasiṃha's translation office represented the bibliographical and academic accomplishments of the Ximingsi monks in the eighth century. An important inference drawn from the newly translated forty-fascicle *Av ataṃsaka sūtra* (Ch. *Sishi huayan* 四十華嚴, T293, *Gaṇḍa-vyūha*) indicates that at least in the early eighth century the official library of Ximingsi was associated with Putiyuan.[59]

Over the course of the first two centuries of the Tang, scriptural translations were joint projects involving both scholar-monks and officials in charge of religious affairs. The famed masters of Ximingsi were expected to engage themselves in this process at their home monastery or other designated institutions. For instance, between 650 and 655, Xuanzang recruited at least five cleric scholars from Ximingsi to join his translation atelier. In an effort to render the seminal treatise of the Sarvāstivādins, the *Abhidharma-mahāvibhāṣā-śāstra* (Treatise of the Great Commentary on the Abhidharma, Ch. *Apidamo da piposha lun* 阿毘達磨大毘婆沙論, T1545) into Chinese, the Ximing prelates took separate positions on the translation team: initial checker (or checkers of meaning, *zhengyi* 證義); editor (or binders of the composition, *zhuiwen* 綴文); drafter (*zhibi* 執筆) and amanuensis (or

---

[58] *SGSZ*, T50, no. 2061, p. 715, b9-12; *Tang Kaiyuan shijiao guangping li zhang*, A098, no. 1276, p. 257, a10-b4; *Xu gujin yijing tuji*, T55, no. 2152, p. 372, b2-6.

[59] *Da fanguang fo huayan jing*, T10, no. 293, p. 849, a9-16; *ZYL*, T55, no. 2157, p. 894, c22-26; *Xu Zhenyuan shijiao lu* 續貞元釋教錄 (Continuation to the *Zhenyuan Catalogue*), T55, no.2158, p. 1052, a13-17; *SGSZ*, T50, no. 2061, p. 721, b15-24. In 798, the King of Uḍa (Ch. *wutu guowang* 烏荼國王) presented a Sanskrit manuscript of the *Āv ataṃsaka Sūtra* as a gift to Dezong. Copied by the Indian king himself to pay his homage to the Chinese emperor, the text was translated by Prājña and his atelier at Congfu Monastery. The king of Uḍa is also known as the king of Odra, or Orissa. He was probably Śubhakaradeva the first (r. 780-800), the founder of the Bhauma-kara Dynasty; see Davidson, *Indian Esoteric Buddhism*, 51. The Singaporean scholar Ku Cheng-Mei 古正美 thinks that the new version of *Āv ataṃsaka Sūtra* reflects the Av ataṃsaka Buddharāja (Ch. *fowang* 佛王) tradition that was associated with the cult of Amoghapāśa (Ch. *Bukong juansuo guanyin* 不空羂索観音) popular in southern India. Like many translated texts from the tradition of Indian tantrism, the submission of this scripture to the emperor certainly assumes the political connotation of the Buddha king. See Ku Cheng-Mei, *Cong tianwang chuantong dao fowang chuantong: Zhongguo zhongshi fojiao zhiguo yishi xingtai yanjiu* 從天王傳統到佛王傳統: 中國中世佛教治國意識形態研究 (Taipei: Shangzhou chuban, 2003), 325-76.

scribes, *bishou* 筆受).[60] In the tripiṭaka described by Daoxuan in the middle of the seventh century, the *Abhidharma-mahāvibhāṣā-śāstra* was contained in twenty book cases, the exact location of which in the early Ximing library was precisely prescribed in the *Neidian Catalogue*.[61] On many occasions such as this, when the major locale of translation was situated elsewhere, it was customary for the Ximing prelates to make copies of the works, so as to enrich their own library. Yuanzhao, who participated as an amanuensis in the new translation of the *Āvataṃsaka Sūtra*, copied the scripture and took it back to Ximingsi. On this occasion, textual evidence bears testimony to the role of the East Pavilion (*dongge* 東閣), situated in the Putiyuan cloister, as the official depot of the renowned Ximing tripiṭaka:

It was the fourteenth year of Zhenyuan of the Great Tang, the lunar year of Wuyin. Śramaṇa Yuanzhao, member of the translation atelier…copied the newly translated scripture and remedied the inadequacy of the tripiṭaka of East Pavilion in the [library] of the Putiyuan cloister at Ximingsi.

大唐貞元十四年，歲在戊寅……翻經沙門圓照……手自書寫此新譯經，填續西明寺菩提院東閣一切經闕.[62]

Reference here to the tripiṭaka of East Pavilion (*dongge yiqiejing* 東閣一切經) attests to the existence of an open Buddhist canon preserved in a major Buddhist hall at Putiyuan. We are familiar with other cases of Chinese pavilions (*ge* 閣) that served as monastic libraries in Chang'an. For instance, the Wenshuge 文殊閣 (Pavilion of Mañjuśrī), superintended by Amoghavajra in the eighth century, was the central repository of Xingshan Monastery, located in the Institute of Sūtra Translation.[63] The

---

[60] *Apidamo da piposha lun* 阿毗達磨大毗婆沙論 (Skt. *Abhidharma-mahāvibhāṣā śāstra*), T27, no. 1545, p. 4, c19-p. 5, a15. Forte, *Political Propaganda and Ideology*, 171-76.

[61] *NDL*, T55, no. 2149, p. 311, c9-18.

[62] Recorded in the long postscript to the narrative chapter *Ru busiyi jietuo jingjie Puxian xingyuan ping* 入不思議解脫境界普賢行願品 (Chapter on the Vows of Samantabhadra) in the forty-fascicle *Avataṃsaka sūtra*; see *Da fangguang fo Huayanjing*, T10, no. 293, p. 849, a9-16; *Mochizuki*, 3404-07. In 755, Buddhist prelates sent the newly-translated *Avataṃsaka Sūtra* to a eunuch-official Ma Chengqian 馬承倩 for proofreading in Guangzhai Monastery (Guangzaisi 光宅寺), another centre of sūtra-replication in Chang'an; see *ZYL*, T55, no. 2157, p. 771, c10-14.

[63] See Wang Xiang, "Beiye yu xiejing," 507-08. On one occasion, at the request of Amoghavajra, the emperor Daizong (r. 762-79) bestowed a tripiṭaka of 5,050 scrolls to his daughter Master Qionghua 瓊華, who was studying under the tutelage of Amoghavajra in the Institute for Sūtra Translation at Wenshuge; see

selection of scriptures to strengthen the Putiyuan collection was not a random decision. Evidence suggests that the Ximing monks had rummaged through libraries in other monasteries or even those collections located as far as in the east capital of Luoyang for an authoritative edition (*zhengben* 正本), so that they might reproduce accurate texts and take the copies back to Ximingsi.[64] According to the *Da Tang zhenyuan xu kaiyuan shijiao lu* 大唐貞元續開元釋教錄 (Addendum to *Kaiyuan Catalogue* Compiled in the Reign-era of Zhenyuan in the Great Tang, T2156), a minor catalogue that was soon subsumed in the authoritative *Zhenyuan Catalogue*, editing and copying a new text required several stages of editing and copying.[65] Textual instability in the age of manuscripts and the custom of culling excerpts from lengthy texts must have produced numerous variant manuscript versions.

The *Da Tang zhenyuan xu kaiyuan shijiao lu* was a Buddhist catalogue compiled by Yuanzhao at Ximingsi in the tenth year of Zhenyuan (794). It must have used the collection of Putiyuan, suggesting by the end of the eighth century, the size of the collection had grown to a point where a new catalogue was needed. From the eighteenth year of Kaiyuan (730) to 794, the four incumbent Tang rulers (Xuanzong, Suzong, Daizong and Dezong) witnessed a large number of new esoteric scrolls

---

BZJ, T.52, no.2120, 839a.

[64] For the case of selecting the authoritative edition of the *Zhuan falun jing* 轉法輪經 (Sutra of Turning the Wheel of the Dharma, T109) among Buddhist libraries in Chang'an; see *Kaiyuan shijiao lu*, T55, no. 2154, p. 692, b25-26.

[65] Yuanzhao described the process this way:

> [We] copied the official edition according to the set of new characters, of which every leaf has 24 lines, each line 25 characters... by the seventh month... we finished proofreading the draft... by the tenth month... we accomplished the transcription of the official edition which is divided into ten fascicles. Consuming 566 sheets, the total number of characters in the text is 330,104.. by the eleventh month, we collated the draft, the official copy and the duplicate.

> 新定字樣謄寫進本. 每紙二十四行, 每行二十五字. 至七月... 初校草本訖. 至十月... 繕寫進本畢, 分成十卷, 用紙五百六十六張, 計文三十三萬一百四言. 又至十一月... 對草本進本副本檢勘.

Da Tang zhenyuan xukanyuan shijiao lu, T55, no. 2156, p. 762, a11-20; See also Fu Xuancong, *Zhongguo cangshu tongshi*, 196. The text discussed by Yuanzhao is the state-sanctioned *Qianding sifenlü shu* 僉定四分律疏 (Commentary on the Dharmagupta Vinaya Edited by the Imperial Order), a text that we have discussed in chapter 4. The three copies of the same text had been proofread with greatest care to compare the scribal variants of the text. This job lasted for about five months, first producing a draft, followed by an authoritative version prepared for the official canon. The final copy was the duplicate (*fuben* 副本) to back up the official copy.

added to the monastic library shelves, the result of the efforts of the tantric masters committed to introducing the Indian esoteric teachings to their Chinese followers. By 794, for fear that the collection of esoteric manuals, the newly-acquired poetic anthology, and memorials as well as inscriptions were lost in the library (*zangnei* 藏 內), Yuanzhao "wrote down what he had seen and heard" and presented his results in the three-fascicle *Da Tang zhenyuan xu kaiyuan shijiao lu*.[66] The short bibliography includes nearly 200 fascicles of esoteric texts translated by foreign monks. In addition to the famous Vajrabodhi, Amoghavajra and Prajña, the list of translators also features Ajitasena (Ch. Azhidaxian 阿質達霰) from northern India; Dharmachandra (Ch. Fayue 法月) of eastern India; the Kuchen master Utpalavīrya (Ch. Lianhua jingjin 蓮華精進) and the Khotanese Śīladharma (Ch. Shiluodama 尸羅達摩), who had generously bequeathed Sanskrit manuscripts to their host monasteries. In addition to a variety of religious documents collected during the Zhenyuan period, the catalogue is replete with collections of *dhāraṇīs*; ritual manuals (Ch. *niansongfa* 念誦法, Skt. *kalpa* or *vidhi*); as well as systematic works such as the *Liqu jing* 理趣經 (Scripture that Transcends the Principle, Skt. *Adhyartdhaśatikā-prajñāpāramitā-sūtra*).[67] This new esoteric texts laid down a solid foundation that established Ximingsi as another center of Chinese tantrism —— a center that would subsequently attract Japanese student monks to study in the rich Ximing library in the ninth century.

The Zhenyuan Catalogue and Japanese Scholar-Monks

Six years after the publication of Yuanzhao's *Addendum to the Kaiyuan Catalogue*, in the fourth month of 800, the status of Ximingsi as the national repository of the Buddhist canon was enhanced by an edict of Dezong ordering Yuanzhao to produce the authoritative *Zhenyuan xinding shijiao mulu* (A Catalogue of [the Texts on] Buddhist Teachings, Newly Collated in the Zhenyuan Era, T2157) as an exemplar for sūtra replication.[68] The major part of *Zhenyuan Catalogue*, titled *zonglu* 總錄

---

[66] *Da Tang zhenyuan xukanyuan shijiao lu*, T55, no. 2156, p. 766, a13-25.

[67] For the definition of *niansong fa* 念誦法 (chanting method), see *Mochizuki*, 501. For a general introduction of the esoteric texts in the catalogue, see Ian Astley, "Esoteric Buddhism, Material Culture, and Catalogues in East Asia," In *EBTEA*, 712. *Liqu jing* 理趣經 (Skt. *Adhyartdhaśatikā prajñāpāramitā sūtra*) is the abbreviated title of the *Dale jin'gang bukong zhenshi samoye jing* 大樂金剛不空真實三摩耶經 (T243).

[68] The catalogue is also known as *Yuanzhao Lu* 圓照錄 (Catalogue Compiled by Yuanzhao). See *Mochizuki*, 3690-691. According to *Xu Zhenyuan shijiao lu*, the catalogue was finished in 799; see Saitō Akitoshi 斎藤

(general catalogue), was a more or less rehashed edition of the prominent *Kaiyuan shijiao lu,* with the addition of a special section explaining why the catalogue was a state-sanctioned project. The second part, entitled *bielu* 別錄 (explanatory bibliography), contains bibliographical listings of 269 scriptures translated by eleven scholars during the preceding seventy-one years. Another feature of the catalogue is the addendum to the last chapter (fascicle 30) where, under the rubric of *Buruzang mulu* 不入藏目錄 (Catalogue of Works Excluded from the Tripiṭaka), 118 apocryphal texts, beginning with *Miji jingang lishi jing* 密跡金剛力士經 (Sutra of the Vajra-Warrior with the Hidden Tracks) and ending with *Gaowang guanshiyin jing* 高王觀世音經 (The Avalokiteśvara Sutra of King Gao), are identified as apocryphal works.[69] For a long period after its completion, the *Zhenyuan Catalogue* represented the classic work of Buddhist bibliography, the impact of which was felt across the boundaries of East Asian countries. The taxonomy adopted by the *Zhenyuan Catalouge* was slightly different from that of the *Neidian Catalogue.*

Zhenyuan xinding shijiao mulu

Year of Compilation: 800 (Zhenyuan 16)
Number of Manuscripts: 7399 fascicles
Existing Collection: 1258 (vol.29 and 30, *Dacheng ruzang lu* 大乘入藏錄 *and Xiaocheng ruzang lu* 小乘入藏錄)[70]

Category	Number	fascicle	Case
Mahayana sūtra (*Dacheng jing* 大乘經)	682	2413	221
Mahayana vinaya (*Dacheng lü* 大乘律)	27	N/A	55
Mahayana abhidharma (Dacheng lun 大乘論)	99	520	50
Hinayana sūtra (*Xiaocheng jing* 小乘經)	240	618	48

昭俊, *Bukkyō nenpyō* 仏教年表 (Tokyo: Shin jenbutsu oraisha, 1994), 83.

[69] *ZYL*, T55, no. 2157, p. 1046, b1-25. See *Sho Ajari shingon mikkyō burui sōroku* 諸阿闍梨真言密教部類 總錄 (or *Hakke hiroku* 八家秘録 [The Tantric Rituals Collected by the Eight Masters]), T55, no. 2176, p. 1115, c19-20.

[70] *ZYL*, T55, no. 2157, p. 1024, a15-26 and p. 1038, c7-17.

Hinayana abhidharma (*Xiaocheng lü* 小乘律)	61	493	50
Hinayana vinaya (*Xiaocheng lun* 小乘論)	36	698	72
Hagiography (*Shengxian ji* 賢聖集)	112	618	7
Total	1258	5, 390	510

Table 2. *Dacheng ruzang lu* 大乘入藏錄 *and Xiaocheng ruzang lu* 小乘入藏錄, from *Zhenyuan Catalogue*

Although the tantric texts listed in the preliminary *Xu kaiyuan shijiaolu* also appear in *Zhenyuan Catalogue*, there is no specific identification of them as pertaining to a particular school or tradition. On the contrary, they are listed in subordinate positions peripheral to those of the major scholastic traditions such as Huayan.[71] In contrast to Daoxuan, Yuanzhao was more flexible in his choice of sanctioned classics, so that his catalogue incorporates a wide variety of indigenous works by Chinese monks. With its coverage of the minute facts of translation and recension and its precise categorization of materials, the *Zhenyuan Catalogue* may be said to represent the culmination of the Tang Buddhist bibliographic catalogues. With the catastrophe of the Huichang Suppression, the manuscript inventory contained in the *Zhenyuan Catalogue* in some sense captured the afterglow of Tang Buddhism and marked the close of two centuries of Buddhist translations since the monumental *Kaiyan Catalogue*. That work, edited by Zhisheng in 730 (Kaiyuan 18), may have set the standard for Buddhist bibliography, but Yuanzhao's catalogue, based on the comprehensive Putiyuan library of Ximingsi at the end of the eighth century, significantly enlarged the coverage.

The experience of the Kashgarian lexicographer Huilin 慧琳 (737-820), who was active in the Ximing library for some twenty years, also provides a snapshot of the Ximing tripiṭaka around the time of the compilation of the *Zhenyuan Catalogue*. Abe Ryūichi 阿部龍一 rightly points out the link between Yuanzhao's scholarship and Huilin's Buddhist lexicon:

Based on the knowledge he had acquired from his collaboration with Prajñā, Yüan-chao produced a concordance of the principle terms in the *Mahāyana Six*

---

[71] Ian Astley, "Esoteric Buddhism, Material Culture, and Catalogues in East Asia." In *EBTEA*, 711.

Pāramitā Sūtra that provided the pronunciation and meaning of each, and, whenever appropriate, the original term in Sanskrit. Yüan-chao's concordance may well have inspired the compilation of a gigantic Buddhist lexicon, the *Pronunciation and Meaning of Words from the Complete Buddhist Scriptures* (*I-ch'eih-ching yin-i*), in one hundred fascicles, by another resident priest of the His-ming monastery, Hui-lin (737-820).[72]

The gigantic lexicon mentioned here is Huilin's *Dazang yinyi* 大藏音義 (or *Yiqie jing yinyi* 一切經音義, T2128), an important work on sanskritology and Chinese scholia (*xungu* 訓詁). Huilin worked on this masterpiece between 783 and 807, based on the precious volumes of both Buddhist and Chinese classics collected at Ximing library.[73] He made use of such lexicographic classics as *Zilin* 字林 (Grove of Character); *Zitong* 字統 (Unification of Character); *Shenglei* 聲類 (Category of Syllables); *Sancang* 三蒼 (Thee Books of Cangxie); *Qieyun* 切韻 (Cutting Rhymes) and *Yupian* 玉篇 (Jade Chapters), along with historical works and Confucian texts readily accessible in the Ximing collection.[74] Huilin's lexicon, which contains technical terms appearing in one thousand two hundred and twenty texts, is central to a full understanding of the Ximing tripiṭaka. As Chinese scholars point out, it provides a glimpse of the ever-changing collections of Ximingsi and scriptures absent in the official *Zhenyuan Catalogue*. It may well serve as an index to the sanctioned canon and extracanonical works readily accessible in the Ximing library. For instance, Fang Guangchang provides a list of sixteen Buddhist texts freshly adopted in the lexicon:

1. *Shishi xilu* 釋氏系錄 (Geneology of the Śākya Clan)
2. *Lishe lunheng* 利涉論衡 (The Balanced Inquiries of Lishe);
3. *Daoyin ding sanjiao lunheng* 道氤定三教論衡 (Disquisitions of Defining the

---

[72] Abe Ryūichi, *The Weaving of Mantra*, 117-18.

[73] Chinese scholars think that the lexcon was completed in 807 (Yuanhe 2) instead of 810; see Wen Yiwu 文亦武, "Huilin *Yiqiejing yinyi* chengshu niandai kaocha ji qita 慧琳《一切經音義》成書年代考實及其他." *Guji zhengli yanjiu xuekan* 古籍整理研究學刊 4 (2000): 18. For a general study of the lexicon, see Yao Yongming 姚永銘, *Huilin 'Yiqiejing yinyi' yanjiu* 慧琳《一切經音義》研究 (Nanjing: Jiangsu guji chubanshe, 2003).

[74] *Zilin* was composed by Lü Chen 呂忱 from the Jin dynasty (265-420); *Qiuyun*, written by Lu Fayan 陸法言 (581-618), is a Chinese rhyme dictionary published in 601 in the Sui Dynasty. For the impact of *Yiqiejing yinyi* on Chinse phonetics, see Yao Yongming, *Huilin 'Yiqiejing yinyi' yanjiu*, 83-104.

Three Religions by Daoyin)

4. *Chongzheng lu* 崇正錄 (Record of Venerating the Right Path)

5. *Huichao zhuan* 慧超傳 (*Hyecho wang o cheonchukguk jeon* 慧超往五天竺國傳, Memoir of a Pilgrimage to the Five Indian Kingdoms)

6. *Wuxing fashi shu* 無行法師書 (Letters of Master Wuxing)[75]

7. *Zhaolun* 肇論 (Sengzhao on Mahāyāna Buddhist doctrines, T1858)

8. *Zhiguan men lun* 止觀門論 (*Zhiguan men lun song* 止觀門論頌, Treatise on the Methods of Cessation and Clear Observation, T1655)

9. *Anle ji* 安樂集 (Paradise Collection, T1958)

10. *Baofa yi lun* 寶法義論 (On the Meaning of the Treasured Dharma)

11. *Baowang lun* 寶王論 (*Nianfo sanmei baowang lun* 念佛三昧寶王論, Treatise on the Invoking the Buddha Samādhi Treasure King, T1967)[76]

12. *Jinpai juemo lun* 金錍決膜論 (On Removing the Cataracts by Adamantine Scalpel)

13. *Guanxin lun* 觀心論 (Treatise on Observing the Mind, T1920)[77]

14. *Qunyi lun* 群疑論 (*Shi jingtu qunyi lun* 釋淨土群疑論, Explanation of Doubts on the Pure Land, T1960)

15. *Shiyi lun* 十疑論 (*Jingtu shiyi lun* 淨土十疑論, Ten Questions on the Pure Land, T1961)

16. *Yuxiang fa* 浴像法 (*Xinji yuxiang yigui* 新集浴像儀軌, Method of Bathing a Buddha-Image, T1322)[78]

Some of the treatises have been passed down to us, while others were only recently found among the extant Dunhuang manuscripts. It is believed that these texts, absent from the *Zhenyuan Catalogue*, reflect the textual diversity of Ximing library in the early ninth century.[79] According to Huilin's biography, the lexicon was stored in the

---

[75] *Jinzhou shamen Wuxing cong zhongtian fushu yu tangguo zhu dade* 荊州沙門無行從中天附書於唐國諸大德, *Yiqiejing yinyi*, T54, no. 2128, p. 928, a1.

[76] Oda, 1586; *Mochizuki*, 4161.

[77] This is probably the work composed by the eminent Chan master Shenxiu 神秀 (606-706); see S646, S2595, P2460, P2657.

[78] Fang Guangchang, "*Huilin yinyi* yu Tangdai Dazangjing 《慧琳音義》與唐代大藏經," in *Zangwai fojiao wenxian: dibaji* 藏外佛教文獻: 第八集 (Beijing: Zongjiao wenhua chubanshe, 2003), 420. Another example is *Qianbo manshushili jing* 千鉢曼殊室利經, a text absent in the *Zhenyuan Catalogue*; see *Xu Zhenyuan shijiao lu*, T55, no. 2158, p. 1048, b22-25.

[79] Circumstantial evidence concerning the Buddhist tripiṭaka in Chang'an during this period is also available

Ximing library along with many extracanonical works absent in the official catalogue. Not until some forty years after its completion was the *Yiqiejing yinyi* approved by the government and entered into the official tripiṭaka.[80] Huilin's marvelous achievement even captured the attention of some Koryŏ monks who sought to purchase the book during the Xiande 顯德 era (954-959) in the Later Zhou Dynasty. However, after a century and a half, the dictionary might have dropped from circulation and they failed to find a copy on sale in the southern province, Zhejiang. Despite the status of the *Zhenyuan Catalogue* as a state-recognized Buddhist bibliography, the scope of its influence seems to have been restricted to Northern China and the copies of the translated works based in it were mostly preserved in the same area.[81]

If we now look eastward to explore the migration of texts from Ximingsi to Korea and Japan, we find there a passion for Buddhist books akin to that shown by the Chinese pilgrims who once took the arduous road to India in search of the Buddhist teachings. The dissemination of materials from the Buddhist collection of Ximingsi, from the ninth century, can be traced along two lines: first, the Japanese monks in residence at the monastery, reflective of the importance of cultural exchange between Tang China and Heian Japan; and secondly, the textual records of special collections found in various contemporaneous sources. As we have seen from previous chapters, starting from the seventh century, Ximingsi served as a large caravanserai for both local masters and scholar monks of foreign extraction, providing a forum for academic exchange and friendly competition. The visitors, foreign monks in particular, must have taken an immediate liking to the rich store of manuscripts deposited in the Ximing library during their pilgrimage in Tang China.

Among a group of about ten Japanese monks who took up residence at Ximingsi, Dōji visited the monastery in the earlier Nara period, predating his fellow monks by about ninety years. Dōji is known as the transmitter of the *Daianjiryū* 大安寺流

---

through Ennin's travelogue and manuscripts excavated from Dunhuang and Turfan. When Ennin visited the *puxian daochang* 普賢道場 (Hall of Samantabhadra) in the Monastery of Gold Pavilion (Jin'ge'si) at Mount Wutai, he found a well-decorated tripiṭaka donated by a patron from Chang'an. See Reischauer, *Ennin's Travels*, 254.

[80] The original text reads: "貯其本于西明藏中," see *Tang jingshi Ximingsi Huilin zhuan* 唐京師西明寺慧琳傳, *SGZZ*, T50, no. 2061, p. 738, a22-b5. Fang Guangchang argues that Huilin was registered at Xingshan Monastery; see Fang Guangchang, *Zhongguo xieben dazangjing yanjiu*, 282.

[81] Su Bai 宿白, *Hanwen foji mulu* 漢文佛籍目錄 (Beijing: Wenwu chubanshe, 2009), 65.

branch of the Japanese Sanronshū 三論宗.[82] The other Japanese monk-scholars made the journey starting from the last quarter of the eighth century. About three decades after Dōji returned to Japan, Eichū, another Sanronshū monk who made the voyage to Tang China in 777 (Hōki 宝亀 8), lodged in Ximingsi for six years and frequented the Putiyuan library. In 805 (Enryaku 延暦 24), five years after Yuanzhao completed his catalogue, Eichū returned to Japan and assumed the post of abbot at Bonshakuji 梵釋寺 (Monastery of Brahmā and Śakra) by the order of Emperor Kanmu 桓武天皇 (r. 781-806, 737-806).[83] The library of Bonshakuji was said to be in possession of the 5000-fascicle tripiṭaka brought back in 735 (Tempyō 天平 7) by Genbō 玄昉 (d.746), a Hossōshū 法相宗 monk who studied Yogācāra doctrine with the eminent Zhizhou 智周 (668-723). The manuscripts that he collected and copied in Chang'an were believed to be based on the standard *Kaiyuan Catalogue* completed in 730. Like other Japanese *gakumonsō* 學問僧 (scholar-monks), Eichū transcribed the newly-translated scriptures and presented some of them to the emperor. The entry of 835 (Jōwa 承和 2) in the *Shoku Nihon kōki* 續日本後紀 (Continued Later Chronicle of Japan), one of the six imperially commissioned Japanese histories, implies a connection and similarity between *Zhenyuan Catalogue* and *Bonshakuji mokuroku* 梵釋寺目錄 (Buddhist Catalogue of Bonshakuji).[84] The wisdom contained in the Bonshakuji collection greatly enhanced the compilation of another important catalogue, *Tōiki dentō mokuroku*, for the latter preserves a short extract of scriptures contained in the former.[85] We are

---

[82] Ōkubo Ryōshun 大久保良峻, Yamaguchi Kōei 山口耕栄, and Udaka Ryōtetsu 宇高良哲, ed., *Nihon bukkyō hennen taikan: hasshū sōran* 日本仏教編年大鑑：八宗総覧 (Tokyo: Shikisha, 2009), 21.

[83] Bonshakuji was established by Emperor Kammu as the Shitennōji 四天王寺 (Monastery of Four Mahārājās) for the posthumous happiness of the former Emperor Tenji 天智天皇 (r. 668-671) in 786 (Enryaku 延暦 5). Nine years later, it was renamed Bonshakuji; see Oda, 1636. For the biography of Eichū, see *Genkō shakusho*, DNBZ 62.149.

[84] Ono, *kaisetsuhen*, 154; *Mochizuki*, 257. See also *Fozu tongji*, T49, no. 2035, p. 399, a26-28; *Darijing yishi* 大日經義釋 (Explanation of the Meanings of the *Mahāvairocana-abhisaṃbodhi tantra*), XZJ 36, p. 985, b2-10. For a popular novel based on the life story of Genbō, see Matsumoto Seichō 松本清張, *Genjin* 眩人 (Tokyo: Chūō kōronsha, 1980). The six ancient Japanese historical collections (*Rikkokushi* 六国史), compiled between the Nara and Heian periods, are: *Nihon shoki* 日本書紀; *Shoku Nihon ki* 続日本紀; *Nihon kōki* 日本後紀; *Shoku Nihon kōki* 続日本後紀; *Nihon montoku tennō jitsuroku* 日本文徳天皇実録 and *Nihon sandai jitsuroku* 日本三代実録.

[85] For a discussion of *Tōiki dentō mokuroku*, see Sueki Fumihiko 末木文美士, Riben fojiao mulu xue de xingcheng —— yi *Tōiki dentō mokuroku* wei zhongxin 日本佛教目錄學的形成 —— 以《東域傳燈錄》為中心, in *Zangwai fojiao wenxian: diqiji* 藏外佛教文獻：第七集, ed. Fang Guangchang (Beijing: Zongjiao wenhua chubanshe, 2003), 429.

unable to ascertain the exact sources of the lost *Bonshakuji mokuroku*, but Ono Katsutoshi argues that it may contain new texts transcribed at the Putiyuan library by Eichū.[86]

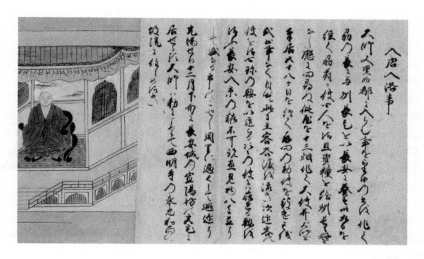

Figure. 51   [Kukai's] Journey to China and the Capital (*Nittō nyūraku koto* 入唐入洛事), from (*Kōya Daishi gyōjō zuga* 高野大師行状図畫), Kōyasan 高野山, Shinnōin 親王院. Source: Tsuji Eiko 辻英子, ed., *Kōya Daishi gyōjō zuga*, 37.

The Ximing cloister where Eichū resided was subsequently occupied by Kūkai (Figure.51), who sailed for China in the sixth month of 804 (Enryaku 23) and arrived at Chang'an by the end of that year.[87] He vowed to travel to China to study the tantras that had puzzled him in Japan. After the official Japanese envoy started home for Japan, Kūkai alone remained behind in Ximingsi in order to learn more about the *Mahāvairocana-sūtra*, which had been translated into Chinese in the 720s and brought to Japan by Genbō.[88] We may reasonably infer that with a copy of the

---

[86] Ono Katsutoshi, "Chōan no saimyōji to nittō guhōsō," 83.

[87] Marian Ury, "Genkō Shakusho, Japan's First Comprehensive History of Buddhism: A Partial Translation, with Introduction and Notes." (PhD diss., University of California, Berkeley, 1970), 216.

[88] *[Go]shōrai mokuroku*, T55, no. 2161, p. 1065, a10-17. The catalogue is also known as the *Jō shōrai kyōtō mokurokuhyō* 新請来經等目錄表 (A Memorial Presenting a List of Newly Imported Sūtras and Other Items). See also John Bowring, *The Religious Traditions of Japan, 500-1600* (Cambridge, UK: Cambridge University Press, 2005), 136.

Zhenyuan Catalogue in hand, Kūkai had made use of the Ximing tripiṭaka of Putiyuan, where he could exchange ideas with Yuanzhao and call on the eminent Buddhist teachers of the capital. It was at Ximingsi that he came into contact with masters capable of reading Buddhist Sanskrit. Abe Ryūichi summarizes Kūkai's activity at Ximingsi this way:

Upon his arrival in 805 at the His-ming monastery, Kūkai must therefore have had immediate access to teachers and materials for his study of Sanskrit, mantra, and Esoteric Buddhist texts in general. Kūkai was the first Japanese pilgrim to bring Yüan-chao's *Chen-yüan Catalogue* to Japan, for example. And because the collection of Buddhist scriptures that had been assembled in Japan was based on Chih-sheng's 730 *K'ai-yüan Catalogue*, Kūkai's access to the *Chen-yüan Catalogue* made it possible for him to identify and import texts hitherto unavailable in Japan.[89]

It seems after meeting with Yuanzhao, Kūkai came to be aware of Prajñā, with whom Yuanzhao had carried out many translation projects. It was even possible that Prajñā was residing at Ximingsi during Kūkai's visit. It is likely that, before Kūkai decided to have a meeting with Huiguo at Qinglong Monastery, he received three Sanskrit manuscripts of the newly translated *Āvataṃsaka Sūtra* and *Scripture of the Six Pāramitā of Mahāyāna* passed from his Sanskrit teacher Prajñā, who told him:

I was born in Kashmir and was initiated into Buddhism while still young and went on a pilgrimage all over India. With the pledge to transmit the torch of the Dharma, I came to China. I wish to sail for Japan, but circumstances do not allow me to fulfill my intention. Take with you the new *Avataṃsaka Sūtra* and the *Ṣaṭ-Pāramitā Sutra*, both of which I have translated, and these Sanskrit manuscripts. I sincerely hope that these will help create conditions [in which to propagate Buddhism] so that people will be saved.[90]

---

[89] Abe Ryūichi, *The Weaving of Mantra*, 118.

[90] Yoshito S. Hakeda, *Kukai: Major Works, Translated, with An Account of His Life and a Study of His Thought* (New York: Columbia University Press, 1972), 149. *[Go]shōrai mokuroku*, T55, no. 2161, p. 1065, c8-13. See also Yoshinori Takeuchi, *Buddhist Spirituality: Later China, Korea, Japan, and the Modern World* (New York: Crossroad, 1999), 177.

Richard Bowring claims that although Kūkai was probably not the inventor of Japanese *kana* 仮名 (Japanese syllabaries), there can be no doubt that the knowledge of the Sanskrit syllabary that he gained in China played a major part in the development of a Japanese script during the course of the ninth century.[91] Abe Ryūichi thinks that the *Six Pāramitā of Mahāyāna* that Kūkai introduced to Japan in 806 provided him with the critical theoretical underpinning for defining Esoteric Teaching (*mikkyō* 密教) as a category distinct from the Exoteric Teaching (*kengyō* 显教).[92] With the help of Takashinano Tōnari 高階遠成 (756-818), the judge and senior secretary of Dazaifu (*Dazai daikan* 大宰大監), Kūkai submitted some of the manuscripts that he collected at Ximingsi, including the compositions by Yuanzhao, to Emperor Saga 嵯峨天皇 (r. 809-823).[93] In addition to the new translations of esoteric Buddhism and some traditional doctrinal treatises, the texts that he imported to Japan also contain scriptures of the two maṇḍalas, siddham and the pictorial presentations of the sacred assembly of deities. Among the 216 scriptures, two of them are concerned with Yuanzhao's bibliographical works: *Zhenyuan xinding shijing mulu* and *Zhenyuan xinfan yijing tuji* 貞元新翻譯經圖記 (The Illustrated Record of the Newly Translated Scriptures During the Zhenyuan Era). Looking into the famous *Sanjū jō sasshi* 三十帖冊子 (Thirty Volumes of Buddhist Teachings, c.805), the famous calligraphical transcription of tantric texts collected by Kūkai, also reveals several scriptures associated with Ximing library, including the new translations of the *Scripture for Humane Kings*, *Avataṃsaka Sūtra*, *Ṣaṭ-Pāramitā Sutra* and another state-protecting sūtra —— *Shouhu guojiezhu tuoluoni jing* 守護國界主陀羅尼經 (Skt. *Āryadhāraṇīśvararāja-sūtra*; Dhāraṇī for Safeguarding the Nation, the Realm and the Chief of State, T997). These scriptures, according to Ono Katsutoshi, were copied by Kūkai in his residence at Ximingsi.[94]

The political instability of the ninth century in China forced several monks,

---

[91] Bowring, *The Religious Traditions of Japan*, 137.

[92] Abe Ryūichi, *The Weaving of Mantra*, 117.

[93] *[Go]shōrai mokuroku*, T55, no. 2161, p. 1060, c5-18. On the interaction between Kūkai and Yuanzhao; see Yoritomi Motohiro, "Fukū · Kūkai o meguru hitobito-2- Saimyōji Enshō (Matsuo Gikai hakase koki kinen) 不空・空海をめぐる人々-2-西明寺円照 (松尾義海博士古稀記念号)," *Mikkyōgaku* 密教學 16 · 17 (November 1980): 183-206. For a discussion of Takashinano Tōnari 高階遠成 in relation to Kūkai's trip to Tang China, see Takeuchi Kōzen 武内孝善, *Kōbō Daishi Kūkai no kenkyū* 弘法大師空海の研究 (Tokyo: Yoshikawa kōbunkan, 2006), 285-88.

[94] Momoi Kanjō 桃井観城, *Kyōten denrai no kenkyū: tsuketari · Heianchō shoki kokusho nenpyō* 経典伝來の研究: 付 · 平安朝初期國書年表 (Osaka: Tōhō shuppan, 1999), 21-30.

especially the last three of the eight *guhō* monks who entered China (*nittō hake*), to travel with merchant missions to the mainland.[95] In the seventh year of Dazhong (853), shortly after the Huichang anti-Buddhist persecution, Enchin, the founder of the future Jimon School (*jimonha* 寺門派) of Tendai Buddhism, sailed for China with a group of Korean merchants. Registered at Fushou Monastery (the former Ximingsi) for six years, he copied some Buddhist manuscripts from the library, including the stone tablet devoted to Daoxuan, the writings of Xuanchang, and the *Zhenyuan Catalogue*.[96] It is clear in his *Nihon biku Enchin nittō gūhō mokuroku* 日本比丘圓珍入唐求法目錄 (Catalogue of Entering China to Seek the Dharma Written by the Japanese Bhikṣu Echin, T2171) that Enchin made use of the section of *Buruzang mulu* in particular as an index to transcribe about eighty-four tantric texts, some of which are believed to be preserved at Enjōji 園城寺 and Jissōji 実相寺 in Japan.[97]

Special Collection: Vinaya Texts and Extracanonical Books

Finally, for the post-catalogue years of Chang'an Buddhism, I want to discuss some special collections connected with certain cloisters or monastic scriptoria of Ximingsi and inquire into their extent. While the academic genealogy of Ximingsi embraces many Buddhist schools —— vinaya, vijñapti-mātratā, esotericism and Chan —— the School of Vinaya was the main thread tying together the leading scholars of different generations. Daoxuan, the leading scholar of the school, possessed a large number of manuscripts in his private library; and the reputation of his collection, with its strength in the *vinaya-piṭaka*, far surpassed similar collections across the country. The biographical sketch of Xuanchang, the Buddhist leader who rose to prominence in the tenth century, reveals that the collection, along with the former residence of Daoxuan, must have been well preserved like a museum at Ximingsi. Before

[95] See *Mochizuki*, 4126; *Iwanami Nihon shi jiten* 岩波日本史辞典, s.v. *nittō hake* 入唐八家. The term was first mentioned by Annen 安然 (841-?) in his *Hakke hiroku*; see *Iwanami Bukkyō jiten*, s.v. *nittō hake*; *Mochizuki*, 2539.

[96] Ximingsi was renamed Fushousi; see chapter 4. See also Ono, *Kaisetsuhen*, 155; Onjōji 園城寺, ed., *Onjōji monjo* 園城寺文書, vol. 1 (Tokyo: Kōdansha, 1998), 342.

[97] *Nihon biku Enchin nittō guhō mokuroku* 日本比丘圓珍入唐求法目錄, T55, no. 2172, p. 1097, b21-p. 1098, b19. It should be remembered that most of the texts that Enchin collected in Chang'an were from Qinglong Monastery; see *Seiryūji gūhō mokuroku* 青龍寺求法目錄 (Catalogue of Scriptures and Items Collected at Qinglongsi, T2172); *Mochizuki*, 2805.

Xuanchang arrived in Chang'an, he expressed his aspiration to peruse the vinaya collection preserved at Ximingsi:

He admired the fact that the imperial Ximingsi preserved the former cloister of the vinaya master Daoxuan. The cloister contained the doctrinal traces of vinaya. He then [went to Chang'an] and studied under the tutelage of the vinaya master Huizheng.

仰京室西明寺有宣律師舊院，多藏毘尼教迹，因栖惠正律師法席.[98]

In early seventh century, Daoxuan reinterpreted the vinaya regulations in his systematic writings on the precepts, creating a standard for the revival of medieval monasticism in Chang'an. Like the private collections of classical scholars, such as Tiberius Julius Celsus Polemaeanus (d. 92), or Saint Jerome (347-420), Daoxuan's library was an outstanding personal collection used in support of his literary career.[99] The "doctrinal traces" (Ch. *jiaoji* 教跡) mentioned here, as defined by the Tiantai master Zhiyi, connotes the teachings of the saints preached at different levels; but its denotation is a collection of Buddhist texts affiliated with a Buddhist sect. Thus, for example, like Xuanchang's interest in the doctrinal traces of vinaya, Ennin made copies of the doctrinal traces of Tiantai (Ch. *tiantai jiaoji* 天臺教跡, Jap. *tendai kyōshaku*) at Dahuayansi 大華嚴寺 on Mount Wutai.[100]

Elsewhere we can find ample evidence of the former residential chamber of Daoxuan from descriptions in early records. One of the catalogues of manuscripts acquired by Enchin, for example, contains the copy of a rubbing of the stone tablet erected in the vinaya cloister of Daoxuan (*Tang Ximingsi gu dade xuangong lüyuan jie* 唐西明寺故大德宣公律院碣), a calligraphic work composed by Liu

---

[98] *SGZZ*, T50, no. 2061, p. 818, a25-27; *Da Tang zhenyuan xu kaiyuan shijiao lu*, T55, no. 2156, p748, b13-14.

[99] The Library of Celsus, located in Ephesus, contained tens of thousands of codices. For a detailed study of Jerome and his personal library, see Megan Hale Williams, *The Monk and the Book: Jerome and the Making of Christian Scholarship* (Chicago: University of Chicago Press, 2006), 167-200.

[100] *Miaofa lianhua jing xuanyi* 妙法蓮華經玄義 (Profound Meaning of the Sūtra on the Lotus of the Marvelous Dharma), T33, no. 1716, p. 810, c12-p. 811, a3; *Fahua wubaiwen lun* 法華五百問論 (Five Hundred Questions on the Sūtra on the Lotus of the Marvelous Dharma), *XZJ* 100, p. 802, a11-14. For Ennin's visit to Mount Wutai, see Ono Katsutoshi, *Nittō guhō junrei gyōki no kenkyū: daisankan* 入唐求法巡禮行記の研究: 卷三 (Kyoto: Hōzōkan, 1989), 64-75.

Gongquan.[101] In his vision of the Jetavana Monastery, Daoxuan himself, combining contemporaneous travelogues and a vision gained from a dream, seems to have conceived the notion of two vinaya cloisters at the Monastery:

> The south of the street at the south end is further divided into two cloisters. The [building on the] west is named Cloister for Vinaya [Teachers] 持律[師]院, and [that on] the east is called Vinaya Cloister of the Ordination Platform 戒壇律院.[102]

We may also note that the *Qianding sifenlü shu* 僉定四分律疏 (Commentary on the Dharmagupta Vinaya Edited by Imperial Order), a project that gathered all the prominent vinaya monks from the capital, was accomplished in the Vinaya Cloister (*jielüyuan* 戒律院) in Anguo Monastery.[103] We may infer from such notices that Daoxuan resided in a vinaya cloister, probably one of the thirteen cloisters of Ximingsi.

It was the collection of this cloister that captured the attention of Xuanchang, who immediately left the remote southern city of Fuzhou and embarked on his journey to Chang'an. As we have seen in chapter 4, Xuanchang would make his mark as the last of the Buddhist heroes of Ximingsi in the service of successive Tang emperors. In a preface (840) affixed to Huilin's *Yiqiejing yinyi*, the Tang literatus Gu Qizhi 顧齊之 praised Xuanchang as a connoisseur of the Ximing tripiṭaka. When Gu Qizhi showed interest in finding his way through the copious collection of Ximing library, Xuanchang guided him through the manuscript labyrinth, with the assistance of Huilin's lexicon used as an index to the manuscripts preserved in the library.[104]

The second case of a special Ximing collection I want to consider here is that

---

[101] *Nihon biku Enchin nittō guhō mokuroku*, T55, no. 2172, p. 1101, b13-14. The rubbing is discussed in chapter 5, see also *Chishō daishi shōrai mokuroku* 智證大師請來目錄 (Chishō Daishi's Catalogue Submitted by Imperial Request), T55, no. 2173, p. 1107, a3-5. During the Dali period (766-779), a Buddha hall devoted to the veneration of Daoxuan (*Daoxuan lüshi tang* 道宣律師堂) was to be found at Ximingsi; see the biography of Daoxua, *SGSZ*, T50, no. 2061, p. 791, b5-10.

[102] Tan Zhihui, "Daoxuan's Vision," 313. *Zhong tianzhu Sheweiguo Qihuansi tujing*, T45, no. 1899, p. 890, c20-22.

[103] *ZYL*, T55, no. 2156, p. 769, a29-b4.

[104] *Yiqie jing yinyi*, T54, no. 2128, p. 311, a5-17; Fang Guangchang, "Huilin yinyi yu Tangdai Dazangjing," 405.

of the library's non-Buddhist texts (*waishu* 外書, or *waidian* 外典). While the work of the monastic scribes was largely taken up with copying Buddhist scriptures, they also devoted a considerable amount of time to transcribe literature. We should recognize that the elite monks did not confine their studies exclusively to Buddhist doctrine and philosophy, but also cultivated a taste for the Chinese classics and general learning.[105] This interest in non-Buddhist materials among Buddhist monks was particularly true in China, where the classics had a much longer history than Buddhist texts in the culture.[106]

The *Mūlasarvāstivāda nikāya vinaya saṃgraha* (Ch. *Genben sapoduobu lü she* 根本薩婆多部律攝, T1458), a text translated by Yijing in 701, stipulates that Buddhist scriptures should be deposited in the library, shared by the saṃgha of the four quarters, whereas the non-Buddhist texts should be sold and divided among the present saṃgha.[107] Again, in his vision of Jetavana, Daoxuan posits the existence of non-Buddhist books in the cloisters on the east side of the Buddha Cloister:

---

[105] Indeed, Chinese monks are renowned for their mastery of both Buddhist texts and classical literature. The Tang-Dynasty monk Shenqing 神清 (d. 820) commented on the notion of "gentlemen monk" (*junziseng* 君子僧) in the history of Chinese Buddhism, saying:

> Zhi Daoling; Chengguan, Kumarajiva, Daoan, Huiyuan, the four saints under the tutelage of Kumarajiva (Daosheng, Sengzhao, Daorong, Sengrui), the Daoan of the Northern Zhou, Yancong of the Sui dynasty, Huijing, Daoxuan, Falin, Minggai at the beginning of this dynasty —— all of them master Buddhist teachings and read classics and history. Their study included prose and poetry. They were all committed to writing.

> 支道林, 澄, 什, 安, 遠. 什門四聖 (生肇融睿), 梁僧祐, 周道安, 隋彥琮, 國初淨, 宣, 林, 概 (慧淨, 道宣, 法林, 明概), 靡不洞閑本教, 該涉經史, 研綜詞翰,咸事著述.

Beishan lu 北山錄, T52, no. 2113, p. 627, b27-c19.

[106] This model contrasts strongly with the case of the Muslim world. Most mosques did not contain many secular books —— especially popular literature, astrology, practical disciplines; see George N. Atiyeh, *The Book in the Islamic World: the Written Word and Communication in the Middle East* (Albany: State University of New York Press, 1995), 10.

[107] *Genben sapoduobu lüshe* 根本薩婆多部律攝 (Skt. *Mūlasarvāstivāda nikāya vinaya saṃgraha*), T24, no.1458, p. 568, a18-20. It is clear in the same text that although the purpose of a monk is to convert others to Buddhism, he may read extracanonical works during the less productive times of the day; see also *Mishasaibu hexi wufenlü* 彌沙塞部和醯五分律 (Vinaya of the Mahīśāsaka Sect), T22, no.1503, p. 174, b6-11 and *Youposai wujie weiyi jing* 優婆塞五戒威儀經 (Scripture of the Five-Precept Deportment of Upāsaka), T24, no.1503, p. 1118, b28-29.

The third cloister on the west is called Cloister for *Yinyang* Books 陰陽書籍院. All kinds of books on [the two principles of] *yinyang* [underlying] ten billions of worlds are all collected in this quarter. It was the Buddha who founded [the cloister so that] monks might sometimes read them for the sake [of understanding] the heterodox....Then, the fourth cloister on the west is called Cloister for Medical Prescriptions 醫方之院. All medical prescriptions under heaven are collected [in this place].[108]

We learn from Daoxuan's work how to distribute books in a textual community like Ximingsi: he classified Buddhist writings into five categories, one of which was Chinese secular works, including Daoism, agriculture, logic, legislation, political affairs and miscellaneous topics. Daoxuan, who might have read an early version of the *Mūlasarvāstivāda nikāya vinaya saṃgraha*, stressed that only Buddhist works can be distributed within the monastic community; however, other secular works should be owned by the community.[109]

The fact that non-Buddhist books were included in catalogues is attested to in the bibliographies brought back to Japan by Tendai and Shingon monks; and the Japanese evidence brings us to another collection that was used by the Tendai monk Ensai, the disciple of Saichō. In 855 (Jōwa 承和 5), Ensai presented fifty questions raised by Japanese Tendai scholars to the Chinese pundits in residence at Mount Tiantai (Tiantaishan 天臺山) and brought their answers, written in a manuscript by the name of *Tōketsu* 唐決, back to Japan. The following year Ensai returned to China and was ordered to be housed at Ximingsi. This time he received the consecration (Skt. *abhiṣeka*) of the Garbhadhātu (Ch. *taizangjie* 胎蔵界, Jap. *taizōkai*) from the eminent tantric guru Faquan. He was credited with the transcription of numerous non-Buddhist texts, especially the Confucian works.[110] Like Kūkai, who stayed in

---

[108] Tan Zhihui, "Daoxuan's Vision," 334-36. For the original Chinese text, see *Zhongtianzhu Sheweiguo Qihuansi tujing*, T45, no. 1899, p. 893, b12-27.

[109] *Liangchu qinzong yi*, T45, no.1895, p. 842, b28-c4; see also Chen Huaiyu, *The Revival of Buddhist Monasticism*, 154-57. Gregory Schopen has discussed the matter as well; see Gregory Schopen, *Buddhist Monks and Business Matters: Still MorePapers on Monastic Buddhism in India* (Honolulu: University of Hawai'i Press, 2004), 91-121.

[110] *Mochizuki*, 301-02; *Da Song sengshi lüe*, T54, no. 2126, p. 249, a15-18. For Ensai's visit to Mount Tiantai, see *Tang Tiantaishan Chanlinsi Guangxiu zhuan* 唐天臺山禪林寺廣脩傳, SGSZ, T50, no. 2061, p. 895, a16-23. For the lineage of Faquan, see *Jintailiangjie shizi xiangcheng* 金胎兩界師資相承 (Instructions from Masters to Disciples in the Two Realms of Vajra and Garbha Maṇḍalas), XZJ 95, p. 991,

the former residence of his predecessor Enchū, the Shingon monk Shōei 宗叡 (809-884), the last of the eight *gūho* monks who visited China, lodged in the "cloister of master Ensai" (Jap. *Ensai hōshiin* 圓載法師院). According to his *Shinshosha shōrai hōmontō mokuroku* 新書寫請來法門等目錄 (Catalogue of the Newly Copied Buddhist Doctrines and Images Obtained in China, T2174a), some of the extracanonical books on the roster, found among the cloistral collection, include hand-copied manuscripts and printed books:

1. *Douli yusi jing* 都利聿斯經 (Scripture of the Yusi Divination in Satruṣṇa)[111]
2. *Qiyao rangzaijue* 七曜禳災決 (Expelling the Seven Planets' Fated Calamities)
3. *Qiyao ershibasuli* 七躍二十八宿曆 (Calendar of the Seven Celestial Bodies and Twenty-Eight Constellations)
4. *Qiyao liri* 七曜曆日 (Calendar of the Seven Celestial Bodies)
5. *Liuren mingli lichengge* 六壬名例立成歌 (Formulas of Quickly Remembering the General Principle of the Liuren Divination)
6. *Mingjing lianshu* 明鏡連殊 (The Lianzhu Style of The Polished Mirror)
7. *Milu yaofang* 祕錄藥方 (The Secret Manual of Prescription)
8. *Xuefa jiayao shuyi* 削繁加要書儀 (The Succint Models for Epistle)
9. *Tangyun* 唐韻 (The Tang Rhyme Dictionary)
10. *Yupian*[112]

Among the ten texts, the *Tangyun* and *Yupian* are literary works printed in Xichuan 西川 (today's Sichuan province). These books tell us that more printed texts were purchased for the Ximing library after the Huichang suppression of Buddhism. From the sixth to the tenth monk in 865 (Xiantong 6), it took Shōei five months to copy the ten manuscripts. Later in the same year, along with more than one hundred other books, the manuscripts were carried to Tōji in Heiankyō for a recount. A preliminary examination of the book titles tells us that the subjects range from numerology,

---

a18. For a detailed study of Ensai and his sūtra-copying activities, see Saeki Arikiyo 佐伯有清, *Hiun no kentōsō: Ensai no sūki na shōgai* 悲運の遣唐僧: 円載の數奇な生涯 (Tokyo: Yoshikawa kōbunkan, 1999); Wang Yong 王勇, "Shinshutsu no tōjin shakyō kara mita Ensai no kyūsho katsudō 新出の唐人寫経から見た円載の求書活動," *Higashiajia bunka kanryū* 東アジア文化環流 1, no. 2 (2008): 168-74.

[111] The text is said to be transmitted to China from Western India, see *XTS* 59.1548. *Duli* 都利 probably refers to Satruṣṇa (Ch. *Sudo lihuina* 窣都利慧那), an ancient city in Turkestan between Kojend and Samarkand.

[112] *Shin shosha shōrai hōmontō mokuroku*, T55, no. 2174A, p. 1111, b20-c6.

calendrical astrology, astral exorcism, medicine, to lexicon and rhyme dictionary. The wide variety of books gives us some sense of Daoxuan's vision of non-Buddhist works appropriate to the monastic library. Not surprisingly, Ennin also transcribed many extracanonical books during his stay in Chang'an, and a study by Kanda Kiichirō 神田喜一郎 (1897-1984) shows that Ennin had a taste for poetry and prose.[113] In sum, then, these bibliographies show us that, in addition to their study of canonical literature, the book-loving prelates of Ximingsi also enjoyed a rich literary life. In addition to such non-Buddhist literary works, the monastic collections also included numerous Buddhist works deemed apocryphal by the catalogers. Indeed, as indicated by Kyoko Tokuno, the period from the Six Dynasties through Tang saw the most prolific production of Buddhist apocrypha, a development that brought Buddhist cataloguers under particular pressure to cope with issues of authenticity.[114]

The Buddhist canon expanded immensely in Chang'an, but any catalogue inevitably remains incomplete and only imperfectly reflects the state of actual library collections. Starting from the late ninth century, in the wake of the Huichang suppression and the subsequent ravages of war, the Buddhist bibliotecas at Ximingsi were decimated. However, the expansion of new entries in the Buddhist catalogues

---

[113] We may compare the extracanonical books preserved at different urban monasteries in Chang'an by investigating records from a variety of Japanese Buddhist catalogues. For instance, among the manuscripts in one of Ennin's catalogues, most of which were acquired in Chang'an, there is a list of secular books he had copied:

A poem sent between Hangzhou and Yuezhou with preface; a new poem by śramaṇa Qingjiang; *Pan yibai tiao* ○ *Dao*, one sheet; *Qiduiyi* [examinational topic], one sheet; *Elegy for Mr. Ren* (by Bai Juyi), one sheet; Winter Chrysanthemum, one sheet; Reading the Prose of Bai Juyi, one sheet; *Eulogy of Morality*, one sheet; one poem; A Celebratory Poem for Yuan Ying, one sheet; Miscellaneous Poems, one sheet; a fascicule of Poems by Former *jingshi* Chi Jianwu, one fascicle; Chinese *changyan*, one fascicle; Portrait of a Persian, one fascicle.

杭越寄和詩并序一帖; 沙門清江新詩一帖; 判一百條別○道一帖; 祇對儀一帖任氏怨歌行一帖(白居易); 寒菊一帖; 攬樂天書一帖; 歐德文一帖; 雜詩一帖; 祝元膺詩一帖; 雜詩一帖; 前進士弛肩吾詩一卷; 漢語長言一卷; 波斯國人形一卷.

See *Jikaku Daishi zai Tō sōshinroku* 慈覺大師在唐送進錄, T55, no. 2166, p. 1078, a22-8; for detailed study of these manuscripts, see Kanda Kiichirō 神田喜一郎, "*Jikaku daishi shōrai gaiten kōshō* 慈覺大師將來外典考證," *Kanda kiichirō zenshū: daisankan* 神田喜一郎全集: 第三卷, (Kyoto: Dōhōsha shuppan, 1984), 287-98.

[114] Tokuno Kyoko, "The Evaluation of Indigenous Scriptures," 33.

continued until the fall of the Tang Dynasty, even as Chang'an lay in ruins. Toward the end of the tenth century, Heng An 恒安, the editor of *Xu Zhenyuan shijiaolu* 續 貞元釋教錄 (Continuation to the *Zhenyuan Catalogue*, T2158), redoubled his efforts to find books south of the Yangzi River and went on a pilgrimage to the various sacred mountains, ferreting out texts absent in Chang'an.[115] When the Northern Song literatus Zhang Li 張禮 ascended the Wild Goose Pagoda in 1086, he lamented the decline of monastic institutions, since all that he witnessed was the obliteration of the scriptures and weeds growing in wanton profusion outside the once magnificent temple buildings.

Although most of the religious manuscripts copied during the Tang Dynasty are now long lost to us, a few are still to found in museums, grottos and even at monasteries off the beaten track. The Buddhist bibliographies and the manuscripts that somehow survived can only give a partial picture of what was once in circulation; and many of the highly specialized texts, apocrypha, or indigenous works in particular were either lost or fell into oblivion in monastic libraries across East Asia. Still, over for the last two centuries, scholar-diplomats and monk-explorers who travelled to abandoned monasteries have made noteworthy discoveries that gave impetus to modern research in Buddhist studies.[116] Even today, due to the unremitting effort of cloistered bibliophiles, Japanese monasteries still preserve a vast number of secular works transcribed in China during the eighth century. For instance, Kōfukuji 興福寺 boasts of a copy of the *Jingdian shiwen* 經典釋文 (Explanation of the Classics) by the Tang-Dynasty Confucian scholar Lu Deming 陸 德明 (d. 630); a manuscript of *Shiji* 史記 (Records of the Grand Historian) can be found on the library shelf of Ishiyamadera 石山寺. Owing to the diligence of Japanese student-monks, scriptures like *Miaosewang yinyuan jing* 妙色王因緣經 (Skt. *Buddhabhāshita-suvarna-rāja-nidāna*, Sūtra on the Cause and Effect of King

---

[115] *Xu Zhenyuan shijiao lu*, T55, no. 2158, p. 1048, b10-c3.

[116] For instance, the advancement of Tibetology in Japan owns much to Kawaguchi Ekai 河口慧海 (1866-1945), a scholar-monk from the Obaku school (Obakushū 黃檗宗) of Zen Buddhism. He visited Tibetan and Nepalese monasteries from 1897 (Meiji 明治 30) to 1915 (Taisho 大正 4), bringing back a set of the Tibetan Buddhist canon along with a rich collection of manuscripts and artifacts; see Saitō Kōjun 斎 藤光純, "Kawaguchi Ekai shi shōrai Tōyō Bunko shozō shahon chibetto daizōkyō chōsa bibō 河口慧海師 将来東洋文庫所蔵写本チベット大蔵経調査備忘," *Taishō daigaku kenkyū kiyō. Bukkyō gakubu・ Bungakubu* 大正大學研究紀要. 佛教學部・文學部 63 (1977): 345-406; Kawaguchi Ekai, *Kawaguchi Ekai shōrai Chibetto shiryō zuroku* 河口慧海請來チベット資料図録 (Sendai: Tohoku daigaku bungakubu, 1986).

Suvarna, T459), a sūtra translated by Yijing and copied at Ximingsi in 703, was preserved intact at Chionin 知恩院 in Kyoto. As a result, today's antiquarians are still able to appreciate those ancient manuscripts of Tang Chang'an, preserved in such proud Japanese collections as Shōsōin 正倉院 (Shōsōin Treasure House); Kunaichō 宮内庁 (Imperial Household Agency) and Shodō hakubutsukan 書道博物館 (Calligraphy Museum).[117]

Across three centuries, Buddhist collections at Ximingsi took on more importance, attracting the most talented translators and compilers to manage the multiplying manuscripts. This chapter presents a many-faceted image of the libraries, the collections and the attendant material culture that coexisted at Ximingsi. In the early days of Ximingsi, the sūtra platform, revealed through textual sources and archaeological discovery, was a ritual library used for state-sanctioned tripiṭaka of the seventh century. Somewhat later, from the eighth to the early ninth century, the Putiyuan library bore witness to multiple projects of scriptural translation, including the gems of esoteric literature that attracted generations of Japanese dharma seekers to cross the ocean. From the beginning of the Ximingsi collection, however, the holdings of the monastic libraries transcended the conventional Buddhist canon and began to absorb secular texts as a supplementary portion. The two major libraries in their designated cloisters, the private libraries, such as the vinaya collection of Daoxuan, and the non-Buddhist books perched on the shelves in the guest cloister inhabited by the Japanese monkish scholars —— all testify to the deeply layered bibliophile culture of Ximingsi.

On the bases of these collections, the Buddhist exegetes at Ximingsi produced two standard sūtra catalogues employed in the subsequent years, as criteria for monastic collections all over the country. Before the Huichang suppression, these remarkable catalogues represented not only the highest achievement in Buddhist bibliography, but also a remarkable testimony to the build-up of the monastic collections at Ximingsi between 658 and 800. Though Buddhist scholars and Chinese bibliographers accorded great importance to the *Kaiyuan Shijiao lu*, the value and impact of the *Neidian Catalogue* and the *Zhenyuan Catalogue* cannot be ignored. Indeed the *Neidian Catalogue* was so influential that even a century after its appearance it was adopted in the Tubo (Tibet)-occupied Dunhuang (787-847) as the

---

[117] Ikeda On 池田温, *Chūgoku kodai shahon shikigo shūroku* 中國古代寫本識語集錄 (Tokyo: Okura shuppan, 1990), 259; Nanjio Bunyū 南條文雄, *A Catalogue of the Chinese Translation of the Buddhist Tripitaka, the Sacred Canon of the Buddhists in China and Japan* (Oxford: Clarendon press, 1883), 109.

prototype for monastic collection.[118] After the *Zhenyuan Catalogue* was transmitted to Japan, it became the benchmark catalogue on which some regional temples in the fledging political entity began to build up their libraries.

In the past three decades, the prominent Buddhist catalogues compiled at Ximingsi have become the focus of some scholars. In addition to research conducted within the field of Buddhist philology, comparison of their content with the Chinese classics and their impact on Japanese literature still require meticulous scholarship. For instance, Aitani Yoshimitsu 會穀佳光 has found that the Buddhist section (*shishilei* 釋氏類) in *Xintangshu* 新唐書 (New Book of Tang) is closely related to the *Neidian Catalogue* and *Xu gaoseng zhuan*. The works by Ono Genmyō 小野玄妙 (1883-1939) and Fang Guangchang also await further attention, as they provide valuable insight still unavailable to western readers.[119]

In summary, Ximingsi is an excellent point of departure for the investigation of a number of topics of Buddhist manuscript culture, including monastic collection, Buddhist bibliography and the rich history of cultural exchange between Tang China and medieval Japan. In spite of the undoubted progress made by Buddhist studies scholars in East Asia, however, the field of Buddhist catalogues and libraries is still in its infancy, with all the questions posed from the perspectives of material culture, doctrinal history, classification, and codicology yet to be properly explored. As the Chinese adage has it, this chapter is "a brick thrown out for a jade " (*paozhuan yinyu* 抛磚引玉), for it is, at this stage, merely a modest study of the Buddhist collection and library history of Ximingsi. In the end, its purpose is simply to induce other scholars to come forward with more valuable contributions.

---

[118] Fang Guangchang, *Zhongguo xieben dazang jing yanjiu*, 145.

[119] Aitani Yoshimitsu 會谷佳光, *Sōdai shoseki shūsan kō: Shintōjo geimonshi shakushirui no kenkyū* 宋代書籍聚散考: 新唐書藝文志釋氏類の研究 (Tokyo: Kyūko shoin, 2004), 55-89. For a representative study of a monastic library in the Tang, see Tejima Isshin, "A Study on a Catalogue of Buddhist Library in Tang's China," in *Seigen hakushi koki kinen ronshū: higashi Ajia bukkyō no shomondai* 聖厳博士古稀記念論集: 東アジア仏教の諸問題 (Tokyo: Sankibō, 2001), 179-93; idem, "'Dai Tō kaigen shakkyō kōhin rekishō' ni tsuite," 24-38. For a study of Dunhuang Buddhist libraries, see Drège, *Les bibliothèques en Chine*, 175-248.

Chapter Seven

Conclusion: The Heritage of Ximingsi

An Unfinished Journey

The current study of Ximingsi offers only a sketch of a major Buddhist monastery long descended into oblivion in Chinese history. A fair treatment of a project like this deserves a series of monographs covering a full range of interregional topics and multidisciplinary approaches. To be sure, among the Buddhist monasteries that flourished in Tang Chang'an, many are worthy of scholastic attention; but none matched Ximingsi in power and opulence, and, though it remains undervalued, none left such a rich cultural legacy to Buddhist Asia.

In the first part of this work, I have provided a chronicle of Ximingsi in the politically tumultuous context of some three centuries, from the monastery's prehistory in the Sui Dynasty, through the height of its prosperity in the Tang, to its closure in the later Liang period. As a de facto public museum and cultural institution, the temple was remarkable for its inspiring architecture, edifying frescos and ornate furnishings; and the second part of this study turns from the institutional history of Ximing to the physical monastery itself. With the help of Japanese and Chinese scholarship, I attempt to probe the artistic world and sacred space of Ximingsi and its association with the Indian Jetavana Monastery and the Daianji Monastery in Japan. In a reassessment of the Illustrated Scriptures by Daoxuan and the *Saimyōjizu* preserved in Japan, the argument draws on historical studies, scriptural sources, and on-site archaeological discoveries. I propose that the illustrated records, the *Saimyōjizu*, in particular, reflect the central part of the monastery's interior space, the main Buddhist cloister located at the heart of Ximingsi. In medieval Sui-Tang society, Ximingsi was also known as the repository of one of the four best Buddhist collections in China. The final section of this work accordingly explores the details of

231

the famed manuscript library and the two major Buddhist bibliographical catalogues compiled at Ximingsi (*Neidian Catalogue* and *Zhenyuan Catalogue*). The study explores not only the development of three centuries of superb scholarship, but also the history of manuscript transmission from China to Japan.

Although the current study attempts to treat Ximingsi as a model of interregional cultural exchange and a network center of East Asian Buddhism, many unsolved problems on the research agenda invites further investigation. First of all, from the perspective of comparative literature, the romance of Ximingsi is also reflected in the classical literature and secular writings composed across the historical and cultural landscape of East Asia. Clearly the literary accounts of the monastery in extant sources are deserving of an entire chapter. Moreover, my particular interest in Ximingsi is connected with "Chang'an Studies," a burgeoning field promoted among Chinese and Japanese historians in particular.[1] Since the monastery was an integral part of the cultural scene of Chang'an, the anecdotal memoirs that colored representations of the monastery can be seen as the epitome of the broader imaginative world of medieval Chang'an.[2] This line of analysis could also be applied

---

[1] In China, traditional scholarship on the city culminated in the volume by the Qing scholar Xu Song, titled *Tang liangjing chengfang kao* 唐両京城坊考 (Investigation of the Two Tang capitals and their wards), where he draws upon 400 sources of literary and historical writings. Most of the topics in this field are concerned with history, politics, commerce, cityscapes, residential wards and the metropolitan life of Chang'an. See Seo Tatsuhiko, "A Draft Bibliography of Works concerning Ch'ang-an City during the T'ang Period," *T'ang Studies* 2 (1984): 129-186; Rong Xinjiang and Wang Jing 王靜, *Sui Tang Chang'an yanjiu wenxian mulu gao* 隋唐長安研究文獻目録稿, http://xiangyata.net/data/articles/d01/321.html, website accessed: Tuesday, May 01, 2012. For a century and a half, many eminent scholars were engaged in the study of Chang'an, including Xu Song; Kuwabara Jitsuzō 桑原隲藏 (1870-1931), Adachi Kiroku 足立喜六 (1871-1949), Yamazaki Hiroshi 山崎宏 (1903-2010), Ono Katsutoshi (1905-1988), Hiraoka Takeo (1909-95); Xiang Da 向達 (1900-66), Ishida Mikinosuke 石田幹之助 (1891-1974), Satō Taketoshi 佐藤武敏, Seo Tatsuhiko, Rong Xinjiang, Victor Cunrui Xiong, Thomas Thilo, and so forth.

[2] Spanning a millennium, six dynasties and eleven governments had established their capitals in Chang'an. A glimpse of the cultural imagination on the city is provided by popular literature; see, e.g., Shiba Ryōtarō 司馬遼太郎, *Chōan kara Pekin e* 長安から北京へ (Tokyo: Chūō kōronsha, 1976); Wang Chongren 王崇人, *Gudu Xi'an* 古都西安 (Xi'an: Shanxi renmin meishu chuban she, 1981); Chang Yao 暢耀, *Qinglongsi* 青龍寺 (Xi'an: Sanqin chubanshe, 1986); Kimura Shōsaburō 木村尚三郎, Iwata Kazuhiko 岩田一彦, and Hisamatsu Fumio 久松文雄, eds., *Chōan no miyako to Shiruku Rōdo Chūgoku to tōzai kōryū* 長安の都とシルクロード: 中国と東西交流 (Tokyo: Shūeisha, 1986); Matsuura Tomohisa 松浦友久 and Ueki Tomohisa 植木久行, *Chōan · Rakuyō monogatari: yūkyūtari ōjō no chi* 長安 · 洛陽物語: 悠久たり王城の地 (Tokyo: Shūeisha, 1987); Huang Xinya 黄新亜, *Xiaoshi de taiyang —— Tangdai chengshi shenghuo changjuan* 消逝的太陽 —— 唐代城市生活长卷 (Changsha: Hunan chubanshe, 1996); Morifuku Miyako 森福都, *Chōan botanka ibun* 長安牡丹花異聞 (Tokyo: Chōan Botanka Ibun 1997); Yamasaki Hisao,

to the related Japanese sources. For instance, Kuranaka Shinobu persuasively argues that the founding tales and biographical compositions concerning Ximingsi influenced the cultural circle of Daianji and promoted the literary writings of the Nara and Heian periods.[3] In the large body of East Asian literature, excerpts from such genres as hagiographies; novels (Ch. *chuanqi* 傳奇), tales (Jap. *monogatari* 物語), stray notes (Jap. *zuihitsu* 隨筆), legends (Jap. *setsuwa* 說話), picture scrolls (Jap. *emaki* 絵巻) and transformation texts (Ch. *bianwen* 變文) collectively constitute another significant resource throwing new light on the richness of the intellectual and literary life of both Ximingsi and Daianji.

Secondly, a reconstruction of the physical monastery would make a valuable contribution to imaginatively filling a void in Sino-Japanese architectural history. Steinhardt has emphasized the importance of understanding the site plans of urban monasteries in Chang'an.[4] In the present study, space permits a listing of only a small number of the works consulted, and the resultant study is only for illustrative purposes. In future work, hopefully in Chinese, I will resume the preliminary effort made in Chapter 5 and provide more complete documentation for the architectural remains and current archaeological reports of Ximingsi. As we have argued, the illustrated manuscript, *Saimyōjizu*, seems to be an authentic map of the cloister of the monastery. Given the great prestige of Ximingsi in ancient Japan, it is worth considering a research project that makes a careful comparison of Daianji, *Saimyōjizu*, the two illustrated scriptures by Daoxuan, and the excavated site of Ximingsi.

Finally, any future research on the topic of Ximingsi should take into account the spiritual legacy and religious issues present in the writings and translations of the scholars associated with the monastery. My future investigation will start with an explication of Ximingsi's academic genealogy. By providing a list of all the known members of the monastic community from its founding until its dissolution, we can map out a chart of lineage for the transmission of numerous sectarian teachings across three centuries. We may also propose the notion of "Ximing School,"

Chōan gensō to shiruku rōdo no tabi.

[3] Kuranaka Shinobu, *Narachō kanshibun no hikaku bungaku teki kenkyū*, 357-427. In this book, she compares the similarity between the biography of Xuanzang (*SZFSZ*) and *Nantenjiku baramon sōjōhi awasete jo* 南天竺婆羅門僧正碑并序 (The Inscription of the Brāhmaṇa Archbisop from southern India and its Preface), the biography of the Indian master Bodhisena (Jap. Bodaisenna 菩提僊那, 704-760) who travelled to Japan. Bodhisena was the "Brahman supervising monk" in residence at Daianji.

[4] Steinhardt, "Seeing Hōryūji Through China," 61-62.

including its Japanese followers, in the matrix of the intellectual history of East Asian Buddhism. Moreover, we hold to the opinion that the religious influence of Ximingsi was to be found not only in East Asia, but also in Tibet and Central Asia. It is clear that, in the tumult of war and rebellion, the knowledge system of Ximingsi had opportunity to shift from the central Chang'an to the peripheral zones. As noted in Chapter 3, the role that Ximing scholars played in the formation of Tibetan Buddhism and the Tobo-occupied Dunhuang invites further scholarly scrutiny. Equally significant, I think, is the task of interpretation of the contents of the ancient monastic scholarship. Although the institution itself declined after the collapse of Chang'an, the Buddhist beliefs and practices prescribed by the wide variety of scriptures translated at Ximingsi remain a living tradition anywhere in East Asia. In a word, it is incumbent upon Buddhist Studies scholars, equipped with the vision of a spiritual seeker, to explicate the soteriological value contained in the many religious tomes composed or translated by past masters at Ximingsi. The fact that these scriptures are still read, practiced and held in high esteem by the modern reading public proves that the Ximingsi heritage remains with us.

Remembrance

When Tang culture reigned over East Asia, Ximingsi stood like a beacon, attracting the ambitions of domestic scholars and the imagination of foreign travelers. Or, again, it was like a canvas, inviting so many Buddhist savants, dharma-seeking explorers and ambitious rulers to insert themselves into the picture. It is easier to lament the fate than to describe the actual condition of Ximingsi when it was reduced to a dilapidated shrine outside the diminished city of Chang'an in the mid-tenth century; but by that time the monastery had long ago transcended its walls.[5] As early as 664, only six years after the founding of the Chang'an Ximingsi, another monastery by the same name was built in Xiuwu 修武 county (Henan's Jiaozhuo city).[6] In the

---

[5] It seems under the aegis of the Song and Yuan dynasties, Chang'an revived again as a provincial center of commerce; but the walled city, which corresponded to the former imperial city in Tang Chang'an, degenerated into a feeble garrison town. The city was again mentioned in *The Travels of Marco Polo* as *Quengianfu*, a place the author is believed to have visited during 1276-1279 on his first mission for Khubilai Khan (1260-94), see Stephen Haw, *Marco Polo in China: A Venetian in the Realm of Khubilai Khan* (London ; New York : Routledge, 2006), 97.

[6] Li Fangmin 李芳民, *Tang Wudai fosi jikao* 唐五代佛寺辑考 (Beijing: Shangwu yinshuguan, 2006), 108.

millennium to follow, the two characters "Ximing" were so widely used that many namesake temples are found across China and Japan. As a name celebrated in poetic fancy and literary imagination, Ximing was long remembered by a succession of writers, travelers and scholars in East Asia.

In classical Chinese literature, some epigraphic collections, such as *Baoke congbian* 寶刻叢編 (General Compilation of Precious Inscriptions, 1229) and *Jinshi cuibian* 金石萃編 (Anthology of the Essence of Bronze and Stone Inscriptions, 1805), gather from various sources a number of anecdotes concerning Daoxuan, Buddhapāla and other unknown masters. The stories were passed down from person to person over the course of a millennium. On the surface of the *dhāraṇī* pillars (*tuoluoni jingchuang* 陀羅尼經幢) standing in monasteries and museums throughout China, the three characters of "Ximingsi" are still inscribed, along with the roster of donors and the votive text of *Uṣṇīṣavijayadhāraṇī*. In the realm of religious practice, whenever any Buddhist picks up the *Suvarṇaprabhāsottama sūtra* or *Xukongzang qiuwenchifa* 虛空藏求聞持法 (Jap. *Kokūzō gumonjihō*), he automatically becomes the beneficiary of the spiritual heritage of Ximingsi.[7] The esoteric method of petitioning the bodhisattva Ākāśagarbha (Boundless Space Treasure, figure.52), practiced in Japan as *gumonjihō*, is becoming increasingly familiar to the Chinese followers of Gangmi 港密, the new sect of Hong Kong Tantrism.[8] While an overall excavation of Ximingsi is still in the future, some of the cultural objects already unearthed, such as the glass fish pendant (*boli yu* 玻璃魚, figure.53) and the stone tea roller (*shi chanian* 石茶碾, figure.54), testify to the manufacturing skill of the High Tang and bear witness to the history of cultural exchange between Chang'an and foreign countries.[9]

---

[7] It is an abbreviation of the title of the *Xukongzang pusa nengman zhuyuan zuishengxin tuoluoni qiuwenchifa* 虛空藏菩薩能滿諸願最勝心陀羅尼求聞持法 (Method of the Victorious, Essential Dhāraṇi for Having Wishes Heard by Space-Store, the Bodhisattva Who Can Fulfill Requests). This tantric belief was popular among Japanese ascetics from the eighth century onwards; see *Mochizuki*, 1136.

[8] The religious order of Gangmi was founded by Li Juming 李居明, an ācāya of Tōmitsu and prominent geomancer (*fengshui shi* 風水師, wind and water intepreter) from Hong Kong. Following the teaching of Kūkai, his main object of veneration (Ch. *benzun* 本尊) is the bodhisattva Ākāśagarbha.

[9] An Jiayao, "Tang Chang'an Ximingsi fajue jianbao," 54; Idem., "When Glass Was Treasured in China," in *Nomads, Traders and Holy Men Along China's Silk Road*, ed. Annette L.Juliano, and Judith A. Lerner (Turnhout: Brepols, 2002), 92.

Conclusion

Figure. 52   The Five Ākāśagarbha Bodhisattvas (Jap. *godai Kokūzō bosatsu* 五大虚空蔵菩薩). Source: Kyōto Kokuritsu Hakubutsukan 京都国立博物館, ed. *Kūkai to Kōyasan: Kōbō Daishi nittō 1200 nen kinen* 空海と高野山: 弘法大師入唐 1200 年記念, 94.

Figure. 53   Glass Fish Pendant (*boli yu* 玻璃魚), Excavated at Ximingsi. Source: An Jiayao, "When Glass Was Treasured in China," in *Nomads, Traders and Holy Men Along China's Silk Road*, ed. Annette L.Juliano and Judith A. Lerner, 92.

Conclusion

Not surprisingly, the Japanese people had a long and special remembrance for Buddhist Chang'an and the monasteries their Buddhist patriarchs had once inhabited. Within centuries of the destruction of Ximingsi, a wealth of semi-fictional tales and folk lore had gathered about its name. The stories of Dōji, Kūkai and other pilgrims to Ximingsi were preserved in classics such as *Konjaku monogatarishū* 今昔物語集 (Tales of Times Now and Past), or in historical tales like *Ōokagami* 大鏡 (The Great Mirror). To demonstrate one direction of future research for scholars interested in Ximingsi, among the corpus of relevant Japanese literary and religious writings, I would like to consider here the example of a case extracted from *Shintōshū* 神道集 (Tales of Shinto), a collection of stories dated from the Nanboku-chō period (1336-1392).[10] According to the section of the work entitled *Kitano tenjin no koto* 北野天神の事, a deity named Tenman daijizai tenjin 天満大自在天神 is capable of travelling within the three realms (Jap. *sangai* 三界, Skt. *traidhātuka or trailokya*; Ch. *sanjie*) of the Buddhist cosmos to edify and convert sentient beings.[11] He said:

> Every day, [I] appear freely at the palace of Śakra, the palace of King Yama, and the palace of the great Brahmā; at the Ximingsi and the Qinglong Monastery in the city of Chang'an in the Great Tang; at the Seongi Museong in the land of Silla; at the royal palaces and the temples and shrines where numinous signs abound in the Five Inner [Provinces] and Seven Districts of Japan.

> 毎日，帝釋宮・閻魔王宮・大梵天宮・五天竺・大唐長安城・西明寺・青龍寺，新羅國禪機武城，日本國の王城および五畿内七道にある霊験あらたかな寺・社などに自由自在に往來する.[12]

---

[10] The ten-fascicle *Shintōshū* was co-authored by writers from a Tendai Buddhist sect by the name of *Agui shōdō kyōdan* 安居院唱導教団 (Buddhist instruction order of the Agui) between the mid fourteenth century and early fifteenth century.

[11] According to the Japanese Shinto tradition, Sugawara Michizane 菅原道真 (845-903), the distinguished courtier of the Heian period (794-1185), turned into an angry ghost who came back to haunt his former enemies after he was maligned and died in exile. A Shinto shrine in the outskirts of Osaka called Dōmyōji Tenmangū 道明寺天満宮 was dedicated to a spirit (*tenjin* 天神) named after him: Tenman daijizai tenjin 天満大自在天神. The deities enshrined in Dōmyōji include the son of Amaterasuoomikami 天照大神 (the Sun Goddess), Amanohohi no Mikoto 天穂日命 and Kakujuni 覺壽尼, the aunt of Sugawara Michizane. Daijizai 大自在, sometimes transliterated as Moxi shouluo tian 摩醯首羅天 (Jap. Makeishura), refers to the Hindu lord Śiva, or Maheśvara; see *Mochizuki*, 3229.

[12] Kondō Yoshihiro 近藤喜博, ed., *Shintōshū* 神道集, Tōyō bunko 東洋文庫, vol. 94 (Tokyo: Kadokawa

Conclusion

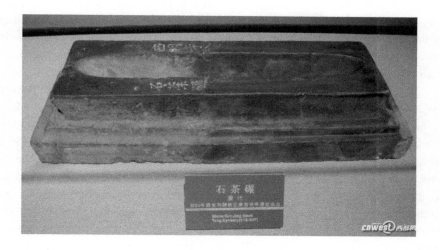

Figure. 54   Stone Tea Roller (*shi chanian* 石茶碾) Excavated at Ximingsi. Xi'an Museum. Source: "Shanxi forum 陝西論壇," accessed February 19, 2012, http://bbs.cnwest.com/thread-733384-1-1.html

The *Shintōshū* was composed by the Tendai Buddhist community of the Agui Temple 安居院 in Kyoto, and the paragraph suggests the glorification of the deity through the invocation of a succession of holy sites valued by the Japanese, or at least by the Tendai community. In another preaching anthology, titled *Gonsenshū* 言泉集 (Anthology of the Spring of Words), the Buddhist order in Agui Temple expressed similar interest in Ximingsi by offering a rare anecdote regarding the Ximing master Xuanze 玄則 that is not available in Chinese sources.[13] These references —— especially the reference in the *Shintōshū* —— are sufficient to suggest the significance of Ximingsi, invoked here along with the famous Qinglong Monastery to represent ideal Buddhist sites in China. The story deals with Ximingsi in such a fascinating way that it invites interrogation of this topic of mythic Ximingsi by religious scholars of both China and Japan. Before proceeding to a final remark, I

---

shoten, 1959), 224. The Gokinai 五畿內 are the five central provinces near Kyoto: Yamato 大和; Yamashiro 山城; Izumi 和泉; Kawachi 河內 and Settsu 摄津.

[13] Nagai Yoshinori 永井義憲 and Shimizu Yūshō 清水宥聖, ed., *Agui shōdōshū* 安居院唱導集 (Tokyo: Kadokawa shoten, 1972), 62.

238

would like to reiterate that the study of Ximingsi, originating from a microscopic survey of one monastery, has now become a fairly large project emphasizing cross-border, trans-regional and interdisciplinary approaches. The study encourages us not only to fully understand a national monastery portrayed in highly exalted terms in history, but also to appreciate its spiritual legacy, which still touches modern souls in search of meaning.

In contemporary Xi'an, the antiquarian passion for the study of Buddhist monasteries by learned professionals and gifted enthusiasts has largely been replaced by the economic impetus to promote domestic and international tourism. With the culture industry undergoing exponential growth, the Xi'an government spares no effort to stress its legitimacy as a historical city that finds its roots in Tang Chang'an. This policy, attributable to economic concerns, has in fact put the ancient heritage in the modern spotlight. The stone tea roller excavated from the site of Ximingsi is now on display in the majestic Xi'an Museum 西安博物院 near the Small Wild Goose Pagoda (*xiaoyanta* 小雁塔).[14] Conferences are also convened in the name of metropolitan Chang'an. The site of Ximingsi, however, has long since sunk into the earth under today's Beilin District 碑林區 of metropolitan Xi'an. On today's satellite map (Figure.55), one can draw a rectangle along the imaginative monastic boundary within the southwestern Baimiaocun area and the southern part of the Northwestern Polytechnic University (Xibei gongye daxue 西北工業大學). Starting from July 2011, the old residential district of Baimiaochun was bulldozed to make way for a new project of urban renewal. However, the southernmost part of the noisy construction field happens to overlap with the northeastern corner of Ximingsi, which gives us a new hope of finding long-buried artifacts.

---

[14] For some modern essays written in commemoration of Ximingsi, see Liao Mingfu 廖明夫, "Wangshi yue qiannian —— jisi Tang mingcha Ximingsi 往事越千年 —— 寄思唐名剎西明寺," *XIbei gongye daxue Bianjiacun qikan* 西北工業大學邊家村期刊 33 (2008), http://www.bjc.org.cn/bjc33/bjc33-05.htm, webpage accessed: Tuesday, February 07, 2012; Shi Zhecun 施蟄存, "Ximingsi 西明寺," In *Beishan sanwen ji* 北山散文集, vol. 2 (Shanghai: Huadong shifan daxue chubanshe, 2001), 779-80.

Conclusion

Figure. 55   Imaginative Monastic Boundary of Ximingsi within the Baimiaocun 白廟村 Area in Modern
Xi'an. Source: "Baidu Map (*baidu ditu* 百度地图)," accessed February 1, 2012, http://map.baidu.com,
drawing by Wang Xiang.

Over three centuries, Ximingsi witnessed the rise and decline of Tang Buddhism,
but it also fulfilled its mission of spreading the dharma across Buddhist Asia. In the
Mahāparinirvāṇa Sūtra, Śākyamuni Buddha refers to the perfect transmission of his
twelve divisions of the Buddhist canon (Skt. *dvādaśāṅgadharmapravacana*, Ch.
shierbu jing 十二部經) to Ānanda as "*xieping* 瀉瓶" (perfect transmission of the
single flavor) —— like water being poured completely and successfully from one
bottle to another.[15] Likewise, in many passages alluding to the transmission of
Buddhist wisdom from master to disciple, Daoxuan draws on the *xieping* metaphor to
express the true mission of a Buddhist monastery.[16] The political activity and
relationship with the imperial court were nothing but a vehicle to make sure that the
lamp of truth was successfully transmitted. In the end, what he expresses in the
Neidian Catalogue seems an appropriate summary of the golden age of Ximingsi:

> To hear and keep the meaning of a doctrine is like water being poured into a
> bottle. [The students] fully understood the skills of *śamatha* (concentration) and
> *vipaśyanā* (observation), and concurrently practice *dhyāna* (meditation) and
> *prajñā* (wisdom). While the master preached the wonderful dharma, the

---

[15] *Da banniepan jing*, T12, no. 374, p. 601, b26-c8, see *Mochizuki*, 2176.
[16] For examples of "*xieping*" in Daoxuan's writings, see *Xu gaoseng zhuan*, T50, no. 2060, p. 456, c12-15;
Guang hongming ji, T52, no. 2103, p. 236, a6-11.

auspicious lotus flowers blossomed in the pond; when the fellow students gathered around their master like clouds, the sweet and refreshing water gushed out from the spring.

聞持教義，類若瀉瓶；深明止觀，雙修定慧．敷揚妙法，池開靈瑞之蓮；學侶雲臻，泉涌輕甘之水．[17]

---

[17] *NDL* T55, no. 2149, p. 284, b26-c6.

Selected Bibliography

I. Abbreviations Used in Bibliography and Footnotes

BZJ	*Daizong chao zeng sikong dabianzheng guangzhi sanzang heshang biaozhiji* 代宗朝贈司空大辨正廣智三藏和上表制集
CFYG	*Cefu yuangui* 冊府元龜
Ch.	Chinese language
DNBZ	*Dai Nihon bukkyō zensho* 大日本佛教全書
EBTEA	*Esoteric Buddhism and the Tantras in East Asia* (Leiden; Boston: Brill, 2011)
FDLH	*Ji gujin fodao lunheng* 集古今佛道論衡
IBK	*Indogaku bukkyōgaku kenkyū* 印度學佛教學研究, Tokyo.
Jap.	Japanese language
JTS	*Jiu Tang shu* 舊唐書
Mochizuki	*Mochizuki bukkyō daijiten* 望月仏教大辭典
NDL	*Da Tang neidian lu* 大唐內典錄
Ono	*Chūgoku Zui Tō Chōan jiin shiryō shūsei* 中國隋唐長安寺院史料集成 (*Kaisetsuhen* 解說篇 and *Shiryōhen* 史料篇)
P	Chinese manuscripts from Dunhuang in the Pelliot Collection, Bibliothèque Nationale, Paris.
Pali.	Pali language
QTS	*Quan Tang shi* 全唐詩
QTW	*Quan Tang wen* 全唐文
S	Chinese manuscripts from Dunhuang in the Stein Collection, British Library, London.
SGSZ	*Song gaoseng zhuan* 宋高僧傳
Skt.	Sanskrit language
SKQS	*Yingyin Wenyuange siku quanshu* 景印文淵閣四庫全書
SZFSZ	*Da Ci'ensi sanzang fashi zhuan* 大慈恩寺三藏法師傳
T	*Taishō shinshū daizōkyō* 大正新修大藏經
TB	*Ximingsi tabei* 西明寺塔碑
Tib.	Tibetan language
THY	*Tang huiyao* 唐會要
XTS	*Xin Tang shu* 新唐書

Selected Bibliography

XZJ	*Xuzang jing* 續藏經
ZYL	*Zhenyuan xinding shijiao mulu* 貞元新定釋教目錄
ZZTJ	*Zizhi tongjian* 資治通鑑

Romanization: Citation of Chinese titles is in pinyin. Scriptures in the Chinese Buddhist canon are cited in the following fashion: Title; Taishō volume number; scripture volume number.

II. Primary Sources

Apidamo da piposha lun 阿毗達磨大毗婆沙論 (Skt. *Abhidharma-mahāvibhāṣā śāstra*). T27, no. 1545.

Baishi changqing ji 白氏長慶集. By Bai Juyi 白居易 (772-846). Beijing: Wenxue guji kanxing she, 1955.

Baoke congbian 寶刻叢編. By Lu Xinyuan 陸心源 (1834-1894). *Shike shiliao congshu* 石刻史料叢書, vol. 79-80. Compiled by Chen Si 陳思. Taipei: Yiwen Yinshuguan. 1966.

Beishan lu 北山錄. By Shenqing 神清 (9th c.). T52, no. 2113.

Bianzheng lun 辯正論. By Falin 法琳 (572-640). T52, no. 2110.

Chang'an zhi: Fu Chang'an zhi tu 長安志: 附長安志圖. By Song Minqiu 宋敏求 (1019-1079). Beijing: Zhonghua shuju, 1991.

Chishō daishi shōrai mokuroku 智證大師請來目錄. By Enchin 円珍 (814-891). T55, no. 2173.

Congshu jicheng chubian 叢書集成初編. Shanghai: Shangwu yinshuguan, 1935.

Da banniepan jing 大般涅槃經 (Skt. *Mahāparinirvāṇa-sūtra*). T12, no. 374

Dacheng baifa mingmen lun kaizong yijue 大乘百法明門論開宗義決. By Tankuang 曇曠 (8th c.). T85, no. 2812.

Dacheng ershier wen ben 大乘二十二問本. By Tankuang (8th c.). T85, no. 2818.

Dafangguang fo huayan jing 大方廣佛華嚴經 (Skt. *Buddhāvataṃsaka-nāma mahā-vaipulya sūtra*). T10, no. 293.

Dai Nihon bukkyō zensho 大日本佛教全書. 100 vols. Edited by Suzuki gakujutsu zaidan 鈴木学術財団. Tokyo: Kōdansha ,1970-1973.

Daizongchao zeng sikong dabianzheng guangzhi sanzang heshang biaozhi ji 代宗朝 贈司空大辨正廣智三藏和上表制集. Yuanzhao 圓照 (8th c.). T50, no. 2120.

Da Song sengshi lüe 大宋僧史略. By Zanning 贊寧 (919-1001). T54, no. 2126.

Da Tang Daci'en si sanzang fashi zhuan 大唐大慈恩寺三藏法師傳. By Huili 慧立 (615-?) and Yancong 彥悰 (627-649, or d.688). T50, no. 2053.

Selected Bibliography

Da Tang gu sanzang Xuanzang fashi xingzhuang 大唐故三藏玄奘法師行狀. By Mingxiang 冥詳. T50, no. 2052.

Da Tang neidian lu 大唐內典錄. By Daoxuan 道宣 (596-667). T55, no. 2149.

Da Tang xiyu ji 大唐西域記 (or *Xiyu ji* 西域記). By Xuanzang 玄奘 (602-664) and Bianji 辯機 (ca. 618-648). T51, no. 2087.

Da Tang xiyu qiufa gaoseng zhuan 大唐西域求法高僧傳. By Yijing 義淨 (635-713). T51, no. 2066.

Da Tang zhenyuan xu Kanyuan shijiao lu 大唐貞元續開元釋教錄. Compiled by Yuanzhao. T55, no. 2156.

Da Zhou kanding zhongjing mulu 大週刊定眾經目錄. Compiled by Mingquan 明佺. T55, no. 2153.

Duli tongkao 讀禮通考. By Xu Qianxue 徐乾學 (1631-1694). *SKQS* vol. 111.

Fangdeng sanmei xingfa 方等三昧行法. Compiled by Zunshi 遵式. T46, no. 1940.

Fanyi mingyi ji 翻譯名義集. By Fayun 法雲 (1088-1158). T54, no.2131.

Fayuan zhulin 法苑珠林. By Daoshi 道世 (596-683). T53, no. 2122.

Fengtian lu 奉天錄. *Congshujicheng chubian* 叢書集成初編, vol. 3834.

Foding zunsheng tuoluoni jing 佛頂尊勝陀羅尼經 (Skt. *Sarvadurgati pariśodhana uṣṇīṣavijayadhāraṇī*). T19, no. 968.

Foshuo Amituo jing 佛說阿彌陀經 (Skt. *Sukhāvatī-vyūha*). T12, no. 366.

Fozu lidai tongzai 佛祖歷代通載. Compiled by Nianchang 念常 (1282-1341). T49, no. 2036.

Fozu tongji 佛祖統紀. By Zhipan 志盤 (fl. 1230). T49, no. 2035.

Fusō ryakki 扶桑略記. By Kōen 皇円 (d. 1169). *Kokushi taikei* 國史大系, vol.12.

Genben sapoduobu lü she 根本薩婆多部律攝 (Skt. *Sarvāstivādavinaya-saṃgrāha*). By Jinamitra (Ch. Shengyou 勝友). T24, no.1458.

Genkō shakusho 元亨釋書. By Kokan Shiren 虎關師錬 (1278-1346). *DNBZ* vol. 62.

Guang hongming ji 廣弘明集. Compiled by Daoxuan. T52, no. 2103.

Guanzhong chuangli jietan tujing 關中創立戒壇圖經. By Daoxuan. T45, no. 1892.

(Gujin tushu jicheng) Shijiaobuhui kao (古今圖書集成) 釋教部彙考. *XZJ* vol. 133.

Gunsho ruijū 群書類従. Compiled by Hanawa Hokinoichi 塙保已一 (1746-1821). Tokyo: Zoku gunsho ruijū kanseikai, 1959.

Honchō kōsōden 本朝高僧傳. By Mangen Shiba 卍元師蠻 (1626-1710). *DNBZ* vol. 63.

Jikaku Daishi zai Tō sōshinroku 慈覺大師在唐送進錄. By Ennin 円仁 (794-864). T55, no. 2166.

Jin'gangding yiqie rulai zhenshi shedacheng xianzheng dajiaowang jing 金剛頂一

Selected Bibliography

切如來真實攝大乘現證大教王經 (or *Jingangding jing* 金剛頂經, Skt. *Vajraśekhara-sūtra*). T18, no. 865.

Jin guangming chanfa buzhu yi 金光明懺法補助儀. Compiled by Zunshi. T46, no. 1945.

Jingde chuandeng lu 景德傳燈錄. By Daoyuan 道原. T51, no. 2076.

Jiupin wangsheng Amituo sanmodi ji tuoluoni jing 九品往生阿彌陀三摩地集陀羅尼經, T19, no. 933.

Ji shamen buying baisu dengshi 集沙門不應拜俗等事. Compiled by Yancong. T52, no. 2108.

Kaiyuan shijiao lu 開元釋教錄. By Zhisheng 智昇 (658-740). T55, no. 2154.

Kōbō daishi nenpu 弘法大師年譜. By Takaoka Ryūshin 高岡隆心 (1867-1939). *Shingonshū zensho* 真言宗全書, vol. 3.

Konjaku monogatarishū 今昔物語集. Edited by Nagazumi Yasuaki 永積安明, Ikegami Jun'ichi 池上洵一. Tōyō bunko 東洋文庫, vol. 80. Tokyo: Heibonsha, 1966-1980.

Kokushi taikei 國史大系. Edited by Kuroita Katsumi 黑板勝美 and Maruyama Jirō 丸山二郎. Tokyo: Yoshikawa kōbunkan, 1951.

Kui tan lu 愧郯錄. By Yue Ke 岳珂 (1183-1243). *SKQS* vol. 865.

Liangbu dafa xiangcheng shizi fufa ji 兩部大法相承師資付法記. By Haiyun 海雲 (9th c.). T51, no. 2081.

Liangjing xinji 兩京新記. By Wei Shu 韋述 (d.757). Taipei: Shijie shuju, 1963.

Lidai sanbao ji 歷代三寶紀. By Fei Changfang 費長房 (6th c.). T49, no. 2034.

Lidai shishi zijian 歷朝釋氏資鑑. Compiled by Xizhong 熙仲. *XZJ* vol. 132.

Longshu pusa zhuan 龍樹菩薩傳. T50, no. 2047a.

Longxing biannian tonglun. 隆興編年通論. By Zuxiu 祖琇 (fl.1164). *XZJ* vol. 130.

Lüyuan shigui 律苑事規. Compiled by Xingwu 省悟, *XZJ* vol.106.

Miaofa lianhua jing xuanyi 妙法蓮華經玄義. Compiled by Guanding 灌頂 (561-632). T33, no. 1716.

Minggong faxi zhi 名公法喜志. Compiled by Xia Shufang 夏樹芳. *XZJ* vol. 150.

Nanhai jigui neifa zhuan 南海寄歸內法傳. By Yijing. T54, no. 2125.

Nihon biku Enchin nittō guhō mokuroku 日本比丘圓珍入唐求法目錄. By Enchin. T55, no. 2172.

Nihon sandai jitsuroku 日本三代實錄. By Fujiwara Tokihira 藤原時平 (871-909). *Kokushi taikei* 國史大系, vol. 4. Edited by Kuroita Katsumi 黑板勝美. Tokyo: Yoshikawa kōbunkan, 1964.

Nittō guhō junrei gyōki 入唐求法巡禮行記. By Ennin. *DNBZ* vol.72.

Nittō shoka denkō 入唐諸家傳考. Edited by Takakusu Junjirō 高楠順次郎

(1866-1945). *DNBZ* vol.68.

[O]shōrai mokuroku 禦請來目錄. By 空海 Kūkai (774-835). T55, no. 2161.

Pinimu jing 毘尼母經 (Skt. *Vinaya mātṛkā-śāstra*). T24, no. 1463.

Qinding gujin tushu jicheng 欽定古今圖書集成. Compiled by Chen Menglei 陳夢雷 (1650-1741). Taipei: Dingwen shuju. 1977.

Quan Tang shi 全唐詩. Compiled by Peng Dingqiu 彭定求 (1645-1719). Beijing: Zhonghua shuju, 1960.

Quan Tang wen 全唐文. Compiled by Dong Hao 董浩 (1740-1818). Beijing: Zhonghua Shuju, 1965.

Quan Tang wenbu bian 全唐文補編. Edited by Chen Shangjun 陳尚君. Beijing: Zhonghua shuju, 2005.

Renwang huguo boruo boluomiduo jing 仁王護國般若波羅蜜多經. T08, no. 246.

Renwang jingshu faheng chao 仁王經疏法衡鈔. Compiled by Yurong 遇榮. *XZJ* vol. 41.

Sangoku buppō dentsū engi 三國仏法傳通緣起. By Gyōnen 凝然 (1240-1321). *DNBZ* vol. 62.

Shanxi tongzhi 陝西通志. Compiled by Chen Qingya 沈青崖. *SKQS* vol. 552.

Shijia fangzhi 釋迦方志. By Daoxuan. T51, no. 2088.

Shimen zhengtong 釋門正統. By Zongjian 宗鑒. *XZJ* vol.130.

Shin Nihon koten bungaku taikei 新日本古典文學大系. Edited by Aoki Kazuo 青木和夫, Sasayama Haruo 笹山晴生, and Yoshimura Takehiko 吉村武彦. Tokyo: Iwanami shoten, 1989.

Shinpen Nihon koten bungaku zenshū 新編日本古典文学全集. Tokyo: Shogakkan, 1994.

Shin shosha shōrai hōmon tō mokuroku 新書寫請來法門等目錄. By Shōei 宗叡 (809－884). T55, no. 2174a.

Shintōshū 神道集. Edited by Kondō Yoshihiro 近藤喜博. Tōyō bunko 東洋文庫, vol. 94. Tokyo: Kadokawa shoten, 1959.

Shishi jigu lüe 釋氏稽古略. By Jue'an 覺岸 (1286-?). *XZJ* 131.

Sho Ajari shingon mikkyō burui sōroku 諸阿闍梨真言密教部類總錄. Compiled by Annen 安然 (841- 915). T55, no. 2176.

Shoku nihongi 續日本紀. *Shin Nihon koten bungaku taikei*, vol. 12-16.

Sifenlü shanfan buque xingshichao 四分律刪繁補闕行事鈔. By Daoxuan. T40, no. 1804.

Song gaoseng zhuan 宋高僧傳. Compiled by Zanning. T50, no. 2061.

Sui shu 隋書. By Wei Zheng 魏徵 (580-643) and others. Beijing: zhonghua shuju, 1973.

Sui tiantai zhizhe dashi biezhuan 隋天臺智者大師別傳. By Guanding. T50, no. 2050.

Taiping guangji 太平廣記. Compiled by Li Fang 李昉 (925-996). Beijing: Zhonghua shuju, 1961.

Taishō shinshū daizōkyō 大正新修大藏經. Edited by Takakusu Junjirō 高楠順次郎 (1866-1945) and Watanabe Kaigyoku 渡邊海旭 (1872-1933). Tokyo: Taishō issaikyō kankōkai, 1924-1932.

Tang huiyao 唐會要. Compiled by Wang Pu 王溥 (922-982). Beijing: Zhonghua shuju. 1955.

Tang Tae Ch'ŏnboksa kosaju pŏn'gyŏng taedŏk Pŏpjang hwasang chŏn 唐大薦福寺故寺主翻經大德法藏和尚傳. By Ch'oe Chiwŏn 崔致遠 (857-904). T50, no. 2054.

Tang kaiyuan shijiao guangping li zhang 唐開元釋教廣品歷章. By Xuanyi 玄逸. *Zhaocheng jinzang* 趙城金藏, vol. 097-98, no. 1276.

Tang wencui 唐文粹. Compiled by Yao Xuan 姚鉉 (967-1020). *SKQS* vol. 449

Tōiki dentō mokuroku 東域傳燈目錄. By Eichō 永超 (1014-1095). T55, no. 2125.

Tsurezuregusa 徒然草. By Yoshida Kenkō 吉田兼好 (1283-1352), *Shin Nihon koten bungaku taikei*, vol. 44.

Tuhua jianwen zhi 圖畫見聞志. By Guo Ruoxu 郭若虛 (11th c.). *SKQS* vol. 812.

Tuoluoni jijing 陀羅尼集經 (Skt. *Dhāraṇī-samuccaya*), T885, no. 901.

Wan Xu zangjing: Zangjing shuyuan ban 卍續藏經: 藏經書院版. Taipei: Xinwen feng chuban gongsi, 1977.

Ximingsi tabei 西明寺塔碑. By Su Ting 蘇頲 (670-727). *QTW* vol. 257.

Xin Tang shu 新唐書. By Ouyang Xiu 歐陽修 (1007-1072) and others. Beijing: Zhonghua shuju, 1975.

Xinxiu kefen liuxue sengzhuan 新修科分六學僧傳. By Tan'e 曇噩. *XZJ* vol. 133.

Xu Gaoseng zhuan 續高僧傳. By Daoxuan. T50, no. 2060.

Xu Gujin yijing tuji 續古今譯經圖紀. By Zhisheng. T55, no. 2152.

Xu Zhenyuan shijiao lu 續貞元釋教錄. By Heng'an 恒安. T55, no. 2158.

Yingyin Wenyuange siku quanshu 景印文淵閣四庫全書. Compiled by Ji Yun 紀昀 (1727-1805). Taipei: Shangwu yinshuguan, 1983-1986.

Yiqiejing yinyi 一切經音義. By Huilin 慧琳 (737-820). T54, no. 2128.

Youyang zazu 酉陽雜組. By Duan Chengshi 段成式 (d. 863). Beijing: Zhonghua shuju, 1981.

Zhaocheng jinzang 趙城金藏. Beijing: Beijing tushuguan chubanshe, 2008.

Zhenyuan xinding shijiao mulu 貞元新定釋教目錄. By Yuanzhao. T55, no. 2157.

Zhiguan fuxing zhuan hong jue 止觀輔行傳弘決. By Zhanran 湛然 (711-782). T46, no. 1912.

Zhongchao gushi 中朝故事. By Yuchi Wo 尉迟偓. *SKQS* vol. 1035.

Zhongtianzhu Sheweiguo Qihuansi tujing 中天竺舍衛國祇洹寺圖經. By Daoxuan. T45, no. 1899.

III.Secondary Sources
(Books and Journal Articles)

Abe, Ryūichi. *The Weaving of Mantra: Kūkai and the Construction of Esoteric Buddhist Discourse.* New York: Columbia University Press, 1999.

Aboshi Yoshinori 網干善教. "Shaeijō to Gion Shōja (Oboegaki 1) 舍衛城と祇園精舍覺書一." *Kansai Daigaku kōkogaku tō shiryōshitsu kiyō* 關西大學考古學等資料室記要 4 (1987): 1-13.

———. "Gion shōja no hakkutsu 祇園精舍の発掘." *Bukkyō shigaku kenkyū* 仏教史學研究 34, no. 1 (1991): 130-47.

Adachi Kiroku 足立喜六. *Chōan shiseki no kenkyū*: 長安史跡の研究. Tokyo: Tōyō Bunko, 1933.

Adachi Yasushi 足立康. *Yakushiji garan no kenkyū* 藥師寺伽藍の研究. Tokyo: Yoshikawa kōbunkan, 1974.

Abu Zayd Hasan bin Yazid, and al-tājir Sulaymān. *Ancient Accounts of India and China.* Translated by Eusèbe Renaudot. London: Printed for S. Harding, 1733.

Acker, William Reynolds Beal, and Yanyuan Zhang, trans. *Some T'ang and Pre-T'ang Texts on Chinese Painting, Translated and Annotated.* Leiden: E.J. Brill, 1954.

Ahir, D. C. *Sravasti, Where the Buddha Spent 25 Retreats.* New Delhi: Buddhist World Press, 2009.

Aitani Yoshimitsu 會穀佳光. *Sōdai shoseki shūsankō: Shintōjo geimonshi shakushirui no kenkyū* 宋代書籍聚散考: 新唐書藝文志釋氏類の研究. Tokyo: Kyūko shoin, 2004.

Akanuma Chizen 赤沼智善. *Indo bukkyō koyū meishi jiten* 印度佛教固有名詞辭典. Nagoya: Hajinkaku, 1931.

An Jiayao 安家瑤. "Tang Chang'an Ximingsi yizhi fajue jianbao 唐長安西明寺遺址發掘簡報." *Kaogu* 考古 1 (1990): 45-55.

———."Tang Chang'an Ximingsi yizhi de kaogu faxian 唐長安西明寺遺址的考古發現." *Tang yanjiu* 唐研究 6 (2000): 337-52.

———. "When Glass Was Treasured in China." In *Nomads, Traders and Holy Men Along China's Silk Road*, edited by Annette L. Juliano, and Judith A. Lerner,

79-94. Turnhout: Brepols, 2002.

Assandri, Friederike. *From Early Tang Court Debates to China's Peaceful Rise.* Amsterdam: Amsterdam University Press, 2009.

Bai Huawen 白化文. *Rutang qiufa xunli xingji jiaozhu* 入唐求法巡禮行記校注. Shijiazhuang: Huashan wenxi chubanshe, 1992.

———, and Li Dingxia 李鼎霞. *Xinglichao jiaozhu* 行曆抄校注. Shijiazhuang: Huashan wenyi chubanshe, 2004.

Barrett, T. H. "Stūpa, Sūtra and Śarīra in China, c. 656-706 CE." *Buddhist Studies Review* 18, no.1 (2001): 1-64.

Barua, Dipak Kumar. *Viharas in Ancient India: A Survey of Buddhist Monasteries.* Calcutta: Indian Publications, 1969.

Beal, Samuel, trans. *Si-yu-ki: Buddhist Records of the Western World.* London: Kegan Paul, Trench, Trübner, 1906.

Beijingshi zhong ri wenhua jiaoliushi yanjiuhui 北京市中日文化交流史研究會. *Zhong Ri wenhua jiaoliushi lunwenji* 中日文化交流史論文集. Beijing: Renmin chubanshe,1982.

Benn, James A., Lori Rachelle Meeks and James Robson, eds. *Buddhist Monasticism in East Asia: Places of Practice.* London: Routledge, 2010.

Berger, Patricia. "Preserving the Nation: The Political Uses of Tantric Art in China." In *Latter Days of the Law: Images of Chinese Buddhism, 850-1850*, edited by Marsha Weidner, 89-124. Lawrence, Kans.: Spencer Museum of Art, 1994.

Bessatsu Taiyō 別冊太陽, *Kūkai: Shingon Mikkyō no tobira o hiraita kessō* 空海: 真言密教の扉を開いた傑僧 (*Nihon no kokoro* 日本のこころ, 187). Tokyo: Heibonsha, 2011.

Bi Fei 畢斐. *Lidai minghuaji lungao* 歷代名畫記論稿. Hangzhou: Zhongguo meishu xueyuan chubanshe, 2008.

Bingenheimer, Marcus. *A Biographical Dictionary of the Japanese Student-Monks of the Seventh and Early Eighth Centuries: Their Travels to China and Their Role in the Transmission of Buddhism.* München: Iudicium, 2001.

Birnbaum, Raoul. "The Manifestation of a Monastery: Shen-Ying's Experiences on Mount Wu-T'ai in T'ang Context." *Journal of the American Oriental Society* 106, no. 1 (1986): 19-37.

Borgen, Robert. "A History of Dōmyōji to 1572 (or Maybe 1575): An Attempted Reconstruction." *Monumenta Nipponica* 62, no. 1 (2007): 1-55.

Bowring, Richard John. *The Religious Traditions of Japan, 500-1600.* Cambridge, UK: Cambridge University Press, 2005.

Buddhaghosa, *The Path of Purification: Visuddhimagga.* Translated by. Ñāṇamoli.

Seattle, WA: 1st BPE Pariyatti Editions, 1999.

Burton, Janet. *Medieval Monasticism: Monasticism in the Medieval West: From Its Origins to the Coming of the Friars*. Oxford: Headstart History, 1996.

Chang Yao 暢耀. *Da Ci'ensi*: 大慈恩寺 Xi'an: Sanqin chubanshe, 1988.

Chen Huaiyu. *The Revival of Buddhist Monasticism in Medieval China*. New York: Peter Lang, 2007.

Chen Jing 陳靜. "Tang Chang'an Ximingsi gouchen 唐長安西明寺勾沉." In *Zongjiao yanjiu lunji* 宗教研究論集, edited by Bai Ming 柏明, 368-73. Xi'an: Shanxi renmin chubanshe, 1994.

Chen Jinhua. "Tang Buddhist Palace Chapels." *Journal of Chinese Religions* 32 (2004): 101-73.

———. "Images, Legends, Politics, and the Origin of the Great Xiangguo Monastery in Kaifeng: A Case-Study of the Formation and Transformation of Buddhist Sacred Sites in Medieval China." *Journal of the American Oriental Society* 125, no. 3 (2005): 353-78.

———. "The Statues and Monks of Shengshan Monastery: Money and Maitreyan Buddhism in Tang China." *Asia Major* 3, no. 19 (2006): 111-160.

———. *Philosopher, Practitioner, Politician: The Many Lives of Fazang (643-712)*. Boston: Brill, 2007.

Chen Jingfu 陳景富. *Xiangji si* 香積寺. Xi'an: Sanqin chubanshe, 1986.

———. "Chaoxian ruxueseng yu Tangdai de fojing fanyi 朝鮮入學僧與唐代的佛經翻譯." *Renwen zazhi* 人文雜誌 2 (1994):105-108.

———. "Yuance yu Xuanzang, Kuiji guanxi xiaokao 圓測與玄奘, 窺基關係小考." *Nanya yanjiu* 南亞研究 3 (1994):17-20.

Chen, Kenneth K.S. *Buddhism in China: A Historical Survey*. Princeton: Princeton University Press, 1964.

———. "The Role of Buddhist Monasteries in T'ang China." *History of Religions* 15, no. 3 (1976): 203-58.

Cheng Longhai 陳龍海. "Liu Gongquan shubei xi niankao 柳公權書碑繫年考." *Huazhong shifan daxue xuebao (Renwen shehui kexue ban)* 華中師範大學學報（人文社會科學版）2 (2000):114-120.

Chikusa Masaaki 竺沙雅章. *Chūgoku bukkyō shakaishi kenkyū*: 中國佛教社會史研究. Kyoto: Dōhōsha shuppan, 2002.

Collcutt, Martin. *Five Mountains: The Rinzai Zen Monastic Institution in Medieval Japan*. Cambridge, Mass: Published by Council on East Asian Studies, Harvard University; distributed by Harvard University Press, 1981.

Coomaraswamy, Ananda. "Sculptures from Mathurā." *Bulletin of the Museum of*

Fine Arts 25, no. 150 (1927) : 50-54.

Copp, Paul. "Voice, Dust, Shadow, Stone: The Makings of Spells in Medieval Chinese Buddhism." Ph.D. thesis. Princeton University, 2005.

Daianji Shi Henshū Iinkai 大安寺史編集委員會, ed. *Daianji shi · shiryō* 大安寺史·史料. Nara: Daianji, 1984.

Davidson, Ronald M. *Indian Esoteric Buddhism: A Social History of the Tantric Movement.* New York: Columbia University Press, 2002.

Dong Zengchen 董曾臣, and Zhang Congxian 張聰賢, eds. *Chang'an xianzhi* 長安縣誌. Taipei: Chengwen chubanshe, 1969.

Doniger, Wendy. *The Implied Spider: Politics & Theology in Myth.* New York: Columbia University Press, 1998.

Drège, Jean Pierre. *Les bibliothèques en Chine au temps des manuscrits: jusqu'au xe siècle.* Paris: Ecole française d'Extrême-Orient, 1991.

Du Doucheng 杜鬥城. *Hexi fojiao shi* 河西佛教史. Beijing: Zhongguo shehui kexue chubanshe, 2009.

Duan Yuming 段玉明. *Xiangguosi: zai Tang Song diguo de shensheng yu fansu zhijian* 相國寺: 在唐宋帝國的神聖與凡俗之間. Chengdu: Bashu shushe, 2004.

Dudbridge, Glen. *Religious Experience and Lay Society in T'ang China: A Reading of Tai Fu's Kuang-I Chi.* Cambridge University Press, 1996.

Dutt, Sukumar. *Buddhist Monks and Monasteries of India: Their History and Their Contribution to Indian Culture.* London: Allen & Unwin, 1962.

Emmerick, R. E. *The Sūtra of Golden Light: Being a Translation of the Suvarṇabhāsottamasūtra.* London: Pali Text Society, 1979.

Fang Guangchang 方廣錩. "'Huilin yinyi' yu Tangdai Dazangjing 《慧琳音義》與唐代大藏經." In *Zangwai fojiao wenxian: dibaji* 藏外佛教文獻: 第八集, edited by Fang Guangchang, 403-424. Beijing: Zongjiao wenhua chubanshe, 2003.

———. *Zhongguo xieben dazang jing yanjiu* 中國寫本大藏經研究. Shanghai: Shanghai guji chubanshe, 2006.

Fan Guangchun 樊光春. *Chang'an daojiao yu daoguan* 長安道教與道觀. Xi'an: Xi'an chubanshe, 2002.

Fan Wenlan 范文瀾, and Zhang Zunliu 張遵驑. *Tangdai fojiao* 唐代佛教. Chongqing: Chongqing chubanshe, 2008.

Fan Jinshi 樊錦詩, and Luo Huaqing 羅華慶, eds. *Dunhuang shiku quanji: 20, Cangjing dong zhenpin juan* 敦煌石窟全集: 20, 藏經洞珍品卷. Xianggang: Shangwu yinshuguan, 2005.

Selected Bibliography

Faure, Bernard. *Visions of Power: Imagining Medieval Japanese Buddhism*. Princeton, N.J.: Princeton University Press, 1996.

———. *The Red Thread: Buddhist Approaches to Sexuality*. Princeton, N.J.: Princeton University Press, 1998.

Feng Chengjun 馮承均. *Lidai qiufa fanjing lu* 歷代求法翻經錄. Shanghai: Shangwu yinshu guan, 1934.

Feng Guodong 馮國棟. "Tang Song wangyi fojiao jinglu congkao 唐宋亡佚佛教經錄叢考." *Zhejiang daxue xuebao(renwen shehui kexue ban)* 浙江大學學報 (人文社會科學版) 5 (2008): 52-60.

Fogelin, Lars. *Archaeology of Early Buddhism*. Lanham, MD: AltaMira Press, 2006.

Forte, Antonino. *Political Propaganda and Ideology in China at the End of the Seventh Century: Inquiry into the Nature, Authors and Function of the Tunhuang Document S. 6502, Followed by an Annotated Translation*. Napoli: Istituto universitario orientale, Seminario di studi asiatici, 1976.

———. "Daiji 大寺 (Chine)." in *Hōbōgirin: dictionnaire encyclopédique du Bouddhisme d'après les sources Chinoises et Japonaises*, vol. 6, 682-704. Tokyo: Maison franco-japonaise, 1983.

———. *Mingtang and Buddhist Utopias in the History of the Astronomical Clock: The Tower, Statue, and Armillary Sphere Constructed by Empress Wu*. Roma: Istituto italiano per il Medio ed Estremo Oriente, 1988.

———. "Chinese State Monasteries in the Seventh and Eighth Centuries." In *Echō ō Gotenjikukoku den kenkyū* 慧超往五天竺国傳研究, edited by Kuwayama Shōshin 桑山正進, 229-230. Kyoto: Jinbun kagaku kenkyūjo, 1992.

———. "The Origins and Role of the Great Fengxian Monastery at Longmen." *Annali* 56 (1996): 365-87.

Fraser, Sarah Elizabeth, ed. *Fojiao wuzhi wenhua: siyuan caifu yu shisu gongyang guoji xueshu yantaohui lunwenji* 佛教物質文化: 寺院財富與世俗供養國際學術研討會論文集. Shanghai: Shanghai shuhua chubanshe, 2003.

Fujita Tsuneyo 藤田經世. *Kōkan bijutsu shiryō: Jiin hen* 校刊美術史料: 寺院篇. Tokyo: Chūō kōron bijutsu shuppan, 1972.

Fujiwara Sukeyo 藤原佐世. *Nihonkoku genzaisho mukuruku* 日本國見在書目録. Taipei: Guangwen shuju, 1972.

Fujiyoshi Masumi 藤善真澄. "Yakushiji tōtō no Satsumei to Saimyōji shōmei · tokushū (Nihon no kentōshi —— hatōbanri · Chōan o mezasu) 薬師寺東塔の擦銘と西明寺鐘銘·特集（日本の遣唐使 —— 波濤萬里·長安を目指す)." *Asia yūgaku* アジア遊學 (Intriguing Asia) 4 (May 1999): 66-80.

———. *Dōsen den no kenkyū* 道宣伝の研究. Kyoto: Kyōto daigaku gakujutsu shuppankai, 2002.

Fu Xuancong 傅璇琮. *Zhongguo cangshu tongshi* 中國藏書通史. Ningbo: Ningbo chubanshe, 2000.

Gernet, Jacques. *Les aspects conomiques du bouddhisme dans la société Chinoise du ve au xe siècle*. Paris: Ecole Française d'Extrême Orient, 1956.

Giles, Lionel, and British Museum. Dept. of Oriental Printed Books and Manuscripts. *Descriptive Catalogue of the Chinese Manuscripts from Tunhuang in the British Museum*: London: Trustees of the British Museum, 1957.

Gimello, Robert. "Changing Shang-Ying on Wu-T'ai Shan." In *Pilgrims and Sacred Sites in China*, edited by Susan Naquin and Yü Chün-Fang, 89-102. Berkeley: University of California Press, 1992.

Gong Guoqiang 龔國強. *Sui Tang Chang'an cheng fosi yanjiu*. 隋唐長安城佛寺研究. Beijing: Wenwu chubanshe, 2006.

Greene, J. Patrick. *Medieval Monasteries*. London: Continuum, 2005.

Guang Xing. "A Buddhist-Confucian Controversy on Filial Piety." *Journal of Chinese Philosophy* 37, no. 2 (June 2010): 248–60.

Guisso, R. W. L. *Wu Tse-T'en and the Politics of Legitimation in T'ang China*. Bellingham, Wash: Western Washington, 1978.

Guo Peng 郭鵬. *Sui Tang fojiao* 隋唐佛教. Jinan: Qilu shushe, 1980.

Hammond, Kenneth J. "Beijing's Zhihua Monastery: History and Restoration in China's Capital." In *Cultural Intersections in Later Chinese Buddhism,* edited by Weidner, Marsha, 189-208. Honolulu: University of Hawai'i Press, 2001.

Han Jinke 韓金科, ed. *98 Famensi Tang wenhua guoji xueshu taolunhui lunwen ji.* 98 法門寺唐文化國際學術討論會論文集. Xi'an: Shanxi renmin chubanshe, 2000.

Hattori Masanobu 服部匡延. "Daianji engi no seiritsu ni tsuite 大安寺緣起の成立について." *Waseda daigaku toshokan kiyō* 早稲田大學図書館紀要 (1961): 92-101.

———. "Daianji wa Saimyōji no moken to iu setsu nitsuite 大安寺は西明寺の模建という説について." *Nanto bukkyō* 南都佛教 34 (1975): 24-39.

Heng, Chye Kiang (*pinyin*: Wang Caiqiang 王才強). *Cities of Aristocrats and Bureaucrats: The Development of Medieval Chinese Cityscapes*. Honolulu: University of Hawai'i Press, 1999.

———. *Tang Chang'an de Shuma Chongjian* 唐長安的數碼重建. Beijing: Zhongguo jianzhu gongye chubanshe, 2006.

Hiraoka Takeo 平岡武夫, and Imai Kiyoshi 今井淸, eds. *Tōdai no Chōan to Rakuyō* 唐代の長安と洛陽. Kyoto: Dōhōsha, 1977.

——— eds. *Tangdai de Chang'an yu Luoyang* 唐代的長安與洛陽. Translated by Li Qing 李慶. Shanghai: Shanghai guji chubanshe, 1989.

Horiike Shunpō 堀池春峰. "Nittō ryūgakusō to Chōan · Saimyōji 入唐留學僧と長安 · 西明寺." In *Nanto bukkyōshi no kenkyū · shoji hen* 南都仏教史の研究 · 諸寺篇, 245-76. (Kyoto: Hōzōkan, 2003), 253.

Hubbard, Jamie. *Absolute Delusion, Perfect Buddhahood: The Rise and Fall of a Chinese Heresy*. Honolulu: University of Hawai'i Press, 2001.

Hucker, Charles. *A Dictionary of Official Titles in Imperial China*. Stanford, Calif: Stanford University Press, 1985.

Huili. *A Biography of the Tripitaka Master of the Great Ci'en Monastery of the Great Tang Dynasty*. Translated by Li Rongxi 李榮熙. Berkeley, Calif.: Numata Center for Buddhist Translation and Research, 1995.

Hu Ji 胡戟. "Ximingsi xilou 西明寺戲樓." In *Shoujie Chang'an fojiao guoji xueshu yantaohui lunwenji disan juan* 首屆長安佛教國際學術研討會論文集第三卷, edited by Zengqin 增勤, 450-51. Xi'an: Shanxi shifan daxue chuban zongshe youxian gongsi, 2010.

Hu Yunyi 胡雲翼, ed. *Tangwenxuan* 唐文選. Shanghai: Zhonghua shuju, 1940.

Ikeda On 池田溫. *Chūgoku kodai shahon shikigo shūroku* 中國古代寫本識語集錄. Tokyo: Ōkura shuppan, 1990.

———. *Tō to Nihon* 唐と日本. Tokyo: Yoshikawa kōbunkan, 1992.

Inobe Jūichirō 伊野部重一郎. "Daianji no sōsō 大安寺の草創." *Nihon jōkoshi kenkyū* 日本上古史研究 3, no. 11 (1959): 199-205.

———. "Daianji no sōsō hoi「大安寺の草創」補遺." *Nihon jōkoshi kenkyū* 日本上古史研究 5, no. 1 (1961): 3-10.

Insoll, Timothy. *Archaeology and World Religion*. London; New York: Routledge, 2001.

Ishida Mosaku 石田茂作. *Bukkyō kōkogaku ronkō 5 Butsuguhen* 仏教考古學論考 5 仏具編. Kyoto: Shibunkaku shuppan, 1977.

Itō Chūta 伊東忠太. "Gion shōja zu to Ankōru watto 祇園精舎図とアンコールワット." In *Tōyō kenchiku no kenkyū* 東洋建築の研究, vol.2, 365-406. Tokyo: Hara shobū,1982.

Itō Daisuke 伊藤大輔, *Shōzōga no jidai: chūsei keiseiki ni okeru kaiga no shisōteki shinsō* 肖像畫の時代: 中世形成期における絵畫の思想的深層. Nagoya: Nagoya daigaku shuppankai, 2011.

Jan Yün-hua, trans. *A Chronicle of Buddhism in China, 581-960 A.D.: Translation from Monk Chih-P'an's "Fo-Tsu T'ung-Chi."* Santiniketan, India: Visva Bharati, 1966.

Selected Bibliography

Ji Xianlin 季羨林. *Datang Xiyu ji jinyi* 大唐西域記今譯. Xi'an: Shanxi renmin chubanshe, 1985.

――― ed. *Dunhuang xue da cidian* 敦煌學大辭典. Shanghai: Shanghai cishu chubanshe, 1998.

Jin Wenming 金文明. *Jin shilu jiaozheng* 金石錄校證. Shanghai: Shanghai shuhua chubanshe, 1985.

Jin Yufu 金毓黻, ed. *Liaohai congshu* 遼海叢書. Shenyang: Liao Shen shushe, 1985.

Kamata Shigeo 鎌田茂雄. *Chūgoku Bukkyō shi · Zui Tō no Bukkyō* 中國仏教史 · 隋唐の仏教. Tokyo: Tōkyō daigaku shuppankai, 1994.

――― ed. *Daizōkyō zenkaisetsu daijiten* 大蔵経全解說大事典. Tokyo: Yūzankaku shuppan, 1998.

Kanda Kiichirō 神田喜一郎. "*Jikaku daishi shōrai gaiten kōshō* 慈覺大師將來外典考證." In *Kanda kiichirō zenshū* 神田喜一郎全集, vol. 3, 287-98. Kyoto: Dōhōsha shuppan, 1984.

Kawaguchi Yoshiteru 川口義照. *Chūgoku bukkyō ni okeru kyōroku kenkyū* 中國仏教における経錄研究. Kyoto: Hōzōkan, 2000.

Kieschnick, John. *The Impact of Buddhism on Chinese Material Culture*. Princeton: Princeton University Press, 2002.

Kimiya Yasuhiko 木宮泰彦. *Nisshi kōtsūshi* 日支交通史. Tokyo: Kinshi hōryūdō, 1926.

―――. *Rizhong wenhua jiaoliu shi* 日中文化交流史. Translated by Hu Xinian 胡錫年. Beijing: Shangwu yinshu guan, 1980.

Kimura Kunikazu 木村邦和. "*Saimyōji enjiki shoin no shintai sanzō itsubun ni tsuite* 西明寺円測所引の真諦三蔵逸文について." *IBK* 26, no. 2 (March 1978): 697-698. .

―――. "*Shintai sanzō no gakuin ni taisuru Saimyōji Enjiki no hyōka ―― Gejinmikkyōsho no baai* 真諦三蔵の學院に対する西明寺円測の評価―― 解深密経疏の場合." *IBK* 30, no.1 (December 1981): 73-76.

Kimura Shōsaburō 木村尚三郎, Iwata Kazuhiko 岩田一彦, Mikami Shūhei 三上修平 and Hisamatsu Fumio 久松文雄, eds. *Chōan no miyako to shiruku · rōdo: chūgoku to tōzai kōryū* 長安の都とシルク·ロード: 中國と東西交流. Tokyo: Shūeisha, 1986.

Kishibe Shigeo 岸辺成雄. *Tōdai ongaku no rekishiteki kenkyū* 唐代音楽の歴史的研究, vol. 2. Tokyo: Tōkyō daigaku shuppankai, 1960.

Knapp, Ronald G. *China's Living Houses: Folk Beliefs, Symbols, and Household Ornamentation*. Honolulu: University of Hawai'i Press, 1999.

Kokushi daijiten henshū iinkai 國史大辭典編集委員會, ed. *Kokushi daijiten* 國史 大辭典. Tokyo: Yoshikawa kōbunkan, 1979.

Kōno Seikō 河野清晃. "Daianji to Kōbō daishi (Kōbō daishi no teradera) 大安寺と 弘法大師 (弘法大師の寺々)." *Bukkyō geijutsu* 仏教芸術 (1973): 16-34.

Kroll, Paul W. *Dharma Bell and Dhāraṇī Pillar: Li Po's Buddhist Inscriptions*. Kyoto: Scuola italiana di studi sull'Asia orientale, 2001.

Kuranaka shinobu 蔵中しのぶ. "*Narachō kanshibun ni okeru Genjō sanzō den no juyō ni tsuite* —— *Chōan Saimyōji to kanbunden jussaku no ba · Daianji* 奈 良朝漢詩文における玄奘三蔵伝の受容について —— 長安西明寺と漢 文伝述作の場 · 大安寺." *Tōyō kenkyū* 東洋研究 120 (1996): 31-48.

———. *Narachō kanshibun no hikaku bungaku teki kenkyū* 奈良朝漢詩文の比較 文學的研究. Tokyo: Kanrin shobō, 2003.

———. "Xuanzang zhuan dao Jianzhen zhuan —— Chang'an Ximingsi yu Da'ansi wenhua quan 從玄奘傳到鑒真傳 —— 長安西明寺與大安寺文化圈." *Yangzhou daxue xuebao (Renwen shehui kexue ban)* 揚州大學學報 (人文社 會科學版) 2 (2010): 87-92.

Kuwayama Shōshin 桑山正進. "How Xuanzang Learned about Nalanda." In *Tang China and Beyond: Studies on East Asia from the Seventh to the Tenth Century*, edited by Antonino Forte, 1-33. Kyoto: Istituto italiano di cultura, Scuola di studi sull'Asia orientale, 1988.

Ku Cheng-Mei 古正美. *Cong tianwang chuantong dao fowang chuantong: Zhongguo zhongshi fojiao zhiguo yishi xingtai yanjiu* 從天王傳統到佛王傳統: 中國中世佛教治國意識形態研究. Taipei: Shangzhou chuban, 2003.

——— ed. *Tangdai fojiao yu fojiao yishu "Qi-Jiu shiji Tangdai fojiao ji fojiao yishu" lunwen ji* 唐代佛教與佛教藝術 "七-九世紀唐代佛教及佛教藝術" 論文集. Xinzhu: Juefeng fojiao yishu wenhua jijinhui, 2006.

Kyōto Kokuritsu Hakubutsukan 京都国立博物館, ed. *Kūkai to Kōyasan: Kōbō Daishi nittō 1200-nen kinen* 空海と高野山: 弘法大師入唐 1200年記念. Osaka: NHK Osaka hōsōkyoku, 2003.

Kyūsojin Hitaku 久曽神昇, Tsukishima Hiroshi 築島裕, and Nakamura Yūichi 中 村裕一, eds. *Fukū Sanzō hyōseishū: hoka nishu* 不空三蔵表制集: 他二種. Tokyo: Kyūko shoin, 1993.

Law, Bimala Churn, and Indian Institute of World Culture. *Early Indian Monasteries*. Bangalore: Indian Institute of World Culture, 1958.

Lee Heungbum 李興範. "Sui Tang shidai de Zhongguo pingdi qielan xingshi yu sixiang 隋唐時代的中國平地伽藍形式與思想." in *Di'er jie Tongchuan Xuanzang guoji xueshu yantaohui lunwen ji, Xuanzang yanjiu* 第二屆銅川玄

奘國際學術研討會文集玄奘研究, edited by Huang Xinchuan 黃心川, 703-729. Xi'an: Shanxi shifan daxue chubanshe, 1999 .

Ledderose, Lothar. *Ten Thousand Things: Module and Mass Production in Chinese Art*. Princeton, NJ: Princeton University Press, 2000.

Lewis, Mark. *China's Cosmopolitan Empire: the Tang Dynasty*. Cambridge, Mass.: Belknap Press of Harvard University Press, 2009.

Lévi, Sylvain, Junjirō Takakusu, Paul Demiéville, and Kaigyoku Watanabe, eds. *Hōbōgirin: dictionnaire encyclopédique du bouddhisme d'après les sources chinoises et japonaises*. Tokyo: Maison franco-japonaise, 1929-1994.

Liang Jianbang 梁建邦. "Yang Su muzhi de faxian yu jiazhi 楊素墓誌的發現與價值." *Weinan shifan xueyuan xuebao* 渭南師範學院學報 1 (1990): 94-98.

Liang Sicheng 梁思成, "Women suo zhidao de Tangdai foshi yu gongdian 我們所知道的唐代佛寺與宮殿." *Zhongguo yingzao xueshe huikan* 中國營造學社彙刊 3, no.1 (1932): 15-46.

Liao Mingfu 廖明夫. "Wangshi yue qiannian —— jisi Tang mingcha Ximingsi 往事越千年—— 寄思唐名刹西明寺." *Xibei gongye daxue Bianjiacun qikan* 西北工業大學邊家村期刊 33 (2008), accessed February 07, 2012. http://www.bjc.org.cn/bjc33/bjc33-05.htm.

Liu Anqin 劉安琴. *Chang'an dizhi* 長安地志. Xi'an: Xi'an chubanshe, 2007.

Liu Bingtao 劉炳濤. "Tangdai Chang'an diqu de siguan yu qi dui huanjing de yingxiang 唐代長安地區的寺觀與其對環境的影響." *Tangdu xuekan* 唐都學刊 2 (2007): 6-9

Liu Gongquan 柳公权. *Liu Gongquan Jingang jing* 柳公权金剛经. Shanghai: Shanghai shuhua chubanshe, 2001.

Liu Shufen 劉淑芬. *Miezui yu duwang: Foding zunsheng tuoluoni jingzhuang zhi yanjiu* 滅罪與度亡: 佛頂尊勝陀羅尼經幢之研究. Shanghai: Shanghai guji chubanshe, 2008.

Liu Suqing 劉素琴. "Xinluo senglü dui Tangdai fojiao de gongxian 新羅僧侶對唐代佛教的貢獻." *Beijing daxue xuebao (zhexue shehui kexue ban)* 北京大學學報 (哲學社會科學版) 1 (1995): 34-36.

Li Yinghui 李映輝. *Tangdai fojiao dili yanjiu* 唐代佛教地理研究. Changsha: Hunan daxue chubanshe, 2004.

Luo Tianxiang 駱天驤, and Huang Yongnian 黃永年, eds. *Leibian Chang'an zhi* 類編長安志. Xi'an: Sanqin chubanshe, 2006.

Luo Xiaohong 羅小紅. "Tang Chang'an Ximingsi kao 唐長安西明寺考." *Kaogu yu wenwu* 考古與文物 2 (2006): 76-80.

Luo Zhufeng 罗竹风, et al. *Hanyu da cidian* 漢語大詞典. Shanghai: Cishu chubanshe, 1986-1993.

Ma Dezhi 馬得志. "Tang Chang'an cheng fajue xin shouhuo 唐長安城發掘新收穫." *Kaogu* 考古 4 (1987): 334-36.

Mae Hisao 前久夫. *Jisha kenchiku no rekishi zuten*: 寺社建築の歴史図典. Tokyo: Tōkyō bijutsu, 2002.

Maezono Michio 前園實知雄, and Han Guohe 韓國河. "Feiniao · Nailiang siyuan qielan peizhi zhi wojian 飛鳥 · 奈良寺院伽藍配置之我見." *Huaxia kaogu* 華夏考古 1 (2003): 91-94.

Makita Tairyō 牧田諦亮. *Chūgoku bukkyō shi kenkyū*: 中國仏教史研究. Tokyo: Daitō shuppansha, 1981-1989.

Matsuura Tomohisa 松浦友久, and Ueki Hisayuki 植木久行. *Chōan Rakuyō monogatari: yūkyūtari ōjō no chi*: 長安洛陽物語: 悠久たり王城の地. Tokyo: Shūeisha, 1987.

McCallum, Donald F. *The Four Great Temples: Buddhist Archaeology, Architecture, and Icons of Seventh-Century Japan.* Honolulu: University of Hawai'i Press, 2008.

McRae, John. "Daoxuan's Vision of Jetavana: The Ordination Platform Movement in Medieval Chinese Buddhism." In *Going Forth: Visions of Buddhist Vinaya: Essays Presented in Honor of Professor Stanley Weinstein*, edited by Stanley Weinstein and William Bodiford, 68-100. Honolulu: University of Hawai'i Press, 2005.

Meng Xianshi 孟憲實. "Tulufan xin faxian de 'Tang longshuo ernian Xizhou Gaochang xian Si'en si seng ji' 吐魯番新發現的《唐龍朔二年西州高昌縣思恩寺僧籍》." *Wenwu* 文物 2 (2007): 50-55.

Miyagi Nobumasa 宮城信雅. *Onjōji no kenkyū* 園城寺之研究. Shiga: Onjōji, 1931.

Miyasaka Yūshō 宮坂宥勝, Kanaoka Shūyū 金岡秀友, and Manabe Shunshō 真鍋俊照, eds. *Mikkyō zuten* 密教図典. Tokyo: Chikuma shobō, 1980.

Mei Lin 梅林. "Lüsi zhidu shiye: jiu zhi shi shiji Mogao kusi jingbian hua buju chutan 律寺制度視野: 九至十世紀莫高窟寺經變佈局初探." *Dunhuang yanjiu* 敦煌研究 1 (1995): 111-19.

Mochizuki Shinkō 望月信亨, Tsukamoto Zenryū 塚本善隆, and Sekai seiten kankō kyōkai 世界聖典刊行協會, eds. *Bukkyō daijiten* 佛教大辭典. 10 vols. Kyoto: Sekai seiten kankō kyōkai, 1954-1971.

Momoi Kanjō 桃井観城. *Kyōten denrai no kenkyū: tsuketari · Heianchō shoki kokusho nenpyō* 経典伝來の研究: 付 · 平安朝初期國書年表. Osaka: Tōhō shuppan, 1999.

Mori Ikuo 森郁夫. *Nihon kodai jiin zōei no kenkyū* 日本古代寺院造営の研究.

Tokyo: Hōsei daigaku shuppankyoku, 1998.

Michihata Ryōshū 道端良秀. *Chūgoku bukkyō shi.* 中國仏教史 Kyoto: Hōzōkan, 1958.

———. *Chūgoku bukkyōshi zenshū.* 中國佛教史全集, vol. 2, *Tōdai bukkyōshi no kenkyū* 唐代
佛教史の研究. Tokyo: Shoen, 1985.

Nagahara Keiji 永原慶二 and Ishigami Eiichi 石上英一, eds. *Iwanami Nihon shi jiten* 岩波日本史辭典. Tokyo: Iwanami shoten, 1999.

Nagai Yoshinori 永井義憲, and Shimizu Yūshō 清水宥聖, eds. *Agui shōdōshū* 安居院唱導集. Tokyo: Kadokawa shoten, 1972.

Nakamura Hajime 中村元, ed. *Iwanami bukkyō jiten* 岩波仏教辭典, 2nd ed. Tokyo: Iwanami shoten, 2002.

———. *Zhongguo fojiao fazhan shi*: 中國佛教發展史. Translated by Yu Wanju 余萬居. Taipei: Tianhua chuban shiye gufen youxian gongsi, 1984.

Nanjio Bunyū 南條文雄, *A Catalogue of the Chinese Translation of the Buddhist Tripitaka, the Sacred Canon of the Buddhists in China and Japan.* Oxford: Clarendon press, 1883.

Nanto kokusai bukkyō bunka kenkyūjo 南都國際仏教文化研究所, ed. *Nanto daianji ronsō* 南都大安寺論叢. Nara: Daianji; Kyoto: Hatsubaimoto rinsen shoten, 1995.

Naquin, Susan, and Chün-fang Yü, eds. *Pilgrims and Sacred Sites in China.* Berkeley: University of California Press, 1992.

———. "Sites, Saints, and Sights at the Tanzhe Monastery." *Cahiers d'Extreme-Asie* 10 (1998):183-211.

Nishiwaki Tsuneki 西脅常記. *Tōdai no shisō to bunka* 唐代の思想と文化. Tokyo: Sōbunsha, 2000.

Okazaki Jōji 岡崎讓治, ed. *Butsugu daijiten* 仏具大事典. Tokyo: Kamakura shinsho, 1982.

Okinoto Katsumi 沖本克己. "Saimyōji to Toban bukkyō 西明寺と吐蕃仏教." *Zengaku kenkyū* 禪學研究 71 (1993): 85-112.

Onjoji 園城寺, ed. *Onjōji monjo* 園城寺文書, vol.1. Tokyo: Kōdansha, 1998.

Ono Genmyō 小野玄妙. *Bukkyō kyōten sōron*: 佛教經典總論. Tokyo: Daitō shuppansha 大東出版社, 1978.

Ono Katsutoshi 小野勝年. "Chōan no Saimyōji to waga nittōsō 長安の西明寺とわが入唐僧." *Bukkyō geijutsu* 佛教藝術 29 (1956): 28-45.

———. "Chōan no Jionji to sono bunka (Chōan ni okeru jiinshi kenkyū）長安の慈恩寺とその文化（長安における寺院志の研究)." *Ryūkoku daigaku bukkyō bunka kenkyūjo kiyō* 竜谷大學仏教文化研究所紀要 (1976): 97-126

———. "Nihon no guhōsōtachi ga mita chūgoku no butsuji (Kitamura Hakase kanreki kinen tokushū) 日本の求法巡禮僧たちが見た中國の仏寺 (北村博士還暦紀念特集)." *Ryūkoku shidan* 竜谷史壇 (1981): 1-20.

———. *Nittō guhō junrei gyōki no kenkyū: daisankan* 入唐求法巡禮行記の研究: 第三巻. Kyoto: Hōzōkan, 1989.

———. *Chuūgoku Zui Tō Chōan jiin shiryō shūsei* 中國隋唐長安寺院史料集成 (*Shiryō hen* 史料篇 and *Kaisetsu hen* 解說篇). Kyoto: Hōzōkan, 1989.

———. "*Chōan no Saimyōji to nittō guhōsō*: 長安的西明寺與入唐求法僧." In *Chūgoku mikkyō* 中國密教 (*Mikkyō taikei* 密教大系, vol. 2), edited by Yūkei Matsunaga 松長有慶 and Yoritomi Motohiro 賴富本宏. Kyoto: Hōzōkan, 1994.

Ōoka Minoru 大岡實. *Nanto shichidaiji no kenkyū* 南都七大寺の研究. Tokyo: Chūō kōron bijutsu shuppan, 1966.

Ookubo Ryōshun 大久保良峻, Yamaguchi Kōei 山口耕栄, and Ryōtetsu Udaka 良哲宇高, eds. *Nihon bukkyō hennen taikan: hasshū sōran* 日本仏教編年大鑑: 八宗総覧. Tokyo: Shikisha, 2009.

Ōta Hirotarō 太田博太郎. *Nanto shichidaiji no rekishi to nenpyō* 南都七大寺の歴史と年表. Tokyo: Iwanami shoten, 1979.

Orzech, Charles D. *Politics and Transcendent Wisdom: The Scripture for Humane Kings in the Creation of Chinese Buddhism*. University Park, Pa.: Pennsylvania State University Press, 1998.

———. Henrik Hjort Sorensen, and Richard Karl Payne, eds. *Esoteric Buddhism and the Tantras in East Asia*. Leiden: Brill, 2011.

Pachow (*pinyin*: Bazhou 巴宙). "Dacheng ershier wen 大乘二十二問." *Zhonghua fojiao xuebao* 中華佛教學報 3 (1990): 83-116.

Pan Guxi 潘穀西, and Guo Daiheng 郭黛姮, eds. *Zhongguo gudai jianzhu shi* 中國古代建築史, vol. 2. Beijing: Zhongguo jianzhu gongye chubanshe, 2001.

Pestell, Tim. *Landscapes of Monastic Foundation: The Establishment of Religious Houses in East Anglia C. 650-1200*. Woodbridge, Suffolk: Boydell Press, 2004.

Pichard, Pierre, and François Lagirarde, eds. *The Buddhist Monastery: A Cross-Cultural Survey*. Paris: École française d'extrême-orient, 2003.

Prip-Moeller, J. *Chinese Buddhist Monasteries: Their Plan and Its Functions as a Setting for Buddhist Monastic Life*. Hong Kong: Hong Kong University Press, 1967.

Proser, Adriana. *Pilgrimage and Buddhist Art*. New York: Asia Society, 2010.

Pulleyblank, Edwin G. *The Background of the Rebellion of An Lu-Shan*. London:

Oxford University Press, 1955.

Qi Dongfang 齊東方, "Fosi yizhi chutuwenwu de jige wenti 佛寺遺址出土文物的幾個問題." In *Fojiao wuzhi wen hua: siyuan caifu yu shisu gongyang guoji xueshu yantaohui lunwen ji* 佛教物質文化: 寺院財富與世俗供養國際學術研討會論文集, edited by Sarah Elizabeth Fraser, 81-91. Shanghai: Shanghai shuhua chubanshe, 2003.

Reischauer, Edwin, trans. *The Record of a Pilgrimage to China in Search of the Law.* By Ennin. New York, Ronald Press Co., 1955.

———. *Ennin's Travels in Tang China.* New York, Ronald Press Co, 1955.

Rosenfield, John. *Portraits of Chōgen: the Transformation of Buddhist Art in Early Medieval Japan.* Leiden, the Netherlands: Brill, 2011.

Robson, James. "Introduction: 'Neither Too Far, nor Too Near': The Historical and Cultural Contexts of Buddhist Monasteries in Medieval China and Japan." In *Buddhist Monasticism in East Asia: Places of Practice*, edited by James Benn, Lori Meeks and James Robson, 1-17. New York: Routledge, 2010.

———. "Monastic Spaces and Sacred Traces: Facets of Chinese Buddhist Monastic Records." In *Buddhist Monasticism in East Asia: Places of Practice*, edited by James Benn, Lori Meeks and James Robson, 43-64. New York: Routledge, 2010.

Rong Xinjiang 榮新江. *Dunhuang xue shiba jiang* 敦煌學十八講. Beijing: Beijing daxue chubanshe, 2001.

———. "Sui Tang Chang'an Yanjiu de jidian sikao 隋唐長安研究的幾點思考." *Tang Yanjiu* 唐研究 9 (2003): 1-8.

———. "Sheng Tang Chang'an yu Dunhuang —— cong E'cang 'Kaiyuan ershijiu nian shoujiedie' tanqi 盛唐長安與敦煌 —— 從俄藏《開元二十九年(741)授戒牒》談起." *Zhejiang daxue xuebao* 浙江大學學報 (Renwen shehui kexue ban人文社會科學版) 37, no. 3 (2007): 15-25.

——— Wang Jing 王靜, eds. "*Sui Tang Chang'an yanjiu wenxian mulu gao* 隋唐長安研究文獻目錄稿." Accessed May 01, 2009. http://xiangyata.net/data/articles/d01/321.html.

——— ed. *Sui Tang Chang'an: xingbie, jiyi ji qita* 隋唐長安: 性別, 記憶及其他. Shanghai: Fudan daxue chubanshe, 2010.

———. "*Dushi kongjian yu wenhu: Suitang Chang'an yanjiu de xin shiye* 都市空間與文化: 隋唐長安研究的新視野." Guangming ribao 光明日報, October 2, 2010.

Ryūkoku Daigaku sanbyaku gojū shūnen kinen gakujutsu kikaku shuppan henshū iinkai 龍谷大学三五〇周年記念學術企畫出版編集委員會. *Bukkyō tōzen:*

Gion Shōja kara Asuka made 佛教東漸: 祇園精舍から飛鳥まで. Kyoto: Shibun kaku shuppan, 1991.

Saeki Arikiyo 佐伯有清. *Hiun no kentōsō: Ensai no sūki na shōgai* 悲運の遣唐僧: 円載の數奇な生涯. Tokyo: Yoshikawa kōbunkan, 1999.

———. *Takaoka shinnō nittōki: haitaishi to kogai densetsu no shinsō* 高丘親王入唐記: 廃太子と虎害伝説の真相. Tokyo: Yoshikawa kōbunkan, 2002.

Saitō Akitoshi 斎藤昭俊. *Bukkyō nenpyō* 仏教年表. Tokyo: Shin jinbutsu oraisha, 1994.

Sakayori Masashi 酒寄雅志. *Bokkaito kodai no Nihon* 渤海と古代の日本. Tokyo: Azekura shobō, 2001.

Saso, Michael R. *Homa Rites and Mandala Meditation in Tendai Buddhism*. New Delhi: International Academy of Indian Culture and Aditya Prakashan, 1991.

Schafer, Edward H. *The Golden Peaches of Samarkand: A Study of Tang Exotics*: Berkeley: University of California Press, 1963.

———. "The Last Years of Chang'an." *Oriens Extremus* 10 (1963): 133-79;

———. *Tangdai de wailai wenming* 唐代的外來文明. Translated by Wu Yugui 吳玉貴. Xi'an: Shanxi shifan daxue chubanshe, 2005.

Schmidt-Glintzer, Helwig. "Buddhism in the Tang Period." *Buddhist Studies Review* 16, no. 2 (1999): 189-206.

Schopen, Gregory. *Buddhist Monks and Business Matters: Still More Papers on Monastic Buddhism in India*. Honolulu: University of Hawai'iPress, 2004.

Seckel, Dietrich. *Buddhistische Tempelnamen in Japan*. Stuttgart: F. Steiner Wiesbaden, 1985.

Sen, Tansen. *Buddhism, Diplomacy, and Trade. The Realignment of Sino-Indian Relations, 600-1400*. Honolulu: University of Hawai'i Press, 2003. .

Seo Tatsuhiko 妹尾達彦. "A Draft Bibliography of Works concerning Ch'ang-an City during the T'ang Period." *T'ang Studies* 2 (1984): 129-186;

———. "The Urban Systems of Chang'an in the Sui and Tang Dynasties A.D. 583-907." In *Historic Cities of Asia: An Introduction to Asian Cities from Antiquity to Pre-modern Times*, edited by Muhammad Abdul Jabbar Beg, 159-200. Kuala Lumpur, Malaysia: Percetakan Ban Huat Seng, 1986.

———. *Chōan no toshi keikaku* 長安の都市計畫. Tokyo: Kōdansha, 2001.

———. "Wei Shu de 'Liangjing xinji' yu bashiji qianye de Chang'an 韋述的《兩京新記》與八世紀前葉的長安." *Tang yanjiu* 唐研究 9 (2003): 9-52

Shahar, Meir. *The Shaolin Monastery: History, Religion, and the Chinese Martial Arts*. Honolulu: University of Hawai'i Press, 2008.

Shi Hongshuai 史紅帥. "'Tang liangjing chengfang kao''Ximingsi' jiaowu 《唐兩京

城坊考》"西明寺"校誤." *Zhongguo lishi dili luncong* 中國歷史地理論叢 1 (1999):184.

Shi Nianhai 史念海. *Xi'an lishi ditu ji* 西安歷史地圖集. Xi'an: Xi'an ditu chubanshe, 1996.

Shi Zhecun 施蟄存. "Ximingsi 西明寺." In *Beishan sanwen ji* 北山散文集, vol.2, 779-80. Shanghai: Huadong shifan daxue chubanshe, 2001.

Shinohara, Koichi and Phyllis Granoff, eds. *Monks and Magicians: Religious Biographies in Asia*. New York: Mosaic Press, 1988.

Shi, Yongyou. *The Diamond Sutra in Chinese Culture*. Los Angeles: Buddha's Light Pub., 2010.

Shōgakkan kokugo jiten henshūbu 小學館国語辞典編集部, ed. *Nihonkokugo daijiten* 日本國語大辭典. Tokyo: Shōgakkan, 2006.

Silk, Jonathan. *Managing Monks: Administrators and Administrative Roles in Indian Buddhist Monasticism*. New York: Oxford University Press, 2008.

Sjoberg, Gideon. *The Preindustrial City, Past and Present*. Glencoe, Ill: Free Press, 1960.

Song Suyi 宋肅懿, *Tangdai Chang'an zhi yanjiu* 唐代長安之研究. Taopei: Dali chubanshe, 1983.

Soper, Alexander Coburn. *The Evolution of Buddhist Architecture in Japan*. Princeton: Princeton University Press, 1942.

———. "A Vacation Glimpse of the T'ang Temples of Ch'ang-An. The Ssu-T'a Chi by Tuan Ch'eng-Shih." *Artibus Asiae* 23, no. 1 (1960): 15-40.

Staikos, K. *The Great Libraries: From Antiquity to the Renaissance (3000 B.C. To A.D. 1600)*. Oak Knoll Press: The British Library, 2000.

Steinhardt, Nancy Shatzman. *Chinese Imperial City Planning*. Honolulu: University of Hawaii Press, 1990.

———. "The Mizong Hall of Qinglongsi: Space, Ritual, and Classicism in Tang Architecture." *Archives of Asian Art* (1991): 27-50.

———. "The Tang Architectural Icon and the Politics of Chinese Architectural History." *The Art Bulletin* 86, no. 2 (2004): 228-54.

———. "Seeing Hōryūji Through China." In *Hōryūji Reconsidered*, edited by Dorothy C Wong and Eric M. Field, 49-97. Newcastle, UK: Cambridge Scholars Pub., 2008.

Su Bai 宿白, *Hanwen foji mulu* 漢文佛籍目錄. Beijing: Wenwu chubanshe, 2009.

Sueki Fumihiko 末木文美士. "Riben fojiao mulu xue de xingcheng —— yi 'Dongyu chaundeng lu' wei zhongxin 日本佛教目錄學的形成 —— 以《東域傳燈錄》為中心." In *Zangwai fojiao wenxian diqiji* 藏外佛教文獻第七集,

edited by Fang Guangchang, 416-35. Beijing: Zongjiao wenhua chuban she, 2000.

Sugimoto Yukio 杉本行夫, ed. *Kaifūsō* 懷風藻. Tokyo: Kōbundō shobō, 1943.

Sun, Xinsheng. "Time and Cause for the Destruction of the Buddhist Statues from the Site of the Longxing Monastery." *Arts of Asia* 31, no.1 (2001): 50-53.

Suwa Gijun 諏訪義純. *Chūgoku chūsei bukkyō shi kenkyū* 中國中世佛教史研究. Tokyo: Daitō shuppansha, 1988.

Takakusu Junjirō 高楠順次郎 and Watanabe Kaigyoku 渡邊海旭. *Taishō shinshū daizōkyō* 大正新修大蔵経. 85 vols. Tokyo: Taishō issaikyō kankōkai, 1924-1932.

Takeuchi Kōzen 武內孝善. *Kōbō daishi Kūkai no kenkyū* 弘法大師空海の研究. Tokyo: Yoshikawa kōbunkan, 2006.

Tamura Enchō 田村圓澄, *Kodai kokka to bukkyō kyōten* 古代国家と仏教経典. Tokyo: Yoshikawa kōbunkan, 2002.

Tanaka Denzaburō 田中傳三郎, ed. *Shoji engishū* 諸寺緣起集. Kyoto: Benrido, 1930.

Tan Zhihui Ai-Choo. "Daoxuan's Vision of Jetavana: Imagining a Utopian Monastery in Early Tang." Ph.D. diss., The University of Arizona, 2002.

Tang Yongtong 湯用彤. *Sui Tang fojiao shigao* 隋唐佛教史稿. Beijing: Zhonghua shuju, 1982.

Teikichi Kida 喜田貞吉. *Nara jidai no jiin* 奈良時代の寺院. Tokyo: Heibonsha, 1980.

Teiser, Stephen F. *The Ghost Festival in Medieval China*. Princeton, N.J.: Princeton University Press, 1988.

———. *Reinventing the Wheel: Paintings of Rebirth in Medieval Buddhist Temples*. Seattle: University of Washington Press, 2006.

Tejima Isshin 手島一真. "A Study on a Catalogue of Buddhist Library in Tang's China." In *Seigen hakushi koki kinen ronshū: higashi Ajia bukkyō no shomondai* 聖嚴博士古稀記念論集: 東アジア仏教の諸問題, edited by Zhonghua foxue yanjiusuo, 179-93. Tokyo: Sankibō, 2001.

———. "'Dai Tō kaigen shakkyō kōhin rekishō' ni tsuite: Tōdai no kyōroku to zōkyō ni kansuru kōsatsu 大唐開元釈教広品歴章について:唐代の経録と蔵経に関する一考察." *Hokke bunka kenkyū* 法華文化研究 29 (2003): 24-38.

Thilo, Thomas. *Klassische Chinesische Baukunst: Strukturprinzipien U. Soziale Funktion*. Leipzig: Koehler & Amelang, 1977.

———. *Chang'an:Metropole Ostasiens Und Weltstadt Des Mittelalters 583-904*. Wiesbaden: Harrassowitz, 1997.

————. *Chang'an: Gesellschaft Und Kultur*. Wiesbaden Harrassowitz, 2006.

Thompson, Michael B. *Cloister, Abbot and Precinct in Medieval Monasteries*. Stroud: Tempus, 2001.

Thompson, James Westfall. *Ancient Libraries*. Berkeley, Calif: University of California Press, 1940.

Tokuno Kyoko. "The Evaluation of Indigenous Scriptures in Chinese Buddhist Bibliographical Catalogues." In *Chinese Buddhist Apocrypha*, edited by Robert Buswell, 31-74. Honolulu: University of Hawai'i Press, 1990.

Tsuji Eiko 辻英子, ed. *Kōya Daishi gyōjō zuga* 高野大師行状図画. Wakayamaken Itogun Kōyachō: Shinnōin gyōei bunko, 2005.

Tsuji Norio 辻憲男. "Daianji hibun o yomu 大安寺碑文を読む." *Shinwa kokubun* 親和國文 32 (1997): 1-25.

Tsukamoto Zenryū 塚本善隆. "Kokubunji to Zui Tō no bukkyō seisaku narabini kanji 国分寺と隋唐の仏教政策並びに官寺." In *Tsukamoto Zenryū chosaku shū* 塚本善隆著作集, vol. 6, 1-50. Tokyo: Daitō shuppansha, 1974.

Twitchett, Denis, and John Fairbank, eds. *The Cambridge History of China*, vol. 3 Cambridge: Cambridge University Press. 1979.

Ueyama Daishun 上山大峻. *Tonkō bukkyō no kenkyū* 敦煌佛教の研究. Kyoto: Hōzōkan, 1990.

Wang Bangwei 王邦維. *Nanhai jigui neifa zhuan jiaozhu*: 南海寄歸內法傳校注. Beijing: Zhonghua shuju, 1995.

Wang, Eugene Yuejin. *Shaping the Lotus Sutra: Buddhist Visual Culture in Medieval China*. Seattle, WA: University of Washington Press, 2005.

————. "Pictorial Program in the Making of Monastic Space: From Jing'aisi of Luoyang to Cave 217 at Dunhuang." In *Buddhist Monasticism in East Asia: Places of Practice*, edited by James Benn, Lori Meeks and James Robson, 65-106. New York: Routledge, 2010.

Wang Guixiang 王貴祥. *Zhongguo gudai jianzhu jizhi guimo yanjiu* 中國古代建築基址規模研究. Beijing: Zhongguo jianzhu gongye chubanshe, 2008.

Wang Huimin 王惠民. "Tang dongdu Jing'aisi kao 唐東都敬愛寺考." *Tang yanjiu* 唐研究 12 (2006): 357-77.

Wang Qinruo 王欽若, ed. *Cefu yuangui* 冊府元龜. Beijing: Zhonghua shuju, 1994.

Wang Shichang 王世昌. *Shanxi gudai zhuanwa tudian* 陝西古代磚瓦圖典. Xi'an: Sanqin chubanshe, 2004.

Wang Xiang 王翔. "Beiye yu xiejing: Tang Chang'an de fojiao tushuguan 貝葉與寫經: 唐長安的佛教圖書館." *Tang Yanjiu* 唐研究 15 (2009): 483-529.

————. "Jiqie yu jiezang: Tang Ximingsi jingzangqun chutan 集篋與結藏: 唐西明

寺經藏群初探", in *Soujie Chang'an fojiao guoji xueshu yantaohu lunwenji disan juan* 首屆長安佛教國際學術研討會論文集,第三卷, edited by Zengqin 增勤, 432-444. Shanxi Norman University Press, 2010.

———. "Buddhist Manuscript Culture in Medieval China: Neidian Catalogue and Monastic Bibliotheca in Early Tang." In *2010 nian foxue yanjiu lunwenji: Diyijie guoji fojiao dacang jing xueshu yantaohui* 2010年佛教研究論文集: 第一屆國際佛教大藏經學術研討會, edited by Li Jixiang 李紀祥, 229-54. Gaoxiong: F.G.S. Foundation for Buddhist Culture and Education, 2011.

———. "From Nalanda to Chang'an: a Survey of Buddhist Libraries." Accepted for publication by Nalanda-Sriwijaya Centre, Institute of Southeast Asian Studies, Singapore, forthcoming in 2012.

Wang Yarong 王亞榮. *Da Xingshansi* 大興善寺. Xi'an: Sanqin chubanshe, 1986.

———. *Chang'an fojiao shilun* 長安佛教史論. Beijing: Zongjiao wenhua chubanshe, 2005.

Wang Yong 王勇 and Ōba Osamu 大庭修. *Zhongri wenhua jiaoliu shi daxi* 中日文化交流史大系, vol. 9. Hangzhou: Zhejiang renmin chubanshe, 1996.

———. "Shinshutsu no tōjin shakyō kara mita Ensai no kyūsho katsudō 新出の唐人寫経から見た円載の求書活動." *Higashiajia bunka kanryū* 東アジア文化環流 1, no. 2 (2008): 168-74.

Watson, Burton, and Haruo Shirane, trans. *The Tales of the Heike*. New York: Columbia University Press, 2006.

Weidner, Marsha Smith, ed. *Cultural Intersections in Later Chinese Buddhism*. Honolulu: University of Hawai'i Press, 2001.

Wei Guohui 魏郭輝. "Fotuoboli yi 'Foding Zunsheng tuoluoni jing' xiangguan wenti kaolue 佛陀波利譯《佛頂尊勝陀羅尼經》相關問題考略." *Dunhuang xue jikan* 敦煌學輯刊 4 (2007): 222-229.

Weinstein, Stanley. "Imperial Patronage in the Formation of T'ang Buddhism." In *Perspectives on the T'ang*, edited by Arthur Wright and Denis Twichett, 265-306. New Haven: Yale University Press, 1973.

———. *Buddhism under the T'ang*. New York: Cambridge University Press, 1987.

———. *Tangdai fojiao* 唐代佛教. Translated by Zhang Yu 張煜. Shanghai: Shanghai guji chubanshe, 2010.

Wei Yanjian 魏嚴堅. "Tangdai Chang'an siyuan zhi yanjiu 唐代長安寺院之研究." PhD diss., Taipei: Zhongguo wenhuan daxue, 2004.

———."Tangdai chang'an siyuan de bihua yu huajia 唐代長安寺院的壁畫與畫家." *Guoli Taizhong jishu xueyuan renwen shehui xuebao* 國立臺中技術學院人文社會學報 3 (2004): 59-78.

Whitfield, Susan, and Ursula Sims-Williams, eds. *The Silk Road: Trade, Travel, War and Faith*. Chicago, IL: Serindia Publications, 2004.

Williams, Megan Hale. *The Monk and the Book: Jerome and the Making of Christian Scholarship*. Chicago: University of Chicago Press, 2006.

Wu Hung. *Monumentality in Early Chinese Art and Architecture*. Stanford, Calif: Stanford University Press, 1995.

Xia Guangxing 夏廣興. *Mijiao chuanchi yu tangdai shehui* 密教傳持與唐代社會. Shanghai: Shanghai renmin chubanshe, 2008.

Xiao Min 肖旻. *Tang Song gujianzhu chidu guilü yanjiu* 唐宋古建築尺度規律研究. Nanjing: Dongnan daxue chuban she, 2006.

Xiao Mo 蕭默. *Dunhuang jianzhu yanjiu* 敦煌建築研究. Beijing: Wenwu chubanshe, 1980.

Xin Deyong 辛德勇, and Du Bao 杜寶, eds. *Liangjing xinji ji jiao, Daye zaji jijiao* 兩京新記輯校, 大業雜記輯校. Xi'an: Sanqin chubanshe, 2006.

Xiong, Victor Cunrui (*pinyin*: Xiong Cunrui 熊存瑞). *Sui-Tang Chang'an: A Study in the Urban History Medieval China*. Ann Arbor: Center for Chinese Studies, University of Michigan, 2000.

———. *Emperor Yang of the Sui Dynasty: His Life, Times, and Legacy*. Albany: State University of New York Press, 2006.

———. *Historical Dictionary of Medieval China*. Lanham, Md.: Scarecrow Press, 2009.

Xu Shiyi 徐時儀. "Chang'an Ximingsi yu Ximingzang kaotan 長安西明寺與西明藏考探." In *Shoujie Chang'an fojiao guoji xueshu yantaohui lunwenji disan juan* 首屆長安佛教國際學術研討會論文集第三卷, edited by Zengqin 增勤, 123-131. Xi'an: Shanxi shifan daxue chuban zongshe youxian gongsi, 2010.

Xu Song 徐松, *Tang liangjin chengfang kao* 唐兩京城坊考. Beijing: Zhonghua shuju, 1985.

———, and Li Jianchao 李健超, *Zengding Tang liangjing chengfang kao* 增訂唐兩京城坊考. Xi'an: Sanqin chubanshe, 2006.

Yamazaki Hiroshi 山崎宏. *Shina chūsei bukkyō no tenkai* 支那中世佛教の展開. Tokyo: Shimizu shoten, 1942.

———. *Zui Tō bukkyō shi no kenkyū*: 隋唐佛教史の研究. Kyoto: Hōzōkan, 1967.

Yamasaki Hisao 山崎久雄. *Chōan gensō to shiruku rōdo no tabi* 長安幻想とシルクロードの旅. Tokyo: Bungeisha, 2002.

Yanase Kazuo 簗瀬一雄. *Shaji engi no kenkyū* 社寺縁起の研究. Tokyo: Benseisha, 1998.

Yang Fuxue 楊富學, and Li Jihe 李吉和, eds. *Dunhuang Hanwen Tubo shiliao jijiao* 敦煌漢文吐蕃史料輯校. Lanzhou: Gansu renmin chubanshe, 1999.

Yao Yongming 姚永銘. *Huilin "Yiqiejing yinyi" yanjiu* 慧琳《一切經音義》研究. Nanjing: Jiangsu guji chubanshe, 2003.

Yee Cordell. "Taking the World's Measure: Chinese Maps between Observation and Text." In *The History of Cartography: Cartography in the Traditional East and Southeast Asian Societies*, vol. 2, bk. 2, edited by J. B. Harley and and David Woodward, 96-127. Chicago: University of Chicago Press, 1994.

Yiru 一如. *Da Ming sanzang fashu* 大明三藏法數. 50 vols. Taipei: Fojiao chubanshe, 1975.

Yishida Mikinosuke 石田幹之助, Ishida. *Zōtei Chōan no haru* 増訂長安の春. Tokyo: Heibonsha, 1967.

Yoritomi Motohiro 賴富本宏. "Fukū·Kūkai o meguru hitobito —— 2 —— Saimyōji enshō (Matsuo Gikai hakase koki kinen) 不空・空海をめぐる人々 —— 2 —— 西明寺円照 (松尾義海博士古稀紀念号)." *Mikkyōgaku*: 密教學 16·17 (November 1980): 183-206.

——— ed., *Mikkyō butsuzō zuten: Indo to Nihon no hotoketachi* 密教仏像図典: インドと日本のほとけたち. Kyoto: Jinbun shoin, 1994

Yoshida Kenkō 吉田兼好. *Essays in Idleness: The Tsurezuregusa of Kenko.* Translated by Donald Keene. New York: Columbian University Press, 1967.

Yoshida Michioki 吉田道興. "Saimyōji enjiki no kyōgaku 西明寺円側の教學." *IBK* 25, no. 1 (1976): 266-68.

Yoshii Toshiyuki 吉井敏幸, and Momose Masatsune 百瀬正恒. *Chūsei no toshi to jiin* 中世の都市と寺院. Tokyo: Kōshi shoin, 2005.

Yoshikawa Tadao 吉川忠夫. *Tōdai no shūkyō* 唐代の宗教. Kyoto: Hōyū shoten, 2000.

Yoshito S. Hakeda. *Kukai Major Works. Translated, with an Account of His Life and a Study of His Thought.* New York: Columbia University Press, 1972.

Yūki Reimon 結城令聞. *Yuishikigaku tensekishi* 唯識學典籍志. Tokyo: Daizō shuppan, 1985.

Yu Xin 余欣. *Shendao renxin: Tang Song zhiji Dunhuang minsheng zongjiao shehuishi yanjiu* 神道人心: 唐宋之際敦煌民生宗教社會史研究. Beijing: Zhonghua shuju, 2006.

Zhang Gong 張弓. *Han Tang fosi wenhua shi* 漢唐佛寺文化史. 2 vols. Beijing: Zhongguo shehui kexue chuban she, 1997.

Cao Erqing 曹爾琴, and Shi Nianhai 史念海. *You Chengnan ji jiaozhu* 游城南記校注. Xi'an: Sanqin chubanshe, 2003.

Zhang Shiqing 张十庆. *Wushan shicha tu yu Nansong jiangnan chansi* 五山十刹图

与南宋江南禅寺. Nanjing: Dongnan daxue chubanshe, 2000.

Zhangsun Wuji 長孫無忌. *Tang lü shuyi* 唐律疏議. Taipei: Hongwen guan chubanshe, 1986.

Zhang Yanyuan 張彥遠. *Lidai minghua ji* 歷代名畫記, edited by Yu Jianhua 俞劍華. Shanghai: Shanghai renmin meishu chubanshe, 1964.

Zhao, Xiaohuan. *Classical Chinese Supernatural Fiction: A Morphological History*. Lewiston, NY: E. Mellen Press, 2005.

Zhou Shaoliang 周紹良, ed. *Quantangwen xinbian* 全唐文新編, vol. 2 .Changchun: Jilin wenshi cubanshe, 2000.

Zhou Wenmin 周文敏, *Chang'an fosi* 長安佛寺. Xi'an: Sanqin chubanshe, 2008.

Zhou Yiliang 周一良. *Tangdai mizong* 唐代密宗. Translated by Qian Wenzhong 錢文忠. Shanghai: Shanghai yuandong chubanshe, 1996.

Zhou Zuzhuan 周祖譔. *Zhongguo wenxuejia dacidian. Tang Wudai juan* 中國文學家大辭典. 唐五代卷. Beijing: Zhonghua shuju, 1992.

Zhu Guantian 朱關田. *Zhongguo shufa shi. Sui Tang Wudai juan* 中國書法史. 隋唐五代卷. Nanjing: Jiangsu jiaoyu chubanshe, 1999.

Zürcher, Erik. "Buddhism and Education in T'ang Times." In *Neo-Confucian Education: The Formative Stage*, edited by William Theodore De Bary, John Chaffee, 19-56. Berkeley: University of California Press, 1989.

———. "Han Buddhism and the Western Region." in *Thought and Law in Qin and Han China: Studies Dedicated to Anthony Hulsewe on the Occasion of His Eightieth Birthday*, edited by. W. L. Idema and Erik Zürcher, 158-82. Leiden: Brill, 1990.

———. *The Buddhist Conquest of China. The Spread and Adaptation of Buddhism in Early Medieval China*. 1959. Reprint, Leiden: Brill, 2007.

Index

Index

Index